Sustainability in the Gulf

Sustainability is a topic of great interest today, particularly for the Gulf Cooperation Council (GCC) countries, which have witnessed very rapid economic and demographic growth over the past decade. The observed growth has led to unsustainable consumption patterns of vital resources such as water, energy, and food, highlighting the need for an urgent shift towards green growth and sustainable development strategies.

Sustainability in the Gulf covers the region's contemporary development challenges through the lens of the UN's Sustainable Development Goals (SDGs), which place sustainability at the centre of the solution to the current environmental, economic, and social imbalances facing GCC countries. The book presents multiple analyses of Gulf-specific sustainability topics, examining the current status, challenges, and opportunities, as well as identifying key lessons learned. Innovative and practical policy recommendations are provided, as well as new conceptual angles to the evolving academic debates on the post-oil era in the Gulf. Through chapters covering sector-related studies, as well as the socio-economic dimensions of the sustainability paradigm, this volume offers valuable insights into current research efforts made by the GCC states, proposing a way forward based on lessons learned.

This is a valuable resource for students, academics, and researchers in the areas of Environmental Studies, Political Economy, and Economics of the GCC states.

Elie Azar is an Assistant Professor of Engineering Systems and Management at the Masdar Institute of Science and Technology, Abu Dhabi, UAE.

Mohamed Abdel Raouf is Sustainability Research Program Manager at the Gulf Research Center, Jeddah, Saudi Arabia.

Routledge Explorations in Environmental Studies

www.routledge.com/Routledge-Explorations-in-Environmental-Studies/book-series/REES

Sustainability in the Gulf

Challenges and Opportunities

Edited by
Elie Azar and Mohamed Abdel Raouf

First published 2018
by Routledge
2 Park Square, Milton Park, Abingdon, Oxon OX14 4RN

and by Routledge
711 Third Avenue, New York, NY 10017

Routledge is an imprint of the Taylor & Francis Group, an informa business

British Library Cataloguing-in-Publication Data
A catalogue record for this book is available from the British Library

Library of Congress Cataloging-in-Publication Data
Names: Azar, Elie, editor. | Abdel Raouf, Mohamed, editor.
Title: Sustainability in the Gulf : challenges and opportunities / edited by Elie Azar and Mohamed Abdel Raouf.
Description: Abingdon, Oxon ; New York, NY : Routledge, 2017. | Series: Routledge explorations in environmental studies.
Identifiers: LCCN 2017012613| ISBN 9781138040687 (hb) | ISBN 9781315174884 (ebook)
Subjects: LCSH: Sustainable development—Persian Gulf States. | Environmental policy—Persian Gulf States. | Sustainability—Persian Gulf States.
Classification: LCC HC415.3.Z9 E576 2017 | DDC 338.9536/07—dc23
LC record available at https://lccn.loc.gov/2017012613

ISBN: 978-1-138-04068-7 (hbk)
ISBN: 978-1-315-17488-4 (ebk)

Typeset in Baskerville
by Apex CoVantage, LLC

Printed and bound by CPI Group (UK) Ltd, Croydon, CR0 4YY

Contents

Figures

Tables

Contributors

Amr Osama Abdel-Aziz is President of Integral Consult in Cairo and works as a consultant. Dr Amr is registered on expert panels with UNEP and UNFCCC for waste and climate change.

Mohamed Abdel Raouf is the Sustainability Research Program Manager at the Gulf Research Center. Dr Raouf was the lead author for UNEP GEO-5 and 6 Reports, West Asia chapter on Environmental Governance section. He is a part lecturer of Environmental Economics and Accounting at various universities in the MENA region. He has published various policy papers on different environmental issues in MENA Region and authored four books. Dr Raouf writes articles and commentaries in Arabic, English, and French in various media outlets in the MENA region and globally.

Ahmed Wafiq Abolnasr has recently been awarded a PhD and works with Dr Amr in Cairo.

Farrukh Ahmad is an Associate Professor in the Department of Chemical and Environmental Engineering (CEE) at the Masdar Institute of Science and Technology (MIST) in Abu Dhabi, UAE. His research interests lie in scientific issues at the intersection of environmental engineering, public health, and sustainability.

Amjad Aliewi is a Research Scientist at the Water Research Center of Kuwait Institute for Scientific Research (KISR). Dr Aliewi is an authority in water resources planning, development, and management. He worked for about 25 years at Newcastle University (UK) as a senior researcher before joining KISR.

Hanan Alrubaiai is currently pursuing a Master's degree in Engineering Systems and Management at Masdar Institute. She is interested in the strategy and socio-economic policies in any field and discipline.

Elie Azar is an Assistant Professor of Engineering Systems and Management at Masdar Institute of Science and Technology in Abu Dhabi, UAE. His research interests lie in sustainable buildings and cities through evaluating and modelling human actions and behaviours. Dr Azar has worked as a construction engineer and building energy analyst in North America, the Middle East, and Europe.

He has also authored more than 25 publications in peer-reviewed journals and refereed conference proceedings, in addition to obtaining multiple best paper awards. Dr Azar received his Doctorate of Philosophy in Civil and Environmental Engineering from the University of Wisconsin–Madison.

Hadeel Banjar has worked with the Gulf Research Center as an Environmental Research Assistant on various reports, articles, and policy papers related to environment and sustainability issues. Banjar's educational background includes a Master's in Global Leadership and Sustainable Development from Hawaii Pacific University, United States and a Bachelor's in Biology from Umm Al-Qura University, Makkah, Saudi Arabia with a Minor Degree in Education.

James Blignaut is an environmental and resource economist. He is a part-time Professor in the Department of Economics, University of Pretoria, and Director of Beatus, ASSET Research, and JAINSA. James specialises in the restoration of natural capital, renewable energy, and economic development, and his aims are to make rural development, conservation, and the restoration of natural capital in sub-Saharan Africa.

Nazli Choucri is Professor of Political Science at Massachusetts Institute of Technology (MIT), United States. Her work is in the area of international relations, most notably on sources and consequences of international conflict and violence. Professor Choucri is the architect and Director of the Global System for Sustainable Development (GSSD), a multi-lingual web-based knowledge networking system focusing on the multi-dimensionality of sustainability. As Principal Investigator of an MIT-Harvard multi-year project on Explorations in Cyber International Relations, she directed a multi-disciplinary and multi-method research initiative. She is Editor of the MIT Press Series on Global Environmental Accord and, formerly, General Editor of the International Political Science Review. She also previously served as the Associate Director of MIT's Technology and Development Program.

Mark Coleman is a recognised voice, business advisor, and consultant on the convergence of sustainability, environmental stewardship, energy, technology, and innovation. Mr. Coleman actively writes for the Huffington Post and IntelligentHQ. He is the author of "Time To Trust: Mobilizing Humanity for a Sustainable Future" (2014) and "The Sustainability Generation: The Politics of Change and Why Personal Accountability is Essential NOW!" (2012).

Paul Dumble is an international waste and resource specialist with over 40 years as Waste Systems Specialist and Industrial Chemist. He was recently Coordinating Lead Author and Lead Author for waste sections of the UNEP GEO6 West Asia Assessment and has previous wide-ranging waste management experience in West Asian and GCC countries, including as Lead Adviser to the Abu Dhabi Waste Enhancement Project in the period 2008 to 2011 where he designed and specified data management systems for the successful Nadafa Programme.

Abdulla Galadari's main research interest is in decision modelling applications, especially for transportation, policy, contract negotiation, and conflict resolution. Dr Galadari holds a PhD in Civil Engineering and has an MSc in Civil Engineering and an MEng in Engineering Management using GIS. He also holds a BSc in Civil Engineering and a BSc in Applied Mathematics. Prior to joining Masdar Institute, he held the position of Head of Data Unit at the GIS Center in Dubai Municipality and Director of Project Management and Development with Dubai Maritime City and Nakheel, respectively. At the same time, he was an Adjunct Faculty of Civil Engineering at the Higher Colleges of Technology and the American University in Dubai. Dr Galadari is currently a registered mediator at the Arbitration Centre of DIFC-London Court of International Arbitration.

Jane Glavan has been a part of the AGEDI team since the organisation's inception in 2003 and has led on a range of AGEDI's milestone projects, including both the Ecosystem Services Assessment and National Blue Carbon project, both extensions of the Abu Dhabi Blue Carbon Demonstration Project. She also led on the Climate Change Programme, the Biodiversity Systematic Conservation Assessment, and the State of the Environment Report for Abu Dhabi.

Alexandre B. Hedjazi is a member of faculty at the University of Geneva where, since 2007, where he has taught courses on comparative politics, environmental governance, and urban transitions. With a doctorate degree in Urban Planning from University of Grenoble, France and a PhD from School of Public Affairs, University of California, Los Angeles (UCLA), Alexandre started his research career on the financing of urban infrastructure and public-private governance in 1996 at the OECD. He joined UCLA in 1998 to conduct research on regional development and lectured on regionalization and geopolitics of energy, including at UCLA Global Studies programme.

Roula Inglesi-Lotz is an Associate Professor in the Department of Economics in the Faculty of Economic and Management Sciences at the University of Pretoria. Her research interests focus on energy and environmental economics, economic growth and development, and applications of time series and panel data econometrics.

Mais Jafari is an architect and urban planner. She studied Architecture and Landscape Architecture at the University of Jordan and received her PhD from the TU Dortmund University (Germany) on transformation of public spaces in Amman, Jordan. She worked in several architectural and planning firms, and as a lecturer at the German Jordanian University (2008–2010). Since 2014, she has been working as a Lecturer and Researcher at the Department of Urban Design and Land Use Planning at the TU Dortmund.

Nagwa El Karawy is a regional environmental and resource specialist built up over 20 years. She is a Member of Arab Renewable Energy Commission (AREC) and recently Coordinating Lead Author for the UNEP GEO6 West

Asia Assessment. Nagwa has held a number of senior roles including Executive Director with AMA Arab Environment Company, Contracts Manager at Center of Waste Management Abu Dhabi, and Alliance Partnership Manager (AGEDI – a UNEP partnership) at Environment Agency Abu Dhabi.

Natalia Karayaneva completed her postgraduate degree in Sustainable Urban Development from the University of Oxford. Originally from Russia, she had a successful career as a serial entrepreneur and a real-estate developer with awarded residential projects in Bulgaria. Ms Karayaneva sought to study the complexity of sustainability in real estate and in 2016 she completed her postgraduate degree in the University of Oxford. As a tech innovator, Ms Karayaneva is interested in smart city concepts, blockchain, and AI applied to community governance and sustainable housing.

Abdullah Kaya is currently working on his PhD degree in the Department of Engineering Systems and Management at Masdar Institute of Science and Technology (MIST) in Abu Dhabi, UAE. He also got his MSc degree from the same department with a thesis titled "Dynamics of Technology Strategy under Changing Regulatory Regimes: An Analytical Framework and a Case Study on the Global Solar Photovoltaic Industry". He holds a BSc degree of industrial engineering from Middle East Technical University in Ankara, Turkey.

Jwen Fai Low has a Master of Science in Computing and Information Science from Masdar Institute of Science and Technology, United Arab Emirates. He currently works as a Research Engineer in Masdar Institute's Department of Engineering and Systems Management. His research interests are in data mining, graph analysis, machine learning, and scientometrics.

Myles Mander is a natural resource economist. He runs a consulting company, Futureworks, focusing on ecosystem services sustainable use and analysis. Myles has extensive experience in environmental economics and has received international recognition for his work on the medicinal plant trade in Africa, as well as in developing economic tools for watershed management in South Africa.

Toufic Mezher is a Professor of Engineering Systems and Management at Masdar Institute of Science and Technology (MIST) since 2008. He is currently affiliated with the Institute Center for Smart and Sustainable Systems (iSmart). Before Joining MIST, he was a Professor of Engineering Management at the American University in Beirut from 1992 to 2007. He earned a BS in Civil Engineering from University of Florida and a Master's and ScD in Engineering Management from George Washington University in 1988 and 1992, respectively. His research interests include Renewable Energy Management and Policy, Sustainable Development, and Technology Strategy and Innovation Systems.

Deepti Mahajan Mittal is Project Manager – Footprint, Climate, and Energy at Emirates Wildlife Society in association with WWF (EWS-WWF). She is leading research and engagement activities in development of sustainable energy policies for the UAE. She manages the Ecological Footprint Initiative, a federal-level partnership geared towards reducing the country's carbon emissions. Deepti was previously with The Energy and Resources Institute (TERI), India, and has wide experience in energy and climate projects, having worked with clients including UN-ESCAP, IUCN, and DfID.

Stephen Parr is an independent consultant ecologist; he has worked mainly in the UK but also Turkey, South Asia, Seychelles, and the Middle East with broad experience of ecological impact assessment, systematic conservation planning, protected area planning, species assessment, and conservation and ecosystem services.

Ashley C. Pilipiszyn is a PhD candidate under the Chair for Energy Efficiency, where she studies Distributed Energy Systems and Digital Technologies. Integrating systems thinking and quantitative analysis, her current research explores the use of blockchain technology applications for microgrids in order to maximise renewable energy use and profitability by increasing self-consumption within a microgrid while trading and shifting demand by use of battery storage. For her Master's thesis, she created the world's first Sustainability-Oriented Innovation Index for Airports© that compares international airports across 10 indicators in relation to their overall sustainability and alignment within a municipality's development strategy through three unique lenses of environmental, social, and technological innovation.

Muhammad Al-Rashed is the Executive Director of the Water Research Center of the Kuwait Institute for Scientific Research (KISR). Dr Al-Rashed is a hydrogeologist with PhD from UCL, London. He is an expert in Kuwait hydrology and strategic planning for the development and management of the water resources in Kuwait. He worked for more than 35 years at KISR. He led and participated in many water research projects, he is an author and co-author of many articles published in refereed journals, international conferences, symposiums, workshops and technical reports, and has vast experience in leading and managing research units and groups.

Andrea Schiffauerova is currently an Associate Professor in the Department of Engineering Systems and Management, Masdar Institute of Science and Technology, UAE, and previously she worked as an Associate Professor at Concordia Institute for Information Systems Engineering at Concordia University, Canada. She obtained her PhD and MEng degrees in Industrial Engineering from École Polytechnique de Montréal, Canada, and BEng from Silesian University, Czech Republic. Her main area of expertise involves economics of innovation and science, and management of knowledge and technology, with a particular interest in innovation networks and knowledge diffusion.

Wolfgang Scholz is an urban planner and researcher. In 2006, he received his PhD in Informal Urbanization in Zanzibar/Tanzania and in 2012 was appointed as Associate Professor for Urban Planning at the German University of Technology (GUtech) in Muscat, Oman. He has more than 15 years of research experience in the field of informal urban development in the Global South, regional development, urban infrastructure, and mobility, as well as teaching experience in urban design, planning theory, theories and models of spatial development, infrastructure planning, and urban planning in the Global South.

I-Tsung Tsai is a professor at Masdar Institute of Science and Technology at the Engineering Systems and Management Department. He holds a PhD degree from MIT while serving as a water strategy consultant for the Singapore government. He was a visiting scholar of the Institute of Financial Research and Management, India in 2006. He focuses on carbon finance, infrastructure policy, and information economics with a special focus of sustainability. He did his PhD dissertation on the implicit incentive mechanism embedded in financial contracts, and the effect of asymmetric information in the online auction markets.

Maryam R. D. Al-Yammahi is a Masters student in the Department of Engineering and Systems Management, Masdar Institute of Science and Technology, UAE. Her research efforts are primarily directed towards investigating the production of scientific knowledge and technological innovations, with a particular focus on the United Arab Emirates and its surrounding region.

Acronyms

10YFP	The 10-Year Framework of Programs on Sustainable Consumption and Production
AAA	American Automobile Association
AADC	Al Ain Distribution Company
AC	Air Conditioning
ADAC	Abu Dhabi Airports Company
ADDC	Abu Dhabi Distribution Company
ADM	Abu Dhabi Municipality
ADQCC	Abu Dhabi Quality and Conformity Council
ADSSC	Abu Dhabi Sewerage Services Company
AGEDI	Abu Dhabi Global Environmental Data Initiative
AIST	(Japan National Institute of) Advanced Industrial Science and Technology
AREE	The Aqaba Residence Energy Efficiency
ASJC	All Science Journal Classification
ASR	Aquifer Storage and Recovery
AST	Activated Sludge Treatment
BCF	Bio-Concentration Factor
BREEAM	Building Research Establishment Environmental Assessment
CBD	Central Business District
CBO	Congressional Budget Office
CCAP	Congestion Charge Auto Pay
CDM	Clean Development Mechanism
Cebr	Centre for Economic and Business Research
CERET	Clean, Efficient, or Renewable Energy Technologies
CFU	Colony-Forming Units
CHONS	Carbon, Hydrogen, Oxygen, Nitrogen, and Sulphur
CMD	Cubic Meters Per Day
CO2	Carbon Dioxide
COP 21	The Twenty-First Session of the Conference of the Parties
COP	Conference of the Parties
CSUD	Climate-Sensitive Urban Design
CUPPS	Common-Use Passenger Processing Systems

CUSS	Common-Use Self-Service
DALY	Disability-Adjusted Life Year
DBP	Disinfection Byproduct
DCS	Departure Control Systems
DEWA	Dubai Electricity and Water Authority
DGNB	Deutsche Gesellschaft Für Nachhaltiges Bauen
DNA	Deoxyribonucleic Acid
DOC	Degradable Organic Carbon
DOT	Department of Transport
DPR	Direct Potable Reuse
DSCE	Dubai Supreme Council of Energy
EAD	Environment Agency Abu Dhabi
EDC	Endocrine-Disrupting Chemical
EF	Economic Freedom
EFI	Ecological Footprint Initiative
EIA	Energy Information Administration
EIU	Economist Intelligence Unit
EmiratesGBC	Emirates Green Building Council
ERP	Electronic Road Pricing
ESCO	Energy Service Company
ESCWA	Economic and Social Commission for Western Asia
ESD	Education for Sustainable Development Unit
ESMA	Emirates Authority for Standardisation and Metrology
EWS-WWF	Emirates Wildlife Society in Association with World Wide Fund for Nature
GBIG	Green Building Information Gateway
GCC	Gulf Cooperation Council
GCxGC-HRMS	Two-Dimensional Gas Chromatography – High Resolution Mass Spectrometry
GDP	Gross Domestic Product
GeSI	Global E-Sustainability Initiative
GHG	Greenhouse Gases
GPS	Global Positioning System
GRIHA	Green Rating for Integrated Habitat Assessment
GSO	Gcc Standardisation Organisation
GW	Groundwater
GWP100	100 Year Greenhouse Gas Warming Potential
HAB	Harmful Algal Blooms
HPLC-MS/MS	High Performance Liquid Chromatography – Tandem Mass Spectrometry
HQE	High Environmental Quality
IAG	Inter-Agency Group
IATA	International Air Travel Association
ICT	Information and Communication Technology
IEA	International Energy Agency

IMF	International Monetary Fund
IPCC	International Panel on Climate Change
IPR	Indirect Potable Reuse
ISI	Institute of Scientific Information
ISWA	International Solid Waste Association
IUs	In-Vehicle Units
IWM	Integrated Waste Management
IWRM	Integrated Water Resources Management
kgoe	Kilogram of Oil Equivalent
KISR	Kuwait Institute for Scientific Research
km/l	Kilometres Per Litre
kWh	Kilowatt Hour
LDPE	Low Density Polyethylene
LED	Light Emitting Diode
LEED	Leadership in Energy and Environmental Design
MAC	Maximum Allowable Concentration
MBR	Membrane Bioreactor
MBT	Mechanical Biological Treatment
MCA	Muscat Capital Area
Mcm/yr	Million Cubic Meter Per Year
MCM	Million Cubic Meters
MDGs	Millennium Development Goals
MEW	Ministry of Electricity of Water
MIGD	Million Imperial Gallons Per Day (1 MIGD = 4.546 CMD)
MIT	Massachusetts Institute of Technology
MNE	Ministry of National Economy
MOH	Ministry of Housing
MPN	Most Probable Number
MRF	Material Recycling Facility
MSQ	Madinat as Sultan Qaboos
MSW	Municipal Solid Waste
MT+Bio	Mechanical Treatment with Biological Treatment – often referred to as Sorting and Composting Plants
MTC	Midfield Terminal Complex
MWNT	Multi-Walled Carbon Nanotubes
NGO	Non-Governmental Organisation
NGS	Next-Generation Sequencing
NIS	National Innovation Strategy
NPDES	National Pollution Discharge Elimination System
NPV	Net Present Value
OECD	Organisation for Economic Co-Operation and Development
ONSS	Omani National Spatial Strategy
PAH	Polycyclic Aromatic Hydrocarbon
PET	Polyethylene Terephthalate
PFRD	Parks & Recreational Facilities Division

PPCPs	Pharmaceuticals and Personal Care Products
QMRA	Quantitative Microbial Risk Assessment
qPCR	Quantitative Polymerase Chain Reaction
R&D	Research and Development
RDF	Refuse Derived Fuel
RO	Reverse Osmosis
RSB	Regulation and Supervision Bureau
SA	Sustainability Assessment
SABIC	Saudi Basic Industries Corporation
SCAD	Statistics Centre Abu Dhabi
SCI	Science Citation Index
SCP	Supreme Council of Planning
SCP	Sustainable Consumption and Production
SCTP	Supreme Committee for Town Planning
SDGs	Sustainable Development Goals
SITA	Societe Internationale de Telecommunications Aeronautiques
SOI	Sustainability-Oriented Innovation
SPE	Solid-Phase Extraction
SSCI	Social Sciences Citation Index
STEP	Strategic Tunnel Enhancement Program
STMP	Surface Transport Master Plan
TDM	Travel Demand Management
TDS	Total Dissolved Solids
THM	Trihalomethane
TSE	Total Sewage Effluent
TWCM	Total Water Cycle Management
U.K.	United Kingdom
U.S.	United States
UAE	United Arab Emirates
UFW	Unaccounted-for-Water
UK	United Kingdom
UN	United Nations
UNEP	United Nations Environment Programme
UNFCCC	United Nations Framework Convention on Climate Change
UPC	Urban Planning Council
US$	United States Dollar
US	United States (of America)
USEPA	United States Environmental Protection Agency
USGBC	United States Green Building Council
VQS	Vehicle Quota System
WDM	Water Demand Management
WEF	World Economic Forum
WFES	World Future Energy Summit

WHO	World Health Organization
WRATE	Waste Resource Assessment Tool for the Environment
WRC	Water Research Center
WTA	Willingness to Accept
WTEEM	Waste, Technology, Economics, and Emission Model
WTO	World Trade Organization
WTP	Willingness to Pay
WWT	Wastewater Treatment
WWTP	Wastewater Treatment Plant

Acknowledgments

This volume is based on a selection of papers presented at the Towards a Sustainable Lifestyle in the Gulf workshop, which was held on 17–19 August 2016 at the University of Cambridge in the United Kingdom. The co-editors would like to extend a warm thank you to all participants of the workshop, totalling 21 scholars and practitioners, who convened over three days to present academic papers and discuss the prospects of sustainability in the six Gulf Cooperation Council member states. The discussions held during the event greatly enriched the chapters of this volume, also helping the co-editors and authors together define a number of overarching themes, challenges, and solutions relating to the topic.

The co-editors are also deeply grateful to the organisers of the 2016 Gulf Research Meeting of the Gulf Research Centre Cambridge (GRCC), under the umbrella of which the workshop took place. In particular, we would like to thank Dr. Abdulaziz Sager, Chairman and Founder of the Gulf Research Center (GRC), Dr. Christian Kokh, Director of the GRC Foundation Geneva, as well as Elsa Courdier at the GRC Foundation, Dr. Oskar Ziemelis, Director of Cooperation at the GRC, and Sanya Kapasi at the GRC, for their tireless work and support.

Dr. Elie Azar
Dr. Mohamed Abdel Raouf
Abu Dhabi and Cairo
June 2017

Part I

Introduction

1 Sustainability issues in the GCC

Elie Azar and Mohamed Abdel Raouf

Introduction

Sustainability is a topic of great interest today, in particular for the Gulf Cooperation Council (GCC) countries, which have witnessed very rapid economic and demographic growth over the past decade (Economist Intelligence Unit 2010). The observed growth is resulting in unsustainable consumption rates of resources such as water, energy, and food. For instance, the International Energy Agency (IEA 2014) ranks all six Gulf countries among the 15 highest energy consumers per capita in the world: Qatar (1st), Bahrain (5th), Kuwait (6th), UAE (9th), Saudi Arabia (11th), and Oman (15th). The current consumption trends highlight the need for an alternative path of more sustainable and green growth to ensure a prosperous future for the current and next generations of Gulf citizens.

In addition to resource-related challenges, additional hurdles exist in various GCC cities and need immediate tackling such as low security and safety levels, low quality and access to education, healthcare problems such as high child obesity rates, low human development levels, to name a few (UNDP 2015). Sustainability challenges are in fact diverse and cover a vast array of disciplines. They also require the active participation of multiple stakeholders including decision-makers from the public sector, private companies and associations, and more importantly citizens, who should be at the core of the transition towards sustainable growth and development. While many definitions exist for the term "sustainable development" or "sustainability", most definitions emphasize the need to balance three equally important pillars that form the "triple bottom line" of sustainability: people (i.e., social), planet (i.e., environmental), and profit (i.e., economic) (Idowu and Mermod 2014).

Arcadis, a consultancy and design firm, and the Centre for Economic and Business Research (Cebr) have developed an index that measures how "sustainable" cities are (Arcadis 2016). The index combines an exhaustive list of indicators that cover the three highlighted pillars of sustainability. Data was then gathered from a variety of sources such as the World Bank and the Energy Information administration (EIA) to rank 100 cities from around the world, including eight cities from the GCC (Arcadis 2016). Unfortunately, Gulf cities appear to be here again occupying lagging positions when compared to cities of developed countries: Doha

(57th), Manama (70th), Dubai (74th), Abu Dhabi (75th), Kuwait City (78th), Jeddah (86th), Riyadh (87th), and Muscat (88th). The current ranking confirms and documents the importance of addressing the sustainability challenges facing GCC cities today.

MDGs, SDGs, and the GCC

Acknowledging the urgent need for action, the GCC countries, along with the international community, have committed to actively work towards addressing a variety of sustainable development challenges. An important milestone in these efforts was the development of eight Millennium Development Goals (MDGs) in the year 2000, where leaders of 189 countries signed the millennium declaration at the United Nations (UN) millennium summit (UN 2000). The MDGs included targets such as reducing poverty rates by half, providing universal primary education, and slowing down the spread of HIV/AIDS. A summary of these targets is presented in Table 1.1, along with their current progress status, which varies from "achieved" to "ongoing" to "progress with difficulties". As can be seen from the table, the progress is not very reassuring, which might indicate a slower-than-needed transition towards a sustainable development path for the GCC.

Table 1.1 GCC countries' performance on the MDG targets (based on national MDG progress reports)

MDG/State	*Bahrain*	*Kuwait*	*Oman*	*Qatar*	*Saudi Arabia*	*UAE*
1 – Eradicate extreme hunger and poverty	Achieved	Achieved	Achieved	N/A	Ongoing	N/A
2 – Achieve universal primary education	Achieved	Ongoing	Ongoing	Ongoing	Ongoing	Achieved
3 – Promote gender equality and empower women	Ongoing	Ongoing	Ongoing	Progress with difficulties	Progress with difficulties	Ongoing
4 – Reduce child mortality	Ongoing	Achieved	Ongoing	Achieved	Achieved	Ongoing
5 – Improve maternal health	Ongoing	Ongoing	Ongoing	Achieved	Achieved	Achieved
6 – Combat HIV/AIDS, malaria, and other diseases	Ongoing	Ongoing	Ongoing	Achieved	Ongoing	Achieved
7 – Ensure environmental sustainability	Progress with difficulties	Progress with difficulties	Ongoing	Ongoing	Ongoing	Ongoing
8 – Develop a global partnership for development	Ongoing	Achieved	Ongoing	Achieved	Ongoing	Ongoing

Source: Mohamed Abdel Raouf and Hadeel Banjar, GRC, Oct. 2016

To follow and extend on the MDGs, more than 150 world leaders adopted in the year 2015 the new 2030 agenda for sustainable development, including 17 Sustainable Development Goals (SDGs) for the period of 2015 to 2030 (UN 2015). Also referred to as "Global Goals", SDGs aim to end poverty, protect the planet, and ensure prosperity for all. A list of the SDGs is presented Table 1.2, highlighting the scale of the commitment that the global community, including GCC countries, has agreed on.

While committing to a more sustainable future is considered a crucial and promising step, the true challenge is to develop and execute the plans that make the sustainable transition a reality. This task is particularly challenging for Gulf countries who have important hurdles to overcome along the three pillars of the triple bottom line (UNDP 2015). Environmental challenges are many and include the need for eco-production and eco-consumption of energy, water, and food. It is

Table 1.2 List of SDGs

SDGs	*Description*
Goal 1	End poverty in all its forms everywhere
Goal 2	End hunger, achieve food security and improved nutrition and promote sustainable agriculture
Goal 3	Ensure healthy lives and promote well-being for all at all ages
Goal 4	Ensure inclusive and equitable quality education and promote lifelong learning opportunities for all
Goal 5	Achieve gender equality and empower all women and girls
Goal 6	Ensure availability and sustainable management of water and sanitation for all
Goal 7	Ensure access to affordable, reliable, sustainable, and modern energy for all
Goal 8	Promote sustained, inclusive, and sustainable economic growth; full and productive employment; and decent work for all
Goal 9	Build resilient infrastructure, promote inclusive and sustainable industrialization and foster innovation
Goal 10	Reduce inequality within and among countries
Goal 11	Make cities and human settlements inclusive, safe, resilient, and sustainable
Goal 12	Ensure sustainable consumption and production patterns
Goal 13	Take urgent action to combat climate change and its impacts
Goal 14	Conserve and sustainably use the oceans, seas, and marine resources for sustainable development
Goal 15	Protect, restore, and promote sustainable use of terrestrial ecosystems; sustainably manage forests; combat desertification; and halt and reverse land degradation and halt biodiversity loss
Goal 16	Promote peaceful and inclusive societies for sustainable development, provide access to justice for all and build effective, accountable, and inclusive institutions at all levels
Goal 17	Strengthen the means of implementation and revitalize the global partnership for sustainable development

Source: United Nations, "Transforming our world: the 2030 Agenda for Sustainable Development", New York, NY, 2015

important to highlight the "nexus" between these three resources given that food production requires important amounts of water, which are mostly obtained through desalinating ocean or seawater. This process is extremely energy-demanding, hence coupling the three mentioned resources and increasing the complexity of managing their supply and demand. In parallel to environmental challenges, economic challenges are also significant, such as the high reliance on oil revenue and the resulting instability due to fluctuations in oil prices. Other economic issues include low employment opportunities and availability of local human capital, leading to high levels of dependence on foreign manpower. Finally, social challenges include security, safety at the workplace, human rights and discrimination, access to healthcare, and the engagement of citizens in decision-making.

In order to start addressing the challenges above, important questions need to be asked and answered. How can key sectors, such as buildings or transportation, contribute to the sustainable transition? What are the social or behavioural drivers that are impeding such transition? What would a sustainability-driven economy in the GCC resemble given the economic, social, and environmental barriers that exist? Finally, and most importantly, what are the current or previous efforts that GCC countries have taken towards sustainable development, and how can they build on these efforts to advance their local sustainability agendas in light of the global SDGs agenda?

In this edited volume, academics and practitioners from various fields investigate sustainability challenges and opportunities as well as case studies from various sectors in the GCC countries. Through chapters covering the sustainability status in the GCC, sector-related studies, as well as the economic and social dimensions of the problem, the book examines the GCC states' quest towards sustainability, proposing a way forward based on lessons learned from experiences in the region and beyond. Prior to outlining the structure and content of the book in Chapter 3, the following chapter evaluates the scholarly publications on sustainability originating from the Gulf region, allowing us to assess the region's previous and current levels of commitment to sustainability efforts and research.

References

Abdel Raouf, M., and Banjar, H. 2016. *Sustainable Development Goals: Challenges and Opportunities for the GCC Countries*. Cambridge, UK: Gulf Research Center.

Arcadis. 2016. *Sustainable Cities Index*. Technical Report. Amsterdam, the Netherlands.

Economist Intelligence Unit. 2010. *The GCC in 2020: Resources for the Future*. Technical Report. The Economist Intelligence Unit Limited, London, United Kingdom.

Idowu, S., and Yüksel Mermod, A. 2014. Developmental Perspective of CSR: An Introduction. In S. O. Idowu and A. S. Kasum (Ed.), *People, Planet and Profit: Socio-Economic Perspectives of CSR*. Surrey: Gower Publishing Limited.

International Energy Agency (IEA). 2014. *IEA Energy Atlas*. Available at: http://energyatlas.iea.org/#!/tellmap/-297203538/4 (Accessed 19 January 2017).

United Nations (UN). 2000. *United Nations Millennium Declaration*. New York, NY: UN.

United Nations (UN). 2015. Transforming Our World: The 2030 Agenda for Sustainable Development. New York, NY: UN.

United Nations Development Program (UNDP). 2015. *Human Development Report*. New York, NY: UNDP.

2 The Gulf region's commitment to a sustainable lifestyle

A bibliometric study

Jwen Fai Low, Maryam R. D. Al-Yammahi and Andrea Schiffauerova

Introduction

A sense of nostalgia permeates the study of scientific production in the Arab world. When achievements in Arab science are discussed, the contributions made by Arab scientists to the field of mathematics, astronomy, and geography during the Islamic Golden Age are inevitably invoked (Maziak 2005; Falagas et al. 2006). Comparisons are often made between past achievements and the current state of Arab science. This situation is understandable, as the scientific output from the Arab world past the medieval age is barely noticeable next to the volume of research pouring out from the US, Europe, and Japan. However, the recent influx of oil wealth and the initiatives taken by visionary leaders over the past decades have made a profound impact upon the state of scientific development in the Arab world. A great number of institutions for higher learning and research were set up and have been operating for a fair number of years, and the resources poured into these institutions as well as other initiatives have begun to bear fruit. At this moment in time, we are witnessing the cusp of a renaissance in Arab science.

The world has moved on since the last time when the Arab world was home to pioneers and leaders of science. While mathematics, astronomy, and geography are still core disciplines of scientific study, many new disciplines have been developed or have branched off since the medieval age. Technological advancement has enabled the creation of some of these new fields of study. Others came into existence due to pressing societal needs. Sustainability science belongs to the latter category. The previously unquestioned policy of reckless resource exploitation with complete disregard for the consequences along with a swelling human population has prompted many to raise their concerns over the pace of human progress. A growing voice within the scientific community began asking if the speed of the current human development model could be sustained for the long term. Extinction of species, depletion of finite resources, pollution rendering areas uninhabitable, and a host of other maladies brought about by the unrelenting march of human consumption threaten the survival of our species.

One industry implicated as a contributor to unsustainable development is the petrochemical industry. The extraction and transport of crude oil have caused a number of environmental disasters and they have the potential to cause many more. Crude oil refinement and the subsequent consumption of the products produce a number of toxic and harmful compounds. Carbon dioxide and a number of greenhouse gases are released when gasoline, one of the major products of petroleum, is burned, trapping heat within the atmosphere and making the planet increasingly unsuitable for human and other life.

As some of the biggest beneficiaries of our civilization's dependence on oil, the nations of the Gulf Cooperation Council (GCC) are acutely aware of the perils inherent to the exploitation of finite petrochemical resources. While much of the resources in the GCC countries have been directed to researching petrochemicals, a non-trivial portion of them are also funnelled to researching sustainability. The countries know that the status quo will not last forever and having contingency plans will ensure their survival in a post-oil era. This investment of resources is not just towards the development of new and better renewable energy technologies, but is also used to make progress in other scientific disciplines which can have an impact on the sustainable lifestyle in the Gulf countries: for instance, desalination and wastewater processing are technologies critical in ensuring that the Gulf countries, which are poor in water resources, remain habitable for humans.

Our literature review revealed that no comprehensive study on the contributions made by GCC countries to sustainability science has been performed to date. This chapter seeks to address this gap. With the aid of bibliometric data of scholarly publications obtained from an extensive source, we chronicled the growth of sustainability science within each country. The collaboration networks built by countries who are working in the sustainability domain are constructed and analysed. In addition, we examined how each country distributes its resources among disciplines within sustainability science.

Literature review

A number of publications on the scientific output of the Arab world exist, although there are slight differences with regards to which countries are considered a part of the Arab world. Waast and Rossi (2010) included only 13 countries in their paper on the scientific production in Arab countries, which were divided into Maghreb (Morocco, Algeria, Tunisia), Machreq (Lebanon, Jordan, Syria), and Gulf (Bahrain, Kuwait, Oman, Qatar, Saudi Arabia, United Arab Emirates) countries. Egypt does not fall into any grouping in Waast and Rossi's work. In a bibliometric study of the industrial wastewater research in the Arab world, Zyoud et al. (2016) included all 22 members of the Arab league in their analysis. The nine additional countries found in the work by Zyoud et al. are Palestine, Iraq, Sudan, Yemen, Comoros, Djibouti, Libya, Mauritania, and Somalia. The majority of the works we surveyed appeared to favour the latter definition of the Arab world being constituted of 22 Arab league member countries.

There appears to be a bias to towards studying the biomedical research output in Arab countries, even after we have accounted for the fact that a majority of this output comes from a single group. The group of collaborators who authored a large number of papers on the bibliometric analysis of biomedical research in the

Arab world – Waleed M. Sweileh, Ansam Sawalha, Sa'ed H. Zyoud, Samah W. Al-Jabi – are all based in An-Najah National University. The topics covered by this collaboration group as well as authors outside the core group include breast cancer, toxicology, urology, nephrology, solid waste, diabetes mellitus, nutrition and dietetics, substance use disorders, osteoporosis, ophthalmology, and water pipe tobacco smoking (Zyoud et al. 2014a, 2014b, 2014c, 2015; Sweileh et al. 2014a, 2014b, 2014c, 2014d, 2014e, 2014f, 2015a, 2015b). Most of the researchers who are not a part of this group conducting bibliometric studies of biomedical literature did not place an emphasis on a specific topic in their works (Salem 1990; Tadmouri and Bissar-Tadmouri 2003; Al-Khader 2004; Falagas et al. 2006; Benamer and Bakoush 2009; Bredan et al. 2011; Afifi 2005). The only instances of studies on non-biomedical research output from the Arab world which we could find are the desalination and industrial wastewater focused papers by Zyoud (a different Zyoud from the one based in An-Najah National University) and collaborators (Zyoud and Fuchs-Hanusch 2015; Zyoud et al. 2016), the papers which focused on overall scientific production in the Arab world authored by Waast and his collaborator (Waast 2010; Waast and Rossi 2010), and the findings published by El Alami et al. (1992) on the international scientific collaboration of nine Arab countries.

Existing studies which examined the research output of just GCC countries have chosen to focus on one particular field and not general scientific production. As is the case with the Arab world, one field which has received a lot of attention is the biomedical field. A 1996 paper profiled the medical research publications by authors from GCC countries using the Medline database, which was then a very nascent field for the GCC countries (Lammers and Tahir 1996). Then, in 2001, the Medline database was used again in a study by Deleu et al. (2001) which analysed the geographical distribution of biomedical and clinical research publications originating from GCC countries. The only bibliometric analysis that we found of research output from GCC countries which did not focus on biomedical research was a 2008 study by Al-Ansari (2008), where the library and information science literature was the focus instead.

Few studies investigate the production of sustainability science research, which encompasses renewable energy, sustainability, and environmental science. Romo-Fernández et al. (2012) authored a paper on world scientific production on renewable energy, sustainability, and the environment which used the Scopus (Elsevier 2017a) database of scientific literature. The analysis is done from a country, institutional, and journal level, covering the period from 2003 to 2008. A more recent publication by Kajikawa et al. (2014) using Science Citation Index (SCI) and the Social Sciences Citation Index (SSCI) provided by the Institute of Scientific Information (ISI) studied more than just the research production in the field of sustainability science. They also investigated the level of interdisciplinary research being carried out over time as sustainability science matures and identified emerging research fields.

Most existing studies tend to focus on a single facet of sustainability science. Renewable energy received the greatest amount of attention from researchers. The most recent publication on the production of scientific knowledge in renewable energy which we found was a 2014 study conducted by Rizzi et al. (2014) which covered all countries and used Web of Science, a citation indexing service, as its data source. A similar global study on renewable energy research production was done earlier in 2013 using the same data source (then known as ISI Web of Knowledge) by Manzano-Agugliaro et al. (2013). An even earlier study on renewable energy research output by Uzun (2002) relied on SCI and SSCI databases. The scope of Uzun's study was global but limited to 25 major countries. Uzun covered a greater number of areas than later works by others, as he included policy issues, low energy architecture, and topics related to renewable energy into his analysis in addition to the five major areas of biomass, geothermal, hydro, solar, and wind power covered by his work and later works.

Aside from renewable energy, researchers have also performed bibliometric analysis of scientific publications related to the resilience, vulnerability, and adaptation of humans to global environmental change; for instance the work by Janssen et al. (2006) used the ISI's Arts and Humanities Index, Social Science Citation Index, and Science Citation Index. Dragos and Dragos (2013) investigated the factors influencing scientific productivity in environmental sciences and ecology in their paper using data from ISI Web of Knowledge, World Bank's World Development Indicators, and Yale University for Environmental Performance Index. Hassan et al. (2014) presented in a paper their findings on the research production in sustainable development and its subfields across the globe from a country, institution, and individual level using the Scopus database. A paper published by Li and Zhao (2015) contains a bibliometric analysis of environmental assessment research around the world across a 20-year period.

Studies on sustainability in the GCC countries did not deal with scientific output, but rather policies implemented. The status, viability, and implementation of renewable energy policies represent the majority of the publications (Doukas et al. 2006; Hertog and Luciani 2009; Reiche 2010; Alnaser and Alnaser 2011; Ferroukhi et al. 2013; Bhutto et al. 2014; Al-Mulali and Ozturk 2014). Water policies have received a lot of research attention as well, and they often are related to desalination due to the region's geography (Bushnak 1990; Abdulrazzak 1994; Al-Zubari 2003; Dawoud 2012). Examples of studies which are not related to either renewable energy or water policies is Spiess's (2008) paper on GCC countries' ability to respond to climate change, Kumetat's (2009) paper on the security and sustainability implications of climate change on the Arabian Gulf countries, Shah's (2010) paper on food security in the GCC countries, and Kannan's (2012) study on the effort put forth by GCC countries in combating desertification.

We did not find any work which dealt with the topic of research production in sustainability science occurring in the GCC countries, a research gap which this work seeks to fill.

Methodology

Scopus is the source of raw data used in our analysis. Publications which were included in our analysis are those which have at least one author whose listed affiliation is one of the GCC countries: Bahrain, Kuwait, Oman, Qatar, Saudi Arabia, and the United Arab Emirates (UAE). Another criterion that must be met is that one of the All Science Journal Classification (ASJC) codes assigned to the publication must be the code for 'Renewable Energy, Sustainability, and the Environment', which is 2105 (Elsevier 2017b). As Scopus does not provide cited references data for documents prior to the year 1996, we opted against the inclusion of documents published before 1996 in our analysis. We are also aware that there is a considerable delay between the time when a document is published and when it is indexed by Scopus (Moed et al. 2016), so we have chosen to exclude documents which are newer than 2012. The total number of documents which were retrieved from Scopus is 1,175.

Time series analysis

To determine the subfield of sustainability that a document belongs to, we used keywords which were assigned to each document by the authors. There is existing literature (Rizzi et al. 2014) which guided us when we selected keywords for renewable energy subfields. The terms which we used can be found in Table 2.1. We failed to find a set of generally agreed-upon categories for subfields of sustainability which are not related to renewable energy. This difficulty might be due to sustainability science being relatively new, with many disciplines falling under the banner of sustainability science only beginning to define themselves and emerge (Kajikawa et al. 2014). Therefore, we did not categorize documents into a subfield if they are not related to renewable energy, with the only exception being publications related to water treatment. Water treatment (e.g. wastewater processing and desalination) is critical to the region due to its scarcity in the region and replaces the spot occupied by hydropower in our analysis since hydropower is virtually a non-entity in the GCC countries and thus not much can be gained from a close examination of subfield. Keywords used for the water treatment subfield are also found in Table 2.1.

Categorizing a work using keywords is not without its shortcomings. For instance, when using 'solar' as a keyword for solar power publications, we will include publications that are unrelated to solar power at all such as publications on solar assisted air conditioning of buildings, which also have 'solar' as a keyword. There

Table 2.1 Search terms used to find documents that belong to a particular subfield of sustainability

Field	*Search terms*
Solar	solar, photo
Wind	wind, aerodynamic
Water treatment	hydro, water
Geothermal	geotherm
Biomass	bio, ethanol, feedstock, gasification, methane, oil, anaerobic, alternative fuel

are also cases where a publication can have keywords which belong to more than one subfield. An example is solar photocatalytic water treatment, which would fall under both solar and water treatment subfields.

For each country and each subfield, comparisons of the number of publications and number of citations were made between documents which are related to sustainability science and the total number of documents. To determine the level of individual productivity, we counted the number of authors who published sustainability papers per year per country.

Network analysis

Country collaboration network

The network for inter-country collaboration is constructed from the group of co-authors found within each paper. A node/vertex in this network represents a single country. If authors from two different countries have collaborated on a paper, a link/edge then exists between the two vertices that represent the two countries. If a paper is authored by a single person, or if the team members who worked on a paper are all affiliated with a single country (they may be from different institutions), then an edge that originates from and terminates at the same vertex exists, which we will refer to as a loop or self-loop edge.

Plotting networks aid in conceptualizing the design of the networks and the interaction of the entities within them. In the plot, the size of each vertex is proportional to the number of papers which are associated with the country represented by the vertex. Larger vertices correspond to more publications while smaller correspond to less. The width of the edge is the number of times that the countries linked by the edge have worked together. Thicker edges mean greater collaboration frequency while thinner mean lesser. In the scenario where there are three authors, one belonging to institution A from country A, one belonging to institution B from country B, and one belonging to institution C from country B, the collaboration frequency between country A and country B is only increased by one. In other words, we deliberately avoid taking duplicate countries in a single paper into consideration. This is because the purpose of the analysis is to examine the collaboration pattern between countries. If we allowed for duplicate countries, then a scenario could occur where two countries are inaccurately portrayed as collaborating very frequently, when in fact there exists only one paper on which researchers of both countries have worked together, but the paper has a large number of authors who originate from those two countries.

To better understand the structure of the collaboration network, a community detection algorithm was used to partition the graph. Rather than having us impose our idea on how the countries in the network should be grouped, the algorithm attempts to discover the groups/blocks within the network. The algorithm which was used is the stochastic blockmodel, specifically the degree-corrected version proposed by Karrer and Newman (2011), which factors each vertex's degree (number of connections to other vertices) when blockmodeling. For the country collaboration network, we specified that a minimum number of three blocks must be discovered from the network.

Getting an idea of how the collaboration network between countries evolved over time requires producing separate plots for different time periods. First, we divided the range of years studied into three roughly equal time periods, which are 1996 to 2001, 2002 to 2007, and 2008 to 2012. Then, a plot is produced from each time period's aggregated data. By using multi-year data for a single plot, the analysis is resistant against the influence of outliers. This strategy also helps reduce the number of network plots. Instead of 17 plots, one for each year of data, there are only three multi-year plots.

Keywords network

Another set of data which was subjected to network analysis are the keywords assigned to each paper by its authors. The motivation behind this analysis is to discover the areas of research which the sustainability publications can be grouped under and infer the GCC countries' research priorities. This analysis also helps address gaps in the time series analysis. In the time series analysis, we defined groups and document membership based on words we assigned to each group. In this network analysis, we work in reverse, using all available words then inferring the existence of groups from word clusters. Although the texts of the title and the abstract of each publication are available to us, we elected not to use them as there may be a lot of noise in the data. Keywords are better at capturing the essence of a publication.

A keywords network was constructed for all GCC countries by aggregating all the countries' data. As in the country collaboration network analysis, three separate plots were made for different time periods (1996 to 2001, 2002 to 2007, and 2008 to 2012) so that the changing research foci of the GCC countries can be observed. Additional keywords networks were plotted for each country in order to compare how each country prioritizes its sustainability research. For these country-level network plots, the data for the entire 1996 to 2012 period are aggregated.

In a keywords network, each vertex represents a single word. While a keyword may have more than one word (e.g. 'solar power'), each word is treated as linked but separate from the others ('solar' and 'power'). Our analysis is conducted at the level of a single word/unigram as it gives a more detailed picture of how words and the type of research they represent relate to each other. For instance, rather than treating 'solar power' and 'solar energy' as two separate entities that may or may not be linked to each other, by conducting analysis at a unigram level, we instead have a model where 'power' and 'energy' are related to 'solar', and through 'solar', a connection exists between 'power' and 'energy'. The size of each vertex is proportional to the frequency of appearance of the word represented by the vertex, with larger vertices representing more commonly occurring words and smaller vertices representing uncommon words.

An edge between vertices exists if two words are found together within a single keyword and when they belong to the same document. As an example, in a document with two keywords, 'solar energy' and 'photovoltaic', an edge exists between 'energy' and 'solar' because they were parts of a keyword, and an edge exists between 'energy' and 'photovoltaic' because both words are found in the same document. Each edge is weighted by their frequency of occurrence within keywords and within documents. From our previous example, the edge between 'solar' and 'energy' would have a weight of 2 since the pairing occurs on both keyword and document levels. However, 'energy' and 'photovoltaic' would only have a weight of 1 since the pairing occurs only at the document level. The weighting scheme is designed so that words which are closely related (i.e. composing a single keyword) have greater weight while looser affiliations (i.e. from different keywords but originating from the same document) result in a lower weight. In the network plots, the width of an edge is fixed and does not reflect the weight of the edge to preserve legibility.

As with country collaboration networks, we produced plots for the keywords networks to aid in our analysis. Words need to cross a certain threshold before they could be plotted. This is due to the large number of unique words found. Plotting all of the words would result in an uninformative graph. The keywords network for each country requires that a word must be found in an edge which occurs more than once before it is included in the plot. The exceptions are Saudi Arabia and the UAE, which required a higher threshold of two edge occurrences before being plotted due to a much larger number of unique words found for each country as a result of their greater number of publications. For the aggregated GCC plots, the threshold is at one edge occurrence as well. The 2008 to 2012 period has a threshold of two edge occurrences due to the greater number of publications resulting in a larger pool of words. As part of the data cleaning step, common English stop words (e.g. 'the', 'and', 'of') were removed from our pool of words prior to constructing the network.

Determining the areas of research within each country or each period is accomplished using a community detection algorithm. Words in the same community can be thought of as belonging to the same area of research. We must emphasize that this is not a strict membership, but merely reflects which community a word is most strongly associated with. For instance, 'energy' may belong in the same community as 'solar' but that does not mean 'energy' is completely divorced from another community that contains the word 'wind'.

The large number of words makes the keywords network a more complex network than the country collaboration network. Consequently, capturing the network structure through a traditional stochastic blockmodel is insufficient. Instead, a nested stochastic blockmodel is used. A nested stochastic blockmodel can be thought of as blockmodeling applied upon blockmodeling, forming hierarchical layers of abstraction (Peixoto 2014). In our application of the algorithm, the modelling is degree-corrected and the minimum number of blocks/communities which are to be found is six. To avoid cluttering the graph, only labels for the 200 largest vertices were plotted.

Analysis

Time series analysis

Countries and fields

To understand each GCC country's sustainability research output relative to its overall research output, we must first get a picture of the country's overall research output. Saudi Arabia is the scientific powerhouse of the GCC countries, as it consistently has the biggest share of all publications throughout all the years (Figure 2.1). While the number of publications of all countries has grown, as seen in Figure 2.2, the rate of growth is uneven. From Figure 2.1, we observe that Kuwait's share of total publications from the GCC countries, which was approximately 20% in 1996, has steadily declined, dropping down to less than 10% in 2012. The shares of all publications attributable to Bahrain and Oman respectively have not changed appreciably over the years. For Saudi Arabia, its share of publications shrunk from 1996 to 2008 before recovering to its 1996 level in 2012. Figure 2.2 shows a greater than linear growth in the number of publications during the 2008 to 2012 period. The UAE, which had the third largest share of publications in 1996, grew to have the second largest share in 2012. Although Qatar had the smallest share of publications in 1996, it has the third largest share in 2012.

The sustainability research output of each country mirrors the overall research output in general (Figure 2.2). The number of sustainability publications from the UAE grows faster than the overall number of publications from 2005 onwards. The same phenomenon is observed in Oman, Qatar, and Saudi Arabia from 2008 onwards. Kuwait's number of sustainability publications grew faster than overall publications from 2006 to 2010 but tapered off from 2010 onwards. Saudi Arabia has the largest share of sustainability publications for a majority of the time period we studied (Figure 2.1). Saudi Arabia's share was greatest from 1996 to 2000, when it was responsible for approximately three-quarters of the GCC countries' sustainability research output. From 2006 to 2008, the UAE briefly closed the gap with Saudi Arabia, producing an equivalent or greater number of sustainability publications. Even though Saudi Arabia took the lead back from 2009 onwards, the share of sustainability publications it reclaimed was less than the share of overall publications it reclaimed. From 2002 to 2008, Kuwait was a significant contributor to the GCC countries' sustainability science literature pool, exceeding its own contribution to the overall scientific literature pool in that time period.

Compared against other countries in the Middle East which are not a part of the GCC, the number of sustainability science publications as a share of total publications is higher in the GCC countries than non-GCC Middle East countries over all the years studied. Based on the data points from the time series of sustainability publications to all-publications ratio, the share of sustainability publications in the GCC countries was higher at the start of our study period (1996) and has steadily declined since, before increasing again from 2005. The share of sustainability publications in other Middle Eastern countries is essentially unchanged until 2005, when it began displaying an upward trend.

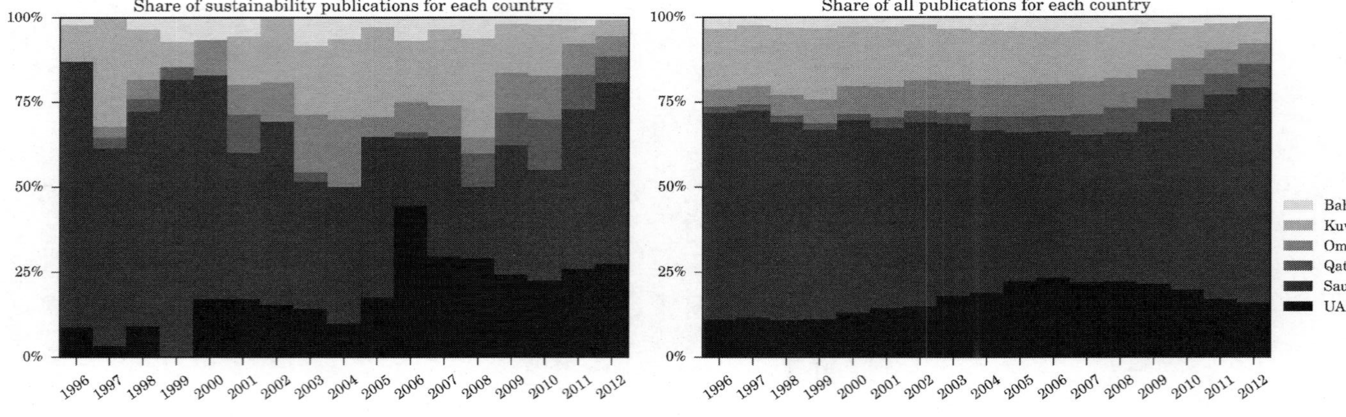

Figure 2.1 Share of sustainability publications compared against share of all publications for each country

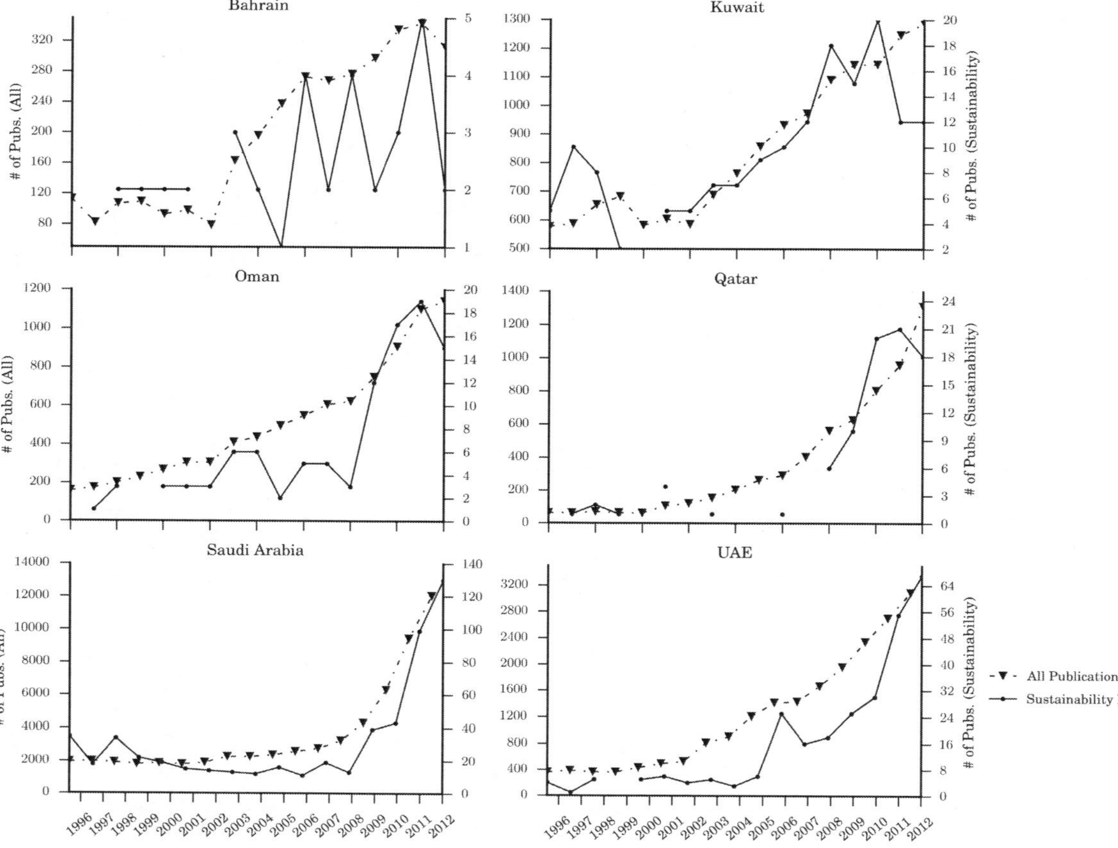

Figure 2.2 Sustainability publications per year compared against all publications per year for each country

Two other ratios which were examined were the ratio of sustainability publications originating from the GCC countries over those originating from non-GCC Middle Eastern countries and the ratio of all publications from GCC countries versus those from non-GCC Middle Eastern countries. The ratio for GCC versus non-GCC Middle Eastern sustainability publications is higher than the ratio for GCC versus non-GCC Middle Eastern publications in all the years we studied in this work. At its height in 1996, the GCC countries produced close to four publications in sustainability for every 10 sustainability publications from non-GCC Middle Eastern countries, while the ratio for all publications is 1.5 GCC publications for every 19 non-GCC Middle Eastern publications. The ratio of GCC and non-GCC Middle Eastern sustainability publications follows the general trend of the all-publications ratio, declining from 1996 to 2008 and increasing from 2008 to 2012. The all-publications ratio in 2012 is close to the ratio in 1996. However, the GCC countries in 2012 did not return to its previously prolific publication of sustainability research found in 1996. Only two sustainability publications were produced by the GCC countries for every 10 that were published by non-GCC Middle Eastern countries.

The analysis of publication numbers for each sustainability subfield, as defined in Table 2.1, showed that in earlier time periods, the focus of sustainability research within the Gulf region is on solar energy, but water treatment grows in importance as time passes. These trends are most readily observed in Kuwait, Saudi Arabia, and, to a lesser extent, Bahrain. Geothermal energy research is practically non-existent in the GCC countries. Wind energy research is consistently carried out in Saudi Arabia, UAE, Bahrain, and Oman throughout the entire period of our study. Kuwait's wind energy research output, however, is intermittent and appears to be on the decline. Qatar's wind energy research is similarly sporadic, although Qatar's publication history is too short for a trend to be conclusively determined.

For the number of publications per author, Kuwait and Saudi Arabia has never had a ratio greater than or equal to 1 in our studied time period of 1996 to 2012. From 2001 to 2004, the UAE has greater than 1 publication per author, although the ratio has declined since 2004. Oman has exceeded the 1 publication per author ratio only once, in 2001. While Bahrain and Qatar have publications per author ratios greater than 1 in their histories, the data for their publications are too sporadic for us to say that these ratios are representative of general trends within the two countries.

Newer publications from Oman, Saudi Arabia, and the UAE have received fewer citations while older publications have received more, which is in line with citation trends of publications worldwide, where the number of citations received slowly grows as the number of years since publication increases (Slyder et al. 2011). Qatar has too few data points for us to draw any conclusions for citation patterns of its publications. While Kuwait's and Bahrain's publication histories are comparable to Oman's and the UAE's, older publications from Bahrain and Kuwait have received far fewer citations on average when compared against Oman and the UAE.

When examining the number of citations which an author receives on average, authors of older publications received more citations on average than expected. Since the number of authors is always several times greater than the number of publications, the number of citations per author is often lower than the number of citations per publication. The exception in the case of the GCC countries is the

UAE during the 2001 to 2004 period, where publications per author exceeded a ratio of 1, which meant that more citations are attributable to an author on average in this time period.

Network analysis

Dynamics of networks are more apparent in graphical plots. Therefore, we have decided to include exemplars of the two types of networks used in this work – country collaboration networks and keywords networks – in the hopes that their presence would help readers digest the results and analyses we present more easily.

For the country collaboration networks, Figures 2.3 and 2.4 were chosen as exemplars. Picking two figures of different time periods helps illustrate the massive surge in collaborative activity from 1996 to 2012.

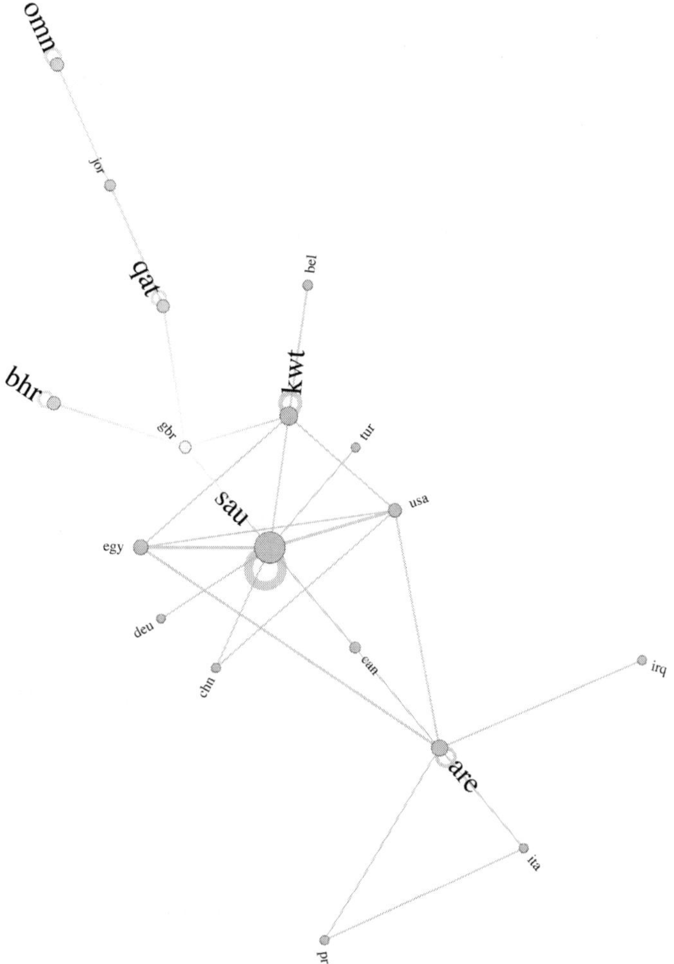

Figure 2.3 Country collaboration network based on sustainability publications, 1996 to 2001

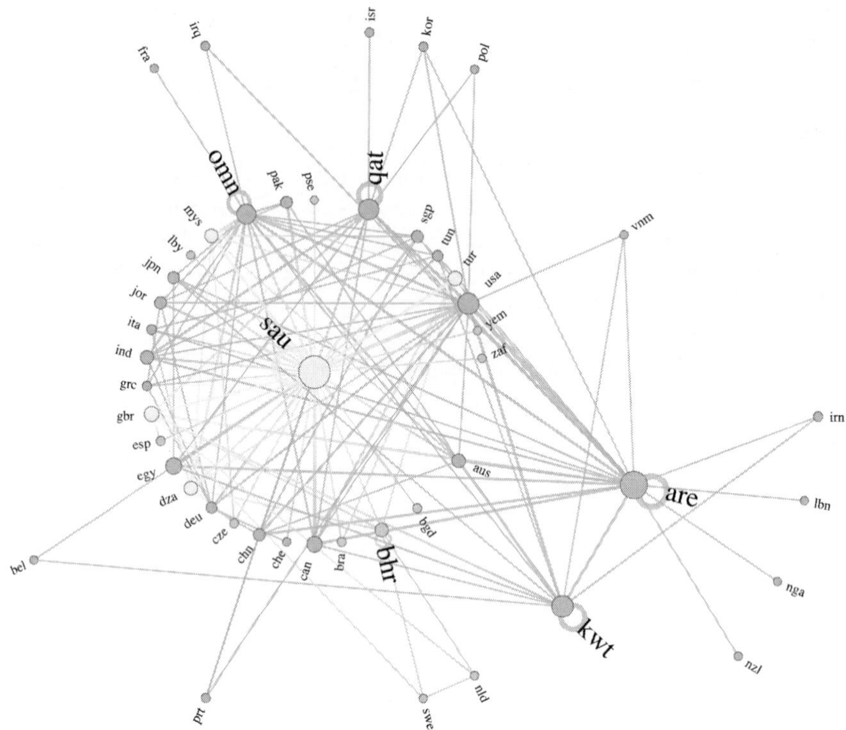

Figure 2.4 Country collaboration network based on sustainability publications, 2008 to 2012

Figure 2.5, which documents keywords usage in the early (1996–2001) period of sustainability research in the GCC region, was chosen as an exemplar of keywords networks as it is sufficiently complex to permit the reader to visually explore it while remaining simple enough that details are not hopelessly lost due to an overcrowding of keywords. In Figure 2.5, readers can attempt to trace the connections between the keywords and observe how keywords are grouped together into communities.

Country collaboration network over time

The passage of time renders the collaboration network for sustainability science research increasingly complex as more and more countries outside the GCC partnered with GCC researchers and GCC member countries increased the frequency of collaboration amongst themselves.

In the earliest period of this study (Figure 2.3), which is 1996 to 2001, half of the GCC countries – Oman (omn), Qatar (qat), and Bahrain (bhr) – are isolated in their sustainability research efforts. None have collaborated with each other

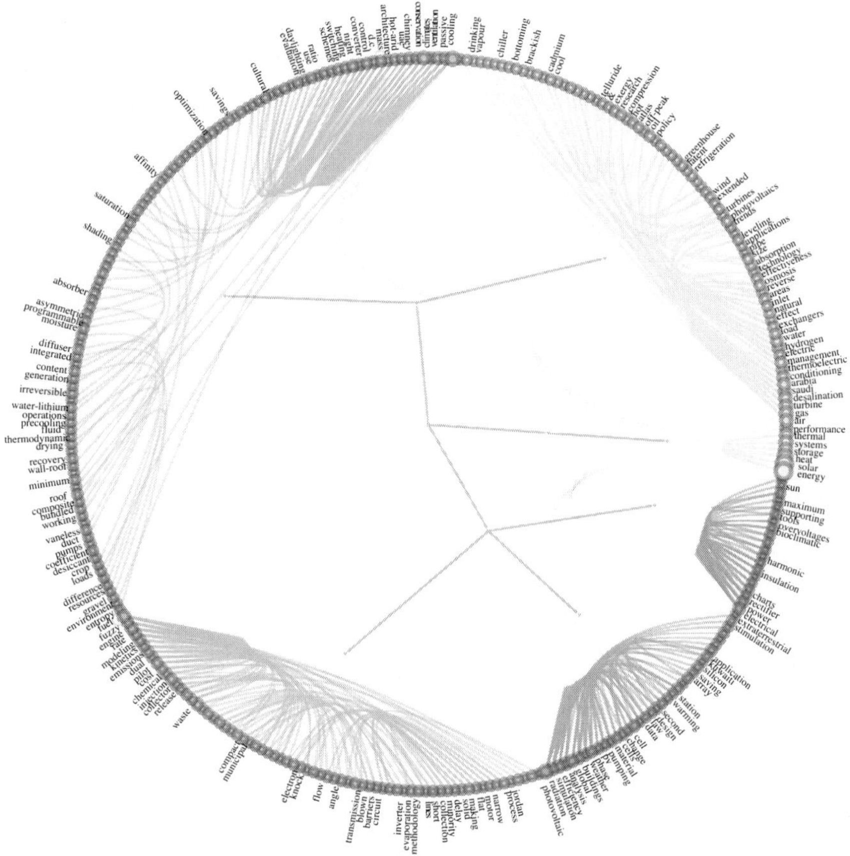

Figure 2.5 Network of keywords used in sustainability publications, 2008 to 2012

although they have shared similar non-GCC research partner countries. Oman and Qatar have collaborated with Jordan (jor), while Bahrain and Qatar have collaborated with the United Kingdom (gbr). The colour assigned to Oman, Qatar, and Bahrain by the community detection algorithm reflects these countries' isolation, as they are separate from Saudi Arabia (sau), Kuwait (kwt), and the UAE (are). The UK serves as a bridging country during this time period, having collaborated with four GCC countries (Qatar, Bahrain, Kuwait, and Saudi Arabia), two of which are from the isolated community and two which are not. Authors for every country showed a preference for working alone or with collaborators from the same country. This tendency is most clearly seen for Saudi Arabia, which has a thick loop edge, despite having collaborated on sustainability research with the largest number of different countries. In contrast, the UAE's loop edge is fairly thin although it has fewer unique collaborator countries.

In the 2002 to 2007 period, the graph has become denser than the earlier period. The number of countries has grown and so has the number of edges connecting the countries. In this time period, the biggest community contains Saudi Arabia, Qatar, the UAE, and Oman in addition to other non-GCC countries. Kuwait was assigned its own partition by the community detection algorithm due to the fact that it collaborated with Belgium and Iran, two countries which no other country, GCC or otherwise, in the network has collaborated with. Bahrain's isolation stems from the fact that it has few collaborators and did not collaborate on sustainability research with any GCC country during this period. Qatar, though similarly having few collaborators and having not collaborated with any GCC countries, is likely assigned to the biggest community by the algorithm due to its connection with the US, whose number of links rivals Saudi Arabia's and the UAE's in this network. Of GCC countries which have a large number of collaborators – Saudi Arabia, the UAE, and Oman – Oman produced the least number of single-author or single-country publications, as evidenced by the thin self-loop.

The latest period in our study is from 2008 and 2012 (Figure 2.4). Saudi Arabia was assigned to a community separate from other GCC countries most likely as a result of its overwhelming number of publications and connections. Countries which were also placed in the same community as Saudi Arabia are its most frequent collaborators, which include Malaysia (mys), the UK, Turkey (tur), Algeria (dza), and Germany (deu). Bahrain is once again isolated into its own partition as it did not collaborate with many countries. Other countries such as Sweden (swe), Netherlands (nld), and Bangladesh (bgd) which were assigned to the same group as Bahrain also have few collaborations with countries in the network. The remaining GCC countries, which are Oman, Qatar, the UAE, and Kuwait, belong to the largest community in this graph that also includes many non-GCC countries. The US (usa) is the most popular collaborator in this time period. While each GCC country's node size is bolstered by publications which originate from itself, non-GCC countries such as the US have their node sizes limited since they cannot include publications which are not done in collaboration with one or more GCC countries and can only include publications which are. Despite this, the US's node size is fairly large and comparable to Oman, Qatar, and Kuwait in size, demonstrating its popularity.

Keywords network: GCC over time

For the 1996 to 2001 period (Figure 2.5), the six communities which were detected can be broadly categorized as solar energy, sustainable buildings, waste management, policy, systems simulation, and materials science, based on the words found in each community. At level one abstraction, waste management and sustainable buildings are grouped together. At level two abstraction, policy, systems simulation, and materials science are treated as one group. The size of the 'solar' vertex suggests that the most intensive research performed in the GCC countries in this time period is solar-related. The communities are well defined and do not have severe inequality in the number of members. This suggests that GCC countries are pursuing traditional avenues of research, which is expected in this time period as sustainability science is a new discipline. The assignment of the word 'photovoltaic' to a community that contains mostly terms associated with sustainable buildings suggests that photovoltaic research has strong links to sustainable buildings in the GCC countries in this period.

In the 2002 to 2007 period, the largest community out of the six detected appears to be a catch-all group for words which do not fit into other communities but are not substantial enough to form their own community. Prominent elements found in this community are associated with the fields of waste management and sustainable buildings. Using the words associated with each of the remaining five communities allows us to categorize them as photovoltaic and non-solar energy sources, thermal solar energy, pollution, materials science, and policy and systems simulation. At level one abstraction, the thermal solar energy, pollution, materials science, and policy and systems simulation communities are grouped together while another grouping is made up of the photovoltaic and non-solar energy sources community and catch-all community. Photovoltaic being grouped with non-solar energy sources, which consist of wind and diesel, demonstrates its relative lower importance compared to solar thermal energy. Some terms found in the catch-all community are there because they are too generic and may be associated with many research topics (e.g. 'flow', 'emissions', 'growth'). Many other terms found there, however, are not. One interpretation of the large catch-all community's existence is that certain research topics found within it (e.g. waste management and sustainable buildings) are deemphasized by the GCC countries in this period. Another interpretation is that the community represents the diversification of research topics in the GCC countries, with the growing scientific community within the countries and the increasing maturity of sustainability science prompting the exploration of new research questions.

The 2008 to 2012 period saw the increase in size of the catch-all community. The other communities in this time period, as described by terms found within them, are solar energy; photovoltaic, non-solar energy, and sustainable buildings; geographical information; systems and policy modelling; and pollution. Higher levels of abstraction/grouping are absent in this network. Photovoltaics are once again associated with sustainable buildings in this time period. The community which contains the word 'solar' also has 'water' as a member, perhaps reflecting a trend within the GCC countries to research ways to use its most abundant resource, solar energy, to solve the problem of water scarcity. Among the larger vertices in the network are wind and hydrogen, which show that both wind energy and renewable hydrogen production are the second most important research topics after thermal solar energy. As before, the increasing number of terms found in the catch-all community could imply the deemphasizing of research topics and could also imply the diversification of research directions. And just as in the 2002 to 2007 graph, some terms in the catch-all groups are found there simply because they are general terms and their associations are diluted among many topics (e.g. 'study', 'knowledge', 'performance').

Keywords network: countries

Bahrain's keywords network is one of the only two which grouped 'wind' and 'energy' together out of all GCC countries' networks, the second keywords network being Oman's. While 'solar' is still very important to Bahrain based on how frequently the term 'solar' is used as a keyword, Bahrain's renewable energy research mix is not dominated by solar unlike most GCC countries. This observation is corroborated by the data on the proportions of sustainability subfields studied by each country, which shows Bahrain's sustainability research output from 2009 to 2012 as having a higher share of wind-related publications compared to other GCC countries. Photovoltaic is the solar energy research focus within Bahrain. Photovoltaic cell materials research terms occur with enough frequency and are sufficiently isolated from other terms that they are deemed a single community by the detection algorithm. Terms such as 'building', 'photovoltaic', 'integrated', and 'turbine' are grouped together in another community, which suggests the integration of photovoltaic panels to buildings and the structural considerations of constructing wind turbines are other major areas of sustainability research in Bahrain. The remaining communities are related to policy and biomaterials, vehicle traffic flow, and a catch-all community which contain terms whose associations with other terms are very spread out such as 'heat' and 'power', as well as terms which are seldom used such as 'tidal'.

Due to a longer and more robust publication history, the keywords network for Kuwait has more communities found in it than Bahrain's. A total of 14 communities exist on the network. The sustainability research foci found in Kuwait are photovoltaic cell material; renewable hydrogen production; sustainable buildings; weather and water; simulations and optimization; solar and photovoltaic; thermodynamics; climate change; climate change, waste management, and electrical grid; waste management and electrical grid; dynamic economic dispatch problem; harmonic elimination pulse width modulation; wind and gas modelling; and a catch-all community. The creation of the 'climate change, waste management, and electrical grid' community is due to the fact that the terms found in this community are strongly associated with both 'climate change' and 'waste management and electrical grid' communities, but the terms are not sufficiently generic to be thrown into the catch-all community. The presence of two separate communities – the dynamic economic dispatch problem community and the harmonic elimination pulse width modulation community – which are specifically related to developing algorithms to improve electrical power systems, shows that Kuwait places a much stronger emphasis on electrical power systems optimization research compared to other GCC countries.

For Oman, their sustainability science research efforts are concentrated on materials science; sustainable development; photovoltaic, wind, biomass, and geothermal energy; water treatment and waste management; power systems simulations; solar power; concentrated solar power; and thermodynamics. The 'wind' keyword's high appearance frequency indicates the importance of wind energy research in Oman and its appearance frequency is comparable to the keyword 'solar' despite solar having two forms of energy production associated with it: concentrated solar power and photovoltaic.

Qatar's keywords network has the following communities: solar, chemicals, feasibility studies, computational models, photovoltaic and power systems, wind and natural gas, pulse width modulation converters, and thermodynamics. The words 'heat', 'flow', and 'reactor', which in the other keywords networks often fall under the catch-all or the thermodynamic communities, are grouped together with 'solar' in Qatar's keywords network, suggesting that sustainability research related to heat, flow, and reactor performed in Qatar is strongly linked to solar. Wind power research is not Qatar's main focus, demonstrated by the 'wind' keyword appearing much less frequently than 'solar'.

As mentioned in the methodology section, the restriction on the number of terms included in the Saudi Arabia keywords network is stricter than the ones placed on other countries in order to facilitate the extraction of insights from the network. This has the effect of reducing the complexity of the network which is why Saudi Arabia's keywords, if they were plotted, would appear simpler than Kuwait's despite Saudi Arabia's greater publication history and volume. The signifier of the maturity of sustainability science research in Saudi Arabia that exists in the network is the large catch-all community which can also be found on the similarly mature UAE's keywords network. Having a more mature research history means that more concepts are explored, resulting in more unique words being found. Exploratory research is often not repeated as a particular avenue of research may prove to yield no useful results. The community detection algorithm will place repeated research into its own community while those that are not repeated will end up in the catch-all community. Aside from the catch-all community, communities found in Saudi Arabia's network are sustainable development, solar, weather, wind and gas, sustainable infrastructure, and turbines. Although we decided to label one community as 'sustainable development', the community actually contains many subfields in it such as water treatment, geothermal, and greenhouse gases. The community detection algorithm's decision to lump all these subfields together into one community suggests that the subfields are often studied together. 'Solar' is not the most commonly occurring keyword in the network, but surprisingly it is 'warming'. This can be interpreted as Saudi Arabia devoting considerable resource on understanding the impact of global warming, which makes Saudi Arabia unlike most GCC countries in that its strongest focus is not the renewable energy aspect of sustainability science. 'Photovoltaic' belongs to the same community as 'solar', suggesting that it is the predominant form of solar energy production. 'Heat', 'radiation', and 'cooling' are also in the same community as 'solar', implying that considerable research efforts are directed at mitigating the effects of solar radiation. Food security is possibly a concern for Saudi Arabia as 'farm' is one of the more commonly found keyword found on the network.

The UAE's keywords network construction uses a higher word inclusion threshold just like Saudi Arabia's keywords network. And, similar to Saudi Arabia's network, the threshold would make the network appear simpler if it was plotted, with only a large catch-all community serving as evidence of mature sustainability science research. Communities other than the catch-all which were detected in the network are chemical thermodynamics, socio-economic policies, renewable energy and power systems, solar energy, and meteorology. Judging by each keyword's appearance frequency, the types of renewable energy which have received the most research attention, in descending order, are solar, hydrogen, and wind. Communities in other countries' networks which are analogous to the UAE's socio-economic policies community are not as clearly defined. The UAE appears to be the only GCC country with a strong exclusive focus on studying socio-economic policies.

Discussion and recommendations

Comparison of the GCC countries' sustainability science output against global production is not possible, as we lack the data to do so. However, we do have data for a comparison against non-GCC Middle Eastern countries which includes regional scientific leaders such as Egypt and Turkey, and this comparison of publication ratios paints the GCC countries' sustainability research productivity in a favourable light. Considering that the research infrastructure in most GCC countries have only been developed fairly recently and there are far fewer countries in the GCC in total than in the Middle East, the GCC countries are performing well by producing two sustainability publications for every 10 from the Middle East in 2012. The GCC countries are also more strongly committed to sustainability science than Middle Eastern countries, as sustainability publications' share of overall publications is higher for GCC countries than Middle Eastern countries throughout the entire 17-year period that we studied. However, this does not mean that the GCC countries should feel comfortable maintaining their current level of effort in sustainability science research. After many years of stagnation, sustainability science's share of overall publication has begun increasing in Middle Eastern countries and appears poised to catch up to that of the GCC countries.

From our network analysis, the sustainability science research efforts of the GCC countries will potentially allow them to meet many of the 17 Sustainable Development Goals (SDGs) adopted at the 2015 United Nations Sustainable Development Summit. The unequal distribution of research focus may mean that certain goals (e.g. 'Life on Land') will be achieved later than others (e.g. 'Affordable and Clean Energy' and 'Clean Water and Sanitation').

The path to affordable and clean energy may be the shortest for GCC countries, as they have invested the greatest amount of effort into researching renewable energy sources, especially those related to solar. The GCC countries' current level of research productivity in renewable energy should be sustained.

Meeting clean water and sanitation goals will likely come as the by-product of the GCC countries' research efforts in addressing the region's potable water scarcity issue. However, the keywords networks we constructed did not indicate that much research has been done on the impact made by the use of certain technologies to address the water scarcity problem, such as desalination increasing the Arabian Gulf's salinity. Attempting to meet the clean water and sanitation goal may have the unintended consequence of making the 'Life below Water' goal, which is about conserving marine resources, difficult to meet. Therefore, we recommend that the GCC countries enact policies that place greater emphasis on environmental and ecology research.

Achieving the goal of decent work and economic growth and the goal of sustainable cities and communities will most likely be achieved by the GCC countries with a more mature scientific research background. This is due to countries with less sustainability research experience favouring the research of renewable energy sources over other aspects of sustainability. In contrast, the more mature Saudi Arabia can and have devoted efforts into making cities sustainable and liveable, while the UAE has a fairly strong research focus on socio-economic policies. Policies which foster the growth of scientific communities for countries with weak sustainability research backgrounds would help these countries achieve the goals of economic growth and sustainable cities.

Climate action as a goal has received some attention of GCC countries, with 'global warming' appearing in many keywords network, although it does not stand out as its own research focus. Policies which incentivizes research into climate action are required for GCC countries.

For the industry, innovation, and infrastructure goal, there are countries which have placed an emphasis on parts of the goal. One of Bahrain's research foci is studying traffic flow, which aids in the development of sustainable infrastructure. A part of the social-economic policies research focus of the UAE involves studying entrepreneurship, which fosters innovation and may promote sustainable industries. Each GCC country could perhaps focus its research on a particular part of the industry, innovation, and infrastructure goal that is most relevant to the country then share the lessons learned with other GCC countries.

Conclusion

In this chapter, bibliometric data for the GCC region has been used to gauge the state of sustainability science research in the GCC countries. The methods used to parse the data are time series analysis and network analysis. From the analysis, we find that GCC countries' sustainability research efforts are mostly directed towards renewable energy, with solar taking priority, followed by wind, hydrogen, and biomass. Water treatment and sustainable development also received considerable attention from GCC-based researchers. The state of the GCC countries' sustainability science research compares well against non-GCC Middle Eastern countries, although the Middle Eastern countries are closing the gap in recent years. A stronger commitment to the study of sustainability as well as a diversification of research topics is required if the GCC countries are to meet the many goals in SDGs.

References

Abdulrazzak, Mohamed J. 1994. Review and assessment of water resources in Gulf Cooperation Council countries. *International Journal of Water Resources Development*, 10(1): 23–37.

Afifi, M.M. 2005. Mental health publications from the Arab world cited in PubMed, 1987–2002. *Eastern Mediterranean Health Journal*, 11(3): 319.

Al-Ansari, Husain H. 2008. Library and information science literature on the Gulf Cooperation Council (GCC) countries: A bibliographic analysis. *Technical Services Quarterly*, 25(3): 21–34.

Al-Khader, Abdulla A. 2004. Enhancing research productivity in the Arab world. *Saudi Medical Journal*, 25(10): 1323–1327.

Al-Mulali, Usama, and Ilhan Ozturk. 2014. Are energy conservation policies effective without harming economic growth in the Gulf Cooperation Council countries? *Renewable and Sustainable Energy Reviews*, 38: 639–650.

Alnaser, W.E., and N.W. Alnaser. 2011. The status of renewable energy in the GCC countries. *Renewable and Sustainable Energy Reviews*, 15(6): 3074–3098.

Al-Zubari, Waleed K. 2003. Alternative water policies for the Gulf Cooperation Council countries. *Developments in Water Science*, 50: 155–167.

Benamer, Hani T.S., and Omran Bakoush. 2009. Arab nations lagging behind other Middle Eastern countries in biomedical research: A comparative study. *BMC Medical Research Methodology*, 9: 26.

Bhutto, Abdul Waheed, Aqeel Ahmed Bazmi, Gholamreza Zahedi, and Jiří Jaromír Klemeš. 2014. A review of progress in renewable energy implementation in the Gulf Cooperation Council countries. *Journal of Cleaner Production*, 71: 168–180.

Bredan, Amin, Hani T.S. Benamer, and Omran Bakoush. 2011. Visibility of Arab countries in the world biomedical literature. *Libyan Journal of Medicine*, 6: 6325.

Bushnak, Adil A. 1990. Water supply challenge in the Gulf region. *Desalination*, 78(2): 133–145.

Dawoud, Mohamed A. 2012. Environmental impacts of seawater desalination: Arabian Gulf case study. *International Journal of Environment and Sustainability (IJES)*, 1(3): 22–37.

Deleu, Dirk, Margaret G. Northway, and Yolande Hanssens. 2001. Geographical distribution of biomedical publications from the Gulf Corporation Council countries. *Saudi Medical Journal*, 22(1): 10–12.

Doukas, Haris, Konstantinos D. Patlitzianas, Argyris G. Kagiannas, and John Psarras. 2006. Renewable energy sources and rationale use of energy development in the countries of GCC: Myth or reality? *Renewable Energy*, 31(6): 755–770.

Dragos, Cristian Mihai, and Simona Laura Dragos. 2013. Bibliometric approach of factors affecting scientific productivity in environmental sciences and ecology. *Science of the Total Environment*, 449: 184–188.

El Alami, J., Jean-Christophe Dore, and Jean-François Miquel. 1992. International scientific collaboration in Arab countries. *Scientometrics*, 23(1): 249–263.

Elsevier. 2017a. *Scopus | The Largest Database of Peer-Reviewed Literature | Elsevier*. Available at: www.elsevier.com/solutions/scopus (Accessed 30 January 2017).

Elsevier. 2017b. *SciVerse Scopus Custom Data Documentation*. Available at: http://ebrp.elsevier.com/pdf/Scopus_Custom_Data_Documentation_v4.pdf (Accessed 30 January 2017).

Falagas, Matthew E., Effie A. Zarkadoulia, and George Samonis. 2006. Arab science in the golden age (750–1258 CE) and today. *The FASEB Journal*, 20(10): 1581–1586.

Ferroukhi, Rabia, Noor Ghazal-Aswad, Stella Androulaki, Diala Hawila, and Toufic Mezher. 2013. Renewable energy in the GCC: Status and challenges. *International Journal of Energy Sector Management*, 7(1): 84–112.

Hassan, Saeed-Ul, Peter Haddawy, and Jia Zhu. 2014. A bibliometric study of the world's research activity in sustainable development and its sub-areas using scientific literature. *Scientometrics*, 99(2): 549–579.

Hertog, Steffen, and Giacomo Luciani. 2009. *Energy and Sustainability Policies in the GCC*. Discussion Paper. Kuwait Program, London School of Economics, London.

Janssen, Marco A., Michael L. Schoon, Weimao Ke, and Katy Börner. 2006. Scholarly networks on resilience, vulnerability and adaptation within the human dimensions of global environmental change. *Global Environmental Change*, 16(3): 240–252.

Kajikawa, Yuya, Francisco Tacoa, and Kiyohiro Yamaguchi. 2014. Sustainability science: The changing landscape of sustainability research. *Sustainability Science*, 9(4): 431–438.

Kannan, A. 2012. Global Environmental Governance and Desertification: A Study of Gulf Cooperation Council Countries. New Delhi, India: Concept Publishing Company.

Karrer, Brian, and Mark E.J. Newman. 2011. Stochastic blockmodels and community structure in networks. *Physical Review E*, 83(1): 016107.

Kumetat, Dennis. 2009. *Climate Change in the Persian Gulf – Regional Security, Sustainability Strategies and Research Needs*. In International Conference "Climate Change, Social Stress and Violent Conflict" in Hamburg (Germany), vol. 19, p. 20.

Lammers, W.J.E.P., and Adnan Tahir. 1996. Profile of medical research publications from the GCC countries, 1990–1994. *Annals of Saudi Medicine*, 16: 666–669.

Li, Wei, and Yang Zhao. 2015. Bibliometric analysis of global environmental assessment research in a 20-year period. *Environmental Impact Assessment Review*, 50: 158–166.

Manzano-Agugliaro, F., A. Alcayde, F.G. Montoya, A. Zapata-Sierra, and C. Gil. 2013. Scientific production of renewable energies worldwide: An overview. *Renewable and Sustainable Energy Reviews*, 18: 134–143.

Maziak, Wasim. 2005. Science in the Arab world: Vision of glories beyond. *Science*, 308(5727): 1416–1418.

Moed, Henk F., Judit Bar-Ilan, and Gali Halevi. 2016. A new methodology for comparing Google Scholar and Scopus. *Journal of Informetrics*, 10(2): 533–551.

Peixoto, Tiago P. 2014. Hierarchical block structures and high-resolution model selection in large networks. *Physical Review X*, 4(1): 011047.

Reiche, Danyel. 2010. Energy Policies of Gulf Cooperation Council (GCC) countries – Possibilities and limitations of ecological modernization in rentier states. *Energy Policy*, 38(5): 378–382.

Rizzi, Francesco, Nees Jan van Eck, and Marco Frey. 2014. The production of scientific knowledge on renewable energies: Worldwide trends, dynamics and challenges and implications for management. *Renewable Energy*, 62: 657–671.

Romo-Fernández, Luz M., Vicente P. Guerrero-Bote, and Félix Moya-Anegón. 2012. World scientific production on renewable energy, sustainability and the environment. *Energy for Sustainable Development*, 16(4): 500–508.

Salem, Shawsky. 1990. Bibliometric aspects of medical information in Arab countries. *Bulletin of the Medical Library Association*, 78(4): 339–344.

Shah, Mahendra. 2010. Gulf Cooperation Council food security: Balancing the equation. *Nature Middle East*. Available at: http://www.natureasia.com/en/nmiddleeast/article/10.1038/nmiddleeast.2010.141 (Accessed 30 April 2017). doi:10.1038/nmiddleeast.2010.141

Slyder, J.B., Stein, B.R., Sams, B.S., Walker, D.M., Beale, B.J., Feldhaus, J.J. and Copenheaver, C.A. 2011. Citation pattern and lifespan: a comparison of discipline, institution, and individual. *Scientometrics*, 89(3): 955-966.

Spiess, Andy. 2008. Developing adaptive capacity for responding to environmental change in the Arab Gulf States: Uncertainties to linking ecosystem conservation, sustainable development and society in authoritarian rentier economies. *Global and Planetary Change*, 64(3): 244–252.

Sweileh, Waleed M., Samah W. Al-Jabi, Ansam F. Sawalha, and H. Zyoud Sa'ed. 2014a. Bibliometric analysis of nutrition and dietetics research activity in Arab countries using ISI Web of Science database. *SpringerPlus*, 3: 718.

Sweileh, Waleed M., Samah W. Al-Jabi, Sa'ed H. Zyoud, Ansam F. Sawalha, and Mustafa A. Ghanim. 2014b. Osteoporosis is a neglected health priority in Arab World: A comparative bibliometric analysis. *SpringerPlus*, 3: 427.

Sweileh, Waleed M., H. Zyoud Sa'ed, Samah W. Al-Jabi, and Ansam F. Sawalha. 2014c. Assessing urology and nephrology research activity in Arab countries using ISI web of science bibliometric database. *BMC Research Notes*, 7: 258.

Sweileh, Waleed M., H. Zyoud Sa'ed, Samah W. Al-Jabi, and Ansam F. Sawalha. 2014d. Bibliometric analysis of diabetes mellitus research output from Middle Eastern Arab countries during the period (1996–2012). *Scientometrics*, 101(1): 819–832.

Sweileh, Waleed M., H. Zyoud Sa'ed, Samah W. Al-Jabi, and Ansam F. Sawalha. 2014e. Substance use disorders in Arab countries: Research activity and bibliometric analysis. *Substance Abuse Treatment, Prevention, and Policy*, 9: 33.

Sweileh, Waleed M., Sa'ed H. Zyoud, Samah W. Al-Jabi, and Ansam F. Sawalha. 2014f. Quantity and quality of obesity-related research in Arab countries: Assessment and comparative analysis. *Health Research Policy and Systems*, 12: 33.

Sweileh, Waleed M., Samah W. Al-Jabi, Yousef I. Shanti, Ansam F. Sawalha, and Sa'ed H. Zyoud. 2015a. Contribution of Arab researchers to ophthalmology: A bibliometric and comparative analysis. *SpringerPlus*, 4: 42.

Sweileh, Waleed M., H. Zyoud Sa'ed, Samah W. Al-Jabi, and Ansam F. Sawalha. 2015b. Contribution of Arab countries to breast cancer research: Comparison with non-Arab Middle Eastern countries. *BMC Women's Health*, 15: 25.

Tadmouri, Ghazi Omar, and Nisrine Bissar-Tadmouri. 2003. Biomedical publications in an unstable region: The Arab world, 1988–2002. *The Lancet*, 362(9397): 1766.

Uzun, Ali. 2002. National patterns of research output and priorities in renewable energy. *Energy Policy*, 30(2): 131–136.

Waast, Roland. 2010. Research in Arab countries (North Africa and West Asia). *Science Technology & Society*, 15(2): 187–231.

Waast, Roland, and Pier-Luigi Rossi. 2010. Scientific production in Arab countries: A bibliometric perspective. *Science Technology & Society*, 15(2): 339–370.

Zyoud, Sa'ed H., Samah W. Al-Jabi, and Waleed M. Sweileh. 2014a. Bibliometric analysis of scientific publications on waterpipe (narghile, shisha, hookah) tobacco smoking during the period 2003–2012. *Tobacco Induced Diseases*, 12: 7.

Zyoud, Sa'ed H., Samah W. Al-Jabi, Waleed M. Sweileh, and Rahmat Awang. 2014b. A bibliometric analysis of toxicology research productivity in Middle Eastern Arab countries during a 10-year period (2003–2012). *Health Research Policy and Systems*, 12: 4.

Zyoud Sa'ed, H., Samah W. Al-Jabi, Waleed M. Sweileh, and Rahmat Awang. 2014c. A Scopus-based examination of tobacco use publications in Middle Eastern Arab countries during the period 2003–2012. *Harm Reduction Journal*, 11: 14.

Zyoud Sa'ed, H., Samah W. Al-Jabi, Waleed M. Sweileh, Suleiman Al-Khalil, Shaher H. Zyoud, Ansam F. Sawalha, and Rahmat Awang. 2015. The Arab world's contribution to solid waste literature: A bibliometric analysis. *Journal of Occupational Medicine and Toxicology*, 10: 35.

Zyoud, Shaher H., Aiman E. Al-Rawajfeh, Hafez Q. Shaheen, and Daniela Fuchs-Hanusch. 2016. Benchmarking the scientific output of industrial wastewater research in Arab world by utilizing bibliometric techniques. *Environmental Science and Pollution Research*, 23(10): 10288–10300. doi:10.1007/s11356-016-6434-6

Zyoud, S.H., and D. Fuchs-Hanusch. 2015. Estimates of Arab world research productivity associated with desalination: A bibliometric analysis. *IDA Journal of Desalination and Water Reuse*, 7(1–4): 3–16.

3 Framework of study and book organization

Elie Azar and Mohamed Abdel Raouf

Introduction

Filling a void in the academic and policy-relevant literature on the topic of sustainability in the Gulf region, this edited volume provides a multidisciplinary analysis of the key themes and challenges related to sustainability in the region, including water, standards and policies, as well as economic and social perspectives. The proposed sustainability-focused approach also aims at generating economic development that increases environmental and social welfare, as well as human well-being and quality of life.

Eleven insightful analyses on Gulf-specific aspects of sustainability are presented, examining the current status, challenges and opportunities, and identifying key lessons learned. The book also provides innovative and practical policy recommendations, as well as new conceptual angles to the evolving academic debates on the post-oil era in the Gulf. It is intended to become a useful academic resource for the region's policymakers and an essential reading for academics and students of the Gulf.

Book structure

The book is divided into five main parts. Part 1: Introduction – which is comprised of three chapters – introduces the readers to main sustainability issues in the GCC and presents a mapping of previous and current sustainability research efforts. Part 2: Infrastructure management and urban solutions – which includes five chapters – covers case studies from sectors or disciplines related to the infrastructure of Gulf countries such as water management, public transit, and climate-sensitive urban design. Part 3: Standards and policies – which is composed of two chapters – present mechanisms used to assess the efficiency and sustainability in different sectors. Part 4: The socio-economic perspective – which includes four chapters – covers the two remaining pillars of the triple bottom line, the profit (i.e., economic) and the people (i.e., social) perspectives. Finally, Part 5: Conclusion presents an outlook towards the future of sustainability in the Gulf. The following paragraphs detail each of the chapters presented in the book starting from the chapters of Part 2, which follow the current introductory chapters.

In Chapter 4, "Water resources sustainability in Kuwait against United Nations Sustainable Development Goals", the authors develop a water resources sustainability plan for Kuwait. This plan includes suitable interventions and strategic policies in response to the local economic, environmental, financial, and cultural conditions in an effort to sustain water supplies for the future of Kuwait and address the UN's SDGs.

Chapter 5, "Towards safe and sustainable reuse of treated wastewater in Abu Dhabi, UAE", covers the Abu Dhabi Emirate's ambitious targets and practices for meeting part of its freshwater demand with treated wastewater. The authors argue that the reuse of treated wastewater offers a sustainable solution in line with the SDGs for limiting the Emirate's carbon footprint and energy demand in freshwater production, while enhancing its food and water security.

In Chapter 6, "Implementation of the Sustainable Development Goals in the GCC countries via application of sustainability-oriented innovation to critical infrastructures", the authors explore the role of global cities in the global governance architecture, specifically with regards to the implementation of the SDGs in the GCC countries. The authors then provide a case study of Abu Dhabi by applying the Sustainability-Oriented Innovation Index for Airports©, with regards to the international airport's capacity to align sustainability strategies through three unique lenses of environmental, social, and technological innovation.

Chapter 7, "Towards sustainable urban development: Challenges and chances of climate-sensitive urban design in Muscat/Oman", proposes consolidated planning strategies that address climate-sensitive urban design (CSUD) and sustainable lifestyle in Muscat/Oman. A comprehensive socio-spatial and environmental approach is introduced through planning a system of urban spaces in Muscat with a focus on transforming the so-called wadis – undeveloped, sloped dry riverbeds which form natural barriers and segment the urban fabric of Muscat – into urban green spaces.

Chapter 8, "The future of sustainable public transit in Abu Dhabi", suggests a transit-oriented development in the new Capital District and its suburbs. In order to support this claim, the study examines the historic and future urban growth trends of the Emirate of Abu Dhabi in relation to the transportation demand. It analyzes them against external and internal factors that affect transit travel demand in order to detect possible travel trends that would encourage further transit developments in the new district.

Chapter 9, "Advancing sustainable consumption: energy efficiency labels and standards in the UAE", examines existing energy efficiency labels and standards of particular relevance to lifestyle consumption, as well as complementary policies that have been – or can be – adopted to help meet the objectives of these regulations. The chapter also examines policymaking models that allow for effective and informed decision-making on design and implementation of standards.

Chapter 10, "Sustainability assessment for real estate in the UAE: the case of Masdar City", aims at identifying issues that determine the efficiency of Sustainability Assessment (SA) tools for buildings such as LEED, BREEAM, and Estidama. A case study on Masdar City has been presented and experts were interviewed to understand the role of SA tools in driving the consumer demand for sustainable projects. The authors argue that mandatory green building certifications such as Estidama play a significant role in driving people's awareness and improving the building stock.

In Chapter 11, "Energy consumption and transition dynamics to a sustainable future under a rentier economy: the case of the GCC states", the authors investigate the energy consumption dynamics of GCC states and market entry barriers for clean, efficient, or renewable energy technologies (CERET) development. The findings suggest that the current rentier economic system, along with population increase, growing economic activity, and the very hot climate of the region, may cause a further increase in energy consumption in the region and associated CO2 emissions per capita. On the other hand, development of CERET in the region depends on the initiatives from the state itself since market entry barriers in the region may block private investments.

In Chapter 12, "Economic value of the Abu Dhabi coastal and marine ecosystem services: estimate and management applications", the authors estimate the value that Abu Dhabi's beachfront hotels derive from coastal and marine ecosystems. The willingness to accept (WTA) compensation in the event of harmful algae blooms was estimated at $141 million per year or 35% of beachfront hotels' average turnover. The findings indicate the reliance on the delivery of ecosystem services, but also the risks as a result of such reliance as ecosystems were under increasing economic development-related pressures.

Chapter 13, "Economic and GHG emission policy co-benefits for integrated waste management planning across the GCC", presents a modelling study to assess future economic and emission co-benefits from the planned increase in integrated waste management capacity, which is necessary to stabilize and reduce future methane disposal emissions. The chapter also presents new time-based metrics that may be used by developing and undeveloped countries to measure policy implementation co-benefits and progress towards the mitigation of municipal solid waste emissions.

The aim of Chapter 14, "Motivating sustainable consumption behaviour through education, incentive programs, and green policies in Saudi Arabia", is to encourage sustainable consumption behaviour of water and energy in Saudi Arabia. The results of a questionnaire conducted in the Makkah region confirm the need for more sustainable consumption behaviours. The authors then propose solutions to alter current behaviours through incentive schemes, green policies, and education initiatives through school curricula.

Finally, Chapter 15, "Outlook towards the future of sustainability in the Gulf", concludes this book with a summary of the findings and the lessons learned, in addition to reflections on the prospects for sustainability in the GCC states and the region.

Part II

Infrastructure management and urban solutions

4 Water resources sustainability in Kuwait against United Nations Sustainable Development Goals

Muhammad Al-Rashed and Amjad Aliewi

Introduction

Water is the source of sustainable life anywhere in the universe. Wherever reliable water resources exist, the means for socio-economic development exist but sustainability of water resources requires additional efforts such as the development of long-term water strategies and plans to conserve and secure sustainable water supply for all demand sectors. The sustainable development, management, use and protection of the limited and scarce water resources in Kuwait are essential for their security and for the quality of life of future generations. This emphasis on sustainability aligns with the Integrated Water Resources Management (IWRM) paradigm. This can be achieved through developing and implementing a clear water policy and associated action plans. Kuwait is located in a hyperarid zone having very limited resources of freshwater. Brackish groundwater aquifers and intermittent wadis which may run a few days in the year are the only natural water resources of Kuwait. The groundwater is replenishable by a limited recharge from rainfall and trans-boundary influx from adjacent countries such as Saudi Arabia. Today, Kuwait is mostly dependent on seawater desalination for supplementing its freshwater needs. Water resources in Kuwait are very fragile, lack reliability and have been used at unsustainable rates with almost no significant economic returns to Kuwait's economy. Kuwait, due to rainfall scarcity, low quality of groundwater, high population growth rates and increased standards of living, fragmented and weak water demand management (WDM), and the practice of expanding irrigated agriculture and industrialization, is suffering severe water supply shortages albeit almost completely compensated from desalination plants. If water shortage problems reach a crisis level, then water will become a limiting factor to further socio-economic, agricultural and industrial developments as well as a limiting factor to advancement in public health. The Kuwaiti government encourages the utilization of treated wastewater, whether from urban or industrial sources. Urban effluent is the only resource of water, which increases with the initial supply level. It can be treated and utilized within the water management plans in Kuwait. It is worth noting that Thames Water International, which serves London, reuses urban water up to nine times as water supply before sea discharge (personal contacts with Thames Water International). Water resources

Table 4.1 Summary of used water in Kuwait (for the year 2015)

Source of water	*Quantity (Mcm/yr)*	*Quality*	*Use*
Desalination plants (consumption)	660	Freshwater	Mainly domestic
Fresh groundwater aquifers	3	Freshwater	Mainly domestic
Brackish groundwater aquifers	250	Brackish water	Agriculture and oil industry
Conventional treated wastewater for reuse	77*	Freshwater to brackish water	Greenery use
Reverse osmosis treated wastewater for reuse	84**	Freshwater	Crops agriculture
Total use of water	1074		

* Only 70% of the wastewater (110 Mcm/yr) tertiary treated is reused for greenery purposes.
** Only 70% of the wastewater (120 Mcm/yr) treated by membranes is reused for crops agriculture (Al-Anzi et al. 2012).

sustainability is a fundamental element in any attempt to formulate a national water policy for Kuwait. There is a need to develop national water policies for Kuwait to overcome water resources problems and related threats. The main water challenge in Kuwait is to manage all available water resources under one umbrella. In this chapter, a discussion is presented about policy statements and principles in order to secure water sustainability in terms of supply and management. According to the records of the Ministry of Electricity of Water (MEW 2015), Kuwait produces approximately 876 Mcm/yr of freshwater from desalination plants and consumes approximately 660 Mcm/yr of freshwater. The summary of used water in Kuwait is presented in Table 4.1.

Table 4.1 illustrates that water supplies for domestic use without desalination in Kuwait are not sustainable. The challenges of water resources sustainability in Kuwait were addressed by a number of authors such as Fadlelmawla (2008), Darwish and Al-Najem (2005), Al-Ruwaih and Almedeij (2007), Al-Damkhi et al. (2009), Al-Otaibi and Kotwicki (2009), Al-Qunaibet and Johnston (1985) and El-Sayed et al. (2015). Water unsustainability and scarcity in Kuwait is regarded as the main constraint to social and economic development as well as a source of wider insecurity. Hadi and Kotwicki (2007) and Kotwicki and Al Sulaimani (2009) pointed out that flexible strategies are needed to deal with the impact of climate change on water resources. The challenges faced with regard to water resources sustainability in Kuwait can be summarized as follows:

Challenge No. 1: heavy reliance on desalination

During the last few decades, Kuwait has been almost 100% reliant on desalination plants to produce freshwater. Kuwait is almost producing freshwater from desalination plants as much as it is consuming. Kuwait blends desalinated water with brackish water and supplies the mixture to pipe networks and elevated towers. Water production through desalination is an energy-intensive process, as it uses up to 70% of electricity consumption in Kuwait (Bachellerie 2012). According to El-Sayed et al. (2015), water subsidies consume 5.9% of the oil export revenues and 2.4% of Kuwait's gross domestic product (GDP). The capital, construction and operating costs of desalination plants are very high. The high operating cost is due to large energy requirements for desalination plants. Energy cost to operate desalination plants is approximately one-third of the desalination cost alone (Ghaffour et al. 2014). Kuwait spends approximately US$4.55 billion annually to operate desalination and energy production plants (Al-Rashed and Akber 2015; and El-Sayed et al. 2010). Kuwait currently uses about 12% and is expected in 2050 to use 50% of its oil production to supply fuel to operate its desalination plants (El- Sayed et al. 2015). However, the high cost associated with desalination does not stop the increasing demand for desalinated water in Kuwait, which makes this challenge even more critical, as reported by El-Sayed et al. (2015); that is, the production of desalinated water will increase by 75% in the near future. The brine is usually diluted and its effect is for a limited distance and mostly thermal effluent only. The emission gases (such as nitrogen, sulphur and carbon dioxide) from these desalination plants cause serious problems to the surrounding environment. These plants are so fragile to polluted seawater which normally results in their shutdown.

Challenge No. 2: limited natural water resources and pollution

Kuwait is located in arid/hyperarid environments with scarcity rainfall and high evaporation rates. Kuwait does not enjoy rivers, lakes and surface reservoirs. The natural renewable water resources are limited to groundwater aquifers, but their water quality is mostly brackish. The wastewater discharge and the industrial effluent loading on the Arabian Gulf are sources of pollution. Also, oil exports' operational services should avoid oil spills so that high hydrocarbon concentrations in the waters of the Arabian Gulf can be avoided. Additionally, where the concentration of hydrocarbons is high, the desalination plants and the environment will also be impacted negatively, especially costs and performance. Today, Kuwait is almost fully supplementing its freshwater needs with seawater desalination.

Challenge No. 3: high water consumption/use

Although Kuwait has limited water resources, the per capita daily consumption is among the highest in the world. Official records of the MEW say that the daily per capita consumption in Kuwait is 442 liters (MEW 2015). Kuwait is among the highest water-consuming countries and among the poorest countries in terms of water resources. In order to meet this high consumption and because water for the residents of Kuwait is a necessity not a luxury, Kuwait constructed desalination plants, which are very expensive. Also, agricultural consumption is far greater than aquifer recharge, causing aquifer water levels to decline considerably and water salinity to increase substantially either by means of saltwater intrusion or by means of saline water up-coning from lower aquifers. Agriculture consumes most of the groundwater produced in Kuwait and provides less than 1% to the GDP, hence supporting imported food with its embedded water, 'the principle of virtual water'. Also, there is an intensive use of agrochemicals to increase productivity as well as over-irrigation washing out salt from soils. The result is groundwater pollution with high levels of nitrates, salinization and water logging. The high water consumption rates increase the risk on the sustainability of non-renewable aquifers. The high rate of water use is not limited only to freshwater in Kuwait. Brackish groundwater is also needed for agriculture as well as for oil processing/injection into oil fields to maintain reservoir pressure and extract crude oil. The demand for brackish water is increasing and plans are required for its sustainable use between agriculture and industry (Aliewi et al. 2015). Pollution is always a concern when industry is involved. The safe disposal of the generated and polluted water associated with oil production wells has become a major problem for the oil industry.

Challenge No. 4: high rates of Unaccounted for Water (UFW) and leakages

The UFW volumes from pipe networks and the leakage volumes into and from sewage collection systems should be reduced. However, leakage from pipe networks in Kuwait is limited and within the least in the world, ranging 7–13%. The UFW and leakages normally lead to: (a) rising groundwater tables in the urban cities of Kuwait, even threatening the stability of building foundations and roads; and (b) increasing aquifer pollution. The heavy use of cesspits and septic tanks makes the shallow unconfined aquifers vulnerable to pollution by raw sewage and thus raises the level of nitrates in these aquifers as well as that of bacteriological challenge.

Challenge No. 5: weak governance

The rapid increase in population and standards of living in Kuwait has increased the annual water demand about 5 times from 1980 to 2000. There is a need of implementing the principles of integrated water resources management (IWRM) (such as equity, socio-economic benefits and efficiency) and governance in Kuwait. There are unclear and conflicting responsibilities among ministries/regional bodies about the regulation of water resources' use and their conservation. The management of water operational services is not fully efficient. The above challenges put Kuwait under pressure to secure water supplies for all demand sectors in a sustainable way following the UN Sustainable Development Goals (SDGs) so as to increase the capacity of the Kuwaiti government to provide adequate quantities of acceptable quality water for sustaining livelihoods and socio-economic development, as well as for preserving ecosystems (UN-Water 2013). In this chapter, the concepts of water resources sustainability and water security are dealt with by emphasizing on the need to develop suitable policies in response to the economic, environmental, financial and cultural conditions in Kuwait in order to achieve sustainable water resources development and management.

Water resources Sustainable Development Goals (SDGs) and security

The UN SDGs are an intergovernmental set of goals covering poverty alleviation, energy, water and sanitation, health and human settlement. The goals address the three dimensions of sustainable development (environment, economics and society) and their interlinkages. In this chapter, the emphasis is given to water issues. The SDGs focus on ensuring the availability of water and the sustainable management of water and sanitation for all. Ensuring access to safe and affordable drinking water for Kuwaiti residents requires investment in adequate water supply infrastructure and sanitation facilities. More efforts are needed to encourage water consumption efficiency and support advanced desalination and treatment technologies. All of the residential areas in Kuwait are served with 100% water supply and sanitation (UNICEF and WHO 2012), but to achieve the SDGs in Kuwait, the management of water supplies and sanitation services needs to be integrated with technical, social and economic aspects. This also requires integration between water and energy through the efficient use of energy for water pumping and treatment. This is an IWRM issue. Water resources sustainability is about the amalgamation between water resources development and management. The sustainable development keeps a balance between the exploitation of natural resources, technology development and implementation in desalination, treatment of wastewater and governance setup to enhance the potential of water supplies to meet human, agricultural and industrial water needs now and in the future (WCED 1987). The sustainable management of water resources as explained by Loucks (1997) is to manage water systems to contribute fully to the objectives of society, now and in the future, while maintaining their ecological, environmental and hydrological integrity. This definition requires the development of water management policies that promote sustainable water resources. The sustainable management of water resources is becoming more difficult to achieve in countries such as Kuwait because of the challenges explained earlier in this chapter.

The water resources sustainability goals for Kuwait should cover the following subjects:

- Assure integration between water availability, environmental concerns and population welfare for future generations.
- Improve water supply reliability and efficiency to meet human water needs and reduce energy demand through using renewable solar and wind energy.

- Investigate new water resources and new water technologies to desalinate seawater and brackish groundwater.
- Improve conjunctive use and management of desalinated water, runoff water from rainfall and treated wastewater for domestic and agricultural purposes in addition to aquifer recharge and reserve.
- Support IWRM that includes reforms, regulations and water laws and policies.

Methodology

Water resources sustainability requires a balance between water supply and demand through an action plan utilizing structural measures (development of internal and external water resources/supplies) and supporting nonstructural measures (demand management imperatives) (CH2MHILL 2002). The methodology in this chapter adopts the stakeholders (participatory) approach in which quite a large number of scientists and managers from different academic and research institutes, in addition to managers from different Kuwaiti authorities, were interviewed about water resources sustainability in Kuwait. The stakeholder dialogue helped arrive at compromise response scenarios that provided the core of the water resources sustainability strategy for Kuwait which will be discussed later in this chapter.

The discussions with the stakeholders were organized as follows:

1. Socio-economic–environmental future for Kuwait. The interviews included discussions on the socio-economic and environmental future of Kuwait in response to water scarcity and sustainability. The influence of internal and external socio-economic forces on the future of water demand in Kuwait is difficult to anticipate. An attempt has been made in the UK (DTI 1999) to define a set of possible global and environmental future scenarios, which would influence water demand in the future. Another attempt was made for Kuwait. The scenarios use social values and socio-economic dimensions. As an example, these scenarios can be used to assess changes in the planning for the future of water demands in Kuwait in terms of socio-economic benefits against environmental values dereliction.
2. Water resources sustainability indicators. Also, the discussion covered the use of indicators which measure the economic, social and environmental performance of the water sector in Kuwait in terms of its sustainability.
3. Interventions. Suitable interventions made in response to the burdens on the sustainability of water resources in Kuwait were also discussed. These interventions can be structural interventions and nonstructural interventions. Desalination is a structural action while demand management is a nonstructural action.

4 Governance and policies. The discussion included the analysis of alternative policy options under the conditions of socio-economic and environmental changes. The burdens on water resources, such as climate change (which controls water availability) and socio-economic development (which can be beyond the control of the water sector), were discussed. These burdens can be reflected in drought frequency and severity, or increasing demand for water associated with population growth or growth in the agricultural, commercial and industrial sectors in response to a high socio-economic change.

Results, analysis and discussions

Possible future of Kuwait within water resources sustainability

In developing possible socio-economic future scenarios for Kuwait, conflicts need to be addressed. For example, industrial activities can contribute to economic growth but may lead to aquifer pollution, resulting in potential water quality problems and longer term degradation unless more restricted regulations are made in industrial water treatment effluent. Over-abstraction to support the expansion of industry or irrigated agriculture may lead to source depletion with consequent impacts on livelihoods. A possible scenario might call at reducing the amount of water allocated to agriculture, which will lead to increased imports of food (virtual water) and investment in abroad agricultural projects. In Kuwait, this scenario is possible and may be favorable. The social values are dominated by consumerist attitudes which emphasize individualism, materialism and private consumption. Concern for the environment focuses on specific problems that impact on the individuals or their immediate local area. In contrast, community-oriented values are concerned with securing long-term social goals such as sustainable economic development. There is a strong emphasis on the enhancement of collective goods and services, reflected in the high priority placed on the use of resources and environmental problems. However, globalisation is characterized by the redistribution of political power and influence away from the nation-state towards global institutions such as the United Nations (UN) and World Trade Organization (WTO). Economic activity is locked into international trading systems, dominated by transnational corporations. This is distinct from regionalization, where national sovereignty is strengthened and there is a movement towards regional devolution and local government. In Kuwait, the economic growth should not be on the expense of the environment and social benefits. High levels of investment in research and development result in the development of innovative clean technologies that benefit the environment. The future of Kuwait as a result of deep discussions may favor globalization and other external developments in the world economy and trade. The way in which the Kuwaiti economy develops in response to globalization and other forces will affect trading and economic opportunities with the Gulf

Cooperation Council (GCC) countries as a whole, which will in turn affect the demand for shared water resources between these countries. A possible scenario for Kuwait's future could be as follows:

- Substantial economic development of the internal market.
- Heavy reliance on oil gradually reduced towards more industrial development.
- Reliance on abroad agriculture investment.
- Changing of economic patterns from oil industry to other industries such as agro-services, skilled tourism and international trading.
- Boom in activities including urban coastal and industrial development, desalination, power generation, oil production and processing, fishing and marine recreational activities.
- Increase in the levels of cooperation and integrated use of shared water resources by the GCC countries.

The following actions should be considered for a sustainable water resources future for Kuwait in close cooperation with other GCC countries:

- Regional water linkage projects.
- Development of shared aquifers and GCC country cooperation to better utilize these aquifers.
- Improved WDM within a unified water policy of the GCC countries.
- To minimize the energy and environmental cost of wastewater treatment and desalination using reclaimed water and renewable energy.
- Full utilization of advanced and tertiary treated wastewater.

Water resources sustainability indicators

A water resources sustainability indicator is normally developed to measure the performance of the selected interventions or management options relative to the desired condition such as to secure water supplies for the residents of Kuwait on a continuous basis (Aliewi et al. 2003; Parkin et al. 2005). Sustainability indicators should measure the impacts of climate variability on the reliability of a water resource system. Reliability is defined as the proportion of the time over which the demand can be met. The indicator in this way is used to evaluate progress towards a range of sustainability conditions. An example of this is the reliability and availability of brackish groundwater for agricultural and industrial use in Kuwait. Another example is to measure how well the desalination plants perform in meeting the demand regime imposed on them. Sustainability indicators should be carefully chosen because they are important to ensure that the resulting evaluation is vigorous and usable by the decision-makers. The emphasis here is on identifying suitable indicators, which can measure water resources/supply sustainability for Kuwait. A group of experts from Kuwait were interviewed to develop water resources sustainability goals and indicators. The following water resources sustainability indicators were developed using a participatory approach:

- Water law for Kuwait is developed and approved.
- Fresh groundwater use in agriculture is gradually reduced.
- The use of treated wastewater in agriculture and oil industry is increased.
- Wastewater is treated to level according to the potential use.
- Water allocated to grow crops with lower economic returns is gradually reduced.
- Virtual water principle is implemented.
- Investment in abroad agricultural projects with countries rich in water is encouraged.
- Per capita consumption is gradually reduced.
- The principles of governance and IWRM are implemented.
- Independent regulator for water resources and water services is established.
- Abstraction from Kuwait Group and Dammam Aquifers are fully regulated.
- Domestic supply meets quality standards at source is ensured.
- Leakages from water supply systems are monitored.
- Groundwater wells are metered.
- Fair water tariff is introduced.
- Water delivered is fully paid for.
- Annual report on the full cost of domestic water supply is produced.

Suitable actions

The suitable actions to be taken cover structural (interventions) and nonstructural (management options) measures (Burton et al. 2005). These actions cover water supply from desalination plants, aquifers, wastewater treatment plants and stormwater in addition to policies, regulations, reforms and other management options. Once the preferred intervention/management option has been identified, the associated investments will be integrated to form a comprehensive investment plan for the entire sector. The following interventions/management options were developed as a result of the participatory approach used in this study.

Interventions

(1) DESALINATION

Desalination is the most strategic option to boost water supply in Kuwait. The use of this option is largely dependent on the cost of consumed energy and transporting the desalinated water from the desalination plant to the demand center. At the moment, desalination is the only viable option for a sustainable life in Kuwait. Also, it is important to investigate what other solutions can offer in meeting the future water demand of Kuwait (Al-Rashed et al. 1998) in terms of environmental and socio-economic benefits. The socio-economic benefits of desalination for Kuwait are great. The job opportunities in this industry form the neck bone for the socio-economic life in Kuwait. Brackish water is less saline than seawater and, therefore, is more cost-effective to desalinate rural brackish water. However, using desalinated brackish water as a source depends on its location. However, desalinating brackish water is still expensive. Kuwait should consider using solar and wind energies to save operational cost, especially since the technology prices of renewable energy sources are declining these days. Also, there are high levels of solar radiation and sunshine durations making solar-based generation of electricity a good option despite harsh weather conditions, which could negatively affect the performance of solar cells (Bachellerie 2012). The use of solar energy technology for desalination is still not applied on a large scale because of huge land requirements (Ghaffour et al. 2014). The policymakers should encourage an integrated approach for the development of the energy and the water sectors (Abdel Gelil 2014). The use of reverse osmosis (RO) desalination has increased in the Middle East (Afonso 2004) as materials have improved and costs have decreased. Today, RO is a leading technology for new desalination plants as they have a better performance and can be applied to a variety of salt-water resources. New technologies in energy recovery and renewable energy will allow greater use of desalination (Greenlee et al. 2009). Because central desalination plants are expensive, there is an increasing interest to use mobile RO units as they can decrease the pressure on these plants.

In summary, Kuwait needs the following:

- New desalination plants to be operated with renewable energy;
- Small-scale brackish groundwater desalination plants;
- Small-scale mobile RO desalination units.

(2) WATER HARVESTING

The number of rainy days in Kuwait is limited to a few days in a year but it is not unusual if this number is increased considerably in some years. Some rainy storms may produce volumes of rainfall that Kuwait is unlikely to receive in a few years. Therefore, there is a good chance to harvest rainwater through the following means:

- Construction of household cisterns to capture rainfall from the roofs of the households.
- Construction of surface dams to capture runoffs in the wadis.
- Aquifer storage and recovery (ASR).

The idea of constructing household cisterns in Kuwait is possible but is not encouraging because the number of rainy days in Kuwait on average is very low.

In some years, it may not rain at all, making the investment in rainfall cisterns economically costly, especially if the maintenance cost of the cisterns is added to the construction cost.

The construction of surface dams to capture runoff waters to be used for irrigation is economically feasible because, when it rains in Kuwait, millions of cubic meters of water will be generated and it can be captured and reused if these dams are located in optimal sites. Studies were not made to assess the potential of this intervention in Kuwait. In the United Arab Emirates (UAE), personal communications with officials from the government were made which revealed that some 300 Mcm/yr can be harvested during the rainy season in UAE. In Kuwait when it rains 100 mm in a rainy season, it is assumed that 20% will be generated as runoff which can be harvested. If runoff from rainwater will be harvested over one-third of the surface area of Kuwait, then for practical and operational reasons, approximately 75 Mcm/yr is the potential for runoff harvesting through dams.

In Kuwait, ASR means the reinjection of desalinated freshwater or advanced treated wastewater into an aquifer for later recovery and use. The latest feasibility study of ASR in Kuwait aquifers was investigated by Mukhopadhyay et al. (2012). Their study was a hydrogeological investigation of Az-Zaqlah depression in north Kuwait to assess the feasibility of storing treated wastewater, by membrane technology, or desalinated water in the underlying aquifer (Kuwait Group Aquifer). The study concludes that it is possible to store a significant volume of good-quality water through artificial recharge and recover it later during high demand periods. The study also made an economic analysis between injecting treated wastewater and injecting desalinated water into the underlying aquifer, which shows that injecting the latter is economically more efficient. In another study by Mukhopadhyay (1996), 17 Mcm/yr of treated wastewater were proposed to be injected to the Kuwait aquifers and recovered. Al-Sumait and Senay (1999) later assessed the feasibility of recharging tertiary treated effluent into groundwater aquifers for a subsequent reuse. The concept is attractive to water resources sustainability in Kuwait and this is why there is now an ongoing project (Mukhopadhyay 2014) of the same type which is led by Water Research Center (WRC) of Kuwait Institute for Scientific Research (KISR). It is planned that any new water resource from desalination plants and treated wastewater beyond 2025 will be injected for ASR schemes. This means that the potential for this option is 100 Mcm/yr from desalination plants and 70 Mcm/yr from treated wastewater, totaling 170 Mcm/yr.

(3) WASTEWATER TREATMENT AND REUSE

Wastewater treatment and reuse have become a significant element in water resources planning and management, particularly in arid regions such as Kuwait. Treated wastewater can be used on a sustainable level in water-scarce environments. Treated wastewater should be reused as an essential element for sustaining agricultural life. Treated wastewater has great potential to supplement the brackish groundwater supplies in irrigation and as a recharge to the aquifers, thus reducing water shortages. The reuse of treated wastewater, however, should not and need not cause any risk to health or environment and socio-economic security. Irrigation with treated wastewater is a potential alternative as it will save a lot of water supply but it needs to be investigated in terms of the level of treatment needed to avoid negative impacts on the quality of groundwater resources, hygiene and health. Treated wastewater can be used in Kuwait for agricultural and landscaping purposes (Al-Anzi et al. 2012). Out of the treated wastewater, only 164 Mcm/yr (70%) is reused for agricultural and greenery purposes. This means that 30% of the treated wastewater is wasted and disposed to the Arabian Gulf. This is a losing situation and does not help the sustainability of water supplies in Kuwait. Strategically, the amount of treated wastewater should be 100% to preserve the Kuwaiti environment. The percentage of the reuse of treated wastewater should be 100% to use this in agriculture in order to release the heavy pumping of brackish groundwater from the aquifers. There are other options regarding treatment of produced water such as drainage from dewatering schemes (Aliewi et al. 2013), irrigation returns and oil field-produced water. Also, Kuwait should develop strategic plans to construct small-scale domestic wastewater treatment plants for small communities and farms.

(4) IMPORTATION OF FRESHWATER

At the moment, Kuwait does not import freshwater for its sustainability. The importation of freshwater from countries rich in water (such as Turkey) is a vital intervention in the long run for Kuwait realizing its scarcity of natural water resources. From where to import freshwater, how (pipelines or other methods) and the cost of 1 m^3 of freshwater when it reaches the consumers in Kuwait will remain important questions to answer before this intervention is considered seriously. However, it should be understood that it is very costly to transport freshwater from other countries, and vulnerable to pollution and failure, but it may be a resilient option in the next 20 years if the water sector of Kuwait does not develop in a sustainable way. A moderate figure should be planned over the medium term of a total of 12 Mcm/yr. Although importation of freshwater from other countries is favorable to increase the socio-economic benefits for Kuwait, it is politically so complicated because it may lead to a situation that puts Kuwait in the position of not having the liberty to consume the freshwater it needs when politics is becoming difficult in the region. The politicians should always find the optimal solutions to trade off for freshwater importation.

Management options

These are nonstructural measures. They mainly aim to reduce the high per capita water consumption. These measures are divided into the following categories:

(1) Economic measures. These are about water prices and tariffs, as well as water subsidies. Water tariffs should be constructed with economic incentives.

It has proven that water prices are the most efficient option to control water consumption. This will bring a lot of socio-economic benefits for Kuwait. The politicians should decide on the issue of water subsidy. The subsidy issue is arguable with respect to social context such that the water provided to the poor for basic needs should be subsidized and the recovery of operating cost should depend on a suitable system of metering. These measures when implemented should be measured against the efficiency and sustainability of water supplies.

(2) Efficiency of the water supply system. The water supply efficiency should be improved through leak detection, household plumbing and maintenance, and installation of water saving and pressure control devices in the households.

(3) Environmental protection. Any activity that will pollute the environment, including groundwater environment, should be regulated. The benefits of protecting the environment are confined to avoid enlarging the gap between water supply and demand due to the pollution of natural water resources. In this context, groundwater protection guidelines should be established. Furthermore, liquid discharge from industrial activities (such as oil refineries, petrochemicals and industrial complexes) to the Arabian Gulf should be minimized to conserve the sustainable future of Kuwait's marine environment. The accumulation of heavy metals in the environment should be monitored, managed and mitigated.

Governance and policies

Governance and policies are efficient means for managing water demand.

Governance

Governance is important in the management of water resources because it includes monitoring mechanisms associated with the enforcement of established laws and standards. Examples of governance measures applicable to Kuwait are as follows:

- Establishment of water law and National Water Council for Kuwait, which will include representatives from the water and the sanitation sectors. The suggested role of the Council is to approve the overall allocation of investments to various water subsectors and approve water sector regulations.
- Establishment of an administrative body that will coordinate activities between the different ministries and authorities with regard to generation and use/reuse of domestic water, agricultural water, treated wastewater, treated urban water, etc.
- Establishment of a unit within the MEW that will be responsible for rainfall/runoff harvesting and reuse.

- Establishment a unit within the related ministry/authority that will be responsible for the reuse of the treated dewatered water and wastewater, especially in urban areas.

Changes to agricultural policies

The changes in agricultural policies in Kuwait should include the following:

- The concept of virtual water was first introduced by Allan (1993) to help countries such as Kuwait to save water. The idea of the virtual water is to import food that includes water supply in it instead of wasting the scarce water resources of Kuwait in irrigation. The trade in food embedded water proved to be helpful for the sustainability of water resources.
- Irrigation with treated wastewater will save a lot of water but it needs to be investigated in terms of the level of treatment needed to avoid negative impacts on groundwater quality, hygiene and health. Kuwait is using only 70% (Table 4.1) of the treated wastewater in irrigation. As a policy, this percentage has to increase.
- Food security consumes a lot of brackish groundwater and treated wastewater. Kuwait subsidizes local agriculture considerably. This subsidy has increased the agricultural lands (3 times) and groundwater extraction volumes (3 times), encouraging farmers to produce crops of low returns, waste a lot of water and pollute groundwater resources. Kuwait should consider using high-tech (hydroponic) agriculture (with soilless cultivation) and biotechnology agriculture. The new agricultural policies should avoid the farming of the water-consumptive crops of low economic values. Farmers should be encouraged to shift from low value vegetables grown in open fields to high-value vegetables grown in greenhouses. Farmers should be stimulated to take into consideration the rate of water application needed for different crops and the value of nutrients in the treated water. The use of modern and efficient irrigation technologies should be encouraged.
- Establish mutual agreements with countries rich in agricultural lands and freshwater to cultivate the major crops that will be transferred to Kuwait (Alrwis 2014).

Other policy principles

The following other policy principles should be considered for water resources sustainability:

- Coherent planning should be required for any additional water supply for effective usage and management to reflect its full economic value.

- Clear linkages should be drawn across water, oil, gas and electricity (water-energy nexus).
- Up-to-date technologies of renewable energies (solar and wind technologies) should be recognized and used.
- Cooperative desalination industries between Kuwait and the GCC countries should be established.
- Water desalination and power generation activities should not have harmful impacts on the ecosystem of the Arabian Gulf given proper design, construction and operation are ensured.
- Construction of mobile RO units should be encouraged to desalinate and treat produced water from dewatering schemes in urban areas for reuse purposes.
- Groundwater aquifers should remain a strategic resource to sustain various water uses and to provide emergency reserves through the ASR concept.
- Non-renewable groundwater resources should be utilized and properly managed.
- Better management of trans-boundary waters and shared aquifers' water should be ensured.
- Water-use efficiencies should be enhanced.
- Water subsidy policy should be evaluated and reformulated.
- Kuwait should consider adopting a policy to monitor UFW.
- Efficient policies about WDM and IWRM should be put in place in Kuwait.
- Institutional strengthening of agencies responsible for water policies should have a high priority.
- Decentralisation and privatisation of water utility operational services should be encouraged.
- Legislation and regulation should be promoted as policies for efficient water resources development and management.

Water resources sustainability plan for Kuwait

Table 4.2 presents a translation of the different interventions and management options into additional volumes of water in order to ease the burden on desalination for a sustainable water resources future for Kuwait. The data of Table 4.2 illustrates that implementing suitable interventions and management options will reduce the water demand from 1074 to 843, from 1482 to 882 and from 2045 to 1031 over the planning horizons of 2016–2025, 2026–2035 and 2036–2045, respectively.

It should be noted that:

- It is planned not to construct additional desalination plants beyond 2045 unless the implementation of the water sustainability plan presented in Table 4.2 fails to achieve its objectives. The added water from desalination plants is reduced gradually from 2016 to 2045.
- The effect of policies and WDM is increasing gradually from 2016 to 2045.

Table 4.2 Additional[1] volumes of water (Mcm/yr) to be generated from different interventions/MO over the three planning horizons of Kuwait's water sector

Parameter	*Planning horizon*		
	2016–2025	*2026–2035*	*2036–2045*
Water demand[1,2]	Current use 1074	1482	2045
Intervention/MO			
Desalination	155	115	30
• Az-Zour South RO plant	50	0	0
• Doha RO Plant-Stage I	100	0	0
• Doha RO Plant-Stage II	0	100	0
• Small RO Units[3]	5	15	30
Brackish groundwater	25	25	33
Water harvesting	25	110	110
• Capture of wadi runoffs	25	25	25
• ASR from desalination plants	0	50	50
• ASR from treated wastewater	0	35	35
Treated wastewater			
• For agricultural use[4]	22	22	22
Importation of freshwater	4	4	4
Reduction of per capita consumption by economic means, regulations and changes in policies including agricultural ones[5]	0	93	215
Total additional volumes of water	231	231+ 369 = 600	231 + 369 + 414 = 1014
Resultant demand	843	882	1031

1 All existing data were obtained from the MEW (2015).

2 The statistical yearbook of water (MEW 2015) shows that the consumption of water increased in a decade at 38%. The same percentage of increase was used for each horizon of planning afterwards.

3 Based on 0.5 Mcm/yr per RO Unit.

4 The agricultural reuse in this plan is proposed to be increased by 66 Mcm/yr over the three planning horizons, which is driven as follows: total planned volume of treated wastewater for reuse – actual volume being used for agriculture – additional volume for ASR = 300 Mcm/yr – 164 Mcm/yr – 70 Mcm/yr = 66 Mcm/yr, realizing that it is planned to increase the total treated wastewater for reuse from the current level of 230 Mcm/yr to 300 Mcm/yr over the three planning horizons. This 300 Mcm/yr is 68.5% of the total generated wastewater, which is 438 Mcm/yr.

5 The current per capita consumption is 442 L/C per day. By implementing a series of WDM such as providing economic incentives, metering, restructuring the tariff system and improving the efficiency of water supplies and services, this per capita consumption rate can be reduced to 400 L/C per day over the second planning horizon and to 350 L/C per day over the third planning horizon. This means that if the number of residents in Kuwait does not increase, then approximately 93 and 215 Mcm/yr respectively can be saved from the current use.

- In the plan, water harvesting, especially using the ASR concept, is important and sizable.

Conclusions

Water resources in Kuwait are not sustainable for a healthy and proper socio-economic life unless huge investment is made in nonconventional water supplies. However, the nonconventional water supplies are expensive and fragile. Water resources in Kuwait have been utilized at unsustainably high rates, with little socio-economic benefits. Water is important to domestic, industrial and agricultural sectors in Kuwait. Therefore, reliable strategic water plans are vital for the sustainability of water resources in Kuwait. The utilization of the available water resources/supplies needs to be optimized for economic, social and environmental benefits using developed policies. In this chapter, suitable policy statements and principles are developed with appropriate interventions and management options towards the sustainability of water resources in Kuwait. A water resources sustainability plan is developed in this chapter. The main elements of this plan are as follows:

- Desalination of water means life for Kuwait; therefore, this option will continue to be the strategic option for Kuwait despite its exorbitant cost and environmental impacts. Applicable policies should be developed to use renewable energy technologies and mobile RO units.
- Changes in agricultural policies – such as the implementation of virtual water, the use of treated wastewater in irrigation, changing of the rigidness of the food self-sufficiency policy, the use of high-tech (hydroponic) agriculture (with soilless cultivation) and biotechnology agriculture, avoiding the farming of high water-consumptive crops of low economic values – and implementation of water demand measures in Kuwait are expected to reduce the total water demand by 93 Mcm/yr and 215 Mcm/yr by 2035 and 2045, respectively.
- It is possible to store a significant volume of good-quality water through artificial recharge and recover it later (ASR principle) during high demand periods. There is a potential to implement ASR in Kuwait: 100 Mcm/yr from desalination plants and 70 Mcm/yr from treated wastewater, totaling 170 Mcm/yr.
- The domestic water consumption in Kuwait can be reduced by implementing reasonable policies regarding pricing and economic incentives. Tariff schemes should be developed and reviewed against full cost recovery to secure financial sustainability while maintaining a reasonable rate of subsidy for low-income citizens.
- Integrated water management principles should be encouraged widely in a way that the MEW implement and monitor water projects while strengthening water institutions with appropriate capabilities to develop suitable water policies.
- Separation between regulatory functions and water services management should be encouraged.

- Establishment of a water law and a National Water Council in Kuwait should be prioritized.
- Commercial orientation of water supply service providers should be encouraged through establishing progressive tariffs and collecting revenues to cover their costs. Also, the participation of the private sector in the operation of water and wastewater services and the decentralisation of water services should be encouraged to promote capital efficiency.
- Policies about the protection of the seawater intakes of desalination plants and the marine environment should be developed. Minimal liquid discharge of wastewater policy and the 'Polluter Pays' principle should be implemented.

Acknowledgements

The authors would like to extend their gratitude and appreciation to the management of the Kuwait Institute for Scientific Research (KISR) for providing financial support and boosting the morale of the study team.

References

Abdel Gelil, I. 2014. Energy-water-food-climate nexus. In *Arab Environment: Food Security: Annual Report of the Arab Forum for Environment and Development*, edited by A. Sadik, M. El-Solh, and N. Saab, pp. 18–29. Beirut, Lebanon: Technical Publications.

Afonso, M., J. Jaber, and M. Mohsen. 2004. Brackish groundwater treatment by reverse osmosis in Jordan. *Desalination*, 164: 157–171.

Al-Anzi, B., A. Abusam, and A. Shahalam. 2012. Assessment of wastewater reuse in Kuwait and its impact on amounts of pollutants discharged into the sea. *Journal of Environmental Protection*, 3: 935–939. doi:10.4236/jep.2012.328108

Al-Damkhi, A.M., S.A. Abdul-Wahab, and A.S. Al-Nafisi. 2009. On the need to reconsider water management in Kuwait. *Clean Technologies and Environmental Policy*, 11: 379. doi:10.1007/s10098-009-0201-z. Kuwait: Public Authority for Applied Education and Training.

Aliewi, A. S., A. Al-Haddad, H. Al-Qallaf, T. Rashid, and J. Al-Kandari. 2015. *Characterization and Evaluation of Groundwater Potential in Abdaliyah Water Field, Kuwait.* Final Report No. WM055C. Water Research Center of Kuwait Institute for Scientific Research, State of Kuwait.

Aliewi, A.S., A. Al-Odwani, H. Qallaf, T. Rashid, M. El Mansour, and S. Al Mufleh. 2013. Design of dewatering schemes using analytical and numerical methods at residential areas in Kuwait. *International Water Technology Journal*, 4(3): 217–231.

Aliewi. A.S., E. O'Connell, and G. Parkin. 2003. *Development of a Framework for Evaluating SUSMAQ Management Options*. Report No. SUSMAQ-SUS#24V1.1. Newcastle University, UK.

Allan, J.A. 1993. Fortunately there are substitutes for water otherwise our hydro-political futures would be impossible. In *Priorities for Water Resources Allocation and Management*, edited by Overseas Development Adminstration, pp. 13–26. London: Overseas Development Administration.

Al-Otaibi, M., and V. Kotwicki. 2009. *Challenges of Water Management in Kuwait.* Paper presented at the 4th Joint KISR-JCCP Environment Symposium, Kuwait, September 2–4, pp. 101–119.

Al-Qunaibet, M.H., and R.S. Johnston. 1985. Municipal demand for water in Kuwait: Methodological issues and empirical results. *Water Resources Research*, 21(4): 433–438.

Al-Rashed, M., and A. Akber. 2015, June. *Water Security in the Kuwait: Challenges and Opportunities*. Paper presented at the 11th Kovacs Colloquium, Hydrological Sciences and Water Security: Past, Present and Future, Paris, France, pp. 119–120.

Al-Rashed, M., M. Al-Senafy, M.N. Viswanathan, and A. Al-Sumait. 1998. Groundwater utilization in Kuwait: Some problems and solutions. *International Journal of Water Resources Development*, 14(1): 91–105. doi:0790-0627/98/010091-15

Al-Ruwaih, F.M., and J. Almedeij. 2007. The future of sustainability of water supply in Kuwait. *Water International*, 32(4): 604–617.

Alrwis, K. 2014. Food security choices in the GCC states. In *Arab Environment: Food Security. Annual Report of the Arab Forum for Environment and Eevelopment*, edited A. Sadik, M. El-Solh, and N. Saab, pp. 30–34. Beirut, Lebanon: Technical Publications.

Alshawaf, M. 2008. *Evaluating the Economic and Environmental Impacts of Water Subsidies in Kuwait*. MSc thesis, Louisiana State University, United States of America.

Al-Sumait, A., and Y. Senay. 1999. *Recharging Tertiary Treated Effluents Into Groundwater System and Storing for Subsequent Reuse*. Water Projects Administration, Ministry of Electricity and Water.

Bachellerie, I.J. 2012. *Renewable Energy in the GCC Countries – Resources, Potential and Prospects*. Published by Gulf Research Center. ISBN: 978-9948-490-05-0, 232pp.

Burton, M., K. Saleh, G. Parkin, F. Contreras-Jimenez, S. Ghannam, E. O'Connell, A. Aliewi, A. Nicol, Y. Shalabi, and A. McDonald. 2005. *Development of Management Options for Sustainable Water Resources Management*. Report No. SUSMAQ – SUS #39 V1.1. Newcastle University, UK.

CH2MHILL. 2002. *Draft West Bank Integrated Water Resources Management Plan*. Palestinian Water Authority, Ramallah, Palestine. A project funded by the USAID.

Chenoweth, J. 2008. Minimum water requirement for social and economic development. *Desalination*, 229(1–3): 245–256.

Darwish, M.A., and N. Al-Najem. 2005. The water problem in Kuwait. *Desalination*, 177: 167–177.

DTI. 1999. *Environmental Futures, Foresight Energy and Natural Resources Panel*. Office of Science and Technology, Department of Trade and Industry, London.

El-Sayed, E. 2010. Assessment of Electrical Power Generation and Water Desalination Plants. Vol 1: General Assessment. Kuwait Institute for Scientific Research, Report No. KISR10404, Kuwait.

El-Sayed, E., M. Abdel-Jawad, M. Al-Tabtabaei, M. Ahmed, and A. Al-Odwani. 2015. *Feasibility Study for Treatment and Effective Usage of High Salinity Oilfield Produced Water in Kuwait*. Final Report No. WT037C. A collaboration project between Kuwait Institute for Scientific Research and Japan Cooperation Center, Kuwait.

Fadlelmawla, A. 2008. Towards sustainable water policy in Kuwait: Reforms of the current practices and the required investments, institutional and legislative measures. *Water Resources Management*, 23(10): 1969–1987.

Ghaffour, N., S. Lattemann, T. Missimer, K. Choon, S. Shahnawaz, and G. Amya. 2014. Renewable energy-driven innovative energy-efficient desalination technologies. *Applied Energy*, 136: 1155–1165.

Greenlee, L., D. Lawler, B. Freeman, B. Marrot, and P. Moulins. 2009. Reverse osmosis desalination: Water sources, technology, and today's challenges. *Water Research*, 43(9): 2317–2348. doi:10.1016/j.watres.2009.03.010

Hadi, K., and V. Kotwicki. 2007. *Some Aspects of the Effects of Expected Climate Change on Water Resources of Kuwait.* Paper presented at the Twelfth Regional Meeting of the Arab IHP National Committees, Al-Ain, United Arab Emirates.

Kotwicki, V., and Z. Al Sulaimani. 2009. Climates of the Arabian peninsula – Past, present, future. *International Journal of Climate Change Strategies and Management*, 1(3): 297–310.

Loucks, D.P. 1997. Quantifying trends in system sustainability. *Hydrological Science Journal*, 42(4): 513–530.

MEW. 2015. *Statistical Year Book of Water in Kuwait.* State of Kuwait: Statistical Department and Information Center, Ministry of Electricity and Water.

Mukhopadhyay, A. 1996. Development of Strategic Reserve of Potable Water Through Artificial Groundwater Recharge: A Pilot Project. Kuwait: Kuwait Institute for Scientific Research.

Mukhopadhyay, A. 2014. Field Assessment of the Use of RO-Treated Wastewater for Artificial Recharge of Dammam Formation Aquifer in Kuwait. Kuwait Institute for Scientific Research, Report No. KISR12807, Kuwait.

Mukhopadhyay, A., M. Al-Senafy, A. Al-Haddad, V. Kotwicki, A. Al-Dousari, and T. Rashid. 2012. *Hydrogeological Assessment of the Az-Zaqlah Depression for Artificial Recharge (WM034C).* Kuwait Institute for Scientific Research, Report No. KISR11334, Kuwait.

Parkin, G., M. Hatem-Moussallem, E. O'Connell, F. Contreras-Jimenez, M. Burton, A. Nicol, Y. Shalabi, A. Aliewi, M. Abu Sada, K. Saleh, and A. McDonald. 2005. *Definition of Sustainability Indicators for Water Resources. Management Options.* Report No. SUSMAQ – SUS #38 V2.1. Newcastle University, UK.

UNICEF, and WHO. 2012. *Progress on Drinking Water and Sanitation: 2012 Update.* Switzerland: WHO Library Cataloguing-in-Publication Data.

UN-Water. 2013. *Analytical Brief on Water Security and the Global Water Agenda.* Ontario, Canada: United Nations Publications.

World Commission on Environment and Development (WCED). 1987. *Our Common Future: The Brundtland Report.* Oxford, UK: Oxford University Press.

5 Towards safe and sustainable reuse of treated wastewater in Abu Dhabi, UAE

Farrukh Ahmad

Introduction

The concept of Total Water Cycle Management (Chanan and Woods 2006) (TWCM), which considers all parts of the urban water cycle as a potential resource, holds a special meaning in arid urban areas such as the coastal cities of the Gulf Cooperation Council (GCC) countries (Al-Zubari 1998). With little or no availability of freshwater, countries along the Arabian Gulf rely heavily on either energy-intensive and high-carbon-generating seawater desalination plants (Aina and Ahmad 2013), or on non-replenishable groundwater reserves (Brook et al. 2006). In contrast to these freshwater production practices, the treatment of municipal wastewater costs only a fraction of desalination (Hering et al. 2013). Furthermore, the reuse of treated wastewater serves to prolong the average residence time of water in the urban water cycle. Therefore, the reuse of treated wastewater offers a sustainable solution to meet the burgeoning water demand in water-scarce regions such as Abu Dhabi, especially for society's functions that require non-potable quality water for beneficial reuse. Safe and sustainable water reuse practices are directly aligned with the Abu Dhabi Economic Vision 2030 (Abu Dhabi Council for Economic Development 2009), as well as the United Nations Sustainable Development Goals of "Clean Water and Sanitation" (Goal 6) and "Sustainable Cities and Communities" (Goal 11) (United Nations 2016). Sustainable water reuse practices hold the promise of limiting the region's carbon footprint and energy demand, while potentially enhancing food and water security with additional treatment.

The Emirate of Abu Dhabi has a long history of water recycling. In fact, the use of water reclaimed from wastewater for landscape irrigation and for date palm irrigation has been practiced in the Emirate since as early as the 1970s. Because of such practices, the UAE has ranked as one of the world's leading nations in treated wastewater reuse on the basis of total volume reused (Jimenez and Asano 2008). Nevertheless, by most recent estimates (Abu Dhabi Executive Council 2015), the Emirate of Abu Dhabi still discharges approximately 80 MIGD or 44.4% of treated wastewater to the environment (Figure 5.1), leaving much room for improvement in its treated wastewater reuse policies and practices. At the Abu Dhabi City level, the discharge percentage of treated wastewater is even more

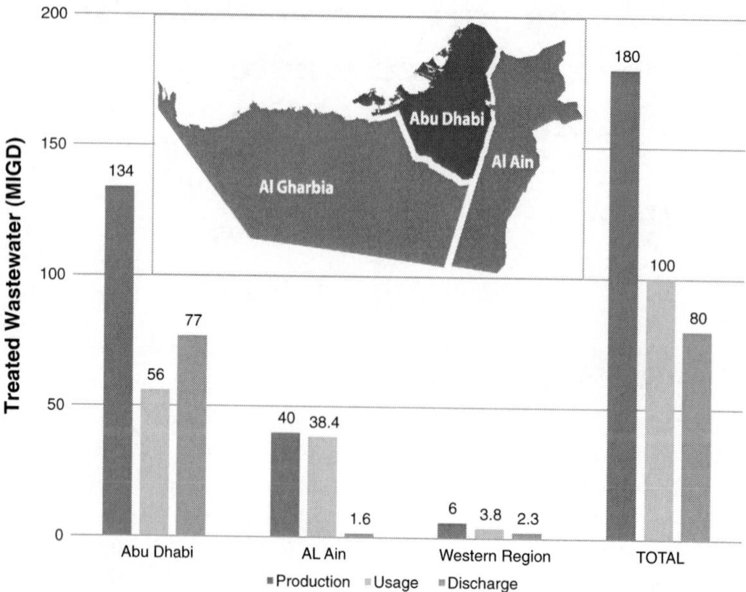

Figure 5.1 Treated wastewater production, reuse, and discharge in MIGD units during 2013 in the three major regions of the Abu Dhabi Emirate

Source: Abu Dhabi Executive Council 2015

significant at 57.5%. To address this concern, in 2015, the Abu Dhabi Executive Council solicited proposals and ideas from universities in the Emirate to work towards the goal of attaining zero wastewater and treated wastewater discharge to the environment, including marine and terrestrial environment, in a time frame of two calendar years. However, significant challenges remain before such a goal can be achieved.

Global state of science in treated wastewater reuse

Around the world, water reclamation and reuse is a growing practice (USEPA 2012, 2004). Generally, recycled water is judiciously matched based on its quality to a specific non-potable end-use (USEPA 2004), such as urban reuse (e.g., landscaping, irrigation, fire-fighting, or cooling (Aina and Ahmad 2013)), industrial reuse, and agricultural reuse (Figure 5.2). Each class of reuse requires water of different quality, not only for operations reasons, but also to minimize nuisance (e.g., aesthetic effects such as odour and algal growth), protect public health via human exposure pathways, and to safeguard the environment (Regulation and Supervision Bureau 2010a) and the animal/ecological organisms or receptors present within it.

The quality of water reclaimed from wastewater, and consequently its type of end-use, depends largely on the level of treatment it undergoes. Most conventional centralized municipal wastewater treatment plants employ the activated sludge

Figure 5.2 Water reuse regulations attempt to manage the various concerns related to different types of non-potable end-use by carefully controlling recycled water quality

treatment (AST) process as secondary treatment followed by filtration and disinfection (Figure 5.3). Some plants may also employ tertiary processes for nutrient removal that render the recycled water safe from nuisance issues such as the occurrence of algal blooms upon discharge. With lower cost and high performance of membranes in the last decade or more, there has been a shift to membrane bioreactors (MBRs) for decentralised treatment. MBRs are modular, allowing easy scalability as a neighbourhood or community grows. MBRs also have a much smaller land footprint, especially in the submerged MBR version of their design, where the membrane module is submerged directly within the aeration tank.

More recently, water scarcity has prompted several regions around the world to consider treated municipal wastewater or reclaimed water for direct or indirect augmentation of drinking water supplies, also known as direct potable reuse (DPR) and indirect potable reuse (IPR), respectively (USEPA 2012). For example, Singapore and Southern California have begun augmenting drinking water supplies with treated municipal wastewater that has undergone advanced treatment via a combination of reverse osmosis followed by advanced chemical oxidation (Tortajada 2006). These "fit-for-purpose" advanced treatment technologies (Figure 5.4) have been touted to produce water of any quality albeit at a significant cost (USEPA 2012). Hence, they offer good economic returns in centralized treatment, especially in water-stressed regions, but might not be the optimal solution at decentralised treatment locations. Advanced treatment techniques have also been applied in Germany and Switzerland for source control to treat wastewater from heavily polluting facilities such as hospitals before the effluent is discharged to the municipal sewer (Köhler et al. 2012, Kovalova et al. 2013, Verlicchi et al. 2010). Still, concerns remain for some of the advanced oxidation unit operations utilized in

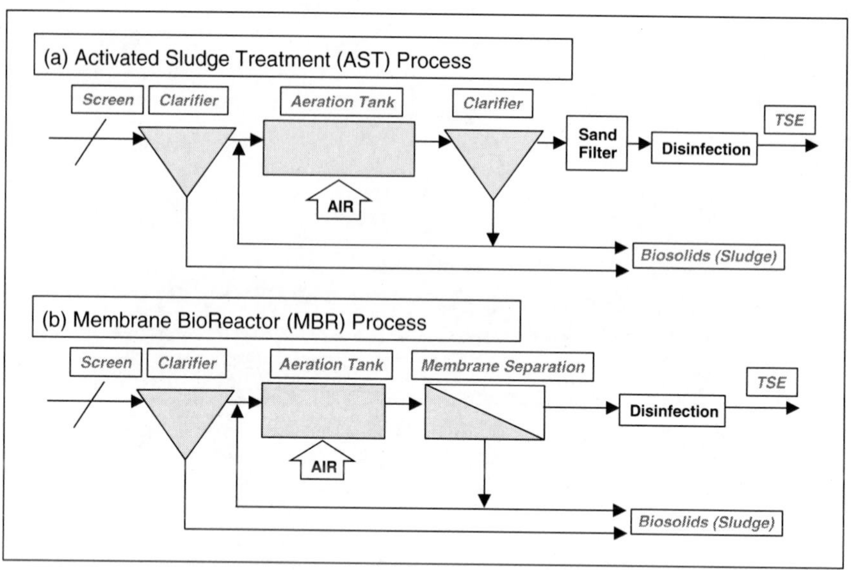

Figure 5.3 Common conventional (e.g., AST) and unconventional (e.g., MBR) municipal wastewater treatment (WWT) processes in use in Abu Dhabi and around the world

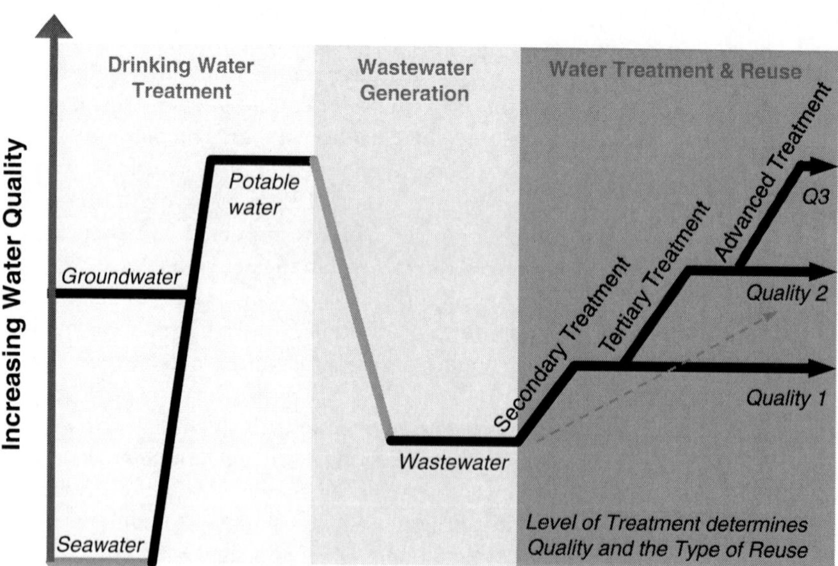

Figure 5.4 The type of recycling activity is directly linked to the quality of water available after treatment, which, in turn, can be controlled by "fit-for-purpose" treatment solutions at the tertiary and advanced treatment levels after conventional WWT unit operations

Source: Adapted from USEPA (2012)

fit-for-purpose treatment, as they have been shown to produce transformed compounds from parent contamination that might actually be more toxic than the parent contaminant (Lee and von Gunten 2016, Li et al. 2016).

The recycling of treated wastewater, especially for possible unrestricted end-use or reuse in places without advanced treatment, has brought several scientific uncertainties or problems into sharp focus. One uncertainty is the chemical and biological fate of the large number of natural (e.g., hormones) and synthetic chemicals, such as pharmaceuticals and personal care products (PPCPs), flame retardants, and preservatives, many of which are endocrine-disrupting chemicals (EDCs) in humans and animals (Snyder et al. 2003). Other compounds, such as antibiotic pharmaceuticals, might not pose a substantial direct risk to human health as they are made for human consumption; however, they pose an indirect risk by increasing antibiotic resistance of microorganisms in the environment, leading to untreatable infections. These "emerging contaminants" or "micropollutants" persist in wastewater at low levels and tend to remain in the treated effluent of conventional treatment processes (Levine and Asano 2004, Snyder et al. 2003, Wintgens et al. 2008). Such micropollutants can now be measured at trace and ultra-trace levels by using a combination solid-phase extraction (SPE) sampling (Baüerlein et al. 2012) with advanced analytical techniques such as High Performance Liquid Chromatography – Tandem Mass Spectrometry (HPLC-MS/MS) (Leendert et al. 2015, Wille et al. 2011) and two-dimensional Gas Chromatography – High Resolution Mass Spectrometry (GCxGC-HRMS) (Dimitriou-Christidis et al. 2015, Godayol et al. 2015).

Another major uncertainty in water reuse is the effective monitoring of pathogens and other biological disease agents present in treated wastewater. All water, even tap water and bottled drinking water (Berry et al. 2006, Loy et al. 2005), contains complex microbial communities that are, for the most part, harmless to humans. Discerning potentially pathogenic microbes from such background diversity of organisms is a formidable task that cannot be achieved by simply monitoring bacterial numbers since these are uninformative regarding the types of microbes present. Moreover, monitoring pathogens using conventional methods based on indicator organisms has been demonstrated to be grossly inadequate in detecting both the presence and levels of pathogens (Blumenthal et al. 2000, Stewart et al. 2008), especially in warm and hot climates. To address this challenging problem, a number of tools have recently been adapted from the field of molecular biology to identify and quantify the types and levels, respectively, of pathogens present in treated wastewater.

Finally, the last uncertainty deals with the assessment of exposure and prediction of disease in human receptors once the levels of contaminants in treated water are known. Exposure models, which rely on behaviour patterns associated with each type of end-use, are employed to this effect, both for chemical exposures and for exposures to specific pathogens. These models guide decision rationales and help establish levels of risk to human health that are acceptable to the communities in which they are deployed. Unfortunately, the toxicity and disease-causing mechanisms of many of the residual chemical and biological contaminants in treated wastewater are largely unknown and an intense area of present-day scientific inquiry. Therefore, safe and sustainable reuse of treated wastewater can only be accomplished with a decision rationale that is deeply rooted in scientific and technical understanding of these and other harmful constituents present in treated wastewater and the health risk they pose to human and animal populations (USEPA 2012; WHO 2006).

Water demand and the urban water cycle in the city of Abu Dhabi

With the absence of fresh surface water resources in the Emirate because of its arid climate and its strategic location at the coast, the city of Abu Dhabi relies primarily on seawater desalination as the main source of potable water production. Data reported for 2012 by the Statistics Centre Abu Dhabi (SCAD) shows desalinated water and groundwater meeting 78.7% and 11.6% of the total water demand, respectively. In 2012, treated wastewater, groundwater, and desalinated water met 9.7%, 11.6%, and 78.7%, respectively, of Abu Dhabi city's total water demand (SCAD 2012). This leaves much room for improvement in treated wastewater reuse, especially since over 40% of the treated wastewater generated in the Emirate is wasted primarily through discharge to the environment (Figure 5.1). Opportunities exist for reducing the city's carbon and energy expenditure for water production by shifting from desalinated water to treated wastewater for meeting its non-potable end-use demand. Such a shift might be inevitable for the UAE, considering UAE's per capita water demand in 2012 of 550L/day was one of the highest in the world and that the regional population is expected to almost double by 2050.

While the possibility of reducing desalination demand with treated wastewater for non-potable use sounds appealing, it is worthwhile to examine the urban water cycle of the city to determine roughly how much treated water is generally produced per cubic meter of desalinated water (Figure 5.5). Using conventional thermal desalination processes, approximately one part of desalinated potable water is produced from ten parts of seawater, with the remaining nine parts of the salt-enriched brine returned to the sea. Roughly 81% of the desalinated water makes it to customers after line losses, and then 60% of the desalinated water is lost via processes such as evaporation and soil percolation. A remaining 21% of the desalinated water is collected as wastewater after primary use, most of which is conserved through wastewater treatment. An interesting point to note is that there is no greywater recycling loop in the Abu Dhabi urban water cycle. Despite the introduction of programs such as the Urban Planning Council's (UPC's) Estidama program, which award points for localized greywater recycling to new developments, such recycling is discouraged by the local water regulator possibly for health or environmental reasons. For example, the Masdar Institute dormitories are piped for single-pass greywater recycling, but Masdar City has to date been unable to gain to approval to use this infrastructure.

Finally, approximately 12% of the original desalinated water is resupplied to the city and other facilities, primarily via the city's total-sewage-effluent (TSE) pipeline as treated wastewater, while the excess 9% is discharged to mainly the marine environment. The TSE to desalinated water consumption ratio, which was 14.8% for the 2009 data in Figure 5.5, is roughly conserved across the Emirate. It fell within

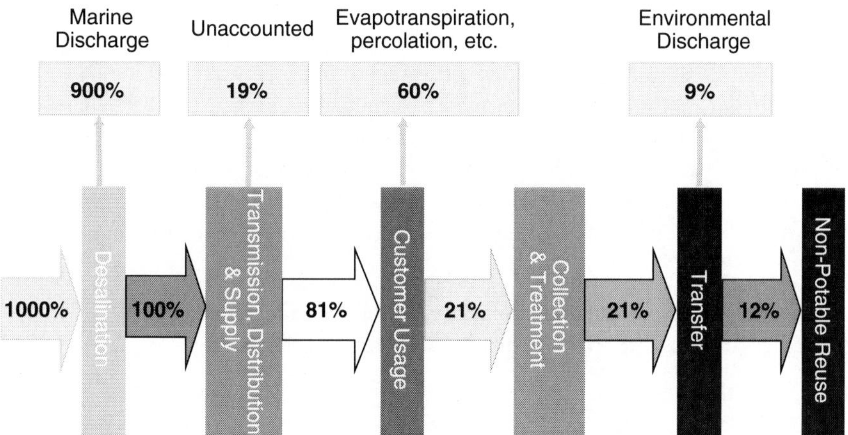

Figure 5.5 Urban water cycle and relative budget for the city of Abu Dhabi based on 2009 data

Source: Adapted from RSB (2010b) and Smith (2013)

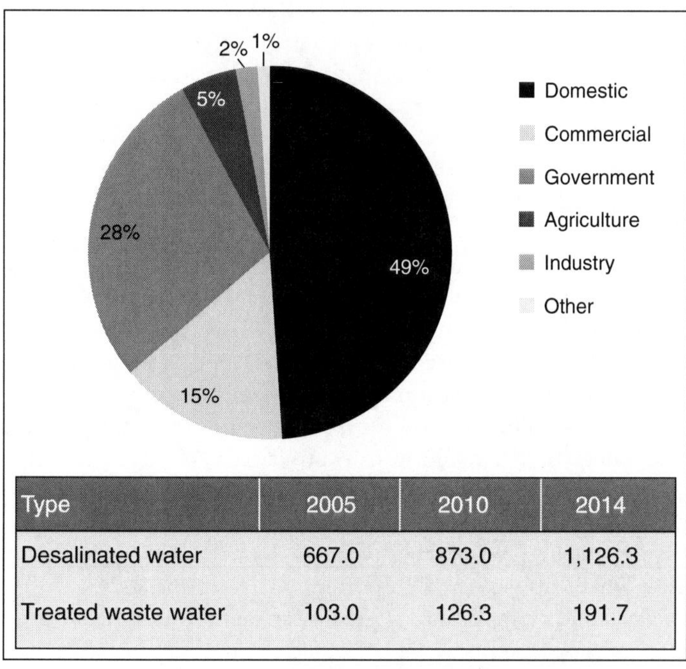

Type	2005	2010	2014
Desalinated water	667.0	873.0	1,126.3
Treated waste water	103.0	126.3	191.7

Figure 5.6 Top: consumption of desalinated water by sector in 2014. Bottom: the unconventional water resource (i.e., desalinated and treated wastewater) consumption in the Abu Dhabi Emirate in MCM

Source: Top: ADDC, AADC, and SCAD (2015). Bottom: SCAD (2015)

a range of 14.5% to 17% from 2005 to 2014 despite rapid increase in water consumption over the years owing to growth (Figure 5.6). As illustrated by Figure 5.5 above, the approximate maximum that this ratio can climb to is 25.9% based on existing infrastructure and desalinated water-use practices. Therefore, in the future as water demand grows, it is important for Abu Dhabi to supplant desalinated water with treated wastewater, especially for non-potable and non-recoverable water use in parts of the industrial, commercial, agricultural, and government sectors.

Wastewater collection, treatment, resupply, and storage infrastructure: merits and constraints

The Abu Dhabi Sewerage Services Company (ADSSC) maintains the municipal sewerage system, which includes the sewerage network that transports the city's sewage to its main municipal wastewater treatment plants (WWTPs) located approximately 40 km inland near Al Mafraq. Discharges to the municipal sewerage system from industry is regulated by the Emirate's water and electricity regulator, the Regulation Supervision Bureau (RSB), via its Trade Effluent Control Regulations (Regulation and Supervision Bureau 2010c). A consent license for discharging industrial wastewater into the municipal sewerage system is granted by the RSB, provided the water contains no "prohibited wastes" (i.e., hazardous, medical, or radioactive wastes) and meets the maximum allowable concentrations (MACs) of a common set of organic and inorganic pollutants with or without pretreatment. The permitting approach is quite different than that of the United States, which has different industry- and discharge volume-specific comprehensive guidelines through its National Pollutant Discharge Elimination System (NPDES) (United States Government Publishing Office (GPO) 2015). Much of the industrial sector of Abu Dhabi city located in Musaffah, which includes hundreds of small workshops, also has direct access to the municipal sewerage system. It is not clear exactly how many licenses for wastewater discharge have been issued by the RSB, but a total of four major- (i.e., greater than 10,000 CMD) and 21 minor-license holding entities are listed on its website (http://rsb.gov.ae/en/sector/licence-holders).

The city has so far employed a pressurized sewerage system that transports sewage approximately 40 km inland to its centralized WWTPs at an approximate pumping elevation of 40 m above that of the island. The sewerage system of the city of Abu Dhabi is not as old as the ones found in major cities of the world, considering that the UAE was established in 1971 and most infrastructure development in Abu Dhabi city occurred only after then. Nevertheless, the sewerage system has been found to be prone to significant saline water intrusion from the underlying hypersaline groundwater below the city (Aina and Ahmad 2013; Environment Agency – Abu Dhabi (EAD) 2013). A hypersaline shallow groundwater band extends approximately 10 km inland from coastline of the Abu Dhabi emirate (Brook et al. 2006). Shallow groundwater salinity levels have been measured as high as 5 times the salinity of the Arabian Gulf's average value of 45 parts per thousand (ppt) total dissolved solids (TDS) in wells at Masdar City. Several reasons for the hypersalinity have been cited; however, a detailed water stable isotope tracking study found it to be a culmination of three factors: (i) high evaporation rates of the shallow groundwater as it discharges into the Gulf; (ii) elevated levels of evaporate minerals in the coastal soils; and (iii) an extremely high mass flux of dissolved salts from the Lower Fars geologic formation, which outcrops into shallower groundwater near the coast (Imes and Wood 2007). To address the saline water intrusion problem, the City of Abu Dhabi initiated construction in 2008 of the Strategic Tunnel Enhancement Program (STEP), which will have a 41 km-long corrosion-protected gravity sewer tunnel that extends all the way from the island to a 30 m^3/s pumping lift station at Al Wathba on the mainland (EAD 2009). The STEP tunnel is scheduled for commissioning by late 2017 in phases to replace the old sewerage system. STEP will be completed at a total investment cost of US$1.9 billion and will have the capacity of 0.6–1.7 million CMD once operational.

As reported by the SCAD, sewage treatment capacity in the Emirate has increased dramatically over the years (Figure 5.7), rising from a total capacity of 135.8 MCM in 2005 to 466.8 MCM in 2014. Much of the capacity comes from WWTPs developed for the city (370 MCM in 2014) (SCAD 2015). The city's oldest centralized WWTP is Al Mafraq at a capacity between 260,000 and 300,000 CMD. The WWTP, located 40 km inland from the city center, has been

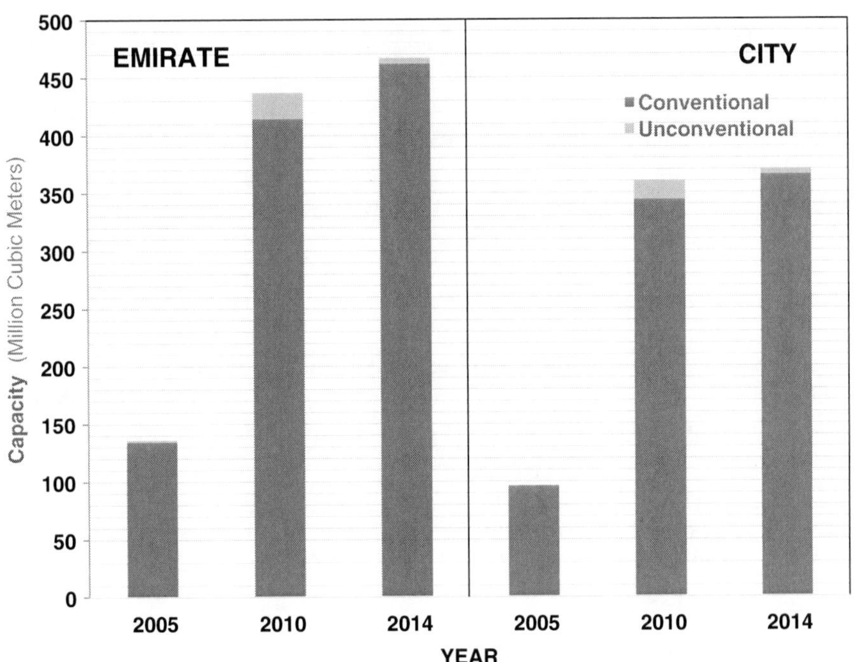

Figure 5.7 Conventional (e.g., AST) and unconventional (e.g., MBR) WWTP capacity in the Emirate and the City of Abu Dhabi

Source: Compiled from ADSSC data in SCAD (2015)

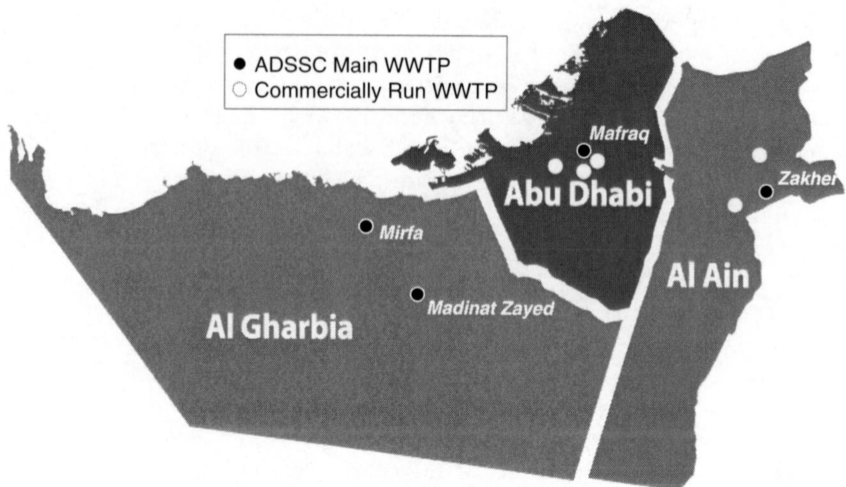

Figure 5.8 Location of the major WWTPs in the Emirate of Abu Dhabi

Source: Adapted from RSB [http://rsb.gov.ae/en/sector/wastewater-at-a-glance]

operational since the 1980s (Kumaraswamy et al. 2014). The newer Al Wathba WWTP at a capacity of 300,000 CMD, has been operational for over three years. It is located further inland from Al Mafraq (Figure 5.8) and receives sewage from a 14 km pipeline that diverts flow from Al Mafraq. Both of these plants employ the conventional activated sludge treatment (AST) process (Figure 5.3).

Smaller MBR-based unconventional treatment plants make up a small fraction of the total capacity (Figure 5.7). For example, the Masdar City MBR WWTP has a capacity of only 1,500 CMD; however, a 57,000 CMD capacity MBR plant is planned for Yas Island, which is located adjacent to Abu Dhabi Island. In contrast to the developed world where decentralised treatment is being increasingly favoured (Hering et al. 2013), there is still a strong trend in Abu Dhabi to centralize wastewater treatment so that there is better control on the level of treatment. The phased commissioning of the STEP tunnel, with its high capacity for sewage conveyance, is likely to further reinforce the centralized AST approach.

Once the wastewater is treated at the central WWTPs at Al Mafraq and Al Wathba, it is transported through ADSSC's TSE network, which now consists of over 177 km of piping (Jarrar 2014). The TSE network originally took treated wastewater only back to the island, but now has been extended to include developments on the mainland and on adjacent islands (Environment Agency-Abu Dhabi (EAD) 2013). The treated wastewater is used for landscape irrigation in public areas through connection to the irrigation network of the Parks and Recreational Facilities Division (PFRD) of the Abu Dhabi Municipality (ADM). The PFRD's main irrigation network consists of over 25 km of its main distribution network and over 920 km of a secondary distribution network (Jarrar 2014).

To date, treated wastewater from municipal WWTPs in Abu Dhabi has been used primarily to irrigate public landscaped areas including public parks, golf courses, and forest trees. The possibility of using treated wastewater in farming has been explored by the government but low acceptance levels remain amongst farmers in the UAE for this reuse application (EAD 2013) – farmers cited health concerns and aesthetic reasons for their unwillingness to use treated wastewater in their farms. To address some of these concerns, the Environmental Agency-Abu Dhabi (EAD) in collaboration with the ADSSC, has been running a pilot test at the Al Nahda Farms near the Al Wahda WWTP since December 2012 (Dawoud et al. 2012). The pilot utilizes municipal treated wastewater from Al Mafraq WWTP, after further advanced treatment, in the farming of edible crops (Dawoud et al. 2012). The advanced treatment system includes ultrafiltration membrane treatment followed by a combination of UV oxidation and chlorine disinfection.

Storage of excess water is a major problem in the Emirate. With a mean annual precipitation that hovers slightly above 100 mm (Brook 2003) (153.9 mm around Abu Dhabi city in 2014 (SCAD 2015)), a measured annual evapotranspiration rate in the range of 2.4–3 m measured around Abu Dhabi city (Jarrar 2014), as well as land limitations, storage of water in surface impoundments is not a viable long-term option. Aquifer storage and recovery or ASR has been considered a valuable storage option for Abu Dhabi, especially since its fresh and brackish water levels have declined substantially owing to over-pumping. Two EAD pilot projects are in place, one in the Al Ain region (Al-Katheeri 2008) and the other in the Liwa region. Both take excess desalinated water from various cogeneration desalination plants located along the coast and pump it into an aquifer located inland near the Liwa region. So far, treated wastewater storage in the subsurface has not been promoted owing to potential health concerns, which can be alleviated only with additional treatment prior to injection (Dawoud et al. 2012). Excess treated wastewater can pose a significant storage problem, especially since the TSE network emanating from WWTPs have a limited capacity. Past rainfall events, the remoteness of the central WWTP to the city, and switching of water supply sources from groundwater to desalinated water have all led to the availability of excessive volumes of treated wastewater without a clear plan for storage. Such events have led to the creation of treated wastewater lakes such as Al Wathba Wetland Reserve in Abu Dhabi City (WGS 24.254379°N, 54.607528°E, adjacent to Al Mafraq WWTP) and Zakher Lake in Al Ain City (WGS 24.089097°N 55.633471°E, near the Al Ain WWTP). For example, Zakher Lake, which was originally created for stormwater relief, grew rapidly when the oasis city of Al Ain city switched from local groundwater resources to desalinated water piped from Fujairah for its potable water needs. These treated wastewater lakes are aerially extensive (Al Wathba Wetland Reserve and Lake Zakher are approximately 5 km^2 and x 1 km^2 in area, respectively) and relatively non-diminishing in size, especially in summer months when evaportranspiration rates are at their peak, indicating that there is a constant influx of water to these surface water bodies. As these lakes are unlined, they serve as slow and uncontrolled recharge basins for underlying groundwater. Hydrogeological modelling for water table mounding and any downgradient effects are needed (Bouwer 2002). Additionally, quality concerns remain for this water as it would require further treatment before recharge into the groundwater. Hence, low-cost technologies are needed to improve the quality of Abu Dhabi's treated wastewater.

Abu Dhabi policy related to recycled water quality and its limitations

An effective framework for water treatment and reuse generally entails a number of activities. These include: (1) demonstrating aggressive wastewater treatment processes that can recover high-quality water; (2) minimizing energy use in water production; (3) establishing the fate of hard-to-treat or recalcitrant compounds present in the waste stream to ensure the safe use of the recovered water; (4) minimizing environmental impacts from the treatment process and the produced water; and, (5) developing human health and ecologically sensitive water quality standards based on the different types of recovered water and their end-use (USEPA 2004). In Abu Dhabi, regulations introduced by the RSB in 2010 took promising steps towards defining a broader framework for managing environmental risk from biological and non-biological agents encountered during water reuse (Regulation and Supervision Bureau 2010b) (Figure 5.9). The RSB defined "points-of-transfer" between treated or partially treated water suppliers and end-users conducting a specific end-use disposal activity such as marine disposal, landscaping, irrigation,

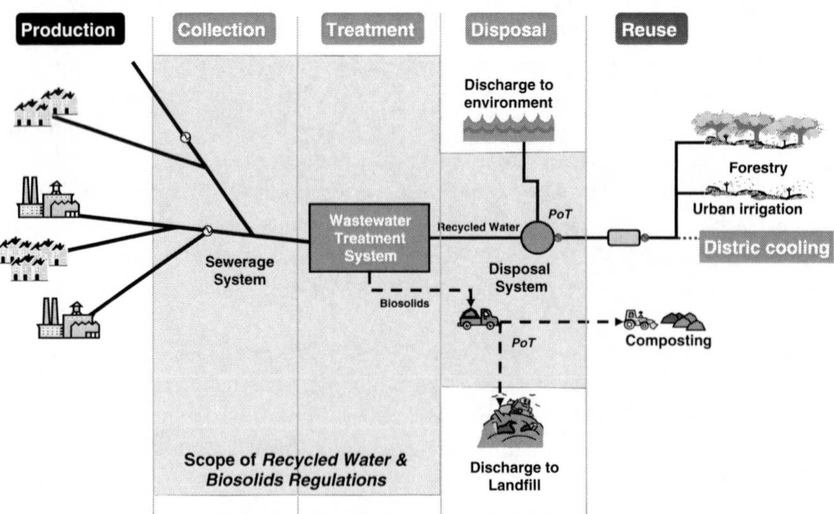

Figure 5.9 The framework for treated water and biosolids recycling of the RSB showing the agency's jurisdiction in the grey-shaded area and "PoT" points or points-of-transfer to different types of end-users and disposal sites

Source: Regulation and Supervision Bureau (2010a)

and industrial reuse. The regulations require that (i) the supplier develop a Safety Plan, including an environmental risk assessment, for the treated water and (ii) the two parties, i.e. supplier and end-user, reach a supply agreement based on the specific end-use activity. Because the quality of water can vary with the different types of end-use, the potential for exposure and consequences of that exposure in human receptors must be assessed for the different qualities of reclaimed water for specific types of reuse. The assessment must take into account the latest scientific understanding of toxicological and contaminant fate and transport principles to assess human risk of exposure to harmful chemicals and pathogens that may be present in recycled water (Regulation and Supervision Bureau 2010b) in order to safeguard human health and the environment. At present, the RSB guidelines and regulations only cover indicator microorganisms (not pathogens), heavy metals, and salinity parameters in reuse options such as irrigation (Regulation and Supervision Bureau 2010a).

Unfortunately, much of the scientific basis to make the RSB framework successful remains uncharted. The health and environmental impacts of many of the residual chemical micropollutants and bacterial and viral pathogens found in treated wastewater remain a subject of ongoing global scientific scrutiny. While the environmental transport and migration parameters of known chemicals and biological agents can be estimated, their toxicity can only be determined via controlled toxicity studies using these or similar contaminants. Combining this with the unique environmental factors found in the GCC region of high temperatures and salinity, the outcome of any risk assessment exercise for the reuse of treated wastewater in the region will be highly unpredictable without thorough baseline characterization and research on exposure for each type of reuse. This phenomenon can be illustrated with the following research work carried out by our group on the following types of contaminants in treated wastewater at the Masdar Institute:

Residual micropollutants and their transformation products

As mentioned earlier, a large number of natural (e.g., hormones) and synthetic chemicals (e.g., PPCPs, flame retardants, and preservatives, many of which are EDCs (Snyder et al. 2003)) have been found to occur in wastewater. These micropollutants persist in wastewater at low levels and tend to remain in the treated effluent of conventional secondary and tertiary treatment processes (Levine and Asano 2004, Snyder et al. 2003, Wintgens et al. 2008). Some have also shown poor removal during advanced treatment (Kimura et al. 2003). The biomagnification and toxicity of such pollutants are an active area of study and of regulatory concern. In 2013, the European Union added 12 such micropollutants to its Water Framework Directive and three more to its watch list (Drewes and Khan 2015). In the US, the USEPA has added several pharmaceuticals and other PPCPs to its Contaminant Candidate List (Drewes and Khan 2015). The fate of micropollutants in conventional and advanced wastewater treatment processes is currently under study in several European countries at the pilot-scale level (Hering et al. 2013), and the feasibility of developing regulatory criteria for direct possible reuse despite the occurrence of micropollutants is currently under evaluation in the State of California (Drewes and Khan 2015).

A baseline micropollutant characterization study was conducted by the Masdar Institute for the Al Wathba WWTP in collaboration of Japan's national institute of Advanced Industrial Science and Technology (AIST). Two month-long rounds of SPE-based passive sampling campaigns using two different types of passive samplers were conducted. After extraction, sample preparation, and derivatization was conducted at the Masdar Institute, the samples were analyzed using GCxGC-HRMS at AIST and matched to their comprehensive library for micropollutants. Almost 2,800 different micropollutants were identified in the effluent (i.e., treated wastewater) samples at appreciable levels. Compound classes that the detected micropollutants fell into included musks, over-the-counter pharmaceuticals, prescribed pharmaceuticals (e.g., antibiotics), industrial chemicals (e.g., plasticizers and corrosion inhibitors), flame retardants, hormones, steroids, polynuclear aromatic hydrocarbons (PAHs), pesticides, fungicides, bacterial biocides, opioid metabolites, and nicotinates. Further work is underway to report findings and to quantify temporal trends of these micropollutants.

Disinfection byproducts

The occurrence of uniquely toxic disinfection byproducts (DBPs) during the disinfection part of wastewater treatment, especially for saline wastewaters, has been well documented in regions such as Hong Kong, where seawater is used for toilet flushing in public toilets (Sun et al. 2009a, 2009b). Salinity intrusion into piping is a common phenomenon in coastal regions of Abu Dhabi because of the occurrence of shallow hypersaline groundwater (Brook et al. 2006, Imes and Wood 2007). In fact, the treated wastewater from Al Mafraq WWTP retains chloride at levels in the 1500 mg/L range (Aina and Ahmad 2013), easily placing the treated water in a slightly brackish quality range. In a study conducted by the Masdar Institute in 2012, the effects of saline water intrusion on the speciation carcinogenic trihalomethane (THM) DBPs were evaluated at the Al Mafraq WWTP (Aina and Ahmad 2013). These were compared to the non-salinity impacted disinfection at the Masdar City MBR WWTP over a monitoring period of one year. The study found a shift in THM DBPs towards brominated compounds. Brominated THMs are known to be far more carcinogenic than their chlorinated counterparts. Upon carrying a detailed quantitative risk assessment for landscape irrigation reuse, which considered only the inhalation and dermal chronic exposure routes for workers and playing children in public parks, the salinity impacted treated wastewater was found to be counter-intuitively less toxic. The main reason for this result was that brominated THMs are significantly less volatile than chlorinated THMs such as chloroform. Had the risk evaluation been performed for a different type of reuse that involves exposure to soluble THM, such as indirect exposure in agriculture of edible crops (i.e., ingestion exposure via biomagnification in crops) or direct exposure to marine animals in marine discharge, the outcome would have been the exact opposite. The study also highlighted the difficulty in conducting a chronic environmental risk evaluation in a region where the majority of the residents are expatriates, who will have a more limited exposure duration than a complete lifetime used in chronic incremental lifetime cancer risk studies.

Pathogens and other biological disease agents

The occurrence of pathogens and other biological agents present in treated wastewater is a widely reported phenomenon. All water contains complex microbial communities that are, for the most part, harmless to humans. Discerning potentially pathogenic microbes from such background diversity is a formidable task. Conventional bacterial measurement numbers used in wastewater treatment (e.g., indicator colony-forming units [CFU] or most probable number [MPN]) are uninformative regarding the types of microbes present. Moreover, monitoring pathogens using conventional methods based on indicator organisms have been demonstrated to be grossly inadequate in detecting both the presence and levels of pathogens, especially in warm and hot climates (Blumenthal et al. 2000, Stewart et al. 2008), where growth rates might be quite faster. A recent study at Masdar Institute developed a new bacterial pathogen screening method using next-generation sequencing (NGS) technology for DNA (Kumaraswamy et al. 2014) sequencing and mapping the sequenced data to the human bacterial pathogen database using a bioinformatics data analysis pipeline. Using this method, a total of 21 different human bacterial pathogens were screened along the WWT train and at least 10 in the treated wastewater after disinfection. The co-occurrence of bacterial pathogens with antibiotic pharmaceutical micropollutants presents a further major public health concern because it can result in antibiotic-resistant pathogens in the environment, which can eventually cause untreatable infections.

In another study conducted by the Masdar Institute, the health risk from agricultural reuse of Abu Dhabi's treated wastewater for growing high-consumption edible crops (i.e., lettuce, cabbage, and cucumber) was evaluated (Amha et al. 2015). For this study, a probabilistic quantitative microbial risk assessment (QMRA) model was developed using *Salmonella spp.* counts enumerated using quantitative polymerase chain reaction (qPCR) for treated effluent from Al Mafraq WWTP. The risk of infection was evaluated using a number of scenarios, and of the three vegetables considered, lettuce displayed the highest risk while cucumber showed the lowest, when compared to the 10^{-6} acceptable disability-adjusted life year (DALY) threshold set by the WHO (WHO 2006). Unfortunately, knowledge on mathematical models for human exposure to pathogens in reclaimed water from end-use activities such as edible crop irrigation is limited to a handful of specific pathogens (Amha et al. 2015). Nevertheless, the study points to the need for additional treatment prior to more sophisticated reuse of treated wastewater such as agriculture.

The way forward

While preliminary studies by the EAD are underway to explore farming-based end-use options using excess treated effluent after additional treatment, unwillingness to use treated wastewater for agriculture remains a major concern amongst the area farmers primarily for health and aesthetic reasons. In order to gain wider public acceptance of treated wastewater recycling in the region, especially for agricultural reuse, confidence-building measures must be initiated with respect to establishing the quality of recycled water. Moreover, the development and implementation of a comprehensive and scientifically backed regulatory framework is needed to ensure public and environmental safety going forward. These objectives can be achieved through additional research on characterization and treatment, as well as standardization of water quality testing methodologies, before more comprehensive guidelines on treated wastewater reuse can be developed.

Development of methodology for detailed treated water quality characterization

There is a dire need for detailed chemical and molecular biological characterization of treated effluent generated from conventional, unconventional, and advanced treatment technologies employed in Abu Dhabi in order to identify potentially problematic MPs, DBPs, and pathogens in the types of treatment practiced in Abu Dhabi. Existing methodology for techniques such as SPE passive sampling, HPLC-MS/MS, NGS, and qPCR need to be adapted for Abu Dhabi wastewater and treated effluent, and standardized with the help of local agencies such as the Abu Dhabi Quality and Conformity Council (ADQCC) and then promulgated in the region with the help the RSB and the ADSSC. Preliminary work in this area has been accomplished at the Masdar Institute but detailed routine monitoring is needed for decision-making related to water recycling and to determine whether the Emirate is on track to attain its goal of zero discharge of treated wastewater.

Polishing technologies development for enhancing treated wastewater quality

Given the large volume of treated wastewater that goes unused, there is a need to use polishing technologies in order to enhance the quality of this water. Once the quality of the treated wastewater is improved and tested, it can help build consumer confidence in the agricultural sector. One such technology was developed at Masdar Institute involved photo-regenerable multi-walled carbon nanotube (MWNT) filters and membranes (Zaib et al. 2013) for treating micropollutants in treated wastewater. The membranes and filters can then be regenerated by the photocatalyst embedded in the composite material by exposure to a light source, leading to sustainable operation. Other off-the-shelf advanced chemical oxidation technologies need testing in conditions relevant to Abu Dhabi before they can be routinely applied.

Exposure models for end-use

End-use-specific mathematical exposure models must be developed for chemical and biological pollutants in treated wastewater so that the potential risk to humans can be characterized and quantified. In the case of edible crop agricultural use, the prospect for micropollutants to bioaccumulate in edible crops must be examined. Based on the residual chemicals detected in treated wastewater, bio-concentration factors (BCFs) can be developed using chemical structure and the type of edible crops grown in this region. For pathogens, some work on pathogen QMRA health risk protocols has already been initiated at the Masdar Institute (Amha et al. 2015).

New guidelines and decision rationale

Finally, new, more comprehensive guidelines that consider recycled water quality, especially for emerging pollutant and pathogen content, in selecting reuse options need to be developed for Abu Dhabi. At present, the RSB guidelines and regulations only cover indicator microorganisms (not pathogens), heavy metals, and salinity parameters in recycling water for irrigation (Regulation and Supervision Bureau 2010a). Detailed decision rationale that utilize the characterization data and exposure models developed for the region for matching treatment, quality, end-use, and exposure are needed for Abu Dhabi.

Conclusion

Complete treated wastewater reuse holds the promise of limiting the region's carbon footprint and energy demand while enhancing food and water security with additional treatment. To this effect, the government of Abu Dhabi has set the ambitious goal of attaining zero wastewater and treated wastewater discharge to the environment, including marine and terrestrial environment, in a time frame of two calendar years. Nevertheless, significant challenges related to (i) treated wastewater quality characterization, (ii) additional treatment, and (iii) health and environmental risk evaluation in different reuse scenarios remain before such a goal can be achieved. To date, the city of Abu Dhabi has relied chiefly on seawater desalination as a source of potable water. On average 21% of water is recovered from the production of desalinated water based on existing patterns of use, sewage collection, and treatment infrastructure. Abu Dhabi relies predominantly on centralized AST WWTP treatment of wastewater, which might limit localized treatment and reuse such as greywater recycling. Instead, a central ADSSC TSE line carries treated wastewater 25–40 km back to the island and interfaces with the PFRD irrigation network of the ADM for landscape irrigation of public spaces. The treated wastewater generated by the central

WWTPs is of a slightly brackish quality owing to saline water intrusion into the sewerage collection infrastructure leading up to the plant. The STEP sewerage pipeline is expected to be commissioned in phases by late 2017 to help alleviate the saline water intrusion problem. Plans are in place to expand the ADSSC's TSE network capacity as approximately 40% by volume of the treated wastewater is discharged to the environment because of limited storage and resupply options. Farming-based end-use with excess discharged water might be one feasible option. Unfortunately, unwillingness to use treated wastewater for agriculture remains amongst area farmers primarily for health and odor reasons. These concerns are not without merit; comprehensive treated wastewater quality characterization work undertaken at the Masdar Institute demonstrates significant levels of chemical (i.e., micropollutants and halogenated DBPs) and pathogen loading in this water that can pose a health and environmental risk for specific types of recycling activities. Additional treatment must be performed to reuse this water in agriculture and to store it as artificial recharge in depleted aquifers. Even before additional treatment, consumer confidence must be established by the standardization of water quality characterization methods and by the development of health-based exposure models for different types of treated wastewater end-use. Such efforts will facilitate the formulation of a scientifically defensible water reuse methodology that will lead to a wider public acceptance of treated wastewater recycling in the region.

References

Abu Dhabi Council for Economic Development. 2009. *The Abu Dhabi Economic Vision 2030*. Abu Dhabi, UAE.

Abu Dhabi Executive Council. 2015. *Treated Wastewater Usage Workshop* (MS PowerPoint Presentation). Abu Dhabi, UAE.

Abu Dhabi Statistics Center. 2012. *Abu Dhabi Health Statistics, 2012*. Publication Reference: SP.S.04.P1.

Aina, Oluwajinmi Daniel, and Farrukh Ahmad. 2013. Carcinogenic health risk from trihalomethanes during reuse of reclaimed water in coastal cities of the Arabian Gulf. *Journal Water Reuse and Desalination*, 3(2): 175–184.

Al-Katheeri, E.S. 2008. Towards the establishment of water management in Abu Dhabi Emirate. *Water Resources Management*, 22: 205–215.

Al-Zubari, W.K. 1998. Towards the establishment of a total water cycle management and re-use program in the GCC countries. *Desalination*, 120(1–2): 3–14.

Amha, Yamrot M., Rajkumari Kumaraswamy, and Farrukh Ahmad. 2015. A probabilistic QMRA of Salmonella in direct agricultural reuse of treated municipal wastewater. *Water Science & Technology*, 71(8): 1203–1211.

Baüerlein, Patrick S., Jodie E. Mansell, Thomas L. ter Laak, and Pim de Voogt. 2012. Sorption behavior of charged and neutral polar organic compounds on solid phase extraction materials: Which functional group governs sorption? *Environmental Science & Technology*, 46(2): 954–961.

Berry, D., C. Xi, and L. Raskin. 2006. Microbial ecology of drinking water distribution systems. *Current Opinion in Biotechnology*, 17(3): 297–302.

Blumenthal, U.J., D.D. Mara, A. Peasey, G. Ruiz-Palacios, and R. Stott. 2000. Guidelines for the microbiological quality of treated wastewater used in agriculture: Recommendations for revising WHO guidelines. *Bulletin of the World Health Organization*, 78(9): 1104–1116.

Bouwer, Herman. 2002. Artificial recharge of groundwater: Hydrogeology and engineering. *Hydrogeology Journal*, 10(1): 121–142.

Brook, M.C. 2003. *Working Towards a Water Resources Management Strategy for the Emirate of Abu Dhabi, United Arab Emirates*. In 2nd International Symposium on Integrated Water Resources Management, Stellenbosch, South Africa.

Brook, M.C., H. Al-Houqani, T. Darawsha, M. Al-Alawneh, and S. Achary. 2006. Groundwater resources: Development & management in the Emirate of Abu Dhabi, United Arab Emirates. In *Arid Land Hydrogeology: In Search of a Solution for a Threatened Resource*, edited by A.M.O. Mohamed, pp. 14–34. London: Taylor & Francis.

Brook, M.C., and M.A. Dawoud. 2005. *Coastal Water Resources Management in the United Arab Emirates*. Paper read at Integrated Coastal Zone Management in the United Arab Emirates, at Abu Dhabi, U.A.E.

Chanan, Amit, and Paul Woods. 2006. Introducing total water cycle management in Sydney: A Kogarah Council initiative. *Desalination*, 187(1): 11–16.

Dawoud, M.A., O.M. Sallam, and M.A. Abdelfattah. 2012. *Treated Wastewater Management and Reuse in Arid Regions: Abu Dhabi Case Study*. In The 10th Gulf Water Conference. Doha, Qatar.

Dimitriou-Christidis, Petros, Alex Bonvin, Saer Samanipour, Juliane Hollender, Rebecca Rutler, Jimmy Westphale, Jonas Gros, and J. Samuel Arey. 2015. GC×GC quantification of priority and emerging nonpolar halogenated micropollutants in all types of wastewater matrices: Analysis methodology, chemical occurrence, and partitioning. *Environmental Science & Technology*, 49(13): 7914–7925.

Drewes, J.E., and S.J. Khan. 2015. Contemporary design, operation, and monitoring of potable reuse systems. *Journal of Water Reuse and Desalination*, 5(1): 1–7.

Environment Agency – Abu Dhabi (EAD). 2009. *Abu Dhabi Water Resources Master Plan*. https://www.ead.ae/SitePages/presscentre.aspx?itemid=52 .

Environment Agency – Abu Dhabi (EAD). 2013. *Annual Policy Brief: Maximizing Recycled Water Use in the Emirate of Abu Dhabi*. https://www.ead.ae/Publications/Maximizing%20Recycled%20Water%20Use%20in%20the%20Emirate%20of%20Abu%20Dhabi/recycled-water-PB-Eng.pdf .

Godayol, Anna, Rafael Gonzalez-Olmos, Juan M. Sanchez, and Enriqueta Anticó. 2015. Assessment of the effect of UV and chlorination in the transformation of fragrances in aqueous samples. *Chemosphere*, 125: 25–32.

Hering, Janet G., T. David Waite, Richard G. Luthy, Jorg E. Drewes, and David L. Sedlak. 2013. A changing framework for urban water systems. *Environmental Science & Technology*, 47(19): 10721–10726.

Imes, J.L., and W.W. Wood. 2007. Solute and isotope constraint of groundwater recharge simulation in an arid environment. Abu Dhabi Emirate, United Arab Emirates. *Hydrogeology Journal*, 15(7): 1307–1315.

Jarrar, A. 2014. Optimization of treated sewage effluent for landscape irrigation. In Proceedings of *Irrigation Australia 2014*. 2–6 June 2014, Gold Coast, Australia.

Jimenez, B., and T. Asano. 2008. Water reclamation and reuse around the world. In *Water Reuse: An International Survey of Current Practice, Issues, and Needs*, edited by B. Jimenez and T. Asano. London: IWA Publishing.

Kimura, Katsuki, Gary Amy, Jörg E. Drewes, Thomas Heberer, Tae-Uk Kim, and Yoshimasa Watanabe. 2003. Rejection of organic micropollutants (disinfection by-products, endocrine disrupting compounds, and pharmaceutically active compounds) by NF/RO membranes. *Journal of Membrane Science*, 227(1): 113–121.

Köhler, C., S. Venditti, E. Igos, K. Klepiszewski, E. Benetto, and A. Cornelissen. 2012. Elimination of pharmaceutical residues in biologically pre-treated hospital wastewater using advanced UV irradiation technology: A comparative assessment. *Journal of Hazardous Materials*, 239: 70–77.

Kovalova, Lubomira, Hansruedi Siegrist, Urs Von Gunten, Jakob Eugster, Martina Hagenbuch, Anita Wittmer, Ruedi Moser, and Christa S. McArdell. 2013. Elimination of micropollutants during post-treatment of hospital wastewater with powdered activated carbon, ozone, and UV. *Environmental Science & Technology*, 47(14): 7899–7908.

Kumaraswamy, Rajkumari, Yamrot M. Amha, Muhammad Z. Anwar, Andreas Henschel, Jorge Rodríguez, and Farrukh Ahmad. 2014. Molecular analysis for screening human bacterial pathogens in municipal wastewater treatment and reuse. *Environmental Science & Technology*, 48(19): 11610–11619.

Lee, Yunho, and Urs von Gunten. 2016. Advances in predicting organic contaminant abatement during ozonation of municipal wastewater effluent: Reaction kinetics, transformation products, and changes of biological effects. *Environmental Science: Water Research & Technology*, 2(3): 421–442.

Leendert, Vergeynst, Herman Van Langenhove, and Kristof Demeestere. 2015. Trends in liquid chromatography coupled to high-resolution mass spectrometry for multi-residue analysis of organic micropollutants in aquatic environments. *TrAC Trends in Analytical Chemistry*, 67: 192–208.

Levine, A.D., and T. Asano. 2004. Recovering sustainable water from wastewater. *Environmental Science & Technology*, 38(11): 201–208.

Li, Man, Bi Xu, Zhiqi Liungai, Hong-Ying Hu, Chao Chen, Juan Qiao, and Yun Lu. 2016. The removal of estrogenic activity with UV/chlorine technology and identification of novel estrogenic disinfection by-products. *Journal of Hazardous Materials*, 307: 119–126.

Loy, A., W. Beisker, and H. Meier. 2005. Diversity of bacteria growing in natural mineral water after bottling. *Applied and Environmental Microbiology*, 71(7): 3624–3632.

Regulation and Supervision Bureau. 2010a. *Guide to Recycled Water and Biosolids Regulation.* Abu Dhabi, UAE.

Regulation and Supervision Bureau. 2010b. *Recycled Water and Biosolids Regulations*. Abu Dhabi, UAE.

Regulation and Supervision Bureau. 2010c. *Trade Effluent Control Regulations*. Abu Dhabi, UAE.

Smith, Richard. 2013. Regulation & Supervision Bureau: Developing a Framework for Safe and Sustainable Wastewater Reuse. Presentation at Masdar Institute.

Snyder, S.A., P. Westerhoff, Y. Yoon, and D.L. Sedlak. 2003. Pharmaceuticals, personal care products, and endocrine disruptors in water: Implications for the water industry. *Environmental Engineering Science*, 20(5): 449–469.

Statistics Centre Abu Dhabi (SCAD). 2012. *Statistcal Yearbook of Abu Dhabi 2012*. Abu Dhabi, UAE.

Statistics Centre Abu Dhabi (SCAD). 2015. *Statistcal Yearbook of Abu Dhabi 2015*. Abu Dhabi, UAE.

Stewart, J.R., R.J. Gast, R.S. Fujioka, H.M. Solo-Gabriele, J.S. Meschke, L.A. Amaral-Zettler, E. Del Castillo, M.F. Polz, T.K. Collier, and M.S. Strom. 2008. The coastal environment and human health: Microbial indicators, pathogens, sentinels and reservoirs. *Environ Health*, 7(Suppl 2): S3.

Sun, Y.X., Q.Y. Wu, H.Y. Hu, and J. Tian. 2009a. Effect of bromide on the formation of disinfection by-products during wastewater chlorination. *Water Research*, 43(9): 2391–2398.

Sun, Y.X., Q.Y. Wu, H.Y. Hu, and J. Tian. 2009b. Effects of operating conditions on THMs and HAAs formation during wastewater chlorination. *Journal of Hazardous Materials*, 168(2–3): 1290–1295.

Tortajada, C. 2006. Water management in Singapore. *Water Resources Development*, 22(2): 227–240.

United Nations. 2016. *Transforming Our World: The 2030 Agenda for Sustainable Development (A/RES/70/1)*. https://sustainabledevelopment.un.org/content/documents/21252030%20Agenda%20for%20Sustainable%20Development%20web.pdf.

United States Government Publishing Office (GPO). 2015. Code of Federal Regulations (CFR) Title 40 Part 122: EPA Administered Permit Programs – The National Pollutant Discharge Elimination System (NPDES). Washington, DC.

USEPA. 2004. Guidelines for Water Reuse (EPA/625/R-04/108). Washington, DC: USEPA.

USEPA. 2012. *Guidelines for Water Reuse*. Washington, DC: Office of Wastewater Management, Office of Water.

Verlicchi, Paola, Alessio Galletti, Mira Petrovic, and Damià Barceló. 2010. Hospital effluents as a source of emerging pollutants: An overview of micropollutants and sustainable treatment options. *Journal of Hydrology*, 389(3): 416–428.

WHO. 2006. WHO Guidelines for Safe Use of Wastewater Excreta & Greywater, Wastewater Use in Agriculture. Geneva, Switzerland: World Health Organization.

Wille, Klaas, Julie A.L. Kiebooms, Michiel Claessens, Karen Rappé, Julie Vanden Bussche, Herlinde Noppe, Nander Van Praet, Eric De Wulf, Peter Van Caeter, and Colin R. Janssen. 2011. Development of analytical strategies using U-HPLC-MS/MS and LC-ToF-MS for the quantification of micropollutants in marine organisms. *Analytical and Bioanalytical Chemistry*, 400(5): 1459–1472.

Wintgens, T., F. Salehi, R. Hochstrat, and T. Melin. 2008. Emerging contaminants and treatment options in water recycling for indirect potable use. *Water Science and Technology*, 57(1): 99–108.

Zaib, Qammer, Bilal Mansoor, and Farrukh Ahmad. 2013. Photo-regenerable multi-walled carbon nanotube membranes for the removal of pharmaceutical micropollutants from water. *Environmental Science: Processes & Impacts*, 15(8): 1582–1589.

6 Implementation of the Sustainable Development Goals in the GCC countries via application of sustainability-oriented innovation to critical infrastructures

Ashley C. Pilipiszyn and Alexandre B. Hedjazi

Introduction

The 2030 Development Agenda and accompanying Sustainable Development Goals (SDGs) is a strategic recalibrating of the Millennium Development Goals by connecting international security to people, the planet, prosperity, peace and partnerships (Sherwood 2016). The objective of these 17 goals is the simultaneous achievement of social, environmental, and economic development, which within the context of the Middle East, underwrites water security as an inherent link to state security (Sherwood 2016). In relation to the GCC countries, the SDGs have relevance with regards to the GCC's long-term strategies to address water insecurity. For example, SDG #6 sets out eight targets to address matters such as access to safe water and sanitation, water quality, water-use efficiency, ecosystem protection, transboundary cooperation, and integrated water resources management (Sherwood 2016). Beyond SDG #6, a number of the other goals indirectly support it either through quantified water-related targets or effective water management for their attainment. These include goals pertaining to health (SDG #3), cities (SDG #11), consumption–production (SDG #12), marine resources (SDG #14), and terrestrial ecosystems (SDG #15). Beyond these, successful water management is required for all SDGs, making it fundamental for the achievement of the overall 2030 Development Agenda, an agenda that, progressively, is underwriting understandings of international security (Sherwood 2016). In the following body of literature, we build upon the arguments of Sherwood (2016) and will focus on SDG #11, cities, in the context of the GCC and where there are opportunities to implement sustainable solutions with a positive impact on the urban environment through critical infrastructure (SDG #9).

The key objectives of this chapter are to contextualize the current state of global cities within the global governance system, link the SDGs to global cities in the GCC, provide a new tool of analysis for urban critical infrastructures within the framework of sustainability-oriented innovation, and finally, explain how actions aligned with achieving the SDGs for global cities in the GCC legitimize the role of these cities in the global governance architecture. The first section presents the current status of global cities of today and explains the role they play in the global governance system. The second explains the methodology of this work by presenting the theory behind the sustainability-oriented innovation framework and the Sustainability-Oriented Innovation Index for Airports©. The third section presents the case study of this sustainability tool applied in Abu Dhabi as a means to achieving the targets outlined in the 2030 Agenda. The fourth section offers a discussion on global cities that utilize an SOI framework like Abu Dhabi. The last section concludes with how Abu Dhabi has the potential to rise to a new level of legitimacy within the global governance architecture through effectively synergizing multiple sustainability agendas within an SOI framework, which will enable greater capacity for SDG implementation.

Global cities today

For the first time in human history, more people now live in cities than in rural areas. Today's experts anticipate that by 2050, 6.5 billion people, two-thirds of all humanity, will live and work in cities (UN 2014). To put this into perspective, cities will experience an inflow of 2.5 billion new urban residents by 2050, more than the current population of India and China combined (WEF 2015). In 1950, fewer than one billion did so. This urban growth of 70 million people annually is roughly the equivalent of adding 35 Stockholms or two Tokyos to the world every single year from now until 2050 (Engelke 2015). And this process is not yet over: by 2100, perhaps 85% of all people will live in cities (OECD 2015). In essence, the city has become the nucleus of the human ecosystem.

Today's global cities are hyper-connected, transcend borders, and impact international agendas. They are magnets for business, people, investment, and innovation. Over time, global cities have been able engage progressively more global through partnerships, collaborations, and agreements with the private sector, academia, and civic society. Nation-states continue to provide frameworks for global governance but it is increasingly today's global cities that are the main actors that provide the energy, enterprise, motivation, innovation, and legitimacy that drives society. While not sovereign, global cities have become increasingly independent and are steering policies that stimulate wider change on the international stage.

According to a recent issue brief by the Atlantic Council, cities generate most of the world's wealth, encourage the majority of its innovation, concentrate much of its poverty, and ultimately feel society's greatest challenges most intensely (Engelke 2015). Smart regulations, effective governance structures, and the development of nimble institutions will be some of the elements required to address these prominent issues (WEF 2016). If these challenges are to be solved during this century, the world's foreign, security, and development policy communities not only must become far more aware of the significance of global urbanization, they also must create the processes that will integrate cities more effectively into global governance structures and processes (Engelke 2015).

Not having the time or patience to wait for the international community to give them formal recognition, cities have built their own parallel global governance architectures in order to address challenges that arise here and now (Pilipiszyn 2016). As a result, cities now have the capacity to exert considerable power at the global scale across a number of key domains, and will continue to increase their influence in the coming years due to their success in solving problems creatively and efficiently. As such, they have become essential actors on the world stage and are forging new mechanisms of transnational relations and forms of global governance (Engelke 2015).

So where are nation-states currently positioned within these shifting dynamics? According to Barber (2015), nation-states have failed on a number of fronts to address these various global challenges such as public health, education, the Internet, natural environments, and employment. According to former U.S. Secretary of State Madeleine Albright, people are talking to their governments on 21st-century technology, the government hears them on 20th-century technology, and then gives people 19th-century responses, which is unacceptable (Albright 2015). Barber (2015) further explains that the key dilemma to this equation is that for the past 400 years, people have seen the nation-state as the centerpiece to political authority and that the solution of the problem lies within government domains. The reality of today is that society is now in a 21st-century world of global interdependence where it is not nation-states that have changed, but the world in which they inhabit (Albright 2015). Furthermore, it is the nature of these global challenges that is changing and nation-states are not equipped with the proper tools to address these problems in this framework of a global interdependent world. On a positive note, it is these changing global challenges that have been able to unite cities with a common thread for innovative problem-solving in domains such as the environment, climate change, and economic development.

In order for cities to advance in their problem-solving capacity on these challenges, they will need to have the institutional and financial support of higher governance spheres (Pilipiszyn 2016). The U.S. Department of State's 2015 Quadrennial Diplomacy and Development Review (QDDR) has called for the need of the department to build stronger relationships with cities given this era of diffuse and networked power in which we live (US Department of State 2015). Similarly, the Atlantic Council's first Strategy Paper, "Dynamic Stability: US Strategy for a World in Transition," has made the case that the U.S. government should craft partnerships with cities and other non-state actors in pursuit of its strategic ends (Pavel and Engelke 2015).

This said, we argue that cities can help national and international governing bodies meet these strategic ends by providing individuals with easier access to education, services, economic opportunities, and ideas. At the same time, cities are dismantling traditional social architecture, crafting new identities, and influencing the way civil society engages in political discourse. As a result, municipalities have evolved into dynamic nodes of power within this fracturing system of global governance. Engelke (2015) of the Atlantic Council argues that the very legitimacy of local governments is under scrutiny by their own citizens as well as the global governance ecosystem, which motivates them that much more to deliver on their promises. Engelke (2015) further explains that, simultaneously, cities have been champions in managing the flux of global challenges with innovative solutions and organic organizational capacity.

So how should power be balanced between these different levels of governance? In the 2016 World Economic Forum report on Urban Development, experts argued that national governments must ensure that cities are not discriminated against through policies favoring suburbs and rural areas (WEF 2016). Additionally, with cities competing at the global stage to attract resources, they must be well integrated in the global value chain through trade, direct and indirect foreign investment, tourism, and foreign talent (WEF 2016). In doing so, national governments can facilitate healthy urban development (Engelke 2015). Where local governance is weak, national governments can provide financial and institutional support for building expertise and governance capacity in city planning and related technical areas (Engelke 2015).

This continuous process of rescaling between governance levels is supported by Barber's concept of "glocality" (a paradoxical fusion of the global and the local), where government is local, focused on neighbors and neighborhood democracy, but also inclusive of universal urban issues and global intercity networks (Barber 2013, 217). As such, we argue that this glocality has facilitated novel ways of organizing, interacting, influencing governmental processes, and increasing the social and political relevance of non-state actors, such as cities. Additionally, with today's increased accessibility and affordability of information and communication technologies, local governments have capitalized the most by improving the rate of information exchange, speeding up the dissemination of both technological and policy innovations (Lemos and Agrawal 2006).

Localizing the SDGs in global cities of the GCC

We argue that in the context of global cities in the GCC countries, sustainable actions taken at the city level will be the drivers in achieving the SDGs and will facilitate the transition towards sustainable lifestyles in the region. More specifically, we believe that these with actions should come a balanced approach of policy mechanisms and physical/environmental planning of critical infrastructure. This balanced approach should be anchored within the core premise of sustainability-oriented innovation, which we believe is the turnkey to successfully achieving the SDGS, both in the GCC and globally. The development indicators of the GCC countries indicate that the region has achieved high levels of human development that is on par with the most developed nations. However, the sustainability indicators of the GCC countries indicate significant environmental costs. The GCC countries are facing challenges related to sustainable development, including lack of adequate supplies of freshwater supplies, inadequacy of internal food production, high demand for energy, high levels of consumption, and economies' reliance on oil exports. The demographic imbalance and high reliance on temporary expatriate workers are also major challenges to achieving sustainable development in the GCC countries towards anchoring capacity building long term. In response, the GCC governments have actively engaged in promoting sustainability initiatives, mainly in relation to education, land development, environmental protection, water, and energy, all of which fall under the targets set for the 2030 Agenda. To turn this promotion into action, new tools of analysis are required to make a tangible impact.

Methodology

According to MIT professor, Sarah Slaughter, innovation is defined as actual use of a nontrivial change and improvement in a process, product, or system, which is novel to the institution developing the change (Slaughter 2010). Slaughter identifies the following four elements as key challenges to innovation: effectiveness, robustness, availability, and ease of deployment (Slaughter 2010). Building upon this definition, the Organization for Economic Cooperation and Development (OECD) states that innovation is crucial for long-term economic growth in both developed and developing countries, as it fosters competitiveness, creates jobs, helps to address environmental and health challenges, reduces inequality and contributes to sustained and inclusive growth (OECD 2016). But innovation-driven growth requires the right mix of multi-sector and multidisciplinary policy actions – in education, research, science and technology, finance, and public procurement, among others (OECD 2016). The OECD further argues that innovation goes well beyond just research and development – it goes beyond the confines of research labs to users, suppliers, and consumers everywhere – in government, business, and non-profit organizations; across borders; across sectors; and across institutions (OECD 2005). The OECD further posits that innovation activities are all scientific, technological, organizational, financial, and commercial steps which actually, or are intended to, lead to the implementation of innovations (OECD 2013). Accordingly, the notion of innovation policy is broad too, going beyond science and technology policy to support knowledge creation, diffusion, and absorption (OECD 2013).

According to Jay and Gerand (2015, who coined the term "sustainability-oriented innovation" (SOI), they define SOI as innovation utilized in order to overcome global change and enabling societies to thrive on a planet with increasingly finite resources (Figure 6.1). The authors explain that SOI is about dispelling the notion of tradeoffs between what seem to be competing goals – performance versus impact, profit versus purpose, human well-being versus environmental protection (Jay and Gerand 2015). From their research, the authors state that a critical barrier to achieving SOI is the "sustainability tradeoff" view of the world, a mental model that says having a positive social and environmental impact must exist as a tradeoff with more traditional business drivers (Jay and Gerand 2015). Jay and Gerand (2015) further explain that embracing diversity dispels the notion of single-person innovation and instead on increasing opportunities for growth and scale through a systemic, multi-dimensional, multi-stakeholder approach. With this wider perspective and more diverse population of stakeholders, it becomes possible to tackle

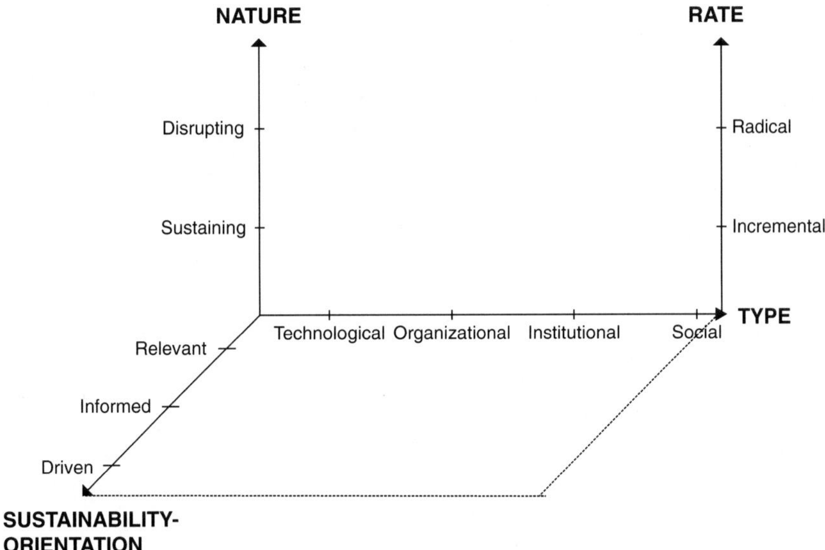

Figure 6.1 Sustainability-Oriented Innovation Dimensions

Source: Jay and Gerand (2015)

the big challenges more effectively and to be part of the solution to create a positive future for business and society at large (Jay and Gerand 2015). It is this definition of sustainability-oriented innovation that we use as the foundation for this chapter in order to support our claims in how global cities attain legitimacy for their position in the global governance framework in order to achieve the SDGs. Furthermore, we build upon Jay's definition of SOI by adding environment as one of the key dimensions. Specifically, we will use the SOI vector of environment, technological, and social innovations within the SOI framework analysis of global cities and their international airports.

Sustainability-Oriented Innovation Index for Airports©

In our analysis of the current literature surrounding SDG action in global cities, we found many valid arguments that supported global cities taking on a leading role within the global governance architecture. Some authors also provided suggestions on how cities should achieve this such as creating a Parliament of Mayors or placing a municipal official in a national office for information sharing. We found that the ultimate equation came down to legitimacy and how innovation can be a driver for achieving this legitimacy in the eyes of all stakeholders and decision-makers. What we found to be a mismatch was that many authors argued for the need of global cities to increase their innovation capacity in order to remain adaptable, responsive, and reflexive, yet many innovations, whether they be technological, infrastructure-based, environmental, or policy-based, come with hidden externalities that can cause unforeseen challenges with unintended consequences. We argue that in order to innovate holistically from a systems-thinking approach, global cities need to anchor their development strategies within a sustainability-oriented innovation framework that aligns strategies of all stakeholders within a given metroregion. As a result, we applied the Sustainability-Oriented Innovation Index for Airports© from Pilipiszyn (2016) in order to analyze how different lenses of innovation applied at GCC airports can create synergies between multiple agendas of decision-makers in the metroregion through a sustainability-oriented innovation framework.

To demonstrate a global cities' true capacity to implement sustainability-oriented innovation and thus legitimize their role in international affairs within the context of GCC countries, we have chosen to analyze the international airport of Abu Dhabi. Our rationale for this choice of analysis is that based on the literature available today regarding the role of global cities in global governance, a very limited number of experts have investigated how the capacity of an international airport of a particular global city to innovate through different lenses impacts that city's legitimacy both locally and globally. This impact can be measured by a city's ability to be adaptable, reflexive, and responsive in the face of global change such as answering to increased urbanization, changing demographics, climate change, and increased globalization. After conducting extensive research, we were unable to find a tool or study that analyzed international airports' agendas in relation to the city they served from an integrated systems perspective, which led us to utilize the world's first Sustainability-Oriented Innovation Index for Airports© by Pilipiszyn (2016). Using this index, we argue that the sustainability agendas of international airports need to be better integrated within the overall development plans of global cities and international communities with regards to sustainability-oriented innovation, especially as airports are entry nodes into the city system between global hubs. Furthermore, air travel is increasing along with population growth and urbanization statistics. According to the International Air Travel Association (IATA), in 2015 more than 3.5 billion passengers flew, which is almost exactly half of today's global population (IATA 2016). That number is predicted to continue to increase as countries such as China and India have a continually growing middle class, allowing more people than ever to be able to afford to fly, making the conversation about the flows in the infrasystems between airports and municipalities an ever more relevant conversation.

To support our claims using the case studies of the international airport of Abu Dhabi, we have used Pilipiszyn's (2016) Sustainability-Oriented Innovation Index© (Figure 6.2) that incorporates the three lenses of innovation we have listed above in addition to their capacity to adapt to change over time. This index specifically looks at the following 10 indicators, which provide an encompassing framework from which to draw conclusions about the relationship between a global city and its airport, and the impact of the sustainability-oriented

Figure 6.2 Sustainability-Oriented Innovation Index for Airports©

Source: Pilipiszyn (2016)

innovations from an airport on a global city's position within the international regime of governance:

- Population of metroregion
- Number of passengers per year at each respective airport
- Number of global city destinations serviced per year per airport compared to total destinations
- Number of flights per week at each respective airport

- Number of connections to municipal public transportation system by type
- Number of connections to municipal energy system by type
- Number of environmental innovations at airport (building certifications, ecological conservation initiatives, nature-based solutions, etc.)
- Number of social innovations at airport (community consultations, joint community projects, social investments)
- Number of technological innovations at airport (in relation to ground handling)
- Level of integration of airport sustainability activities into city development plan

These 10 indicators were created within the context of airports based on the A. T. Kearney Global Cities Index and Outlook metrics of: Business Activity, Human Capital, Information Exchange, Cultural Experiences, Political Engagement, Personal Well-Being, Economics, Innovation, and Governance (A. T. Kearney 2016).

Case study: Abu Dhabi

In this case study we contextualize the role of smart cities within the discourse on global cities, briefly review the key features of Abu Dhabi's metropolitan area and international airport; we explain the challenges and technological dimension of Abu Dhabi's metroregion; we present the Sustainability-Oriented Innovation Index for Airports© portfolio of Abu Dhabi; we study the technological innovations implemented by the Abu Dhabi Airport; and finally we look at how these innovations have contributed to the overall adaptability, reflexivity, and responsiveness of the Abu Dhabi metroregion in relation to the implementation of the SDGs.

Smart cities for sustainable innovation

According to the 2015 Mobility Report by Ericsson, there are 2.6 billion smartphone subscriptions globally and it is predicted that there will be 6.1 billion smartphones in circulation globally by 2020 (Ericsson 2015). Realizing the gravity of this statistic, there is a great deal to be said about what cities are doing currently to employ technology as a creative means to improve efficiency, sustainability, governance, and citizen outreach (Barber 2013, 262). According to Barber (2013, 242), digitally linked, so-called smart cities are on the cutting edge of urban innovation. He explains that smart cities are self-consciously interdependent cities that use technology to enhance communication, hoping to make smart cities wireless nodes in a global network and reinforce their natural inclination to connectivity and collaboration (Barber 2013).

Boyd Cohen extends Barber's claims and calls cities "smart" when they use information and communication technologies (ICT) to be more intelligent and efficient in the use of resources, resulting in cost and energy savings, improved service delivery and quality of life, and reduced environmental footprint – all supporting innovation and the low-carbon economy (Cohen 2012). Barber posits that truly smart cities will rely first not on instrumental technology but on the primary intelligence of citizens and the judgment of mayors in solving the (not just urban) problems of an interdependent world (Barber 2013, 267). The utilization of technology by these "smart" citizens has become one of the key drivers of this sustainable urban transformation and is also driving the emergence of the new urban services paradigm (WEF 2016).

Building upon these claims about the role of technology in urban city systems, we argue that the meaningful utilization of technology by all stakeholders has the capacity to significantly enhance a global city's ability to innovate and thus increase its adaptability, responsiveness, and reflexivity in given challenges. We further support the arguments by Barber that technology itself is not the solution – technology is a tool for citizens to use in order to find solutions to problems. Since the birth of the Internet, the 21st century has seen an exponential growth in the evolution of technologies for both individuals and business alike. Similar to Madeleine Albright's earlier words, today's citizens are already utilizing 21st-century technologies, businesses are becoming increasingly agile and making their way into the 21st century, but it is governments that seem to struggle in breaking out of the 19th century when it comes to technology.

Citing the work of Goldsmith and Crawford (2014), it is local governments who have the most gain from this urban paradigm shift due to their inherent agility and responsiveness. Furthermore, the use of new technologies can facilitate citizen empowerment and, thus, perpetuate a flow of sustainability-oriented innovation that can help a municipality achieve its development plan goals. In the case of global cities, in particular, the increased implementation of technological innovation can aide in the efficiency and overall citizen experience within the city, thus giving legitimacy to the global city within international decision-making. We specifically use the OECD definition of technological innovation, which states that technological innovations comprise new products and processes and significant technological changes of products and processes (OECD 2013). As a global city, we argue that Abu Dhabi has been able to quickly capitalize on the benefits of such technological innovations, especially with regards to the implementation of their E-government platform for the municipality as well as integrating their goals with the UAE National Innovation Strategy.

Overview of Abu Dhabi's accelerated growth

According to the Abu Dhabi Municipality, over the years the United Arab Emirates has witnessed almost unsurpassed development and prosperity, recording comprehensive growth across all sectors (Abu Dhabi Municipality 2016). They have set forward a goal of sustainable growth by decreeing that infrastructure of the highest standard is to be put in place to anticipate and drive future developments (Abu Dhabi Municipality 2016). The Municipality of Abu Dhabi City was established in 1962 as the "Department of Abu Dhabi Municipality and Town Planning" (Abu Dhabi Municipality 2016). In 1969, a royal decree was issued to appoint the first municipal board for the city of Abu Dhabi, with the task of providing

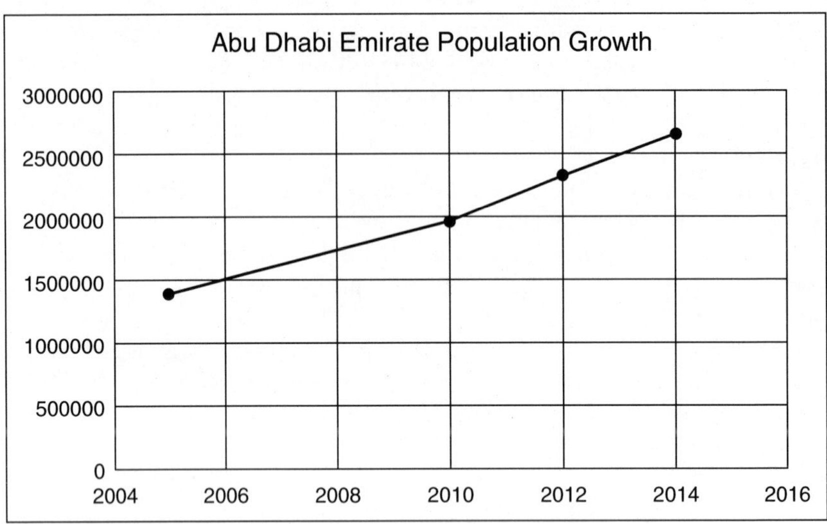

Figure 6.3 Population of Abu Dhabi Emirate 2005–2015

Source: UAE Census Data [accessed via www.citypopulation.de/UAE]

comprehensive services to the public and ensure proper planning of the developing city, with regularized road networks, maintenance services, sewerage, lighting works, launching the Agriculture Development Plan in the Emirate and establishing public markets in various areas (Abu Dhabi Municipality 2016). With all of these infrastructure developments came a steady population growth over the past 10 years (Figure 6.3).

The Municipality of Abu Dhabi has, since its inception, developed a number of key objectives, notably the implementation of projects aimed at establishing modern infrastructure for the city including bridges, drainage systems, road networks, modern means of transportation, and consolidation of comprehensive development projects (Abu Dhabi Municipality 2016). In line with the policies of the government which aim at making Abu Dhabi a modern capital city, it is the Municipality of Abu Dhabi's priority to create an ideal living environment for city residents, with unmatched quality of life and modern amenities (Abu Dhabi Municipality 2016). According to the stated mission of the Abu Dhabi Municipality, the vision of the city is to be recognized as an efficient world-class Municipal System that ensures sustainable development and enhances the quality of life (Abu Dhabi Municipality 2016). Furthermore, the Municipality of Abu Dhabi is committed to the following values: customer service, development, accountability, excellence, knowledge sharing, collaboration, and innovation (Abu Dhabi Municipality 2016).

Abu Dhabi's rapid development and urbanization, coupled with the relatively high average income of its population, has transformed the city into a large and advanced metropolis (Abu Dhabi Municipality 2016). Today the city is the country's center of political and industrial activities, and a major cultural and commercial center, due to its position as the capital (Abu Dhabi Municipality 2016). The UAE's large hydrocarbon wealth gives it one of the highest GDP per capita in the world and Abu Dhabi owns the majority of these resources – 95% of the oil and 92% of gas (Isthmus Partners 2010). However, Abu Dhabi has recently begun to invest substantially in real estate, tourism, and retail as part of an active diversification and liberalization program to reduce the UAE's reliance on the hydrocarbon sector (IMF 2016). This goal is further exemplified in the amount of attention Abu Dhabi is giving to its International Airport as it seeks to attract different types of people.

In 1969, Abu Dhabi International Airport was opened in its first form at the heart of Abu Dhabi Island, which has since been transformed into today's Al Bateen Executive Airport (ADAC 2014a). In 1982, a decade after the unification of the seven Emirates to form the United Arab Emirates under the patronage and guidance of the late Sheikh Zayed bin Sultan Al Nahyan, Abu Dhabi International Airport was inaugurated at its current location 50 km outside of the capital city (ADAC 2014b). Originally designed to handle 5 million passengers per year, today Abu Dhabi International Airport has broken traffic records and raised its annual capacity to 23 million passengers (ADAC 2014a, 2016). Looking forward, plans are in place to reach 40 million passengers by 2017, with the addition of the new Midfield Terminal Complex (MTC), in line with the Government Plan "Abu Dhabi 2030" (ADAC 2014a). (Figure 6.4).

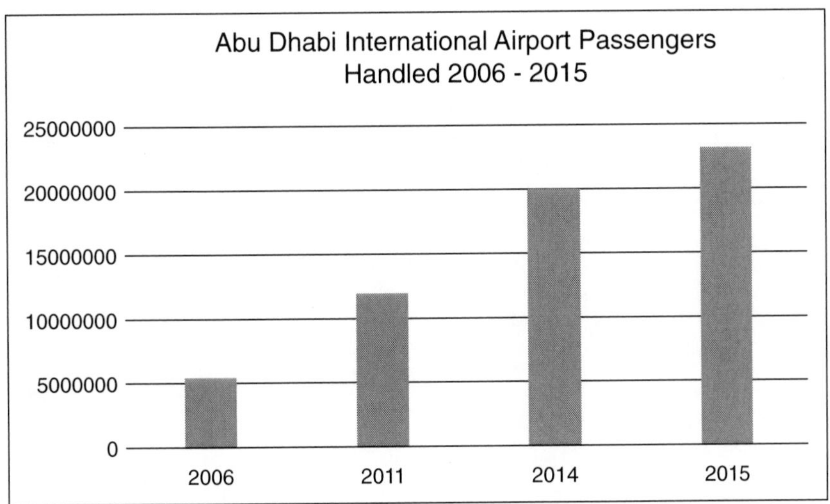

Figure 6.4 Number of passengers handled 2006–2015

Source: Abu Dhabi Airport Company Traffic Data

In 2011, the Abu Dhabi International Airport was awarded the 2nd Best Airport in the Middle East of the Airport Service Quality Awards by the Airports Council International (Airports Council International 2012). In 2012, the airport celebrated its 30th anniversary (Abu Dhabi Airport 2012). Given this incredible growth in such a short time frame, both the city and airport of Abu Dhabi have had to adapt to this demographic challenge and provide the best service possible. As I will explain in the following sections, it is the implementation of new technologies that has helped Abu Dhabi to leap-frog from a small fishing town in the desert to a truly global metropolis and accelerate its own progress.

The technological dimension of innovation in Abu Dhabi

In the GCC countries, as in most other natural resource-driven economies, innovation policy has been at the core of the economic diversification policy agenda (Abu Dhabi Department of Economic Development 2016). In Abu Dhabi, the Economic Vision 2030 sets an ambitious plan to drive innovation and move towards a knowledge-driven economy (Abu Dhabi Department of Economic Development 2016). The plan includes strategic distinct sub-goals related to ICTs, education, infrastructure, and many other intermediate goals towards the ultimate objective of a full transition towards a sustainable knowledge-based economy (Abu Dhabi Department of Economic Development 2016).

Since its inception in 1971, the UAE has constantly been distinguished as an icon for innovation and creativity, enhancing its social and economic status and transforming into a primary destination for talents and businesses in record time (UAE NIS 2015). With such a rapid development in less than 100 years' time, Abu Dhabi has been able to demonstrate the power of being adaptable, responsive, and reflexive to global challenges such as diminished oil prices, impacts of climate change, and the pivotal transition to a sustainable energy future.

One of these examples has been the creation of Masdar City, which is a nearly zero-carbon city located within the metroregion of Abu Dhabi. The Mubadala Development Company, which is owned by the Abu Dhabi government, established Masdar as a wholly owned subsidiary in 2006:

> Masdar is guided by The Abu Dhabi Economic Vision 2030, in order to stimulate new sources of income for the Emirate and strengthen its knowledge-based economic sectors. Masdar takes a holistic approach to its organization, with four business units that are interconnected and a research arm that complements their work. The business units are Masdar Clean Energy, Masdar Special Projects and Masdar City. Masdar Institute, an independent, research-driven graduate university, rounds out the organization. With each unit focused on a key component of the value chain, Masdar operates with the broad scope needed to meet the most pressing sustainability challenges of tomorrow, which keeps Abu Dhabi at the global forefront of the clean energy industry in the pursuit of pioneering commercially viable technologies and systems. As a result, Masdar

> City is one of the most sustainable urban development prototypes in the world. Powered by renewable energy, Masdar City combines passive and intelligent design to showcase how an urban environment can accommodate denser populations with fewer resources. Designed as a clean technology cluster with special economic incentives, the city attracts nearly 200 companies to commercialize and deploy new energy technologies in the Middle East.
>
> (Masdar 2016)

This being said, one of the fundamental building blocks of both Abu Dhabi and the country as a whole has been innovation. According to the UAE Prime Minister's Office, innovation is defined as the aspiration of individuals, private institutions, and governments to achieve development by generating creative ideas and introducing new products, services, and operations that improve the overall quality of life (UAE NIS 2015). Furthermore, innovation is key to promoting economic growth, increasing competitiveness, and providing new job opportunities (UAE NIS 2015).

Looking at technology infrastructure specifically, the UAE National Innovation Strategy has three main aims:

- Set up a first-class technology infrastructure that enables innovation
- Ensure the optimal use of ICTs in acquiring, disseminating, and sharing knowledge to promote innovation
- Ensure competitive and cost-effective technology infrastructure

This report stresses that technology is of paramount importance in today's world. Given the primary role it plays in shaping the future, there is a growing need for innovation in technology tools and systems to ensure a better quality of life for everyone (UAE NIS 2015). The UAE has accordingly launched a range of innovative technology initiatives, namely The Smart Government and The Smart City initiatives, which secured it a global leadership position in record time (UAE NIS 2015). Moreover, Mubadala wholly owns Global Foundries, the world's second largest semiconductor manufacturer (UAE NIS 2015). In addition, the UAE developed a multitude of advanced technology research centers, including The Institute Center for Microsystems (iMicro), The Institute Center for Smart and Sustainable Systems (iSmart), and Khalifa Semiconductor Research Center (KSRC) at Khalifa University (UAE NIS 2015).

In addition, the UAE National Innovation Strategy aims to promote innovation in technology through the development of smart cities, software, and applications, as well as the enhancement of the ICT industry to improve the quality of services provided (UAE NIS 2015). The report explains that innovation in technology will also be achieved through the manufacturing of advanced technology in areas of global interest such as artificial intelligence, semiconductors, nanotechnology, and 3D printing, in addition to the quick adoption of future technology trends across various industries (UAE NIS 2015).

Looking deeper into these building blocks of the UAE National Innovation Strategy, it is clear to see how technology innovation is present at all three levels and unites all of the other core components. According to the Abu Dhabi Innovation Index, one of the city's key strengths lies within the ICT dimension of Internet use, which is bolstered by Abu Dhabi's high level of connectivity (Abu Dhabi Innovation Index 2016). We demonstrate in the following sections how the connectivity of the Abu Dhabi International Airport and its utilization of technological innovations propels the city of Abu Dhabi into the framework of global governance through its capacity to be adaptive, responsive, and reflexive, which facilitates greater opportunities for SDG implementation (Table 6.1) (Appendix I).

Table 6.1 Sustainability-Oriented Innovation Index for Airports©

Metro Region Population	**1.5 million (2014)**	*Abu Dhabi City Municipality*
Airline Passengers	**23 million (2015)**	*Abu Dhabi Airports*
Airport Connectivity	**Total Destinations: 103** **Global City Connections: 62**	*Abu Dhabi Airports* ** Global city connections as according to A>T. Kearney's 2015 Global City Index*
Weekly Flights	**3,323 flights per week**	*Abu Dhabi Airports*
Municipal Transportation Connectivity	**7 connections**	*- Etihad Rail (forthcoming 2019)* *- Musanda Abu Dhabi Metro (forthcoming 2020)* *- Bus A1, Bus 490, Bus 211, Bus 240, Bus X81*
Municipal Energy Connectivity	**1 connection**	*- Mubadala Petroleum*
Environmental Innovation	**6 innovations**	*- 1st Carbon Accredited airport in Asia-Pacific from AIC Europe and AIC Asia-Pacific* *- Midfield Terminal 3 Pearl Estidama rating* *- Energy Management Program* *- Recycling of construction materials* *- Water Management Program* *- Waste Management Program*
Social Innovation	**4 innovations**	*- Sponsorhip of UAE Red Crescent* *- Sponsorship of Women Union in Abu Dhabi* *- Advertising space reserved for Abu Dhabi Environment Agency & Police* *- CityGuard App*
Technological Innovation	**11 innovations**	*- Automated Passenger Mobility System* *- Airport Management Solution Tool (SITA)* *- AirportConnect Open (SITA)* *- BagManager (SITA)* *- Smart Travel Process* *- X-Design of Midfield Terminal (KPF)* *- Airport Vision (SITA)* *- Airport Resource Manager (SITA)* *- Airport Central (SITA), iValidate (SITA)* *- City Terminal*
Municipal Development Plan Integration	**YES**	- ***Abu Dhabi Vision 2030:*** *This strategy plan focuses on creating a sustainable Emirate that protects resources for current and future generations; supports and enables economics diversification and growth; raises the standard of living across the Emirate; protects, enhances, and promotes Arab and Emirate culture and traditions; and embraces contemporary living and respecting the diverse cultures of those residing in Abu Dhabi.*

Source: Abu Dhabi Portfolio

The role of technological innovations in achieving sustainability goals for global cities

In 2008, The Climate Group on behalf of the Global e-Sustainability Initiative (GeSI), with independent analysis by McKinsey & Company, found that ICT is a key sector in the fight against climate change and could enable emissions reductions of 7.8 Gt CO2e in 2020, or 15% of business-as-usual emissions (Climate Group 2008). But it must keep its own growing footprint in check and overcome a number of hurdles if it expects to deliver on this potential (Climate Group 2008). In the case of Abu Dhabi, this information is very significant for both the city and the airport as they continue to invest and implement these new technologies that can deliver state-of-the-art services but can also cause unintended challenges. Climate change has already begun to impact Abu Dhabi with persistent, increasing temperatures, water scarcity, increased acidity and salinity of the Persian Gulf, and coastal erosion (EAD 2009). The use of any technologies requires not just the proper infrastructure to be built, but also massive amounts of energy to keep these technologies operational and not overheat.

We argue that the Abu Dhabi International Airport's implementation of an integrated systems management approach for their ICTs is a crucial step in the right direction to address this externality. By applying a systems model, the system as whole runs more efficiently, thus saving energy and avoiding potential gaps. As discussed earlier, Abu Dhabi is in a transition phase towards a knowledge-based economy and thus must attract a variety of different people to the city in order to cultivate a truly diverse economy. As the global entry point to the city, the Abu Dhabi International Airport has been able to adapt to the city's rapid demographic growth as well as passenger capacity by implementing a suite of technologies that go from the structural design to save energy to passenger mobility to security improvements to connectivity and further development of the public transportation system and more. In the implementation of these technologies and associated services, such as the City Terminal, the Abu Dhabi International Airport has been able to facilitate the legitimization of the city's role in the global governance architecture as it continues to respond and be reflexive to shifting dynamics of change, whether it is the new economy, changing climate, or speed of urbanization. We argue that as the Abu Dhabi International Airport aspires to be one of the "smartest" airports, it must also strive to be one of the most sustainable to align itself with the City of Abu Dhabi's Agenda 2030 and thus bolster the entire metroregion's capacity to respond to local challenges with global impacts.

The Abu Dhabi Midfield Terminal Building has also become a regional benchmark for sustainable airport design by achieving a Estidama 3 Pearl Rating in 2013 and aims to achieve a 4 Pearl Rating by 2017. The Estidama Pearl Rating System, similar to LEED certification, is a framework for sustainable design, construction, and lifecycle operation for communities, buildings, and villas. Estidama is a program developed by the Urban Planning Council that was conceived to promote a new mindset that reflects the intellectual legacy of the late Sheikh Zayed bin Sultan Al Nahyan and his visionary governance in promoting thoughtful and responsible development through the creation of a balanced society based on four equal pillars of sustainability: environmental, economic, social, and cultural (Abu Dhabi Airports 2014b). This utilization of the Estidama framework is thus directly linked to SDG #9 (Industry, Innovation, and Infrastructure) and SDG #11 (Sustainable Cities and Communities).

With its construction of the new Midfield Terminal Complex, the Abu Dhabi International Airport demonstrates its capacity to innovate and use technological innovation to meet multiple challenges at the same time, which is supported by its own agility. According to the Climate Group, while the sector plans to significantly step up the energy efficiency of its products and services, ICTs largest influence will be by enabling energy efficiencies in other sectors, an opportunity that could deliver carbon savings 5 times larger than the total emissions from the entire ICT sector in 2020 (Climate Group 2008). This information should be taken seriously, especially in the context of both the Abu Dhabi International Airport and the City of Abu Dhabi utilizing an exuberant amount of digital technologies. These technologies can improve efficiency but the core component to these technologies should be anchored in sustainability-oriented innovation in order to avoid exacerbating other externalities the city faces, such as water scarcity or climate change. By aligning its goals with the Abu Dhabi municipal development plan, Agenda 2030, the Abu Dhabi International Airport can further demonstrate the capacity of an international airport to enhance urban problem-solving and integrate creative methods of sustainability-oriented innovation that benefits both urban citizens and global visitors.

Discussion

Based on our findings, we argue that true global cities must be able to have a constant birds-eye-view on both local and global challenges in order to address these challenges swiftly and efficiently. To do so, global cities must recognize their own connectivity and networks within their metroregion infrasystems and align development and sustainability strategies with key stakeholders in order to optimize the city's responsiveness, reflexivity, and adaptability (Pilipiszyn 2016). When the city's responsiveness, reflexivity, and adaptability are optimized, the city has the greatest potential to obtain a legitimate position within the global governance architecture, as conferred by both civil society and decision-making authorities (Pilipiszyn 2016). According to Barber, cities don't have to wait for states; they can act to achieve a measure of security or a degree of sustainability whether nations are dysfunctional or not. Civil society doesn't have to wait for city government; it can take action of its own even when mayors hesitate. Citizens don't have to wait for civil society; they can work with one another and impel civil society and leaders to act (Barber 2013, 139).

This capacity of global cities to implement sustainability-oriented innovation is the winning card that cities have available in their policy toolkit in order to succeed where nations have not and impact global decision-making. Barber argues that this optimism about the future arises out of the nature of cities themselves due to the fact that they are already networked and naturally disposed to creative interactivity and innovative cross-border experimentation and collaboration; they are relational, communal, and naturally interdependent (Barber 2013, 171). Whether we call it global governance or simply cosmopolitanism as praxis and whether or not it is underwritten by a parliament of mayors or some other global association, cities will play an increasingly crucial role in making decisions across borders on behalf of humanity (Barber 2013, 171).

In addressing these numerous claims about the role of global cities within the framework of international decision-making, this chapter analyzed the case study of Abu Dhabi through the application of Pilipiszyn's (2016) Sustainability-Oriented Innovation Index for Airports© with regards to the international airport's capacity to align sustainability strategies through three unique lenses of environmental, social, and technological innovation. This chapter demonstrated how the collaborative responsiveness, reflexivity, and adaptability of a city and its respective airport breeds the kind of legitimacy called for by citizens and solidifies the role of cities in today's global governance architecture as a main actor.

Conclusion

This chapter found that cities legitimize their role as local governments in the face of global challenges by optimizing their responsiveness, reflexivity, and adaptability, which bolsters a city's capacity to solve problems. This legitimacy is bestowed upon the city by variety of stakeholders the metroregion serves. We also found that cities are equipped to negotiate the transition of hybrid governance models through capitalizing on the strengths of the infrasystems that form the multi-dimensional helix of a city's genetic composition. One of these infrasystems, in particular, is the systemic flow and synergies between a global city and its international airport. Serving as the entry and exit point of a global city, its international airport has the capacity to facilitate greater legitimacy of the metroregion through its ability to deliver the services that is expected of it. Finally, this chapter found that the implementation of sustainability-oriented innovation frameworks served as a significant mechanism for international airports to contribute to the legitimization of its city within the global governance architecture and advance the implementation of the SDGs goals and targets. Through the utilization of an SOI model, cities can collaborate with nation-states and international authorities to tackle global challenges based on one another's key strengths and create synergies between local and national agendas.

With respect to the Municipality of Abu Dhabi and the Abu Dhabi International Airport, it is clear that technological innovation is the key driver for change within the SOI framework of this metroregion. In analyzing the complete menu of options that are offered with regards to these various digital technologies that are being implemented at the Abu Dhabi International Airport, these innovations contribute to the legitimacy of the City in increasing the efficiency, attractiveness, and user-friendliness of the airport. We argue that these technological innovations are extremely important for the legitimacy of a city, but should not unintentionally create more challenges further down the road. As all of these digital technologies require vast amounts of energy and infrastructure to run properly, we suggest that sustainability must be put at the core of these operations. For example, in order to reduce the use of petroleum to power the airport's activities, the airport could diversify some of its energy mix by obtaining power from the Shams1 solar power plant. In addition, Masdar City is an achievement in itself, but lacks the connectivity of public transportation to connect between downtown and the airport. The potential to optimize these innovative technologies within a sustainability plan is significant because, since both the financial capital and technologies exist, it is a matter of connecting the dots of the city infrasystem. Once these dots are connected, the City of Abu Dhabi has the potential to rise to a new level of legitimacy within the global governance architecture through effectively synergizing multiple sustainability agendas within an SOI framework, which will enable greater capacity for SDG implementation.

With the rapid development, growth, and change in the UAE, sustainability and the successful implementation of the SDGs is more important than ever. Sustainability is carries universal value as it can provide both major opportunities and risk in the short, medium, and long term. Key sustainability drivers in the region, for both businesses and individuals, include: energy efficiency; compliance with regulatory and corporate social responsibility policies relating to the environment; efficient waste management and disposal (including recycling); the sourcing and use of water; the food supply chain; and air, water, and ground emissions (Norton Rose Fulbright 2015). The importance of these drivers on a large scale can be seen in the recent Arab Spring, which many analysts stated was partially driven by the scarcity of resources and their rising cost (Norton Rose Fulbright 2015). On a smaller scale, such factors affect the everyday bottom line of businesses and the social and economic well-being of individuals (Norton Rose Fulbright 2015).

In conclusion, global cities do have the tools and mechanisms to justify their legitimacy to make decisions at the global level in their capacity to implement sustainability-oriented innovations that optimize the metroregion infrasystems, which allow for adaptability, responsiveness, and reflexivity in the face of global challenges. For future research, we plan to investigate other urban critical infrastructures (such as hospitals, bridges, and ports) within an SOI framework in other GCC cities to better understand the power of urban infrasystems as vectors towards new global governance and SDG implementation.

Appendix I

Technological innovations of the Abu Dhabi International Airport

Automated passenger mobility system

This is a light rail system that will transport passengers from the Midfield Terminal building to satellite concourses currently being planned to meet the significant growth of Etihad (ADAC 2015). This project is the cornerstone of the future developments of the Abu Dhabi International Airport.

SITA Airport Management solution

SITA Airport Management is a suite of integrated software applications that support and enhance airport operations from landside to airside, from landing to take off (SITA 2016). Airport Management enables airport operators to be proactive and simplifies their day-to-day tasks by providing them with an effective way to share information with their stakeholders enabling common situational awareness and supporting processes for working together (SITA 2016).

SITA AirportConnect Open

SITA's AirportConnect Open provides the standard communications between all the peripherals required for passenger processing including printers, passport readers, boarding card readers, and bag tag printers (SITA 2016). It also supports self-boarding gates and self-bag drop (SITA 2016). AirportConnect Open is the only platform capable of providing an integrated approach to common-use terminal equipment (CUTE), common-use passenger processing systems (CUPPS), and common-use self-service (CUSS) kiosks, hosted on one platform (SITA 2016).

SITA BagManager

According to SITA, every minute, 40 bags get mishandled worldwide. In 2014, that amounted to more than 24.1 million mishandled bags, costing the air transport industry US$2.4 billion (SITA 2016). More often than not, these bags go astray during the transfer process (SITA 2016). By providing real-time information on baggage status, SITA BagManager cuts mishandled transfer rates by 20%, providing positive return on investment (ROI) from Day 1 (SITA 2016). Suitable for airports, airlines, and ground handlers, it provides industry-leading functionalities for loading, reconciling, tracking, tracing, and managing baggage operations (SITA 2016). It's also available through SITA's ATI Cloud, providing quick implementation with no server equipment requirements onsite (SITA 2016). This new baggage system is designed to process over 19,000 bags per hour with than 22 kilometers of conveying lines (ARUP 2015).

Smart Travel process

The initiative, implemented in partnership with the Ministry of Interior and Abu Dhabi Police, allows passengers to check in and move through immigration and security, interacting only with innovative technology (Al Kuttab 2016). This pioneering system consists of self-check-in and baggage drop facilities, automated passport control gates equipped with biometric verification functions and facial recognition technology, along with smart boarding gates (Al Kuttab 2016). These "Smart Travel" processes will replace the previously used e-gates and enhance passenger experience by decreasing processing times within the airport by up to 70% (Al Kuttab 2016). For the airport and airlines, a quicker flow of passengers will also effectively increase capacity and throughput of the available facilities (Al Kuttab 2016).

Design of midfield terminal

The architect behind the midfield terminal complex's master plan, Kohn Pederson Fox, revealed that it will have an "X" design (Airport Technology 2016). The KPF team adopted structural solutions that created a large, column-free zone that will allow for future space planning needs (Airport Technology 2016). The X-shaped plan involves a large ticketing hall framed by a series of long-span steel arches supporting the roof (Airport Technology 2016). Upon completion, the hall will lead into a central area with a garden, a reference to Abu Dhabi's reputation as the "Garden of the Gulf" (Airport Technology 2016). This terminal was designed to achieve considerable reduction in annual energy consumption through the specification of an appropriate and climate responsive building form and façade and systems, which will feature high-performance low-e double glazing to reduce solar gain and low U-values specified for the walls and roof to minimize heat gain (ADAC 2014a).

SITA AirportVision

SITA's AirportVision is a flight information display system (FIDS) that supports the seamless flow of passengers through an airport (SITA 2016). AirportVision enables targeted advertising to specific groups of passengers and include local community messaging as well as incorporating advertising on FIDS or on advertising-dedicated displays (SITA 2016). The interactive voice response system lets passengers receive real-time information via their mobile device through email or SMS (SITA 2016).

SITA AirportResource Manager

AirportResource Manager is a flexible resource management system for fixed airport resources, such as departure gates, baggage carousels, and check-in desks (SITA 2016). It is equally suitable for managing mobile resources for ground handling or capacity planning for secondary resources such as immigration desks or security points (SITA 2016). SITA's AirportResource Manager coordinates the real-time management of equipment and staff and serves as a powerful scheduling tool designed for airports that need to react to large numbers of passengers or a high degree of seasonal fluctuations (SITA 2016).

SITA AirportCentral

With one integrated touch-point, SITA's AirportCentral allows airport managers to access data management tasks and automated functions for receiving, processing, and distributing consolidated data (SITA 2016). When multiple users access the system at the same time, AirportCentral can calculate and prioritize data, giving users the most accurate information available (SITA 2016).

SITA iValidate

SITA's Airport iValidate enables security agents to verify passengers' bar-coded boarding passes (BCBPs) quickly and efficiently, resulting in a better passenger experience (SITA 2016). Airport iValidate focuses on BCBP validation, including duplicate checking, validation against flight information within the airport operational database (AODB)/flight information display system (FIDS), and validation against airline departure control systems (DCS) (SITA 2016). The system includes four security lanes with automatic gates, four mobile/paper boarding pass scanners, and four hand-held wireless boarding pass scanners (SITA 2016).

City Terminal

Located in the center of Abu Dhabi's business district and within easy reach of many major international hotels, the City Terminal is easily accessible offering convenient early check-in for passengers and luggage (Abu Dhabi Airport 2014a). Passengers travelling from Abu Dhabi Airport can check in their baggage and get hold of their boarding passes up to 24 hours before the flight (Abu Dhabi Airport 2014a). The facility, which is located in Abu Dhabi's Tourist Club area, allows travelers to confirm their seats and reach the airport only an hour before the departure of their flight (Abu Dhabi Airport 2014a).

References

Abu Dhabi Airport. 2012. *Three Decades of Success.* Available at: www.abudhabiairport.ae/english/airport-information/about-abu-dhabi-airport/three-decades-of-success.aspx

Abu Dhabi Airport. 2014a. *Midfield Terminal Building Receives Estidama 3 Pearl Rating.* Available at: www.adac.ae/english/media-centre/press-releases/2013/2013-09-03-Midfield-Terminal-Building-Receives-Estidama-3-Pearl-Rating

Abu Dhabi Airport. 2014b. *Remote Check-In.* Available at: www.abudhabiairport.ae/english/airport-information/check-in-and-passport-control/remote-check-in.aspx

Abu Dhabi Airport. 2016. *Record Year for Abu Dhabi International Airport.* Available at: www.abudhabiairport.ae/english/media-centre/press-releases/2016/2016-01-31-RECORD-YEAR-FOR-ABU-DHABI-INTERNATIONAL-AIRPORT.aspx

Abu Dhabi Airport Company. 2014a. *Midfield Terminal – Sustainable Development.* Available at: www.adac.ae/english/mtp/MTP/sustainable-development

Abu Dhabi Airport Company. 2014b. *Who We Are: Evolution.* Available at: www.adac.ae/english/who-we-are/who-we-are/evolution

Abu Dhabi Airport Company. 2015. *The Future Automated Passenger Mobility System.* Available at: www.adac.ae/english/mtp/MTP/latest-news/2015-07-30-The-future-Automated-Passenger-Mobility-System – -Video

Abu Dhabi Airport Company. 2016. *Traffic Data.* Available at: www.adac.ae/english/doing-business-with-us/airline-development/traffic-data/

Abu Dhabi City Municipality. 2016. *Municipality History & Vision, Mission and Values.* Available at: www.adm.gov.ae/en/Menu/index.aspx?TWVudUlEPTU5JmFtcDtDYXRJRD01OSZhbXA7bW51PUNhdCZhbXA7ZGl2PUNhdA==#

Abu Dhabi Department of Economic Development. 2016. *The Abu Dhabi Innovation Index.* Available at: https://centres.insead.edu/innovation-policy/publications/documents/En_IndexReport.pdf

Abu Dhabi Environment Agency. 2009. *Climate Change: Impacts, Vulnerability, & Adaptation.* Available at: www.ead.ae/Documents/RESEARCHERS/Climate%20change%20impacts%20-%20Eng.pdf

Airport Technology. 2016. *Abu Dhabi International Airport (AUH/OMAA), United Arab Emirates.* Available at: www.airport-technology.com/projects/abu_dhabi/

Airports Council International. 2012. *Airport Service Quality – Best Airport by Region.* Available at: www.aci.aero/Airport-Service-Quality/ASQ-Awards/Current-Winners/Best-Airport-By-Region/Middle-East

Albright, M. 2015. *The Foreign Policy of Global Cities*. Chicago Forum on Global Cities.

Al Kuttab, J. 2016. Abu Dhabi's first airport in region to create "smart travel". *Khaleej Times.* Available at: www.khaleejtimes.com/business/aviation/abu-dhabi-airport-first-in-region-to-create-smart-travel

ARUP. 2015. ICT, Sustainability, and Smart Airports. Available at: http://aci-na.org/static/entransit/greenit_bell.pdf

Barber, B. 2013. *If Mayors Ruled the World: Dysfunctional Nations, Rising Cities*. Yale University Press. New Haven, Connecticut.

Barber, B. 2015. *Foreign Policy of Global Cities Panel.* Chicago Forum on Global Cities.

Cohen, B. 2012. Top Ten Smart Cities. Available at: www.fastcoexist.com/1679127/the-top-10-smart-cities-on-the-planet

The Climate Group. 2008. *SMART 2020: Enabling the Low Carbon Economy in the Information Age.* Available at: www.smart2020.org/publications/

The Economist Intelligence Unit. 2016. *Worldwide Cost of Living Survey*. Available at: www.economist.com/blogs/graphicdetail/2016/03/daily-chart-4

Engelke, P. 2015 October. *Foreign Policy for an Urban World: Global Governance and the Rise of Cities.* The Atlantic Council. Issue Brief. Washington, DC.

EAD. 2009. *Environmental Performance Index for Abu Dhabi Emirate.* Environment Agency Abu Dhabi. Available at: http://archive.epi.yale.edu/files/finaladepi_published.pdf

Ericsson. 2015. *Ericsson Mobility Report.* Available at: www.ericsson.com/mobility-report

Goldsmith, S., and S. Crawford. 2014. *The Responsive City: Engaging Communities Through Data-Smart Governance.* John Wiley & Sons, Inc. Somerset, NJ.

IATA. 2016. *Annual Review 2015.* Available at: www.iata.org/about/Documents/iata-annual-review-2015.pdf

International Monetary Fund. 2016. *Economic Diversification in Oil-Exporting Arab Countries.* Available at: www.imf.org/external/np/pp/eng/2016/042916.pdf

Isthmus Partners. 2010. *Abu Dhabi Investment Environment.* Available at: http://mec.biz/term/uploads/EPART-30-03-2010.pdf

Jay, J., and M. Gerand. 2015. Accelerating the Theory and Practice of Sustainability-Oriented Innovation. MIT Sloan School of Management.

Kearney, A.T. 2016. *Global Cities Index.* Available at: www.atkearney.com/research-studies/global-cities-index

Lemos, MC. and Agrawal, A. 2006. *Environmental Governance.* Annual Review of Environment and Resources. Vol. 31:297-325. Available at: http://www.annualreviews.org/doi/abs/10.1146/annurev.energy.31.042605.135621

Masdar. 2016. *About Masdar.* Available at: www.masdar.ae/en/masdar/our-story

Norton Rose Fulbright. 2015. *10 Things to Know About Sustainability in the UAE.* Available at: www.nortonrosefulbright.com/knowledge/publications/125011/10-things-to-know-about-sustainability-in-the-uae

OECD (2005). Oslo Manual: Guidelines for Collecting and Interpreting Innovation Data, 3rd Edition. Paris, France.

OECD 2013. *Regions and Innovation: Collaborating across Borders.* OECD Reviews of Regional Innovation, OECD Publishing. Available at: http://dx.doi.org/10.1787/9789264205307-en.

OECD. 2015. The Metropolitan Century: Understanding Urbanization and Its Consequences. Paris: OECD, p. 20.

OECD (2016). *The Innovation Policy Platform.* Available at: https://www.innovationpolicyplatform.org/

Pavel, B. and P. Engelke. 2015 April. *Dynamic Stability: US Strategy for a World in Transition.* Washington, DC: Atlantic Council. Available at: www.atlanticcouncil.org/publications/reports/dynamic-stability-us-strategy-for-a-world-in-transition.

Pilipiszyn, A. 2016. *Sustainability-Oriented Innovation: Urban Infrasystems & the Global Governance Architecture.* Masters thesis, Graduate Institute of International & Development Studies Geneva.

Sherwood, L. 2016. *Water Security in the GCC.* Available at: http://trendsinstitution.org/?p=1882

SITA. 2016. *AirportCentral.* Available at: www.sita.aero/solutions-and-services/products/airportcentral

SITA. 2016. *Airport Connect Open.* Available at: www.sita.aero/solutions-and-services/products/airportconnect-open

SITA. 2016. *Airport iValidate.* Available at: www.sita.aero/solutions-and-services/products/airport-ivalidate

SITA. 2016. *Airport Management Solution.* Available at: www.sita.aero/solutions-and-services/solutions/airport-management

SITA. 2016. *Airport Resource Manager.* Available at: www.sita.aero/solutions-and-services/products/airportresource-manager

SITA. 2016. *AirportVision.* Available at: www.sita.aero/solutions-and-services/products/airportvision

SITA. 2016. *BagManager.* Available at: www.sita.aero/solutions-and-services/products/bagmanager

Slaughter, S. 2010. *Innovations in Buildings and Infrastructure Systems.* MIT Research and Development Conference.

UAE Census Data. 2016. Available at: www.citypopulation.de/UAE.html

UAE Prime Minister's Office. 2016. *Abu Dhabi Innovation Index.* Available at: www.uaeinnovates.gov.ae/ecosystem/iIndices

UAE Prime Minister's Office at Ministry of Cabinet Affairs. 2015. *National Innovation Strategy.* Available at: http://uaecabinet.ae/en/the-national-strategy-for-innovation

United Nations. 2014. *World Urbanization Prospects.* Available at: https://esa.un.org/unpd/wup/publications/files/wup2014-highlights.Pdf

US Department of State. 2015, April. Quadrennial Diplomacy and Development Review: Enduring Leadership in a Dynamic World. Washington, DC: US Department of State.

World Economic Forum. 2016. Inspiring Future Cities & Urban Services – Shaping the Future of Urban Development & Services Initiative. Available at: http://www3.weforum.org/docs/WEF_Urban-Services.pdf

7 Towards sustainable urban development

Challenges and chances of climate-sensitive urban design in Muscat/Oman

Mais Jafari and Wolfgang Scholz

Background and motivation

In December 2015 at the United Nations Climate Conference on Change (COP 21), 195 countries finally reached an agreement to reduce global greenhouse gas emissions, thus limiting the effect of climate change. In addition to the direct climate change measures, attention should be directed to the negative effects of daily life practices and inherited norms that equally threaten our cities. This urges the need to re-think the forms of urban development. An example of a city which is exposed to this kind of climatic condition as well as to other socio-spatial and economic challenges that influence its urban development is Muscat, the capital of the Sultanate of Oman.

This chapter is based on a joint research project "Challenges of Rapid Urbanization in Muscat, Oman" of the Department of International Planning Studies at TU Dortmund University, Faculty of Spatial Planning (Germany) and the Department of Urban Planning and Architecture at the German University of Technology in Oman (GUtech) conducted in the academic Winter Semester 2015/2016. The joint research project included a student workshop at the GUtech in Muscat in which the empirical part of this research, including site visits, interviews, and group discussions, was conducted.

The joint research project aimed to read and analyze the urban development in Muscat which is undergoing an intense social and spatial transformation process triggered by socio-economic dynamics, population growth, an increase in the foreign workforce, high rates of internal and international migration, and the concentration of economic activities in urban areas. Therefore, it aims to develop regeneration frameworks and sustainable proposals that meet the challenges caused by rapid urbanization.

The main challenges associated with rapid urban growth in the capital of Muscat identified in the joint research project "Rapid Urbanization in Muscat, Oman" were (Joint Research Project 2016):

- Provision of infrastructure especially stormwater and sewage;
- Transportation, based on individual vehicles;
- Uncontrolled consumption of energy and land resources;

- Uneven land-use distribution and concentration of mixed-use development along main highways;
- Low-density land-use pattern at the urban fringe; and
- Climate-sensitive urban design (CSUD), responding to the urban growth and reflecting the local culture in Oman.

Just as in other GCC states, the urbanization and internationalization processes have led to the introduction of specific forms of space and society and typical suburban conditions with extremely low densities, villa-type houses as social housing programs, huge motorways, and a low efficiency in energy use in Muscat. A specific problem, which is also identified in this joint research project, is the so-called land lottery which provides every Omani citizen a plot to build his/her own house without any choice of the location and proximity to the main services and social infrastructure. This has led to creating low-density residential areas at the periphery of the city and concentration of services in the central areas in Muscat. This has in return contributed to the emergence of certain lifestyle society patterns which are highly dependent on using private transport modes and energy consumption.

Based on the topics covered in this research, this chapter will investigate the interrelated socio-spatial and environmental aspects of Muscat, focusing on the following questions: what social-spatial measures could be implemented at the city, neighbourhood, and individual levels to achieve CSUD in Muscat? How can existing undeveloped spaces in Muscat be converted into environmental spaces that contribute to CSUD? How can producing green open spaces encourage walkability and contribute to overcoming the transportation and energy-consumption problems in Muscat? Which measures could also be implemented to improve and encourage walkability? Finally, how can land-use promote CSUD while addressing sustainability in regions with extreme climatic conditions? This chapter seeks to identify consolidated strategies that address sustainable planning concepts such as climate-sensitive design with a focus on achieving social integration and promoting an environmentally friendly lifestyle.

General overview

Muscat is the capital city of the Sultanate of Oman and the economic centre of the country. It is located in the north-eastern part of the country on the coast of the Gulf of Oman in the Indian Ocean. The traditional natural harbour serves as a transhipment point for goods from Arabia, India, and Europe. The city is located approximately 20 m above sea level and the total city area is approximately 3,500 km^2. The total urban area covers an area of 5 to 10 km wide and 60 km long between the coast and the mountains. The capital area of Muscat is the largest agglomeration and only metropolis in Oman and represents the demographic and economic growth of the country. While Oman has 4,236,057 inhabitants (World Bank Data 2016), more than 30% of the population is living in the metropolitan Muscat. The core of the city has a population of approximately 30,000, but the greater Muscat area, including the outskirts, is home to over 1,201,089 people (NCSI 2015) with a population density of about 300 p/km.

Muscat has a semi-arid tropical climate with high humidity around the year with only a few days of precipitation. The average annual temperature is about 28.4 °C. The average annual rainfall measures about 106 mm. In summer, temperatures rise to more than 40 °C and make it difficult to perform outdoor activities within the daylight hours. Until the 1970s, Oman was undeveloped and more than 80% of its inhabitants were living in rural areas (UNWUP 2007). Since the discovery and exploitation of oil in Oman in the early 1970s, the country has witnessed a period of unprecedented urban growth, which resulted in the concentration of economic activities in the urban areas (see Figure 7.1). This has caused a massive migration from rural into urban areas to search for better job opportunities and a better lifestyle. In 2015, urbanization reached 73% in Oman and it is expected to rise up to 86% by 2050 (UNWUP 2014)

In addition to the socio-economic related issues that led to the concentration of urbanization in certain areas in Muscat, the distribution of its urban population amongst some isolated parts of the country is a result of its topographical and geographical natural settings. This is also part of the reason why the Arabic meaning of Muscat is "falling space," referring to the separation of the city from its hinterland by rough, mountainous slopes. The distinctive geographical mountainous feature in Muscat is part of the Hajar mountain range, which extends down

Figure 7.1 Urban agglomeration in Muscat

Source: © OpenStreetMap contributors and the GIS user community, www.openstreetmap.org

from the north in a great arc from Ras Musandam to the Arabian Peninsula's most south-easterly point, overlooking the Indian Ocean. At its highest point in the Jabal al Akhdar region, the Hajar range reaches a height of 3,000 meters.

At the spatial level, Muscat can be divided into residential areas, which are mostly located on the outskirts of the city and the commercialized central area distributed along the main arterial road "Sultan Qaboos Highway." The height of the buildings is determined by the usage and type of building but limited to eight floors by building regulations. In the traditional residential and modern housing areas, the economic development height of the buildings rarely exceeds three floors (Building Regulations for Muscat, Muscat Municipality 1992). Building regulations combined with the system of land lottery, which is regulated and operated by the Ministry of Housing (MOH) and gives every citizen, both women and men, the right to own a residential land lot of 600–1,000 square meters, have led to a fragmented low-density city. As a result of the low density and large commuting distances, inhabitants have become highly dependent on private modes of transportation. Also, the random distribution of residential land lots does not consider individuals' geographical preferences, time required to reach main facilities, and their job locations.

The following decades after the discovery of oil and gas in 1967 witnessed a huge economic development known as the Omani Renaissance, in which economic development and population growth focused on the Muscat Capital Area (MCA) (Von Richthofen and Langer 2015). As hundreds of thousands of foreign workers moved to Muscat, its population has increased exponentially. Between 1970 and 2010, the population of Muscat grew from 63,000 to 730,300 inhabitants (MNE 2010). Due to this more than ten-fold expansion in a 40-year timespan, together with globalization, the urban development of the city can be described as "rapid urbanization" (Al Gharibi 2014). Most of the labour force in the oil and gas sector is foreign-born. According to the 2016 census, more than 45% of the inhabitants of Oman are expatriates, with 46% of them living in Muscat and thus making up more than 65% of its population (NCSI 2017).

The heterogeneous transnational migrants have brought with them various spatial practices that have caused a cultural shift and reshaped the socio-spatial structure of Muscat society. Individualism, materialism, and mono-functional spaces, along with other consequences of urbanity in post-industrial societies in Europe, can also now be seen in modern Muscat. Spatially, this has manifested through the demand for Western-style buildings in the commercial and residential areas in Muscat and the adaptation of villa-style single-family houses which are often developed in blocks in the so-called gated communities (see Figure 7.2). Not only have the foreign transnational workers encouraged the adaption of this style, but globalization has also encouraged many of the Omanis to prefer modern architectural Western-like forms over their traditional vernacular architecture. Through the import of Western architectural patterns, the abstracted global spaces such as highways and business administration buildings have dominated the spatiality of Muscat. In addition, as individualism and single-family style has been introduced, the distances between houses and services have increased and destinations cannot

Figure 7.2 Al Mouj gated community

Source: Esri, DigitalGlob, GeoEye, Earthstar Geographics, CNES/Airbus Ds, USDA, USGS, AEX, Getmapping, Aerogrid, IGN, IGP, swisstopo, and the GIS User community

be reached within walking distance as in old Muscat. In addition, this has fragmented the urban centres and contributed to the fact that Muscat is one of the least densely populated capitals worldwide at 300 p/km (NCSI 2015).

Most of the residential areas in Muscat do not have commercial facilities or even workplaces. This means that for every kind of activity, the use of a car is necessary because the hot climate in Oman makes it difficult for most people to walk. This has been especially reinforced by the absence of walking accommodations such as wide shaded walkways and shading elements or even walkways along roads at all. This in return leads to a high car dependency and a huge dependency on oil which adds to negative ecological impact. This ongoing process requires that the urban planners must urgently react to the socio-spatial and environmental consequences of rapid urbanization in Muscat.

Omani planning system: gaps and challenges

Most of the Omani administrations, including the planning system, changed during the political transformation process that started in 1970. The establishment of the Higher Development Planning Board and the Directorate of Planning and

Development in 1972 created various linkages between spatial planning and economic development and made planning and the economic situation interdependent (ONSS 2014). The implementation of these two institutions can be considered a step towards a structured planning system which has an immediate relation to the economic situation of the country.

While the Higher Development Planning Board and the Directorate of Planning had a more legislative function providing a comprehensive planning framework for all sectors, they also provided planning power to the Ministry of Land Affairs in 1975. The Ministry of Land Affairs was the most important planning department in Oman on the national as well as on the regional and local levels as it was in charge of any planning issues such as defining and planning land for residential, commercial, and industrial purposes, and coordinating the work between all ministries and departments that were involved in the planning process.

Furthermore, the Ministry of Land Affairs developed the first mapping system which also made provisions for land use and finally worked out the so-called Five-Year-Plans which were meant to guide Oman's development for the next five years. Until today, eight Five-Year-Plans have come into action, where the last one covered the period from 2011 until 2015 (ONSS 2014).

In addition to the Ministry of Land Affairs, the Supreme Committee for Town Planning (SCTP) was established in 1985. This committee was primarily in charge of planning issues on a regional and local level. Seven planning regions and several main centres were identified. This "general framework for town planning provisions" was then transferred to detailed development or structure plans which were taken into account – for future strategic as well as physical planning approaches. Planning standards and processes were codified in the late 1980s to guarantee a nationwide consistent planning system for the planning regions and the actors in charge. Today, urban planning is made by the Supreme Council of Planning (SCP), the successor of the SCTP and the MOH, which was formerly part of the Ministry of Land Affairs. The task of the SCP is to guide economic development as well as to elaborate national and urban spatial planning policies whereas the MOH is responsible for land distribution to citizens – a process commonly known as land lottery. The MOH additionally manages land allocation and sizing.

As briefly indicated at the beginning of this chapter, this land lottery system has led to several problems. First, applicants can only choose the region of their future plot, not the specific location. This means that the distributed plots could be far away from the location of their jobs or families, creating long distances to travel. Second, not all distributed plots are or will be developed by the plot owner due to several reasons. For example, a married couple only needs one plot to build a house, but both partners might individually own plots. Another issue is that some plots are kept free from development due to speculation as the plot owner wants to sell it on the land market when the land prices are assumed to increase because of further development of the area around. Undeveloped plots are the main problem of the distribution system. These undeveloped parcels cut through and break up neighbourhoods. For instance, between 1990 and 2010, all developable land in Muscat could have accommodated a total of 800,000 people while it only provided room for 300,000 people. This indicates a large consumption and demand for land created by the land lottery system, which Muscat will not be able to serve in the future (ONSS 2014).

Consequently, the population density of Muscat has decreased rapidly in the last decades although the urban growth rates remain high. The consequences of this process can only be stopped by a revision of the plot distribution system in parallel with an alteration of the urban sprawl strategy that should focus on densification and defining urban infill areas for the future (Kader 2015).

Climate-sensitive urban design and sustainability

Awareness of environmental issues and climate-sensitive urban design (CSUD) came into urban planning considerations in the late 1960s. New terms and approaches such as ecology, sustainability, energy efficiency, green architecture, and urbanism appeared and became more studied and implemented. Ever since, these concepts and measures have increasingly influenced how planners and architects find solutions for the environmental challenges associated with urbanization and globalization.

This chapter adopts CSUD that addresses sustainability with its three dimensions (ecological, economical, and social) which tackle the socio-spatial and environmental consequences of rapid urbanization in Muscat. To achieve sustainability, coordination between different planning sectors in Muscat is required. Promotion of sustainability through CSUD is formed by three normative assumptions which are essential for the implementation process by first guaranteeing ecological functions for future generations, second enforcing global norms of justice between and among generations, and third permanently preserving individual quality of life (Renn et al. 2007; Kawakami et al. 2013). The idea of CSUD is to elaborate a comprehensive approach which directly addresses the challenges of globalization, climate change, and energy consumption and their effects on daily life. Re-designing cities to manage the mentioned external effects makes it necessary to establish a sustainable approach that takes all these evolutions into account (Oktay 2002).

To successfully implement CSUD, it is necessary for a broad spectrum of actors to be involved in the process. This means that political stakeholders, the business community, and citizens with individual attitudes toward the surrounding environment must all be included. This, however, requires a re-thinking of the traditional and long-term actions and measures.

Measures need to be implemented to alter transportation; production and use of energy; land consumption; street design; the distribution of residential, commercial, and industrial areas; and the current design of residential units. Therefore, it is very important to integrate CSUD measures in existing urban planning policies while respecting "the traditional urban patterns and current planning practices" along with economic and ecological preconditions (Kawakami et al. 2013).

The main impact of CSUD deals, on the one hand, with the reduction of energy use, which may affect forms of transportation, air conditioning and heating, building techniques, use of scarce resources, and urban patterns. On the other hand, its other impacts relate to the increase of outdoor space comfort which can be maximized by lowering the temperature, establishing high-quality green open spaces, and improving the air quality. This has to be managed by making use of the local climate conditions to create a more liveable city (Kawakami et al. 2013).

In connection to this chapter, CSUD is seen as a framework to cope with current challenges in Muscat as extreme climate conditions, spatial planning on regional and neighbourhood levels, and other factors challenge lifestyle patterns in consumption societies. It is further suggested in this chapter that CSUD can be implemented on different spatial levels: on the city, district/neighbourhood, architectural, and individual levels. While the macro-scale at the regional and city level requires structural changes and policymaking, the neighbourhood level could be achieved through urban design interventions. The household level needs individual adjustments and mainly appeals to architectural knowledge. However, adjusting the surrounding environment results in shifting the perception and the behavioural patterns of individuals towards sustainable everyday practices such as walking and friendly use of the surrounding environment.

Why public space?

The city space through history has always been an integral part of its inhabitants' everyday lives. The agora in ancient Greece, Forum in ancient Rome, market place in European cities, and bazaar in Islamic cities served as places for social, political, and cultural exchange. Roads, streets, and spaces between buildings formed another system of connective spaces for everyday discourses (Lefebvre 1991; Gehl et al. 2006). However, due to the rapid urbanization and population growth of cities, the role and character of public space have changed and many questions have been raised such as what role a public space plays within new societies and what kind of public space would respond to contemporary lifestyles. From these proposed questions and many others, it is clear that the ongoing changes of society's lifestyle and technology's intervention in everyday life have multiplied and complicated the role of public space in the current urbanized and modern life.

From a social point of view, public space is defined with a particular emphasis on the social temporal dimension (Madanipour 2014, 2003). In this sense, public urban space does not refer only to all the buildings, objects, and spaces in the urban environment, but also to the people, events, and relationships within them. Social space is a fundamental part of everyday life, and "our spatial behaviour" is defined by the space around us. In other words, defining space is an integral part of our social existence and identity (Madanipour 2003).

Looking at spaces in contemporary Muscat, public space tends to be abstract, fragmented, and broken into sectors: transportation and road network with large highways, urban nodes, trade and commerce by large shopping malls, and separated office block business districts with their labour force. These spaces are global, conceived, and perceived for consumption. Also, they do not function as an arena for everyday life practices, yet this space needs to be transformed into qualitative space, "consumption of space," rather than "space of consumption" (Lefebvre

1991). The spatial layout of the Muscat metropolitan area is characterized by highways and fragmented residential areas. Thus, the provision of public spaces with different hierarchies is a key measure to achieve a sensitive climate design that addresses the social and ecological components of sustainability, yet this requires focus on small-scale urban spaces and neighbourhood parks.

In planning standards, small- to medium-sized open spaces are generally recommended more than the city-scale and regional ones. The effect of smaller green areas in respect to CSUD is much more than only providing a few city and regional parks which cannot be reached within walking distance. Small-scale open spaces can be implemented in a better way within existing neighbourhoods, and their positive effects on the local climate are much higher. In addition, small neighbourhood parks are easily accessible by the inhabitants of the surrounding neighbourhoods who will also accept this park as their own and can better contribute to its management. Walkability is encouraged by integrated pocket parks and therefore car dependency is reduced. This will also potentially lead to a social control over these spaces increasing the sense of safety and privacy.

It is argued in this chapter that the provision of parks and urban space is a fundamental approach to improve the outdoor comfort. Public spaces can best be integrated at the neighbourhood level for social and ecological values since at this level such spaces act on the one hand as a melting point where people from different backgrounds meet and socialize and on the other hand they function as connection channels between the segregated neighbourhoods. Additionally, given the rapid urbanization and dependency on cars in Muscat, it is believed that unless walkability is encouraged at the neighbourhood level, the residential streets within these neighbourhoods might gradually turn into highways as traffic volume increases and reduces the level of pedestrian service (Tawil et al. 2014).

Consolidated planning strategies towards sustainable development in Muscat

Based on the project literature review and empirical research, it is evident that the provision of public spaces at the city and neighbourhood levels contributes to climate-sensitive urban design. In order to address all dimensions of sustainability, it is essential to enforce CSUD by integrating a mixed land-use policy, densification, and urban infill of vacant neighbourhoods, thereby reducing travel distances and introducing walkability increasing the sense of belonging and safety. Based on the empirical work, the following sustainable measures are suggested:

Converting undeveloped wadis into parks

A special topographic feature in Muscat is the wadis, dry undeveloped riverbeds, which channel water during heavy rains from the mountain south of Muscat through the city and into the Indian Ocean. These wadis stay dry most of the time but experience flash floods for a couple of days. The rainwater partly remains in the wadis for a few days and disrupts traffic. In extreme cases, the water might flood adjacent shops and houses. In addition to the flood hazard aspect, wadis form natural barriers and breaks in Muscat's urban development. They segregate the city and neighbourhoods into fragments. Wadis can only be crossed by bridges in a few locations. Citizens of Muscat perceive them as undeveloped areas with a negative effect on the local climate. Most sections along the wadis are composed of gravel and dust and do not provide living space for vegetation and heat up on hot, sunny days (see Figure 7.3). As indicated in the introduction, wadis are considered spatial challenges for urban development in Muscat but also offer opportunities for climate-sensitive urban design.

In their current form, wadis do not contribute positively to their surroundings (see Figure 7.5). However, their locations, orientation, and linear form make them a good starting point to implement linear parks within the neighbourhoods they pass through. Since they have to be kept free from building development, as a blocked wadi will cause flooding in the city, converting them to parks which can be temporally flooded is a favourable solution on different levels.

Parks in wadis have a positive effect on the local climate – much similar to those of common parks. Furthermore, due to their linear form that runs through different neighbourhoods, wadi parks as green infrastructure can be easily crossed on foot or by bike as a shortcut. Furthermore, offering comfortable walkways and connections to other neighbourhoods, facilities, or open spaces could increase the walkability of people and, in turn, limit car dependency. Thus, developing wadi parks is a good measure for urban planning to develop areas which are generally not usable for development.

Figure 7.3 Undeveloped Al Azaiba wadi in Ruwi district

Source: Joint research project 2016

At the present time, only one wadi park project is realized in Muscat, namely, in the Al Azaiba neighbourhood. Al Azaiba Wadi Park is located in the southern part of the Al Azaiba neighbourhood between Sultan Qaboos Highway and the arterial road 48 Way. It was transformed into a park in 2012 by "Atelier Jacqueline Osty & Associés," a French architectural firm. This wadi is part of the municipal city plan for new urban parks and planning strategies.

The design of the Al Azaiba Wadi Park considers the unique topography of the wadi. It was created on two different levels. First, on the street level people can enter the park at the southern and northern entrance to the pathways. This walkway inside the park provides a walkable shortcut from the main road that runs through the Al Azaiba neighbourhood and the Sultan Qaboos highway. The other level of the park is one to two meters below street level and is formed by the actual riverbed of the wadi. On dry days, the wadi can be crossed by the riverbed whereas this crossing is blocked during rainfall events. To maintain the original function of the wadi, which is to transport rainwater from the southern parts of the city to the Indian Ocean, the riverbed has to be kept free from blocking elements. This is already a part of the management and the design concept of the park. To achieve this, the ground of the riverbed is covered with gravel, which allows the water to flow further and also enables standing water to seep into the ground. Even in the riverbed, vegetation has been seeded to increase the ecological function of the wadi park. The zone between the lower and the upper level is covered with grass and features large steps which can be also used as sitting space (see Figure 7.4).

Figure 7.4 Al Azaiba park wadi after development

Source: Atelier Jacqueline Osty & Associés [www.osty.fr]

The field visits and analysis of Al Azaiba Park illustrate that more conversions of wadis to parks is recommended. However, for a successful implementation in terms of climate-sensitive urban design, the original form of the wadi has to remain unchanged. This maintains the vital function of the wadi which is to drain the different neighbourhoods of the city in case of heavy rain and prevent them from flooding damage and nuisance. Furthermore, the extensive new vegetation growth inside the park facilitates CSUD by increasing outdoor comfort. Palm trees provide shadow and thereby lower the temperature in the nearer surroundings. In combination with the other plants, the air filter function and production is enhanced. Lastly, rainwater from the wadis could be collected and stored for irrigation purposes, which is a cheap and ecological-friendly solution to the current form of irrigation. The combination of all these functions makes a trip in the park functional and comfortable for its users (see Figure 7.5).

Future improvements to consider should include the implementation of furniture and further facilities such as playgrounds, toilets which facilitate use of the park, communication, fitness through increased walkability, and reduced car traffic, thereby reducing energy consumption and overall sustainable development. Moreover, a comprehensive design is finally recommendable for implementation on other wadis in the area of Muscat (see Figure 7.6).

Improvement of the pedestrian areas

As mentioned previously, Muscat's urban development is oriented towards accessing important facilities by car. To counteract this process, walkways and pedestrian

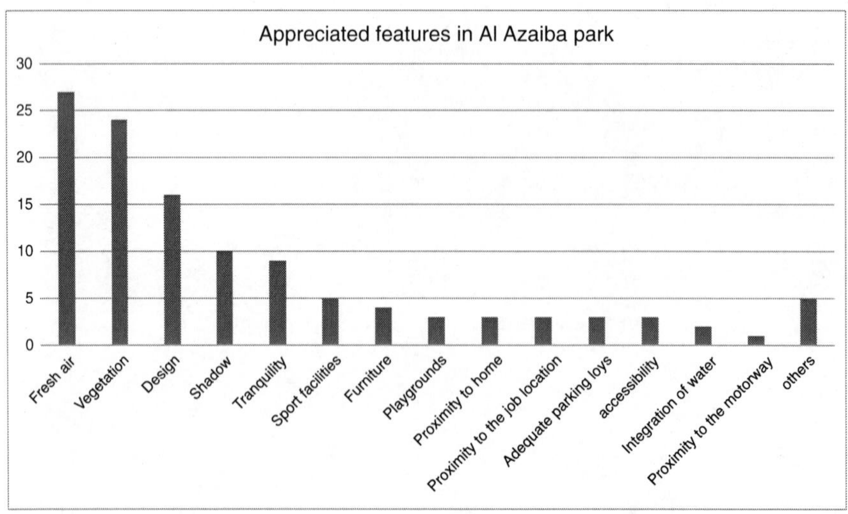

Figure 7.5 Activities appreciated by a variety of users of Al Azaiba park

Source: Joint research project 2016

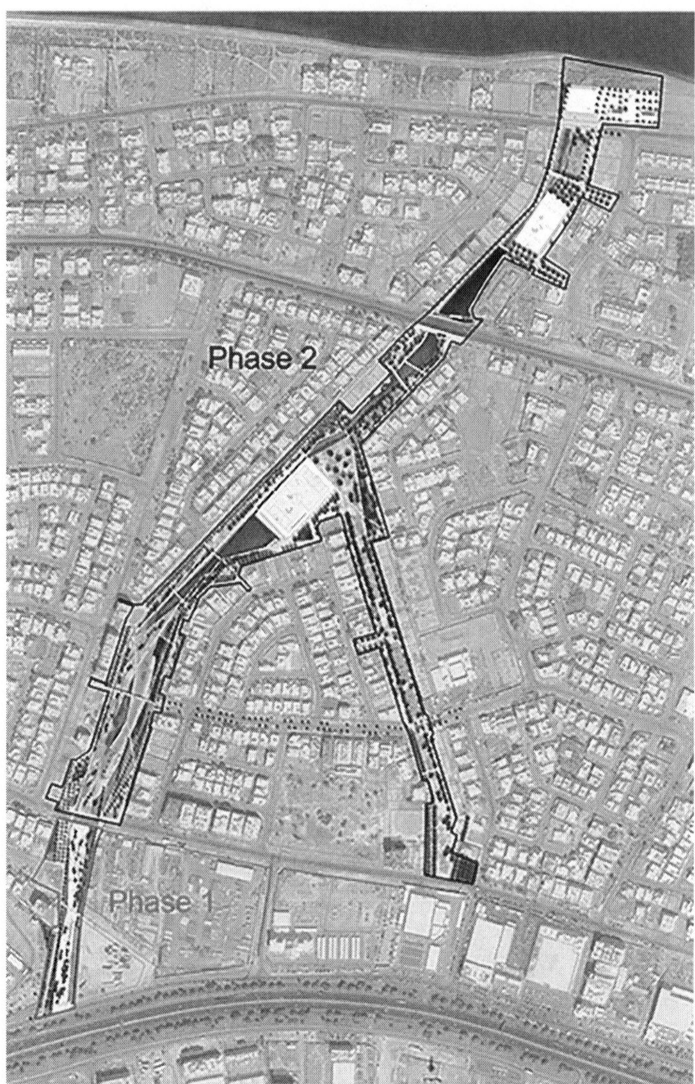

Figure 7.6 Al Azaiba park, Muscat, park area and planned development

Source: Atelier Jacqueline Osty & Associés [www.osty.fr]

networks have to be established. The analysis and field visits in Muscat revealed that a walking lifestyle is not encouraged due to two main issues. First, the outside climatic conditions are not suitable for walking due to high temperatures and humidity rates. Second, the surrounding built environment is not designed to encourage walking (see Figure 7.7 and Figure 7.8). Not all neighbourhood streets

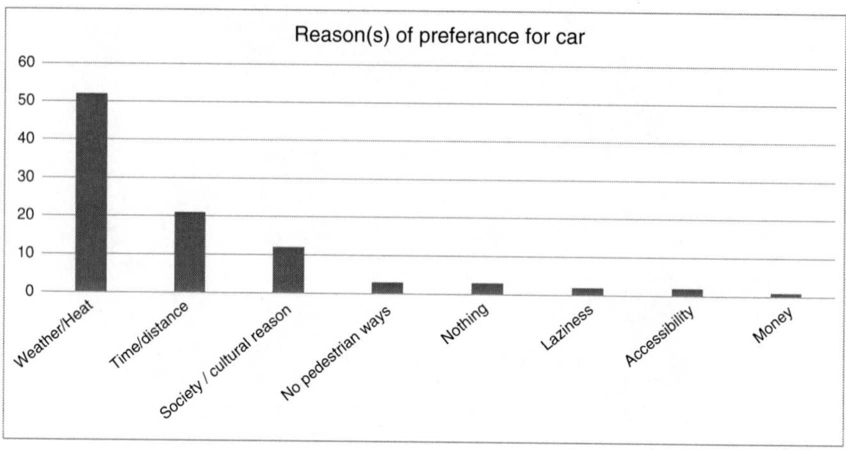

Figure 7.7 Factors affecting walkability of neighbourhoods in Muscat

Source: Joint research project 2016

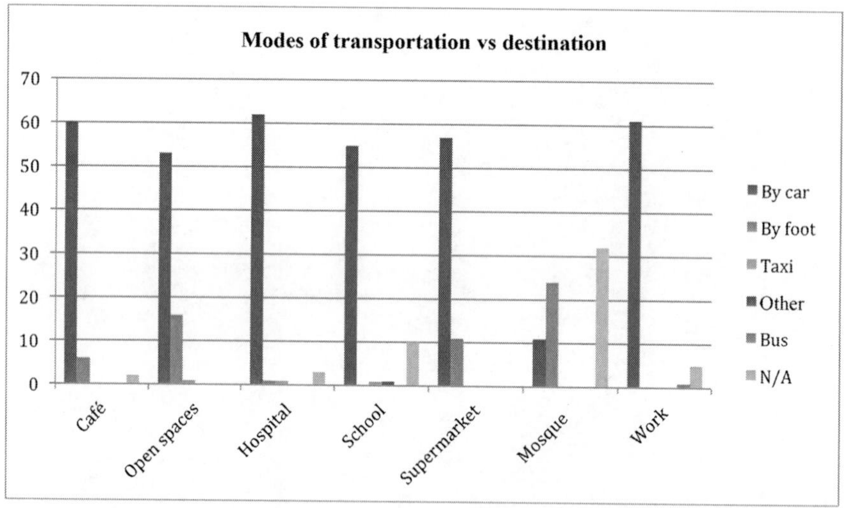

Figure 7.8 Modes of transportation in Muscat

Source: Joint research project 2016

are served with sidewalks and some of the existing ones are not adequately maintained for pedestrians. Resultantly, this reduces safety in the surrounding environment, especially for vulnerable social groups (women, children, elderly people, and people with disabilities). Moreover, walkways are often used as parking spaces which force pedestrians to use the streets for walking activities. This causes the vehicular and pedestrian movement to mix, much to the disadvantage of pedestrians.

When implementing CSUD, many measures have to be taken into account to prioritize pedestrian traffic over car traffic. These measures have to increase the outdoor comfort, safety, and good accessibility for pedestrians. Therefore, green open spaces need to be integrated and connected with the wadi parks to create a spatial network in the city of Muscat. Through this, it is clear that improving the pedestrian areas would improve the outside comfort.

Another analyzed problem is the lack of shading elements in the street (see Figure 7.9). Muscat is located in an arid and humid climate. Therefore, it is necessary to provide shading elements along the walkways. Otherwise, people will be in favour of using their private cars even for short distances. This in return increases traffic congestion and car and oil dependency, and therefore Muscat citizens' ecological footprints. By outlining these problems, pedestrian areas have to be improved at the neighbourhood level in order to accentuate the outside comfort and thus the implementation of CSUD.

Figure 7.9 Missing vegetation and shading elements in pedestrian walkways – Madinat As Sultan Qaboos Neighbourhood (MSQ)

Source: Joint research project 2016

Spatial sustainability: urban connectivity is a key measure towards social, economic, and environmental prosperity in Muscat

In a city like Muscat where the car is the main mode of transportation, roads can cut through pathways and decrease the outside comfort of the walkers. A solution to this conflict could be to implement green bridges along the highways. Another main element for the successful implementation of climate-sensitive urban design is the establishment of a green network on the macro, meso, and micro scales. At regional and city levels, the existing open spaces have to be integrated into a larger network of green corridors which will cross and connect the transformed wadis and extend as a green infrastructural grid. At the district and neighbourhood scale, urban spaces and pocket parks on undeveloped plots connect the spaces at the city level (Figure 7.10). Green connections on the neighbourhood level will encourage walkability within neighbourhood and reduce the need to use their cars. The reduced car dependency through integrating an efficient public transport system, along with the positive local climate effect caused by the alteration of the built environment, will contribute to reduce traffic, encourage walkability, and promote an active lifestyle.

Mixed land-use development

Land-use policies and management determine the effect of human impacts on natural resources, the travel-time pattern, the degree of segregation among land

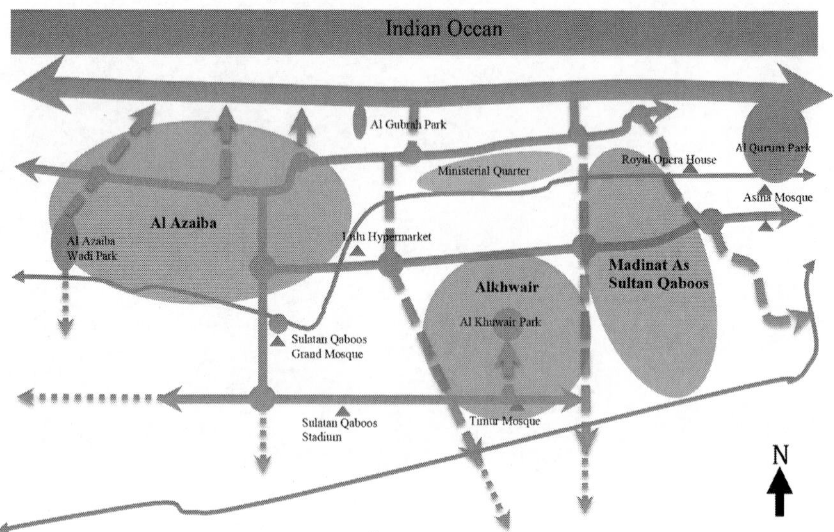

Figure 7.10 Muscat vision Green Network, formulation of strategies resulting from the analysis

Source: Joint research project 2016

uses, and therefore the mode of transport required to travel between those land uses. According to OECD (2010), "many metropolitan regions have used land-use planning to create 'sustainable neighbourhoods' or 'eco-neighbourhoods' that combine transportation, natural resource preservation, building, energy, waste and water policies to respond to climate change and reduce the urban environmental footprint."

However, land-use in Muscat is not mixed but characterized by low-density residential areas on the outskirts of the city and with commercial and mixed-use development mainly along the Sultan Qaboos highway. An adjustment in the distribution of the social services has to be an integrated approach in the future development of Muscat. It should equally fulfil the needs of traffic and public, commercial, industrial, and residential areas, all while decreasing car use and preserving the service network. This can only be achieved by limiting the travel distances from homes to work locations, commercial areas, schools, or mosques. While the city urban network is developed in Muscat, the network within neighbourhoods has to be strengthened.

In addition to the road network in the neighbourhoods, it is essential to implement a parallel network of suitable walkways and cycling paths to support pedestrian and bike traffic as counterpart to car traffic. Establishing a network like this is possible, as many streets have spare space alongside for further road expansion. Social facilities such as small shops and markets have to be favourably and more densely located to supply on the neighbourhood level as opposed to the car-owner preferred development of mega-markets at highway exits. Daily travel time and distance to local services would therefore decrease and in relation car traffic on the main roads and highways especially in times of the rush hour would also. The same is applicable to other facilities and areas. The distribution of offices and other forms of commerce would allow citizens to work inside their neighbourhood instead of commuting between their residences and job locations. This development would have a positive effect in the course of climate-sensitive urban design on different levels. Besides the economic benefits from mixed land-use areas, it would also help to save energy and strengthen the social cohesion within a neighbourhood. Unlike the provision of neighbourhood parks, mixed land use requires new building regulations and policies which enable commercial activities in residential areas.

Meanwhile, the vacant plots produced from the land lottery system would be a good alternative for supporting mixed-use policies. Although these plots belong to their owners, urban planning and municipal administration have to think how to deal with this phenomenon. Key considerations include encouraging plot owner through incentives to develop their plots in a specific urban form to allow infill development and/or to reinforce existing regulations to develop the given plot in a certain period.

An undeveloped plot is a brown field with limited or no function for society. Embodied in these plots is the potential for small commercial initiatives, institutional facilities, or even green open spaces that connect to a larger network. To establish a green network, it is at first necessary to map the existing green spaces and locate their distribution in the city. The next step is to envision how a potential network could stretch all over the city. For this network, two key regards should be observed. The first approach to developing this network is the activation of wadis as accessible open spaces. As the wadis run in a south-north direction through large parts of the city, they could serve as initial points and backbones for a green network. Accordingly, they would serve as green corridors running from the beach side in the hinterland while crossing the main arterial roads. The connection of the wadis with the beach is therefore the framework for a green network. The beach serves as the main west-east axis whereas the wadis help to enter the city on a green pathway.

The next step could be to integrate the existing green open spaces into this vision. Therefore, green cross-connection axes from the existing parks towards the wadis have to be implemented. At this point of development, a green grid traverses the city offering space for recreation and sports, facilitating positive impacts on the local climate and outdoor comfort, and providing walkable shortcuts for citizens who have to travel short distances without a car. Green cross connections can be designed in different ways and on different scales. Since wadis serve as large connected green corridors, residential roads can help to establish green connections into the neighbourhoods. In addition to this, green bridges could be installed in order to cross broader streets or areas which cannot be transformed into green open spaces. This is essential to guarantee a closed network.

The last step to establish a green network is to implement pocket parks in the neighbourhoods. Similarly, undeveloped plots could be used for commercial development such as supermarkets and small retail shops. Small pocket parks are accessible spaces for the citizens of the surrounding neighbourhood to meet and enjoy outdoor activities. Due to their small size, they are affordable with regards to installation and maintenance. By this same token, pocket parks can be operated and maintained also by the society of the neighbourhood. Through this, social cohesion is enhanced; safety and privacy are then guaranteed to a certain degree as mostly locals will be involved in the management process. These pocket parks are therefore the smallest units within their catchment areas that can be linkages to the bigger green connections and corridors.

Conclusions

This chapter uses one converted wadi in Muscat as an example to explore how the issue of CSUD in undeveloped areas can be further addressed. This is feasible by integrating the concept of environmental design with pedestrian space design combined with mixed land-use development, densification, and urban infill of vacant plots and thus formulate consolidated planning strategies that could be implemented not only in Muscat but also in other GCC regions with challenges similar to those in Muscat, Oman. The urban design project of the Al Azaiba Park development of the wadi system includes an urban regeneration project that aims at adjusting urban design elements of the existing natural environment to promote the concept of climate-sensitive urban design (CSUD).

Urban planning should focus on the neighbourhood level instead of solely on the regional, city, or architectural scale. This means that key and frequently visited facilities which are important for daily life have to be present in the neighbourhood. Consequently, people will not have to rely on cars to travel to the next urban amenity or work location. Promoting walkability will help to decentralize the urban life in Muscat and make it more sensitive to the local climate.

Finally, CSUD in Oman contributes to achieving four of the sustainable development goals (SDGs) addressed at the Paris Agreement on climate change in December 2015, namely goal 3 which states *ensure healthy lives and promote well-being for all at all ages*; goal 9 which states *build resilient infrastructure, promote sustainable industrialization and foster innovation*; goal 11 which says *make cities inclusive, safe, resilient, and sustainable*; and goal 13 which asserts *taking urgent action to combat climate change and its impacts* (SDGs 2016).

References

The 2030 Agenda for Sustainable Development and the Sustainable Development Goals (SDGs). 2016. Available at: https://sustainabledevelopment.un.org/sdg (Accessed 16 June 2016).

Al Gharibi, Hamad. 2014. *Urban Growth From Patchwork to Sustainability Case Study: Muscat.* PhD dissertation, TU Berlin University.

Atelier Jacqueline Osty & Associés. 2016. Available at: www.osty.fr (Accessed 1 October 2016).

Gehl, Jan, Lars Gemzøe, and Karen Steenhard. 2006. *New City Spaces*. Copenhagen: Danish Architectural Press.

Joint Research Project. 2016. *Master Planning Studio. Rapid Urbanisation in Muscat/Oman.* Final students report of TU Dortmund University, Faculty of Spatial Planning and 5th semester students of German University of Technology in Oman. Both supervised by authors. Unpublished report.

Kader, Alexander. 2015. Design proposals for a more sustainable urban development of residential quarters in Oman. *Trialog 114: A Journal for Planning and Building in Global Context*, 3. Sonja Nebel and Wolfgang Scholz (volume editors): Oman – Rapid Urbanisation.

Kawakami, Mitsuhiko, Zhenjiang Shen, Jen-te Pai, Xiao-lu Gao, and Ming Zhang, eds. 2013. *Spatial Planning and Sustainable Development: Approaches for Achieving Sustainable Urban Form in Asian Cities*. Series: Strategies for Sustainability. Dordrecht: Springer.

Lefebvre, Henri. 1991. *The Production of Space*. Translated and edited by Donald Nicholson-Smith. Oxford, UK: Blackwell.

Madanipour, Ali. 2003. *Public and Private Spaces of the City*. London and New York: Routledge.

Madanipour, Ali. 2014. Urban Design, Space and Society: Planning, Environment, Cities. New York, NY: Palgrave Macmillan.

Ministry of National Economy (MNE), Final Result Report. Census 2010.

Muscat Municipality. 1992. Muscat Municipality Local Order No. 23/92. *Building Regulation For Muscat*, 1992 available at: http://www.mm.gov.om/Page.aspx?PAID=1#Details&MID=7&PGID=403 (Accessed 30 April 2017).

National Centre for Statistics and Information (NCSI). 2015. *Statistical Year Book*. Available at: www.data.gov.om/en/DataAnalysis/ (Accessed 22 July 2016).

National Centre for Statistics and Information (NCSI). 2017, April. *Monthly Statistical Bulletin*. available at: http://www.mm.gov.om/Page.aspx?PAID=1#Details&MID=7&PGID=403 (Accessed 30 April 2017).

Oktay, Derya. 2002. Design with the climate in housing environments: An analysis in Northern Cyprus. *Building and Environment*, 37 (10): 1003–1012.

Oman National Spatial Strategy (ONSS): Phase One. 2014. Unpublished draft report.

Organisation for Economic Co-operation and Development (OECD). 2010. *Cities and Climate Change*. OECD Publishing. doi:10.1787/9789264091375-en (Accessed 21 July 2016).

Renn, Ortwin, Deuschle Juergen, Jaeger Alexander, and Weimer-Jehle Wolfgang. 2007. Leitbild Nachhaltigkeit: Eine Normativ-Funktionale Konzeption und Ihre Umsetzung [A Normative-Functional Concept of Sustainability and Its Indicators]. Wiesbaden: VS Verlag fuer Sozialwissenschaften.

Tawil, Maram, Reicher Christa, Ramadan Zeyad, and Jafari Mais. 2014. Towards more pedestrian friendly streets in Jordan: The case of Al Medina street in Amman. *Journal of Sustainable Development*, 7(2) 144–158. Canadian Centre of Science and Education. Advance online publication. doi:10.5539/jsd.v7n2p144

United Nations World Urbanization Prospects (UNWUP). 2007. Available at: www.un.org/esa/population/publications/wup2007/2007WUP_Highlights_web.pdf (Accessed 16 June 2016).

United Nations World Urbanization Prospects (UNWUP). 2014. Available at: https://esa.un.org/unpd/wup/Publications/Files/WUP2014-Highlights.pdf (Accessed 16 June 2016).

Von Richthofen Aurel, and Langer Sebastian. 2015. Evaluating the urban development and determining the "peak space" of the Muscat capital area. *Trialog*, 411(3): 4–8.

World Bank Data: Oman. 2016. Available at: http://data.worldbank.org/country/oman (Accessed 14 July 2016).

8 The future of sustainable public transit in Abu Dhabi

Hanan Alrubaiai and Abdulla Galadari

Introduction

The Emirate of Abu Dhabi is setting the stones of its new Urban Structure Framework Plan and transportation policies as a crucial step in achieving Abu Dhabi Economic Vision for 2030. The new urban framework recognizes the need for public transit to meet the travel demand of the anticipated three million residents in the city of Abu Dhabi, as well as commuters from neighbouring cities. Ongoing work is focused on improving the connectivity and mobility of the Central Business District (CBD), while future work will involve the development of a second pivotal center, a Capital District, along with setting the boundaries of the capital industrial zones.

The Capital District is positioned around major new Emirati neighbourhoods. It will become the new face of Abu Dhabi as the center of government and knowledge, while the CBD transforms into the finance and commerce center. High-Tech and clean industries will concentrate east of the Capital District around the airport. The centers will carry similar weights of jobs and office space, distributing the jobs between two employment centers. Both centers will be surrounded by residential districts, with the hope of redirecting the traffic flow into several directions and avoiding traffic congestion.

The Emirati residential neighbourhoods surrounding the capital are built around high-density commercial nodes. Most of the residential neighbourhoods are of low density, but higher density alternatives are also included to provide a variety in housing choice. The proposed new residential neighbourhoods are mixed-used developments. The urban design is configured for family housing clusters that encourage walking.

This study suggests the implementation of transit-oriented development in the new Capital District and its suburbs, instead of the current design of assigning "zones" for each function and then facilitating the movement between these functional zones with roads and public transit. In order to support this claim, the study examines the historic and future urban growth trends of the Emirate of Abu Dhabi in relation to the transportation demand. It analyzes them against external and internal factors that affect transit travel demand in order to detect possible travel trends that would encourage further transit developments in the new district.

An important external factor to transit demand is fuel price. In alignment with the recent elimination of the fuel price subsidy in the United Arab Emirates (UAE), the study examines the potential effect of fluctuating fuel prices on Abu Dhabi public transit demand by analyzing the trends of cross-elasticities of public transit demand with respect to fuel price for a number of countries around the world.

The study also examines policies and legislations that could encourage Abu Dhabi vehicle users to use public transit modes. By looking at the different congestion pricing schemes applied in New York, Singapore, Stockholm and London, the study examines how congestion pricing schemes can similarly influence commuters to move towards public transit in Abu Dhabi.

The aim of the study is to help the policymakers in Abu Dhabi as well as other cities of similar conditions in the region develop sustainable cities using transit-oriented development by presenting some of the economic incentives and the implementation tools that are important in realizing such development.

Background

Abu Dhabi

Abu Dhabi was part of the Trucial States along the coast of the Gulf. Abu Dhabi experienced a rapid growth in the past few decades due to oil discovery and extraction, which unravelled a well of wealth to the Emirate. During the 1930s, when major and energy-thirsty countries around the world were hunting for energy sources to tap into, oil surveys were conducted in Abu Dhabi both on-shore and off-shore. Concessions were given to foreign companies to explore and extract oil in Abu Dhabi (Hajash 1967). By the 1950s, several oil fields were discovered in the Emirate of Abu Dhabi (Hassan and Azer 1985). This brought in major interest by foreign companies to come to Abu Dhabi to work on the new-found wealth. These companies brought in a large workforce of technicians and engineers to work on oil exploration and extraction. In the meantime, as Abu Dhabi found wealth in its hands, it started building its infrastructure and planning its land-use development. By 1971, several of the prominent Trucial States, including Abu Dhabi, formed a union and declared independence as the UAE.

The UAE has grown rapidly, both in terms of population and land-use development. Due to the nations' wealth, major investments were made to its infrastructure construction, real estate development, financial institutions, and services industry. Since the indigenous population was very small, the region required a massive amount of skilled and unskilled workforce for the development. As such, the nation became a home to many expatriate workers, which fuelled its population growth. Figure 8.1 provides an overview of the population growth in the UAE (formerly known as the Trucial States) between 1950 and 2015.

The estimated population in 1950 was around 70,000 inhabitants. By 1970, after the major oil discoveries, extractions, and exports were made, the population increased to around 235,000 inhabitants in order to cater to the increasing demand for workforce. Ever since, the population boomed very rapidly as the wealth, which

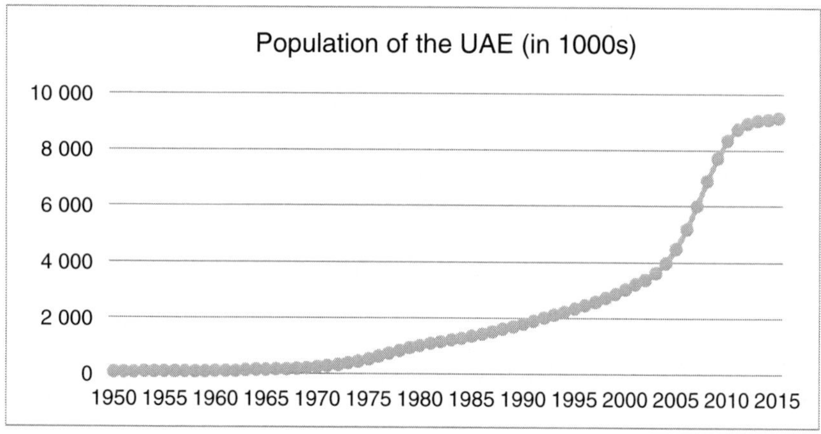

Figure 8.1 UAE's population growth (1950–2015)

Source: United Nations, Department of Economic and Social Affairs, Population Division (2015). *World Population*.

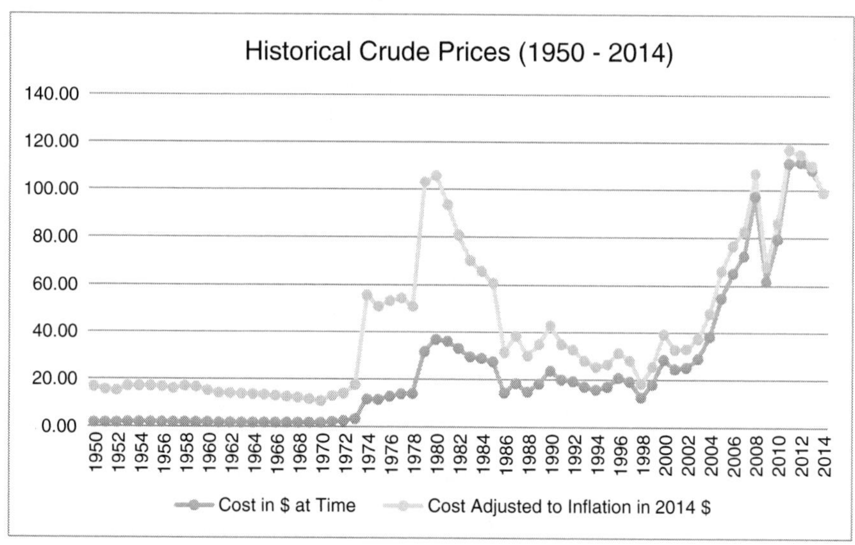

Figure 8.2 Historical crude prices, 1950–2014, showing both cost at the time and cost adjusted due to inflation

Source: The Editor, BP Statistical Review of World Energy 2015 (London: BP, 2015).

was mainly derived from the surge of oil prices after the Arab oil embargo in 1973 as seen from Figure 8.2, was being invested in its infrastructure. By 1980, the population exceeded one million inhabitants. During the advent of the new millennium, the population exceeded three million inhabitants. Also, oil prices started to surge again during the beginning of the third millennium. Accumulating massive wealth, the UAE economic productivity increased and with it the investments on a wide range of developments. By 2015, the estimated population of the UAE rose to about 9.1 million.

Abu Dhabi holds the most significant amount of oil wealth among the seven emirates that make up the UAE. As such, the extensive wealth amassed by Abu Dhabi allowed it to create several sovereign wealth funds and invest in various economic sectors and land developments in the city of Abu Dhabi.[1] Census data was first collected in 1975 and for every five years until 2005. Data after 2005 is mainly obtained via estimates from citizen registry and visa issuance. In 1975, the population of the Emirate of Abu Dhabi was a little over 210,000. This amount was more than doubled by 1980 and further more than doubled by 1995. In 2005, Abu Dhabi had around 1.4 million inhabitants. The estimated resident population of the Emirate of Abu Dhabi in mid-2014 was estimated to be around 2.65 million, of which a little short of 1.5 million live in urban areas (i.e. the city of Abu Dhabi and the city of al-Ain). The city of Abu Dhabi is home of around 1.15 million by mid-2014 (Abu Dhabi Statistics Center 2015).

Abu Dhabi's transportation infrastructure

One can imagine the vast expansion of the transportation infrastructure in Abu Dhabi in the last decades to cater for the growing travel demand. In 2011, there were 785,076 motor vehicles licensed in Abu Dhabi (Abu Dhabi Statistics Center 2015). We identify the historic trend of land use-transportation infrastructure in Abu Dhabi to estimate future growth.

The Department of Abu Dhabi Municipality and Town Planning was established in 1962. Halcrow and Co. were commissioned to create Abu Dhabi's planning, which included a road network that was not based on straight lines. The plan included the demolition of the original settlement, with the exception of Hosn Palace, to pave the way for new infrastructure, development, and land-use plan (Yasser Elsheshtawy 2008). At the time, Abu Dhabi was described as a "tribal society existing at subsistence level" (Trench 1994).

In 1966, there was a change in leadership in Abu Dhabi when Sh. Zayed Al-Nahyan became the ruler. With new leadership and a fresh vision that wanted to make a mark on history, many changes occurred, beginning with the Five Year Development Plan (1968–1972) under the supervision of Mahmoud Hassan Jum'a, an Iraqi who at the time was the Director of Planning. The purpose of the plan was to move from haphazard growth to orderly development. The main objective was to provide infrastructure within five years (Mallakh 1970).

In 1968, Arabicon was appointed to take over Halcrow's plans under the supervision of Dr. Abd al-Rahman Makhlouf, an Egyptian consultant. They were appointed to provide Abu Dhabi's new master plan. Makhlouf became the father of Abu Dhabi's modern urban development (Elsheshtawy 2011). The first municipal board was appointed in 1969 with the task to provide public services and infrastructure, including road networks. The municipalities program in the Five

Year Development Plan (1968–1972) had the task to do town planning and street improvements in towns throughout the Emirate of Abu Dhabi (664 km) (Mallakh 1970). Main roads in the northern part of the island of Abu Dhabi, where the city was first established, were designed to have straight lines in which crossing roads were parallel to each other, becoming a grid system (Yasser Elsheshtawy 2008).

With a change in leadership after the death of Sh. Zayed in 2004 and oil prices rising, a further new vision embarked Abu Dhabi on the path to being transformed into a global city by introducing the era of mega-projects (Yasser Elsheshtawy 2008). In 2007, the Abu Dhabi Urban Planning Council published its new master plan for 2030, which included many ambitious projects geared for sustainable development (Abu Dhabi Urban Planning Council 2007).

The urban growth trend of Abu Dhabi

When compared to the hectic nature of Dubai's development, Abu Dhabi is usually featured as more organized (Davis 2006). However, the difference in the laws pertaining to land ownership between Abu Dhabi and Dubai makes the socio-structure attractiveness of these two cities to foreign investment in different balances (Davidson 2007). This perhaps can be measured by contrasting the population size of both cities. Although the Emirate of Abu Dhabi, which includes al-Ain, oil fields' towns, and other rural villages, has a population size that surpasses the Emirate of Dubai, but the population size of the urban city of Dubai exceeds that of the urban city of Abu Dhabi. As described earlier, the population size by mid-2014 in the city of Abu Dhabi was estimated at around 1.15 million, while the city of Dubai is home to an estimated inhabitants of 2.3 million in 2014, which is double the population size of the city of Abu Dhabi (Abu Dhabi Statistics Center 2015; Dubai Statistics Center 2014). Nonetheless, Abu Dhabi, in recent years, tried to mimic the urban revolution in Dubai, especially through its ambitious master plan, in order to attain its symbolic power as the UAE's political center (Acuto 2010). This has put Abu Dhabi competing in its own urban revolution in the era of mega-projects (Ponzini 2011).

With the current drop of oil prices since September 2014, the era of the mega-projects has been tested for its sustainability. As such, forecasting the future travel demand in the city of Abu Dhabi may become a little more challenging. However, Abu Dhabi, and the UAE, generally, have shown in the past to be resilient during challenging times. The UAE is situated in a region that has been embroiled in conflicts, with the Iran-Iraq War that struck the region from 1980 to 1988, the Gulf War from 1990 to 1991, the invasion of Iraq in 2003, and the instability of the region since the Arab Spring in 2011 and the rise of terrorism. Not only was the UAE tested for its political stability in an otherwise unstable region, but the oil prices have fluctuated throughout these events, reaching a low in 1998, as shown in Figure 8.2. Nonetheless, that did not stop the population growth and the development of the UAE, even during the meagre years. Notwithstanding, the era of mega-projects truly boomed in the turn of the new millennium when oil prices started to rise again to unprecedented highs.

The mega-project frenzy in the Gulf region started in Dubai at the turn of the new millennium (Pacione 2005). It was adopted by Qatar and later by Abu Dhabi (Rizzio 2013; Ponzini 2011). Although the UAE has shown to be resilient to political instability in the region, its financial resilience was also tested during the 2008 economic crisis. The economic crisis created a huge impact in the financial viability of many of the mega-projects for one main reason: the expected population growth of Dubai had been heavily exaggerated. As such, the ambitious plans of many of the mega-projects were reviewed based on more realistic growth. It comes to no coincidence that many of the mega-projects that were planned in Dubai have been shelved, such as Palm Deira and the Universe projects. Nonetheless, although Dubai scaled down its mega-projects program, it mainly extended the time period in which many of these projects would be completed.

Abu Dhabi's 2030 Surface Transport Master Plan

The 2030 Surface Transport Master Plan (STMP), part of the Urban Structure Framework Plan, published in 2007, did not consider the impact of the economic crisis in 2008 and the fluctuations of the oil prices. As such, many of the planned mega-projects in Abu Dhabi also had to be revised, along with the forecasted growth. In similar instances as that of Dubai, Abu Dhabi scaled down its proposed mega-projects and extended the time frame for their completion. Given this information and the current state of affairs, forecasting the future population growth for Abu Dhabi and with it the travel demand becomes somewhat of a challenge. Adding to this challenge is forecasting the utility of public transport in Abu Dhabi.

Since the inception of Abu Dhabi's master plan in 1968, public transport was not an issue. The population size was small. Therefore, the city was planned to be mainly car-friendly. With the booming times, the plan has always been car-friendly transportation development. Although Abu Dhabi's 2030 plan is to increase the use of sustainable transport, such as public transit, such ambitious plans need to remain in focus with the current state of travel demand. We can easily compare Dubai's utility of public transportation with Abu Dhabi's future plans.

In Dubai, passengers using public transport increased by a meagre 4% between 2005 and 2008. Car ownership has been identified in one study as one of the major dummy variables that causes a negative marginal effect in the utility of public transport. It means that car owners in Dubai are less likely to use public transport. It has been suggested that restrictions on car ownership may cause more individuals to utilize public transport and therefore decrease traffic congestions and improve air quality. However, implementing such policies has proven to be difficult in the region (Worku 2013). Nevertheless, to Dubai's advantage, even though residents may not be utilizing the public transport as authorities would like, it has been shown that it has increased Dubai's attractiveness as a tourist destination, as it is being used by tourists (Parahoo, Harvey and Radi 2014). Dubai's public transport system does indeed connect to many tourist attractions and especially its connection with Dubai International Airport. This is something that may need to be considered by Abu Dhabi, especially since it is trying to promote tourist attractions, such as the museums planned in the Saadiyat Cultural District. Also, connecting Abu Dhabi's CBD with Abu Dhabi International Airport may also be considered vital.

Generally, with Dubai Metro as a close comparison for learning how to deal with public and rapid transit in the region, it has been found that factors that impact ridership on the metro are level of education, nationality, purpose of travel, as well as walking time between station and work. On the other hand, owning a car, crowded cabins, speed, frequency of stops, and weather discouraged individuals from using the metro (Alkaabi 2014). The same issues would be expected if Abu Dhabi chooses to adopt a rapid transit system as well.

Our study focuses on the transportation network that is necessary between Abu Dhabi CBD and the new proposed Capital District. We can perhaps state that the built-up area of Abu Dhabi's CBD is near saturation. In other words, the future population of the CBD area may not necessarily significantly increase, unless there is extant change in land use. Nonetheless, transforming it to a financial district and moving government entities to the new Capital District will cause the need for a transportation backbone between those two districts.

Although Dubai's public transport demand is based on the fact that it is more dense, as a city, than Abu Dhabi, that should not necessarily discourage Abu Dhabi's future plans. Qatar, which has been experiencing a great amount of growth and development by unleashing its natural gas and oil wealth in building its infrastructure, is constructing a metro network in Doha that is planned as rapid transit. Although Doha has a smaller population than Dubai, and may be comparable to that of the city of Abu Dhabi, the Doha Metro is planned to be operational ahead of the Qatar 2022 World Cup (Gardner 2014). This again brings us to the ideal of attractiveness of a city by tourists for having good public transport, as has been seen in Dubai. Nonetheless, Doha's metro system is meant to serve and connect Qatar's mega-projects in Doha including Hamad International Airport (Rizzio 2013). It is indeed a project that Abu Dhabi planners need to keep an eye on to learn from its challenges and solutions.

Having a master plan for sustainable development in the Gulf region has been questioned by contemporary scholars. Citizens of the Gulf region expect subsidies on utilities, land, education, and development. They also expect a public-sector job, which is usually different from other societies. A top-down sustainability agenda may prove itself to be challenging, according to current theories and practice (Gardner 2014). This means that Abu Dhabi's ambitions for future sustainable development would be considered an experiment which we will all be learning from.

Given the details put forth in this chapter about Abu Dhabi's historic development and the move within the region to have a public transit agenda, such as in Dubai and Doha, the expected travel demand for Abu Dhabi's public transit will remain low, consistent with findings from within the region. It will also prove to be financially unfeasible within the 2030 master plan, given the low travel demand for using public transport, unless major policies are introduced, which is unlikely. This is especially the situation since the new Capital District would not be fully developed at the time. However, the 2030 master plan may become a 2040 master plan, by which time a newer generation of citizens will emerge and fewer subsidies may be provided by the government, and public transit may become an option.

Congestion pricing

Traffic congestion is a common issue in large cities around the world. It imposes a significant burden in the form of lost time and additional travel (Richard and Small 1994; Palma and Lindsey 2011; Weisbrod, D. Vary and G. Treyz 2003; Wallis and Lupton 2013; Mabrouk and Abdennadher 2016). In 2010, the cost of traffic congestion in the UK, Germany, and France was 1.5%, 1.3% and 0.9% of the national GDP, respectively (Palma and Lindsey 2011).

Abu Dhabi exhibits low vehicle travel speed due to congestion. In 2009, the average vehicle travel speed in Abu Dhabi CBD was low, at around 20 kph, and that is further reduced to almost 15 kph during the peak morning hours. The vehicle driving speed in the CBD is almost 40% lower than that of the outer regions of Abu Dhabi, and 25% lower than the average vehicle speed in al-Ain City (D. O. of Transport Abu Dhabi 2012). The current status of driving speed and the population growth rate indicates a possibility of more severe congestion conditions in the CBD in the future.

Several studies have proven that an increase in road capacity results in an equivalent increase in traffic volume. Therefore, the "predict and provide" strategy is not a viable solution to traffic congestion (Mohring 1999; Porter 1999; Cervero 2003). A number of cities have opted for measures of travel demand management (TDM) instead. The TDM measures' primary objective is to influence the travel behavior of individuals through restrictions on private vehicle ownership and use in addition to providing alternative options (Sammer 2016).

A Pigovian tax quantifies the negative externalities of traffic congestion and materializes it into a Toll Charge to raise the price of driving into one that is socially optimal. The first Toll Charge was introduced in 1920, designed to be equal to the marginal damage due to the negative externality of congestion. Such toll charges are known as congestion pricing (Brueckner and Verhoef 2010). The difference between congestion pricing and other TDM policies, such as parking fees, gasoline taxes, and subsidies for transit fares, is that it influences the travel behavior and decisions made in the short and long terms, such as the number of daily trips and the housing location, instead of penalizing the consequences of congestion (Palma and Lindsey 2011).

There are three elements to congestion pricing, the first of which encompasses the Congestion Scheme which determines the area in which driving is to be charged for traffic congestion. This can be based on a congested zone, a congested road facility or a facility leading to a congested area. Furthermore congestion can be charged per entry to congested zone or per distance travelled within/to a congested zone. The second element is charging based on travel time; the choice is between a fixed flat charge (this is predetermined on the time of day, day of week or season; for example it would be higher during peak hours and lower during weekends) or a time varying charge that depends on the current congestion level. The third and last element is the congestion pricing technology used to collect the toll; the current technologies include Automatic License Plate Recognition (ALPR) and GPS (Palma and Lindsey 2011; Lehe and Daganzo 2015; Decorla-Souza 2006; Ukkusuri et al. 2008; U.S. Department of Transportation (DOT), Federal Highway Administration 2015). In most cases, the critical decision in congestion pricing is in choosing the type of congestion scheme; that is, using facility-based schemes or area-based schemes. Furthermore the choice of the time variation type and the toll technology depends on the number cars in the congestion area and the areas' geography. Both choices are made after choosing the congestion scheme most suitable for the area (Commin 2009). Therefore, and for the purpose of implementing a congestion pricing on the Island of Abu Dhabi, we are mainly concerned with the type of the congestion pricing scheme.

There are three types of a congestion schemes: 1) facility-based schemes, where tolls are imposed fully or partially on the facilities of roads, bridges, and tunnels; 2) area-based schemes, where vehicles are charged for entering, exiting, or traveling within the zone suffering from traffic congestion; and 3) distance-based schemes that charges based on the distance travelled within the congestion zone or on the congested facility (Palma and Lindsey 2011; Decorla-Souza 2006). Distance-based schemes are usually used for highways leading to the area of congestion. We are mainly concerned with managing traffic congestion inside the Island of Abu Dhabi. Hence, the focus will be on the first and second scheme types.

Facility-based schemes

New York

The New York electronic toll collection system E-ZPass imposes tolls on four out of the seven bridges and tunnels that lead to south of 60th street in Manhattan, the area known as Midtown Manhattan, or in other words the CBD of New York. Manhattan is an island that is connected with its surroundings through multiple tunnels and bridges. Hence, it may be relevant to the Island of Abu Dhabi from a geographic perspective (Zupan and Perrotta 2003).

Established in 1987, the E-ZPass Inter-Agency Group (IAG) was formed in the states of New York, New Jersey and Pennsylvania by seven toll agencies, all of which have a control point that leads to Manhattan. In 2015, about 45% of all toll revenue in the U.S. was collected in New York and New Jersey (Zupan and Perrotta 2003; IBTTA 2015).

According to the New York City DOT, since 2003 the traffic entering the CBD declined by 6.5%, while the public transit ridership into the CBD increased by 11.3%. Furthermore, traffic volumes into the CBD through bridges have not experienced a significant change since 2008 (New York City Department of Transportation 2012). Despite the slight decrease in traffic volume, the E-ZPass system did not achieve adequate congestion reductions, reflected by an average taxi speed as low as 9.3 mph, that had not changed significantly since the implementation of the tolls, causing the mean travel time to work in New York City to be 30% lower than the rest of New York County (New York State Department of Motor Vehicles 2007, 2015).

Two reasons were identified as the reason behind failing to reduce the congestion. First, the toll is not imposed on all the bridges and roads leading to the CBD, which allows most drivers to avoid them. In 2000, the traffic volume statistic indicated that only 22% of the vehicles entering Manhattan CBD were tolled (Zupan and Perrotta 2003; New York City Department of Transportation 2012). The second reason is the increasing number of vehicles. In 2015 the number of vehicle registrations in New York County alone was approximately 1.9 million, an increase of almost 7% since 2007, which is higher than any other county in New York State (New York State Department of Motor Vehicles 2007, 2015).

The Partnership for New York City, an organization made of New York's top corporate, investment, and entrepreneurial leaders working together to enhance the economy and culture of the city, estimated that in 2015 alone, traffic congestion had cost the New York City metropolitan area over $14.7 billion in lost productivity and other costs. Furthermore, the number of jobs in the city is expected to increase by 21% over the next 25 years and the population is expected to grow by 12%; consequently, more traffic will attempt to reach Manhattan (Partnership for New York City 2006).

In 2007, a cordon schemes for New York Manhattan Island was proposed by its then mayor, Michael Bloomberg, as part of a city sustainability reform. The mayor proposed a flat daily charge of $8 for cars entering or leaving Manhattan CBD, $21 for trucks, and a discounted $4 for intra-zonal trips. These fees were applicable on weekdays between 6 am and 6 pm. The fees could be paid using the E-ZPass electronic tolling system, the Internet, by phone, or at retail stores. The revenue from the congestion fees would be reinvested in public transportation improvements. However, only 40% of public opinion voters approved the mayor's scheme (Schaller 2010). In January 2008, a modified version was proposed that reduced the areas of cordon zones and only considered inbound trips. It also replaced the intra-zonal toll with parking charges and surcharges on taxi trips. The modified scheme reduced the cost of building and operating the system, while targeting the trips that are more severe to congestion. This proposal was also rejected by public poll voters, mainly because of a public distrust that toll revenue would be used for public transportation improvement rather than it being diverted to the city's general fund. Similar schemes were rejected for the same reason in Hong Kong and Edinburgh (Schaller 2010; Manville and King 2013).

Area-based schemes

Congestions schemes present at Singapore, London, and Stockholm are amongst the main operating area-based schemes designed to control congestion around the world. There are two types of area-based schemes, i) a cordon scheme charges for inbound, outbound, or both directions trips, while exempting trips made inside the cordon that does not cross the cordon boarder; and ii) a zonal scheme charges for any trip made inside the zonal area, whether it was generated inside or outside the zone's border (Palma and Lindsey 2011; Decorla-Souza 2006).

Stockholm

Stockholm congestion charges follow a cordon scheme. The cordon surrounds the city center and has 18 control points. The tolls are imposed on both inward and outward trips made at the arterial roads leading to the city center (Palma and Lindsey 2011; Gullberg and Isaksson 2009). After the success of the London congestion charge, the national government approved a trial for congestion pricing in Stockholm. The Congestion Tax Act was issued on June 2004 and the cost of the trial was paid by the national government (Clee 2007).

At the beginning of 2006, the city implemented a seven-month trial of the cordon scheme designed to reduce the traffic congestion; however a year before the trial's commencement, the public transport network in Stockholm was expanded with 197 new buses and 16 new bus lines. New park and ride facilities were also added. The aim of the trial was to test whether congestion charges can improve the traffic system, with traffic volume reduction goal of 10%–15% during rush hour (Manville and King 2013). The toll charge was between $1.5 and $3, depending on the time of day. The maximum daily payment per vehicle was $9. The charging period on weekdays is between 6 am and 6 pm. The trial achieved a 20–25% reduction in traffic, as well as better air quality, and a total toll revenue of around 48 million dollars during the trial period. In 2007, a referendum was held and the majority voted to keep the congestion charge, and the charge was officially launched (Clee 2007; Gullberg and Isaksson 2009).

A study that controlled for the external factors that could have contributed to the reduction in traffic volume, such as employment rates and fuel prices, found that the congestion charges maintained a significant reduction effect of almost 27–30% between the years of 2007 and 2011 (Börjesson et al. 2012).

Hårsman and Quigley (2010) analyzed the public opinion on the congestion charge in Stockholm. They found that the support for the tolling system was not significantly influenced by the cordon area share of public transit commuters. Rather, the support for the charge was determined by the level of reduction of the travel time. Hence, the most influential voter group was the middle-income driving voters, who are more likely to benefit from a congestion toll (Hårsman and Quigley 2010; Manville and King 2013).

Singapore

Singapore was one of the pioneers in cordon charges with the first cordon pricing scheme introduced in 1975. The current scheme, however, is a hybrid cordon-facility based scheme known as the Electronic Road Pricing (ERP). The EPR was implemented in 1998 and was at the time the first electronic toll collection system. The congestion scheme covers expressways and arterial roads that lead to three cordon areas in the CBD to regulate the traffic demand during peak hours. Tolls vary over time during the day and are imposed for each entry. The toll collection is done through In-vehicle Units (IUs) that are installed on vehicles. The units have an integrated sim card from which charges are deducted when a vehicle passes through an overhead gate at a charging point (Goh 2002; Pike 2010).

It must be noted, however, that between the years of 1975 and 1998, in which the cordon and facility tolls were implemented, mass rapid transit, such as light rail, was developed throughout Singapore to increase the ridership of public transit. In addition, a number of supplementary TDM policies were implemented; prior to the implementation of the cordon scheme in 1975, an additional registration fee was imposed on car purchases which increased the open market vehicle price by 5% to 140%, based on the type of the car (Goh 2002). By 1988, the effect of the cordon scheme was offset by the increase in vehicle ownership that reached 77% in the CBD since 1975, due to the increase in the employment rate. As a result, another congestion measure was taken in 1990; a Vehicle Quota System (VQS) was introduced which capped the annual car population growth to 3%, which was later reduced to 1.5% in 2009, and the right to own a vehicle was auctioned (Goh 2002; Der and Leong 2009). Of all the TDM policies implemented in Singapore, the cordon schemes had the greatest influence on reducing private vehicle traffic volumes. The first cordon scheme implemented in 1975 maintained an almost unchanged traffic reduction of about 45% in the zone until 1988. Therefore, in 1988, an ERP facility toll that was implemented on the highways leading to the CBD, resulting in a 42% drop in traffic volume on those highways and a 16% increase in the travel speed of the public buses (Goh 2002; Pike 2010). In May 1991 the average vehicle speed during peak hours reached 35 kph, almost twice the current speed in the City of London (Phang and Toh 2004).

London

In 1964, a report produced by the Ministry of Transport concluded that vehicle taxes had little impact on congestion in London and recommended the introduction of direct road user charges. Years later, in 2000, a study determined a suitable charging scheme, suggesting an area-based license for driving within the congestion zone (Central London) and using video cameras to detect the vehicle plate number for the license (Leape 2006).

A zonal congestion scheme was finally implemented in 2003. A charge of $10 per day is levied on weekdays from 7 am to 6:30 pm for driving anywhere within the zone or for parking on public roads. The charge applies only once a day, no matter how many times the vehicle enters or exits the congestion charge zone. Residents of the zone receive a 90% discount and only pay if they use public parking within the zone (Clee 2007; Leape 2006). Video cameras record the license plate numbers of vehicles to match with the list vehicle payments. The payment can be made in two ways: i) an advance payment through the Internet, phone, or at selected shops; or ii) using the Congestion Charge Auto Pay (CCAP), which is an automated payment deduction from a debit or credit card each month (Transport for London 2016).

In 2003, the number of private cars in the zone was reduced 34% to make up just over one-third of the traffic in central London. The average traffic speed increased by 37%, from 13 kph to 17 kph, the bus congestion delays declined by 50%, and the overall public transport traffic share increased by a little over 20% for taxis and buses, as well as 28% for bicycles (Leape 2006; Litman 2006).

Abu Dhabi

TDM measures were proposed for Abu Dhabi in 2007 as part of the STMP, which is part of the Abu Dhabi 2030 vision. The measurements included parking charges and cordon tolls. The parking charge scheme was implemented in 2009, but not the cordon toll scheme. The cordon tolls were to be applied on all the access facilities to Abu Dhabi Island, namely all the bridges, charging for the first entry to the cordon area of Abu Dhabi on any day (D. O. Transport of Abu Dhabi 2009). This scheme seems most reasonable as bridges are the only access points to the Island of Abu Dhabi and are connected to some of the most congested roads in Abu Dhabi, such as Sheikh Zayed Road.

A sensitivity analysis was produced for the effectiveness of these cordon tolls on travel modes in the year 2030, on the assumption that a public transit network is fully developed across the Island of Abu Dhabi. The transit network includes a metro line running horizontally across the Island that is connected with the areas around it with feeder buses and trams. The results revealed little to no influence on private vehicle mode share based on a daily toll of $11. The same sensitivity analysis was performed for the parking charge and the tax on vehicle purchase. The most statistically significant correlation to private vehicle mode share was the vehicle purchase tax (D. O. Transport of Abu Dhabi 2009).

To understand these results, the Singaporean experience could give an explanation, as the congestion charge implemented in 1975 lost its effect as purchase power of the citizens grew and more people were able to purchase vehicles, for which the city reacted by introducing the annual vehicle quota. The increase in the population of Abu Dhabi, which was estimated to increase by approximately four folds by 2030, and the similar increase trend in the workforce could explain the lack in sensitivity. However, we do know now that these estimates were over-ambitious. The sensitivity analysis results for the tax on vehicle purchase in Abu Dhabi should encourage its implementation in conjunction with the proposed cordon scheme (D. O. Transport of Abu Dhabi 2009). Additionally, a common factor between the cities discussed here is the presence of a large public transit network that carries a large share of the daily travel demand, which was able to take in the new commuters resulting from the congestion pricing. This would suggest that Abu Dhabi might need to have a similar transit network in place before imposing any meaningful congestion charge.

Fluctuating fuel prices and public transit

In August 2015, after the drop in oil prices that lasted for months, the UAE decided to remove the transport fuel subsidies. Fuel prices in the country were deregulated and linked with the global prices (Carpenter and Khan 2015). Travel in Abu Dhabi is almost completely reliant on private vehicles. According to the 2009 Abu Dhabi Emirate Household Interview Survey, less than 1% of trips were made by public bus, the only mode of public transit in Abu Dhabi (D. O. Transport of Abu Dhabi 2010). The question is whether fluctuating petrol prices would have a significant impact on travel behavior that could affect the public transit ridership or the demand for public transit.

Fuel prices are considered an external influencing factor to transit ridership. External factors (such as income, parking charges, employment, and car ownership) are found to have greater effects on transit ridership in comparison to internal factors. Some studies found the fluctuation in fuel prices to have less effect on transit ridership compared to other external and internal factors, such as service quality and consumer income. The reason behind this could be due to the relatively low levels of variation in the average fuels prices between different areas. The fuel cost is found to comprise a small share of the total driving cost, compared with the cost of purchasing a vehicle (Taylor et al. 2009; Taylor and Fink 2003; Cohn 1999; Chen, Varley and Chen 2011).

The United States

In the U.S., several studies looked at the role of fuel prices on public transit ridership and found a significant effect during the 1970s and 1980s. The research was mainly encouraged by the oil crisis faced during the 1970s due to the Arab oil embargo. The relationship found was significant but mostly inelastic (Agthe and Billings 1978; Horowitz 1982; Nizlek and Duckstein 1974; Lane 2010; Wang and Skinner 1984).

The oil crisis effect

Agthe and Billings (1978) looked at the relationship under an oil crisis in Tucson between 1973 and 1976. They found a significant but inelastic effect on transit ridership, with a 4.2% increase in transit ridership for every 10% increase in fuel prices. Wolff and Clark (1982) found a significant correlation between fuel prices and transit ridership, with most new transit trips taking place from the suburbs to the CBD during the peak periods. The impact was not confirmed by all the studies; Horowitz's (1982) results indicated that vehicle mode of travel is relatively insensitive to fuel price changes. Most of the reduction response comes from low-income households, where cost is a more influential factor. He explained the lack of shift towards transit ridership as a result of trip chaining and reductions in the number of trips, and hence a modal shift is the last resort.

Finding of the 21st century

Studies investigating the relationship during the 21st century found similar results to those observed after the 1970s (Currie and Phung 2007; Lane 2012; Maghelal 2011).

Lane (2010) analyzed the relationship between variable petrol prices and transit ridership from 2005 to 2008, a period that witnessed a significant surge in petrol prices. He focused on nine major U.S. cities and found a small, but statistically significant, correlation between transit ridership fluctuation and fuel prices. However, the attitude towards increasing the cost of driving was different for different cities. Cities with a prevalent public transit network shifted towards public transit, whereas auto-oriented cities were more inclined to respond with increasing the purchase of more fuel-efficient vehicles. The study also found a greater sensitivity towards the increase in the cost of driving in more auto-dependent cities, greater elasticity on rail systems compared to bus systems, and evidence of the influence of seasonal variation of transit ridership.

Lane (2012) examined the relationship between fuel prices and public transit ridership for the period 2002 to 2009 for 33 metropolitan areas. He found a small, but consistently significant, amount of fluctuation in transit ridership due to fuel prices. Every 10% increase in fuel price lead to an increase of up to 4% for bus services ridership and an 8% increase for rail services ridership. In addition, it was noted that rail service capture riders more consistently than bus service. Currie and Phung (2007) calculated a slightly lower fluctuation in ridership with a total transit demand increase of 1.2% for every 10% fuel price increase. U.S. light rail was found particularly sensitive to fuel prices, with an increase in ridership by 2.7% to 3.8% for every 10% increase in fuel price, while bus services were the least sensitive with only 0.4% increase in ridership. Lane (2012) observed that whereas bus services tend to have a complementary impact on rail ridership, the opposite applies to the rail services' impact on bus ridership. The research also noted a relatively lower magnitude of sensitivity of public transit ridership to fuel price fluctuations in cities with more extensive transit systems, as opposed to cities that are more auto-dependent. Nonetheless, transit-oriented cities in the study also experience a significant sensitivity to fluctuations in fuel prices. In addition they are more capable of capturing the travellers moving to public transit due to increasing fuel prices. Maghelal (2011) also confirms the positive association by analysing fuel prices and transit ridership in 2008. The results also discerned that the transit ridership was not affected with the decreases in fuel prices at the beginning of 2009.

In 2005, The Urban Land Institute (2005) stated that new urbanism concepts are becoming mainstream with property developers. Nonetheless, the same developers do not expect the American population preference of suburban lifestyle to change, despite traffic issues and increasing fuel prices. It also found that the majority of drivers were willing to accept the increase in driving cost so as not to compromise their ability to drive. Several studies suggested the improvement of public transit services, where it is not sufficient, in anticipation of the demand as a response to increasing fuel prices. If not prepared, even well-established public transit agencies may not be well equipped to handle the increase in demand. As a result, they may suffer increases in operating deficits (Agthe and Billings 1978; Horowitz 1982).

In the U.S., the Congressional Budget Office (CBO) report in 2008 provided a good estimate of the number of trips that differed from the roads to the transit network due to increase in fuel price by looking at highway traffic count data. The estimate was that the traffic volume on highways with parallel transit rail services were reduced by 0.7% on weekdays for a 20% fuel price increase, whereas highways without transit rail services witnessed no traffic reductions (Austin 2008).

The fuel-efficient vehicle market

Other studies examined the relationship by looking at the effect of fuel prices on the volume of vehicle purchases of different fuel economies. Associated with expectation of changes in fuel costs in the future, the studies observed a shift towards high fuel economy vehicles, as a reaction to increasing fuel prices or in anticipation of it happening based on previous trends (Busse, Knittel and Zettelmeyer 2013; Allcott 2013; Klier and Linn 2010; Anderson, Kellogg and Sallee 2011). Studies also concluded that consumers have a healthy perception of the value of fuel economy. Allcott (2013) estimated that the American driver is willing to pay just $0.61 per gallon to reduce the expected discounted fuel expenditures by $1. Busse et al. (2013) estimated the effect of a $1 per gallon increase in fuel prices on the sales of different vehicle fuel economies. They found sales in the highest fuel economy increased by 10% to 12%, while sales in the lowest fuel economy fell by 27% to 28%.

U.S. versus Europe

Klier and Linn (2010) compared the effect of fuel prices on vehicle fuel economy in the U.S. with the average of the vehicle fuel economy of the eight largest Western European markets between the years 2002 and 2007, while controlling for factors that could influence the results, such as policies and consumer preferences. The study found that fuel prices have a statistically significant effect on the average of the vehicle fuel purchase economy in Europe. However, the elasticity of the effect was only half of the one estimated for the U.S. Overall, substantial changes in fuel prices would have relatively small effects on the average fuel economy of new vehicles sold in Europe, even if the price change was substantial. One reason for the different magnitude of reaction between the U.S. and Europe could be that European cities, in general, are less auto-dependent than most U.S. cities, similar to the observation found when looking at the effect of fuel price fluctuation on public transit ridership.

The direct effect of changing fuel prices on public transit ridership in Europe was measured by the TRACE report in 1999, a comprehensive research program carried out by a number of European consultancies and universities with the financial support of the European Commission. The purpose was to demonstrate the elasticity relationship between travel costs, time, and the demand for car travel in the short and long term for various types of travel modes for numerous European cases. The report estimated that a 10% increase in fuel prices increases the transit ridership by 1.6% in the short term and by 1.2% in the long term as an EU average. However, some cities have higher fuel price elasticities of the number of vehicle kilometres, such as Italy, due to a larger share of long-distance trips. The decline in the long-term response is due to a consumer shift to more fuel-efficient vehicles (Jong 1999).

U.S. versus Australia

In a comparison of the cross elasticity of transit ridership to fuel price between the U.S. and Australia, Currie and Phung (2006, 2008) found that in Australia the impact has been 20% to 30% higher, with a 2.2% increase in transit ridership for every 10% increase in fuel prices, while it increased on average by 1.2% in the U.S. Both countries showed much larger responses for rail services and longer distance travel compared to bus service and shorter distance travel. In Melbourne, Australia, the medium-term cross-elasticities of public transit demand in response to changes in fuel prices was 4.5% for heavy rail for every 10% increase in fuel price.

Abu Dhabi

In general, the observed elasticity of public transit ridership in relation to changing fuel prices ranges from 1.2% to 2.2%, with larger values that do not exceed 5% under the condition of an oil crises. This suggests that fluctuating fuel prices may not be considered as a significant influencer on public transit ridership.

To better understand the impact of fuel price changes on Abu Dhabi vehicle use, we need to look at the driving cost in Abu Dhabi relative to fuel cost. In 2010, the Abu Dhabi DOT estimated the vehicle operating cost in Abu Dhabi at $0.31/km for private vehicles; the cost is estimated to remain constant, as increases in fuel costs are offset by improvements in vehicle efficiency, maintenance cost and increase in wages. In 2008, the American Automobile Association (AAA) estimated the vehicle driving cost in U.S. at 0.839 $/km for vehicles that drive for 2400 km per year; hence we can assume that the public transit ridership sensitivity towards fluctuating fuel prices in Abu Dhabi would be less than that of the U.S. (American Automobile Association 2008).

Nonetheless, studies did observe this sensitivity to be more significant for travellers of low income. When looking at the Abu Dhabi 2012 statistics of employee compensation per economic activity and comparing it with the number of employees at each economic activity, we find that almost 70% of the workforce in Abu Dhabi were earning 89% to 50% less than the rest of workforce from the highest paid economic activity. This indicates that a large population of Abu Dhabi can be considered as low to medium income, who could shift from vehicle use to public transit if fuel prices increase (Statistics Center of Abu Dhabi 2015). In the U.S., in

2011, the low-income population made 32% of the total population while the number was 20.9% for the U.K. Relative to these countries, Abu Dhabi could have a high potential in capturing new riders through a public transit network (Department for Work and Pensions 2014; Population Reference Bureau 2013).

Rail services tend to capture more travel due to fuel price increase more consistently compared to other public transit modes. This could suggest that the future public transit network development in Abu Dhabi should have a larger mix of rail services to increase public transit modal share. Another indicator to the assumption that increasing fuel prices in Abu Dhabi could have a positive impact on public transit ridership in the future is the larger sensitivity responses of change transit ridership in cities with less available public transit services, which is the case in Abu Dhabi.

Conclusion

This chapter discusses some aspects of the transport plans for the city of Abu Dhabi that have been proposed in the Abu Dhabi STMP for 2030. Our analysis of the previous and current trends in Abu Dhabi, which would define the size of the public transit network, concludes that the current level of demand for public transport and the existing policies of transport do not encourage the development of a more extensive transit network in Abu Dhabi, such as the one proposed in the STMP. Certain policies will have to be implemented for the plan to become viable in the future.

We have also looked at a number of implemented congestion pricing schemes to try and identify a suitable scheme for Abu Dhabi that would help relieve the traffic congestion. We recommend a future study on the impact of a vehicle number control policy to explore if such a policy may be beneficial to Abu Dhabi in combination with or without the congestion scheme.

After analyzing the possible effects of fluctuating fuel prices on the travel behavior in Abu Dhabi, we believe that although the response to higher fuel prices may be small, Abu Dhabi could use it as an opportunity to attract more travellers to its existing public transit network, if that network was made more available to users.

Note

1 Examples of these sovereign wealth funds by the government of Abu Dhabi include: Abu Dhabi Investment Authority (ADIA), Abu Dhabi Investment Council (ADIC), International Petroleum Investment Company (IPIC), and Mubadala Development Company.

References

Abu Dhabi Statistics Centre. Wages and Compensation: Economic Surveys Results. 2015. Accessed February 2016. https://www.scad.ae/en/pages/themesreleases.aspx?themeid=6&SubThemeID=22

Abu Dhabi Urban Planning Council. 2007. *Plan Abu Dhabi 2030*. ADUP Council, Abu Dhabi.

Acuto, M. 2010. High-rise Dubai urban enterpreneurialism and the technology of symbolic power. *Cities*, 27(4): 272–284.

Agthe, Donald E., and Bruce R. Billings. 1978. The impact of gasoline prices on urban bus ridership. *The Annals of Regional Science*, 12(1): 90–96.

Alkaabi, Khaula. 2014. Analyzing the travel behaviour and travel preferences of employees and students commuting via Dubai metro. *The Arab World Geographer*, 17(1): 42–65.

Allcott, Hunt. 2013. The welfare effects of misperceived product costs: Data and calibrations from the automobile market. *American Economic Journal: Economic Policy*, 5(3): 30–66.

American Automobile Association (AAA). 2008. *Your Driving Costs*, 2008 Edition. AAA, Heathrow, FL. Accessed December 2016. http://exchange.aaa.com/wp-content/uploads/2015/08/2008-YDC-Final.pdf

Anderson, Soren T., Ryan Kellogg, and James M. Sallee. 2011. *What Do Consumers Believe About Future Gasoline Prices?* National Bureau of Economic Research, No. w16974.

Austin, David. 2008. Effects of Gasoline Prices on Driving Behavior and Vehicle Markets. Congressional Budget Office.

Börjesson, M., J. Eliasson, M.B. Hugosson, and K. Brundell-Freij. 2012. The Stockholm congestion charges – 5 years on. Effects, acceptability and lessons learnt. *Transport Policy*, 20: 1–12.

Brueckner, Jan K., and Erik T. Verhoef. 2010. Manipulable congestion tolls. *Journal of Urban Economics*, 67(3): 315–316.

Busse, Meghan R., Christopher R. Knittel, and Florian Zettelmeyer. 2013. Are consumers myopic? Evidence from new and used car purchases. *The American Economic Review*, 103(1): 220–256.

Carpenter, Claudia, and Sarmad Khan. 2015. UAE removes fuel subsidy as oil drop hurts Arab economies. July 22. Available at: www.bloomberg.com/news/articles/2015-07-22/u-a-e-to-link-gasoline-price-to-global-markets-effect-aug-1 (Accessed 15 March 2016).

Cervero, Robert. 2003. Road expansion, urban growth, and induced travel: A path analysis. *Journal of the American Planning Association*, 69(2): 145–163.

Chen, Cynthia, Don Varley, and Jason Chen. 2011. What affects transit ridership? A dynamic analysis involving multiple factors, lags and asymmetric behaviour. *Urban Studies*, 48(9): 1893–1908.

Clee, A. 2007. Driving Away the Traffic: What Lessons Can New York Learn From London and Stockholm's Experiences With Congestion Charging. A thesis, Tufts University.

Cohn, Harold M. 1999. *Factors Affecting Urban Transit Ridership*. Statistics Canada.

Commin, Harry. 2009. The Congestion Charging Schemes of London and Singapore: Why Did London Choose Different Technology, and Was This a Mistake. Master dissertation, pp. 1–18.

Currie, Graham, and Justin Phung. 2006. *Exploring the Impacts of Fuel Price Increases on Public Transport Use in Melbourne*. In 29th Australasian Transport Research Forum, Gold Coast.

Currie, Graham, and Justin Phung. 2007. Transit ridership, auto gas prices, and world events: New drivers of change? *Transportation Research Record: Journal of the Transportation Research Board*, 1992(1): 3–10.

Currie, Graham, and Justin Phung. 2008. *Understanding Links Between Transit Ridership and Auto Gas Prices: US and Australian Evidence*. In Transportation Research Board Annual Meeting, 87th, Washington, DC.

Davidson, Christopher. 2007. The Emirates of Abu Dhabi and Dubai: Contrasting roles in the international system. *Asian Affairs*, 38(1): 33–48.

Davis, M. 2006. Fear and money in Dubai. *New Left Review*, 42: 47–68.

Decorla-Souza, Patrick. 2006. *Congestion Pricing: A Primer.* Washington, DC: Federal Highway Administration.

De Jong, Gerard 1999. *Elasticity Handbook: Elasticities for Prototype Contexts*. Prepared for the European Comission Directorate-General for Transport, Contract No. R)-97-Sc-2305.

Department for Work and Pensions. 2014. Re-Grossed Households Below Average Income (HBAI) Estimates 2002/03 to 2011/12. Gov.UK.

Der, Lew Yii, and Wai Yan Leong. 2009. Managing congestion in Singapore – A behavioural economics perspective. *Journeys*, 15.

New York State Department of Motor Vehicles. 2015. "Vehicle Registrations in Force (2015)."

New York State Department of Motor Vehicles. 2007. "Vehicle Registrations in Force (2007)."

Department of Transport in Abu Dhabi. 2009. *Surface Transport Master Plan: A Vision for Connecting Abu Dhabi, The Plan – Appendices A-C*. Abu Dhabi: D. O. Transport of Abu Dhabi, pp. 239–249.

Department of Transport in Abu Dhabi. 2010. *Abu Dhabi Travel Patterns Highlights of the 2009 Survey Results.* Abu Dhabi: Department of Transport in Abu Dhabi, pp. 5–6.

Department of Transport in Abu Dhabi. 2012. Media Center. Public Announcements. Travel Surveys. *Abu Dhabi Travel Patterns Highlights of the 2009 Survey Results*, pp. 5–6. Accessed December 2016. https://dot.abudhabi.ae/en/mediainfo/Travel_Surveys

New York City Department of Transportation. 2012. *2012 Sustainable Streets INDEX.* New York: New York City Department of Transportation.

Dubai Statistics Center. 2014. Website. Accessed May 2017. https://www.dsc.gov.ae/en-us.

Elsheshtawy, Yasser. 2011. Informal encounters: Mapping Abu Dhabi's urban public spaces. *Built Environment*, 37(1): 92–113.

Gardner, Andrew M. 2014. How the city grows: Urban growth and challenges to sustainable development in Doha, Qatar. In *Sustainable Development: An Appraisal From the Gulf Region*, edited by Paul Sillitoe, pp. 343–366. New York: NY: Berghahn Books.

Goh, M. 2002. Congestion management and electronic road pricing in Singapore. *Journal of Transport Geography*, 10(1): 29–38.

Gullberg, Anders, and Karolina Isaksson. 2009. Fabulous success or insidious fiasco. In *Congestion Taxes in City Traffic: Lessons Learnt From the Stockholm Trial*, edited A. Gullberg and K. Isaksson, 11–168. Lund, Sweden: Nordic Academic Press.

Hajash, G.M. 1967. *The Abu Sheikhdom: The Onshore Oilfields History of Exploration and Development.* In 7th World Petroleum Congress, Mexico City, Mexico, pp. 2–9.

Hårsman, B., and J.M. Quigley. 2010. Political and public acceptability of congestion pricing: Ideology and self-interest. *Journal of Policy Analysis and Management*, 29(4): 854–874.

Hassan, T.H., and S. Azer. 1985. *The Occurrence and Origin of Oil in Offshore Abu Dhabi*. In Middle East Oil Technical Conference and Exhibition, Bahrain, pp. 11–14.

Horowitz, Joel. 1982. Modeling traveler responses to alternative gasoline allocation plans. *Transportation Research Part A: General*, 16(2): 117–133.

International Bridge, Tunnel and Turnpike Association (IBTTA). 2015. 2015 Report on Tolling in the United States.

Klier, Thomas, and Joshua Linn. 2010. The price of gasoline and new vehicle fuel economy: Evidence from monthly sales data. American Economic Journal: Economic Policy, 2(3): 134–153.

Lane, Bradley W. 2010. The relationship between recent gasoline price fluctuations and transit ridership in major US cities. *Journal of Transport Geography*, 18(2): 214–225.

Lane, Bradley W. 2012. A time-series analysis of gasoline prices and public transportation in US metropolitan areas. *Journal of Transport Geography*, 22: 221–235.

Leape, J. 2006. The London congestion charge. *The Journal of Economic Perspectives*, 20(4): 157–176.

Lehe, Carlos F., and Lewis J. Daganzo. 2015. Distance-dependent congestion pricing for downtown zones. *Transportation Research Part B: Methodological*, 75: 89–99.

Litman, Todd. 2006. London congestion pricing: Implications for other cities. *Victoria Transport Policy Institute*, 10: 5–6.

Mabrouk, A., and C. Abdennadher. 2016. Estimation of time loss and costs of traffic congestion: The contingent valuation method. *International Journal of Social, Behavioral, Educational, Economic, Business and Industrial Engineering*, 10(3): 683–687.

Maghelal, Praveen. 2011. Investigating the relationships among rising fuel prices, increased transit ridership, and CO2 emissions. *Transportation Research Part D: Transport and Environment*, 16(3): 232–235.

Mallakh, Raggei El. 1970. The challenge of affluence: Abu Dhabi. *Middle East Journal*, 24(2): 135–146.

Manville, M., and D. King. 2013. Credible commitment and congestion pricing. *Transportation*, 40(2): 229–249.

Mohring, Herbert, 1999. "In Congestion", In Title: *Essays in Transportation Economics and Policy: A Handbook in Honor of John R. Meyer*. 2011. Edited by: Jose A. Gomez-Ibanez, William B. Tye, and Clifford Winston. pp. 181–222. Washington, DC: Brookings Institution Press.

The New York State Department of Motor Vehicles. 2007. *Vehicle Registrations in Force (2007)*. New York: The New York State Department of Motor Vehicles.

The New York State Department of Motor Vehicles. 2015. *Vehicle Registrations in Force (2015)*. New York: The New York State Department of Motor Vehicles.

Nizlek, Martin C., and Lucien Duckstein. 1974. A system model for predicting the effect of energy resources on urban modal split. *Transportation Research*, 8(4–5): 329–334.

Pacione, M. 2005. Dubai. *Cities*, 22(3): 255–265.

Palma, André de, and Robin Lindsey. 2011. Traffic congestion pricing methodologies and technologies. *Transportation Research: Emerging Technologies*, 19(6): 1377–1399.

Parahoo, Sanjai K., Heather L. Harvey, and Gihad Y.A. Radi. 2014. Satisfaction of tourists with public transport: An empirical investigation in Dubai. *Journal of Travel & Tourism Marketing*, 31(8): 1004–1017.

Partnership for New York City. 2006. Growth or Gridlock? The Economic Case for Traffic Relief and Transit Improvement for a Greater New York. New York: Partnership for New York City.

Phang, Sock-Yong, and Rex S. Toh. 2004. Road congestion pricing in Singapore: 1975 to 2003. *Transportation Journal*, 43(2): 16–25.

Pike, P.E. , The International Council on Clean Transportation. Transportation planning. *Congestion charging: Challenges and opportunities*. 2010.

Ponzini, Davide. 2011. Large scale development projects and star architecture in the absence of democratic politics: The case of Abu Dhabi, UAE. *Cities*, 28(3): 251–259.

Population Reference Bureau. 2013. *U.S. Low-Income Working Families Increasing*. Accessed March 2016. http://www.prb.org/Publications/Articles/2013/us-working-poor-families.aspx.Porter, Richard C. 1999. *Economics at the Wheel: The Costs of Cars and Drivers*. The Academic Press. Cambridge, MA.

Richard, Arnott, and Kenneth Small. 1994. The economics of traffic congestion. American Scientist, 82(5): 446–455.

Rizzio, A. 2013. Metro Doha. *Cities*, 31: 533–543.

Sammer, Gerd. 2016. Travel Demand Management and Road User Pricing: Success, Failure and Feasibility. Routledge. Oxford, UK.

Schaller, B. 2010. New York City's congestion pricing experience and implications for road pricing acceptance in the United States. Transport Policy, 17(4): 266–273.

Statistics Center of Abu Dhabi. 2015. *Economic Survey Result 2013*. Abu Dhabi: Statistics Center of Abu Dhabi.

Taylor, Brian D., and Camille N.Y. Fink. 2003. *The Factors Influencing Transit Ridership: A Review and Analysis of the Ridership Literature.* Berkeley, CA: University of California Transportation Center. http://www.uctc.net/papers/681.pdf.

Taylor, Brian D., Douglas Miller, Hiroyuki Iseki, and Camille Fink. 2009. Nature and/or nurture? Analyzing the determinants of transit ridership across US urbanized areas. *Transportation Research Part A: Policy and Practice*, 43(1): 60–77.

Transport for London. 2016. *Paying the Congestion Charge.* Available at: https://tfl.gov.uk/modes/driving/congestion-charge/paying-the-congestion-charge (Accessed 15 May 2016).

Trench, Richard. 1994. *Arab Gulf Cities*. Slough: Penguin Books, p. 248.

Ukkusuri, Satish V., Ampol Karoonsoontawong, S. Travis Waller, and Kara M. Kockelman. Filip N. Gustavsson (ed). 2008. Congestion pricing technologies: A comparative evaluation. In *New Transportation Research Progress*, 121–142. Nova Science Publishers, Inc. New York, NY.

The Urban Land Institute (ULI), and PricewaterhouseCoopers LLP. 2005. *Emerging Trends in Real Estate 2005*. Washington, D.C: ULI – the Urban Land Institute.

U.S. Department of Transportation, Federal Highway Administration. 2015. *Technologies That Enable Congestion Pricing: A Primer*.

United Nations, Department of Economic and Social Affairs, Population Division (2015). World Population.

Wallis, I.P., and D.R. Lupton. 2013. *The Cost of Congestion Reappraised.* Wellington: NZ Transport Agency.

Wang, George H.K., and David Skinner. 1984. The impact of fare and gasoline price changes on monthly transit ridership: Empirical evidence from seven US transit authorities. *Transportation Research Part B: Methodological*, 18(1): 29–41.

Weisbrod, G., D. Vary, and G. Treyz. 2003. Measuring economic costs of urban traffic congestion to business. *Transportation Research Record*, 1839: 98–106.

Wolff, G.J., and D. M. Clark. 1982. Impact of Gasoline Price on Transit Ridership in Fort Worth, Texas. *Journal of Transportation Engineering*, 108.TE4.

Worku, Genanew B. 2013. Demand for improved public transport services in the UAE: A contingent valuation study in Dubai. *International Journal of Business and Management*, 8(10): 108–125.

Yasser Elsheshtawy, ed. 2008. The Evolving Arab City: Tradition, Modernity and Urban Development. Abingdon: Routledge, 266pp.

Zupan, J.M., and A. Perrotta. 2003. *An Exploration of Motor Vehicle Congestion Pricing in New York.* New York: Regional Plan Association, pp. 3–11.

Part III

Standards and policies

9 Advancing sustainable consumption

Energy efficiency labels and standards in the UAE

Deepti Mahajan Mittal

Introduction

In terms of per capita energy consumption and carbon emissions, the member countries of the Cooperation Council for the Arab States of the Gulf (also known as the Gulf Cooperation Council), including the United Arab Emirates (UAE), figure amongst the highest in the world. Lifestyle consumption, supported by the burning of fossil fuels, is a major contributor to UAE's high energy use. While consumer awareness remains an important part of the drive towards low-carbon lifestyles, regulatory interventions are required to create the right conditions for sustainable lifestyles. These interventions are geared towards access to efficient technology, communication of appropriate market signals, and provision of infrastructure conducive to sustainable choices.

Power consumption and energy use for mobility are key components of lifestyle energy consumption. In energy product markets, government regulation is instrumental in driving producers and consumers alike towards energy efficiency. For consumers, this may involve policies that reduce informational and transaction costs, and even limit choice (by banning inefficient products, for instance). For producers, governments rely on standards and incentives to encourage and/or mandate the supply of green products and services. In a number of cases, governments themselves are suppliers of services and large procurers, and therefore have a significant opportunity to lead by example.

The UAE federal government and Emirate-level government agencies have adopted a range of labels and standards to push the household sector towards efficiency. This chapter examines existing energy efficiency labels and standards of particular relevance to lifestyle consumption, complementary policies that help meet the objectives of these regulations, and potential tools at the disposal of the government in the domain of advancing efficient technologies. The chapter also examines policymaking models that allow for effective and informed decision-making. The views expressed in this chapter are solely those of the author and do not necessarily reflect the views of any organisations the author is affiliated with.

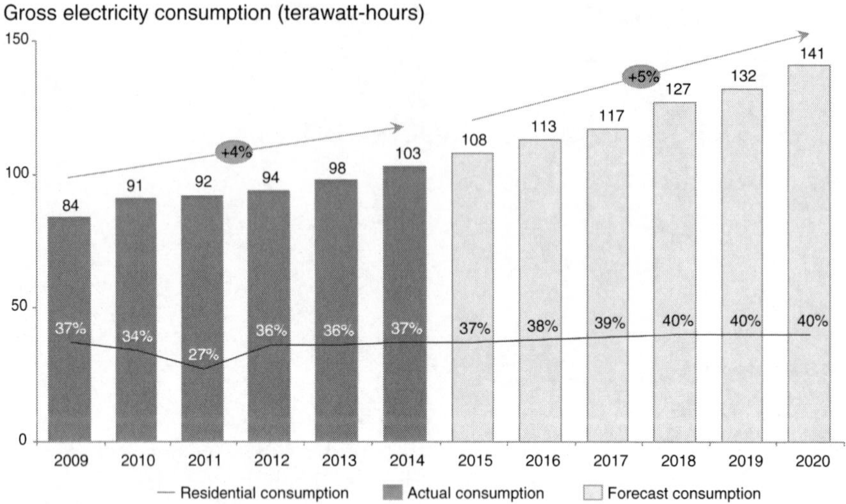

Figure 9.1 Total power consumption and residential percentage of total

Source: Karlsson et al. (2015)

Understanding lifestyle choices in the UAE

UAE is amongst the world's highest per capita energy consumers. In 2013, per capita primary energy use stood at 7,691 kilogram of oil equivalent (kgoe) as compared to 6,914 kgoe in the United States and 6,363 kgoe in Saudi Arabia (The World Bank 2014a). The total electricity consumption in the UAE has more than doubled between 2005 and 2010, growing at an annual average of 4% between 2009 and 2015, and projections up to 2020 show a steady increase (Karlsson et al. 2015) (see Figure 9.1). In 2013, the registered peak load was 19.7 GW, up from 15.6 in 2009 (UAE Ministry of Energy 2016). In the year 2012, over 75% of the oil consumed in the UAE was for transportation needs (The Abdullah Bin Hamad Al-Attiyah Foundation for Energy & Sustainable Development 2015).

Lifestyle energy consumption is broadly comprised of electricity use by households and commercial establishments such as offices and passenger transport. According to the International Energy Agency (IEA), the transport sector, residential sector, and commerce and public services comprised 28%, 23%, and 8%, respectively, of world total final energy consumption respectively in 2013 (IEA 2015a). Consumer demands form a significant component of energy consumption and its environmental impacts: for instance, direct influences due to home energy use and personal travel form 4% of the United States' Gross Domestic Product (GDP), but account for 28% and 41% of the country's energy use and CO_2 (carbon dioxide) emissions respectively, while economic activities that support these demands account for an additional 57% of US energy use (Bin and Dowlatabadi

2005). According to the UAE State of Green Economy Report 2014, the residential sector consumed 35% of the electricity consumed in the UAE in 2012. Of the total UAE consumption of petroleum products in 2013, 75.4% was in the transport sector (UAE Ministry of Energy 2016).

Given the hot and arid climate in the UAE, power demand for cooling is significant: a breakdown of electricity consumption per end-use in Abu Dhabi showed that 57.5% of the consumption in 2009 was for chillers (Executive Affairs Authority cited in Afshari et al. 2014). For 2013, the World Bank reported UAE's per capita electricity consumption at 10,904 kilowatt hour (kWh) while the average for high-income countries stood at 9084 kWh (The World Bank 2014b). In the domain of transport, private cars remain the mainstay of passenger mobility in the country. Car ownership in the UAE is at 480 per 1,000 people, amongst the highest in the world (van Leijen 2015). The UAE is one of the world's fastest growing vehicle markets; in 2010, the sales of light-duty vehicles (passenger cars, SUVs and light trucks) stood at 212,300, with the number more than doubling to 478,872 in 2014 (Marklines vehicle database, cited in International Council on Clean Transportation 2015).

Moving energy consumers in the UAE from resource-intensive lifestyles to green, sustainable ones can significantly contribute to an energy transformation powered by curbing wasteful use of energy and energy efficiency. Curtailing wasteful use involves cutting down on use of an energy service, such as switching off extra lights in a room or maintaining AC levels. This is distinct from energy efficiency, where the effort is directed towards getting the same energy service with use of lesser energy.

Harnessing the potential of energy efficiency

The economic and environmental opportunities offered by energy efficiency need to be utilised in order to meet individual countries' and the international community's environment and development goals as well as to keep to related resource consumption limits. The drive towards energy efficiency resonates with a number of Sustainable Development Goals (SDGs), part of the 2030 Agenda for Sustainable Development agreed at the United Nations Sustainable Development Summit in 2015 (United Nations 2016). SDG 7, 'Ensure access to affordable, reliable, sustainable and modern energy for all', focuses specifically on energy and includes a target to double the rate of improvement in energy efficiency by 2030, globally. Resource efficiency is also emphasised in SDG 8 which addresses sustainable economic growth, SDG 11 which looks at sustainable cities and human settlements, and SDG 12 which focuses on sustainable consumption and production patterns. The critical role that energy resources play in powering the engine of economic growth, and the reality of constrained energy supplies, frames efficiency as a cornerstone of sustainable development policy.

In 2014, the then-UAE Ministry of Environment and Water (now called the Ministry of Climate Change and Environment) released a report titled *UAE State of Green Economy* which drew from a macroeconomic model that evaluated business as usual and a range of green economy scenarios (with the measures including use of efficient energy products, raising the efficiency of built space and increasing use of public transport) (UAE Ministry of Environment and Water 2014). The evaluated scenarios presented significant opportunities for energy and carbon savings: decreased consumption of oil by 7–10% per year, natural gas by 7–20%, and electricity by 11–15% through 2030; and a reduction in carbon intensity ranging between 18–25% of cumulative emissions between 2013 and 2030. That the UAE's energy demand is set to increase considerably over the coming years implies that improvements in energy efficiency will be integral to enhancing energy security and reducing greenhouse gas (GHG) emissions.

Prudent and efficient use of energy can lead to a direct reduction in the energy footprint of the country. The potential that energy efficiency holds for relative decrease in energy use and decoupling of energy demand from GDP growth has led to energy efficiency being referred to as the "first fuel" and an "invisible powerhouse" (IEA 2014). Global energy intensity – an "imperfect proxy" for energy efficiency, showed an improvement of 1.3% annually over the 20-year period from 1990 to 2010 (The World Bank and IEA 2015). Positive estimates abound for the potential of energy savings held by energy efficiency. The total savings potential from the global use of energy-efficient products is nearly as much as the annual electricity consumption of the European Union (Global Energy Efficiency Accelerator Platform 2016). Though energy efficiency applications and measures involve upfront costs for consumers, the payback from energy savings helps recover invested capital. High technology costs are often cited as a barrier to energy efficiency uptake, and a clear communication of costs and benefits, as well as payback periods, can alleviate consumers' concerns on financial implications.

The benefits of energy efficiency are not limited to enhanced energy security alone. Energy efficiency has the potential to provide about 40% of the emissions reductions required by 2050 in order to limit global temperature rise to less than 2 degrees Celsius, thus contributing to address the challenge of climate change (IEA 2015b). In addition to tackling GHG emissions, energy efficiency can help reduce release of local pollutants – linked with adverse health impacts. While air pollution has been a policy concern in the UAE, with efforts having been made to adhere to the World Health Organization's air-quality guidelines, the issue came into prominence like never before when, in 2015, the World Bank's *The Little Green Data Book* ranked the country highest on PM2.5 pollution (The World Bank 2015). Though the reported UAE data was disputed by government authorities, it drove the issue of ambient air quality further up on the policy agenda. The air quality impacts of policies that help reduce energy consumption and carbon emissions are thus of specific policy relevance in the UAE context.

The synergies between renewables and energy efficiency need to be borne in mind while planning energy system transformations; increase in energy efficiency can facilitate further deployment of renewables. Combining energy efficiency applications with renewables influences utility load curves, as efficiency improvements reduce overall demand and renewables (such as solar) generate power during peak hours (Prindle et al. 2007). The synergies are equally relevant when looking at transforming the subset of household consumption. Energy efficiency can help reduce energy demand and maximise equipment efficiencies whereby allowing a larger fraction of a building's/household's consumption to be provided by a renewable energy installation; and, conversely, integrating renewable energy can allow for larger peak power demand reductions than efficiency measures alone (Building Efficiency Initiative 2010). For those looking to invest in installing a home-based renewable energy system, efficiency improvements make renewable energy more affordable: the short payback periods that characterise investments in energy efficiency ensure the availability of "incremental cash flow to pay for the longer payback renewable energy systems" (Building Efficiency Initiative 2010).

The choices that energy consumers make in their daily lives and the attitude they adopt to energy use is determined by a range of factors. These include availability of efficient technology choices; ease of use and appropriate infrastructure; relative pricing of different options; and consumer behaviour. Consumers are generally, and rightly, invested with the power of agency in discussions on sustainable lifestyles. But it is important to note that consumer agency is aided and influenced by a range of factors, including availability of the right technology options and empowerment to make sustainable technology choices. Governments have at their disposal a range of levers to act on this front and shift consumer behaviour towards the 'green' end of the spectrum.

Role of energy efficiency labels and standards

Stringent and effective regulatory frameworks that are informed by the benefits of energy efficiency – enhanced productivity and energy security, reduced pollution, and climate mitigation – have a key part to play in keeping the efficiency market robust. These may involve top-down measures that limit consumer choice, such as a ban on inefficient bulbs or air conditioners, or bottom-up processes such as consumer engagements that seek to transform energy attitudes. Government-led institutions are well placed to influence lifestyle choices through these measures and, in this domain, energy labels and standards constitute a global best practice that has been in existence since the 1970s (IEA 2015c). The Emirates Authority for Standardisation and Metrology (ESMA) is charged with the development of energy efficiency labels and standards in the UAE.

At the outset, it would be important to understand what labels and standards imply. In *Energy Efficiency Labels and Standards: A Guidebook for Appliances, Equipment and Lighting*, Stephen Wiel and James McMahon define energy efficiency labels as informative labels on products that describe its energy performance (Wiel and McMahon 2001). These can take the form of endorsement labels, comparative labels, or informational labels. Endorsement labels are approvals awarded according to specified criteria. Comparative labels, as the name suggests, allow consumers to compare performance among similar products "using either discrete categories of performance or a continuous scale." Information-only labels simply state a product's performance. Labels allow consumers to make informed purchase decisions while creating competition for manufacturers in the favour of average efficiency of products.

Energy efficiency standards are defined as procedures and regulations that "prescribe the energy performance of manufactured products" (Wiel and McMahon 2001). These are distinct from labels as they set performance requirements for products or a classification of products. According to ESMA, a standard "provides requirements, specifications, guidelines or characteristics that can be used consistently to ensure that materials, products, processes and services are fit for their purpose" (ESMA 2014). ESMA also refers to a mandatory standard as a technical regulation, one that is mandatorily applied as per UAE Cabinet resolution. Energy standards can be of three kinds: prescriptive standards; minimum energy performance standards, or class-average standards (Wiel and McMahon 2001). Prescriptive standards make a particular feature or device mandatory for all new products. Performance standards prescribe minimum efficiencies that a product must achieve to qualify for sale in the governed market. Class-average standards specify average efficiency of a product, thus allowing each manufacturer the flexibility to select the level of efficiency of each model as long as the average is achieved. Energy standards and labels can complement each other as well as function as stand-alone policies, and both draw on defined testing protocols. They can also be deployed to set high-performance benchmarks and encourage innovation, as exhibited by Japan's Top Runner programme (Hart 2013, 34).

A McKinsey and Company report released in 2007 suggested that targeted policies that overcome market imperfections and distortions can help capture opportunities for increased energy productivity (Bressand et al. 2007). The implementation of labelling and standards schemes hold out such an opportunity. A global assessment of appliance standards and labels by the IEA in 2015 revealed that one-off improvements of over 30% have been observed in markets where few efficiency programmes existed previously and new energy efficiency standards and labelling programmes were introduced. Mature, long-running national schemes that cover a broad range of products "are estimated to save between 10% and 25% of national or relevant sectoral energy consumption." According to one estimate, by 2020, efficiency standards for appliances in the U.S. will have helped avoid 20% of the country's planned new power generation with expected savings of more than $100 billion (Meyers et al. 2003). Co-benefits include industry competitiveness, improved air quality and better human health (IEA 2015c).

The UAE has already adopted labels and standards in an effort towards better demand side management and supply of state-of-the-art energy technologies to the country. There is, however, scope for improved implementation of current regulations, as well as the need for further regulatory interventions that promote uptake of efficient technologies and consumption best practices.

Regulating technologies and infrastructure for energy efficiency

Technology development and scientific innovation have been the most significant propellers for reducing energy intensity and decoupling growth from increased consumption of energy. A study commissioned by the European Union, *Savings and benefits of global regulations for energy-efficient products*, states that global harmonisation of minimum energy performance requirements for product energy efficiency in 2015 would have implied a 9% lower final energy consumption worldwide – the saved energy being equivalent to the closure of 165 coal power plants (Molenbroek et al. 2015).

Technology standards and codes adopted by government are critical in determining what kind of energy technologies are available in country markets. Government regulation can play a role in making sure that state-of-the-art technology options are available to consumers and outdated, inefficient technologies are not. The setting of minimum energy performance standards can make the sale of inefficient technologies illegal and wipe out the market for low-efficiency products in one go.

It is notable that in the UAE, energy sector management is largely a sub-national subject of governance, managed by Emirates. In the Emirate of Dubai, the Dubai Supreme Council of Energy (DSCE) is charged with energy strategy development and works through implementing members, including Dubai Electricity and Water Authority (DEWA), Dubai Aluminium, Emirates National Oil Company, Dubai Municipality, Roads and Transport Authority – Dubai (RTA - Dubai), amongst others. DSCE has developed the Dubai Integrated Energy Strategy that sets the Emirate a target of reducing its energy consumption by 30% by 2030. In order to meet this target, a targeted Demand Side Management Programme, Taqati, was launched under the framework of the Supreme Council of Energy in 2016 to advance building regulations, building retrofits, district cooling, standards and labels for appliances and equipment, water reuse and efficient irrigation, outdoor lighting, demand response, and rooftop solar. Similarly, Abu Dhabi and the northern emirates have their own governance structures. In Abu Dhabi, the Emirate's Regulation and Supervision Bureau has been implementing demand management initiatives along with the Abu Dhabi Water and Electricity Authority and its subsidiaries, as well as the Executive Affairs Authority. Sharjah has its own water and power authority, and the northern Emirates are governed by the Federal Electricity and Water Authority. Energy standards and labels are, however, developed and implemented federally. National standards play a key role in meeting the efficiency and sustainability targets set by Emirate-level entities for their energy sectors. The sections below examine labels and standards adopted by the UAE for improved efficiencies in household electrical appliances, vehicles, and buildings.

Electrical appliances

ESMA has, over the last few years, developed an Energy Efficiency Standardisation and Labelling Programme which covers a range of household goods and appliances. The UAE energy labelling programme which came into effect in 2013 – a strong consumer education tool – covers a range of products including washing machines and dryers, household refrigerating appliances, storage water heaters, household air conditioners, and commercial and central air conditioners. The country also has a star rating system to grade products in terms of their efficiency, providing for a comparative label. This rating system covers household electrical appliances, air conditioning systems, and lighting products, and adds to the efficacy of labelling by empowering consumers with a clear, relative assessment of products. In an effort to push manufacturers to produce quality products and importers to bring more efficient products to the market, the star rating system incorporates a fee for products that are assigned a rating of one, two, or three stars.

The application of labels and standards to the most prevalent and energy-intensive appliances in a country, such as refrigerators and air-conditioning systems, generally generates larger benefits than the cost of implementing the programmes and producing the more efficient products. Savings on less common and less energy-intensive goods are often not enough to justify the costs (Wiel and McMahon 2001). In the UAE, cooling forms a substantial proportion of the energy consumed in households and air conditioners were amongst the first products subjected to a labelling system in 2011. ESMA announced that beginning in January 2012, only AC units that comply with the label system would be allowed to enter the UAE market. It was estimated then that one in five AC units could be banned for failing to meet efficiency requirements (Todorova 2011).

The country has a regulation for indoor lighting products that sets a minimum energy performance standard for these products and bans the import and sale of inefficient ones. It ensures that the light bulbs being sold in the country are efficient, high-quality, safe, have limited hazardous chemicals, and can be safely disposed of. The UAE market, with the implementation of this standard, is supplied by compact fluorescent lamps, light emitting diodes, and halogens – products more efficient than incandescent bulbs. The import of non-compliant products was banned in July 2014 and the ban on sale of non-compliant products came into force on 1 January 2015. Lighting products to be sold in the UAE market need to follow the Emirates Conformity Assessment Scheme which requires manufacturers, traders, and suppliers to provide third-party test reports of their products, providing proof that they meet the requirements of the lighting regulation, in order to receive a certificate of conformity and obtain the UAE energy efficiency label (Abdullatif and Alam 2014).

The move to better technology holds significant potential for energy savings and related economic and environmental savings. At the launch of the star rating scheme, it was estimated that the system would save the UAE government AED 400 million annually by 2016 due to energy savings on air conditioning units alone. The potential savings from the implementation of the lighting standard are much higher. The estimated financial savings from the standard stand at AED 668 million per year in net savings from households' reduced electricity bills and in government savings from reduced subsidies. The lighting standard's implementation has the potential to reduce UAE's energy consumption by 500 Megawatts annually, equivalent to not using an average gas power station for six months (EWS-WWF 2014).

Vehicle technologies

Besides electrical goods, another domain where consumers' technology choices need to be informed by sustainability is mobility. With exponentially growing sales, it is clear that an early intervention to bring more efficient cars to the UAE market can bring significant long-term energy and environmental benefits. Notably, an advance on vehicle efficiency programmes has been registered at the regional level in the GCC. The GCC Standardisation Organisation (GSO) developed and adopted a technical regulation titled "GSO No. 42/2015: General Requirements – Motor Vehicles" in 2015 (to be enforced 2018 model year onwards), aimed at ensuring high levels of vehicle safety, energy efficiency, anti-theft performance, and environment protection. This regulation puts forth requirements that all vehicle manufacturers have to comply with to be able to sell their light-duty vehicles (passenger cars and light trucks) in the GCC market. Amongst other provisions, the regulation includes requirement of 'Fuel Consumption Measurement and Label'. It mandates that all vehicles with weight equal to or less than 3500 kilograms shall carry a label on fuel consumption efficiency. The label categorises the vehicles from Very Poor (equal to or below 12.49 kilometres/litre (km/l)) to Excellent (equal to or above 14.7 km/l). The regulation prescribes the minimum details the label should include, stipulating that the fuel consumption measurement procedure shall also include documentation of the rolling resistance and wet grip of tyres (through a tyre label) – a factor that influences efficiency of the vehicle.

To build on this regional success and drive vehicle efficiency improvements in the UAE, the country is currently in the process of developing domestic vehicle fuel economy policies. A technical assessment was undertaken by the Ecological Footprint Initiative, a federal-level cross-sectoral partnership, in order to provide the scientific basis for the policies. According to the assessment, a Corporate Average Fuel Economy (CAFE) standard that sets annual average sales-weighted fuel economy targets for each manufacturer up to 2028, has the potential to improve the UAE fleet's fuel efficiency from the current average of 12.1 km/l to 20.8 km/l by 2028 (International Council on Clean Transportation, and Emirates Wildlife Society in association with WWF 2016). This would result in cumulative fuel savings of 171 billion litres and cumulative CO_2 savings of 400 million tonnes by 2050. In annual terms, the country would save 8.8 billion litres of fuel in 2050 and avoid carbon equivalent to the removal of 6.6 million cars off the roads. The analysis also shows that, across different fuel price scenarios, the incremental cost of purchasing an efficient vehicle would be recovered within a short span of time with the fuel savings that will accrue to the consumer (International Council on Clean Transportation, and Emirates Wildlife Society in association with WWF 2016).

While improving the efficiency of conventional light-duty vehicles that run on hydrocarbons, a UAE CAFE standard would also create regulatory conditions for manufacturers to bring more hybrid vehicles and plug-in hybrids into the country. It would even offer the scope to include clauses that encourage supply of electric vehicles by manufacturers. In comparison to internal combustion engines, electric vehicles are about three times more efficient (International Renewable Energy Agency 2015). Not surprisingly, there has been growing policy interest in electric cars. In February 2009, the Department of Transport of the Emirate of Abu Dhabi launched a Surface Transport Master Plan – 'A Vision for Connecting Abu Dhabi' – and in pursuance of the objectives set out by the Plan, in May 2016, the Abu Dhabi

Executive Council approved the Low Emission Vehicle Strategy which aims to bring more environment-friendly vehicles to the Emirate, run on electricity or natural gas (The National 2016). DEWA and RTA - Dubai are working towards increasing the uptake of electric vehicles in the Emirate of Dubai. Notable is DEWA's Green Charger initiative that aims to build infrastructure for electric vehicles.

Buildings

Infrastructure – and the lifestyle choices it necessitates and offers – is an important component of the matrix that determines energy lifestyles. Buildings account for about 40% of global energy use and emit approximately one-third of the world's GHG emissions (United National Environment Programme 2016). In the UAE, about 60% of the electricity produced is consumed by the buildings sector. The buildings and construction sector in the UAE is a vast sphere of activity, which has received a boost from Dubai's successful bid to host EXPO 2020. It is critical for government bodies to ensure that the new buildings being built to house UAE's growing population and provide accommodation to visitors are resource efficient. A best practice followed globally to transform built infrastructure is to promulgate voluntary/compulsory building codes that lay down guidelines or requirements for building envelope and system design elements, site planning and construction practices, materials and technologies used for construction, and maintenance, amongst others.

In the UAE, the two emirates of Abu Dhabi and Dubai have green building regulations. Green building standards are under development in Ajman (Al Shamsi 2016). In Abu Dhabi, the Estidama Pearl Building Rating System was developed by the Urban Planning Council and implemented in November 2014. The Pearl Rating System is organised into seven categories with both mandatory and optional credits. To achieve a Pearl rating of 1, the complete set of mandatory credit requirements must be met. All new projects in the Emirate are required to achieve a minimum rating of 1 to receive approval and permits from the Abu Dhabi planning authorities while government-funded buildings must achieve a minimum 2 Pearl rating Abu Dhabi (Urban Planning Council and Municipality of Abu Dhabi City 2016). Also, beginning in October 2014, the Abu Dhabi International Building Code (including the International Energy Conservation Code) was made compulsory for all government projects. The Emirate of Dubai has adopted and implemented the *Green Building Regulations and Specifications in the Emirate of Dubai* that apply to all new buildings (DEWA and Dubai Municipality 2011). The regulations cover resource effectiveness and set minimum energy efficiency requirements for heating, ventilating, and air conditioning equipment and systems. In 2016, Dubai launched its own green building evaluation system, Al Sa'fat.

In line with demand side management in buildings, another area that Emirate-level governments are looking into is retrofitting the existing stock of buildings. Dubai aims to retrofit 30,000 buildings by 2030 during the first phase of its work through Etihad ESCO, a venture of DEWA (Zawya 2016). Fulfilment of the retrofit target would yield energy savings of 1.7 TWh and reduce CO_2 emissions by one million tonnes by 2030 (Etihad ESCO 2014).

Maximising the benefits of labels and standards

Energy labels and standards are one part of a larger ecosystem of energy policies that formulate a market transformation strategy (Energy Charter Secretariat 2009). Consumer education on the impacts of lifestyles on resource availability and the environment, and awareness programmes on labels and standards themselves, can be enablers for these regulations. Also, an integrated systems approach that focuses on the provision of cleaner power and fuel can multiple the energy and carbon savings that can be achieved by labels and standards alone. The sections below highlight select policy measures that governments can put in place to maximise the efficiency potential offered by labels and standards.

Consumer education

Lifestyles are effectively about individual decisions and behaviours. Even with available and accessible technology and infrastructure, consumer behaviour determines if these amenities are utilised and how. In an oil- and gas- rich country such as the UAE where lifestyles are energy-intensive, consumers often do not consider resource scarcity and the impacts of their choices on the environment in their lifestyle decisions. Regulatory interventions such as minimum performance standards that eliminate inefficient technologies from the market become even more important in such a social and economic context.

While energy labelling is directed at providing relevant product information to consumers, educating them on the need to move to better technologies and rational use of resources is pertinent for the success of labels. Often when making energy technology and infrastructure choices, consumers do not have enough information on available options, and their pros and cons. Regulatory frameworks for technology labels and performance standards thus need to include a strong public communications element that covers traditional and online media, social networks, point-of-sale information, targeted messaging through circulars, and consumer engagement events. For example, in line with the objectives of the fuel economy label, to assist consumers in making decisions when buying passenger cars or light trucks, ESMA has made available a web-based tool to allow consumers to check vehicle specifications, including fuel efficiency, of a range of makes and models. What is important, however, is to advertise such tools well so that they attract consumer traffic and reach a wide audience.

In addition to encouraging consumers to choose the right technologies, there is a need to alter consumer attitudes and behaviours to reduce wasteful use of energy. The UAE Ministry of Energy, for instance, provides an online application that allows a consumer to compare the electricity consumption of his home with an average UAE household and gives tips for reduction in consumption. Encouraging consumers not to waste power and water has also been a focus for public messaging campaigns of electricity and water authorities in the UAE. These authorities share energy-saving tips with their consumers through door-to-door messaging as well as online portals. DEWA has instituted consumer awards to honour those who use energy rationally and reduce usage of resources. The Regulation and Supervision Bureau of Abu Dhabi runs the Powerwise programme which aims to foreground energy and water consumption best practices. In 2016, the Sharjah Electricity and Water Authority has also set a target of reducing power and water use in the Emirate by 30% by the year 2021 (Sharjah Electricity and Water Authority 2015). In order to meet this target, SEWA is working to increase consumer awareness on the need for conservation and maintenance and use of appliances. Energy labelling programmes for appliances – such as those being advanced by UAE's ESMA at the federal level, is a highly recommended strategy to advance consumer knowledge.

Since consumption patterns are difficult to alter and efficient technologies can have high upfront costs, educating consumers on the monetary benefits they may accrue from energy-saving technologies and behaviours is an important component of a public engagement strategy. The mantra of 'saved energy is equivalent to saved money' needs to be highlighted. Given relatively lower costs, a consumer may choose to buy a two-star rated inefficient air conditioner vis-à-vis a more efficient one given the incremental price difference. A developer may be wary of equipping her properties with efficient appliances and electrical fittings and passing on the cost to the buyer/tenant who would be looking for a good bargain in the property market. These situations necessitate building local knowledge on potential energy savings and monetary benefits that are a result of using efficient technologies. Energy and environmental savings, as well as cost recovery periods, should be adequately advertised to consumers through media as well as point-of sale communication.

Pricing and financial incentives

The pricing of energy inputs – power and fuel, and technologies themselves – is one of the most important determinants of consumer decisions. Subsidised input prices and high technology costs keep consumers from moving to efficient products. In order to better understand barriers to energy and water efficiency in the private sector, Emirates Wildlife Society in association with WWF (EWS-WWF) conducted a statistically representative efficiency survey, in 2014–2015, across small and medium enterprises in Abu Dhabi, Dubai, and Sharjah (Rouchdy and Alam 2015). The survey brought to light three main perceived barriers to efficiency. These include: a) high costs of energy efficiency technologies; b) low availability of efficient products and lack of market accessibility; and c) limited understanding of power and water subsidies. Though the survey focused on the private sector, the results do help identify the way consumers think and act when making energy consumption decisions and holds learnings for understanding of household consumption. To address these barriers, the private sector respondents identified rebate schemes as a potential solution for high technology costs. For products availability and market access, capacity building on available technologies and institution of more minimum energy performance standards stood out as two solutions polled for. Awareness and capacity building on the issue of subsidies was highlighted as a solution to deal with lack of understanding of energy pricing and inherent subsidies.

Since energy expenditures command consumer attention, cost-reflective pricing of power sends a strong signal to consumers to transition to sustainable household technologies, with the opportunity for monetary savings. Tariffs for electricity across emirates in the UAE – though having been through a series of revisions – need to be re-evaluated and informed by the true costs of energy including environmental costs. The UAE government spent US$ 3.6 billion on subsidisation of fossil fuel-based electricity in 2014 (IEA 2015d). In 2015, the UAE government deregulated fuel prices, linking them to the international market. A fuel price committee now reviews prices against international prices every month. With continuing low fuel prices relative to other parts of the world, there is strong prevalence of energy-guzzling high-performance vehicles and 'driving pleasure' is relegated second to choosing fuel-efficient vehicles and eco-driving.

Consumer concerns about high costs of technology can be alleviated with interest-free loans, cash hand-outs and rebates. What is also critical here, as discussed above, is to communicate possible energy savings and payback timelines effectively. In the case of buildings, to promote developers to invest in efficient buildings and urban habitats, government regulation needs to address the challenge of split incentives where the technologies are fitted by the developer but the efficiency savings are reaped by the occupier of the property. Mandatory regulatory codes for new buildings can help address this to some extent by creating a level playing field for developers and owners. Also, financial incentives such as mortgage discounts for sustainable construction and renovation plans can make the sustainable habitats market more attractive (Krane 2010). Both supply and demand side actors in the residential buildings sector need to recognise sustainability, and its price implications, in transactions.

Leading by example

Government authorities themselves procure large numbers of energy goods and services, and provide infrastructural facilities. This affords them the opportunity to set an example for the community and alter consumption trends. The UAE has a range of government-led pilot projects on energy efficiency and renewable energy to demonstrate benefits, but government efforts in this domain need to be upscaled for wider and stronger consumer impact.

Sustainable procurement policies need to be put in place by all government entities that are large procurers of energy goods. Transforming public infrastructure can alter public perceptions and encourage private deployment of sustainability solutions. In this context, one initiative that can be cited is sustainable street lighting. Dubai Municipality has an ongoing programme to reduce energy consumption by following measures such as replacement of regular lights with light emitting diodes (LEDs) in public parks, use of electronic ballasts in municipal facilities, and installation of solar-powered lamp posts. The Emirate of Abu Dhabi has a Sustainable Public Lighting Strategy under which traditional lights in a number of areas have been replaced with efficient LEDs. It is estimated that, by 2035, the implementation of the Abu Dhabi strategy will bring down the total cost of public lighting by about 60–75%, power consumption by 60%, and CO_2 emissions by about 75% (Abu Dhabi City Municipality 2015). Further, to tackle the largest energy demand component of cooling, Abu Dhabi's Comprehensive Cooling Plan (2011–12) presented a mitigation strategy for consumption and recommended pilot projects for optimising chiller performance that were implemented over the following years.

Dubai's RTA and Abu Dhabi's TransAD, entities that manage cab fleets, have been bringing more hybrids into the UAE fleet of taxis. RTA has announced that 50% of Dubai cabs would be hybrid by 2021 (WAM 2016). Currently, DEWA is pioneering the use of electric vehicles. In Abu Dhabi, the Low Emission Vehicle Strategy, while setting an Emirate-wide target of converting 20% of the fleet to low emission vehicles by 2030, sets a 100% target for the government fleet for the same period.

Smart and sustainable infrastructure

It is important to note that an electrical appliance's impact on the environment is determined largely by the source of energy that is used to generate electricity to run it. Technology can bring energy and environmental savings, but an integrated energy systems approach needs to be followed to maximise the benefits of such interventions. In this context, one of the foremost structural changes that can propel energy consumers towards sustainable lifestyles is the establishment of sustainable power infrastructure. This would include increasing the share of renewables in the electricity mix, and therefore investing in renewables-based power generation facilities. Of critical importance also is the establishment of smart grid infrastructure that can link across different sources, and minimise losses, as well as provision of smart meters and services that allow closer monitoring of private consumers' consumption and provide data for policy planning. Decentralised renewable energy applications and energy efficiency can be combined through a smart grid, demand-response mechanisms, and energy storage systems.

The UAE has strategic plans and initial efforts in place to transition to such power infrastructure, including DEWA's launch of a Smart Power Plant – a centralised information system that gathers data from control systems in real time. DEWA and the Abu Dhabi Water and Electricity Authority have both rolled out smart meters. DEWA targets installing over a million smart meters by 2020 whereby current and historical meter readings would be made available to consumers to monitor their consumption (DEWA 2016).

Institutionalising cross-sectoral collaboration for an energy transformation

In order for efficiency labels and standards to achieve set sustainability targets, a range of stakeholders need to be involved in design and implementation. A policymaking process devoid of consultation may lead to promulgation of regulations that are not adequately informed by technical and practical aspects and/or do not have buy-in of implementers.

This chapter does not include regulatory compliance and market surveillance in its scope, but it is important to highlight that implementation mechanisms and definition of associated roles and responsibilities are critical for the efficacy of label and standard programmes. Strict adherence to product testing protocols and regular government checks are necessary to ensure that regulated manufacturers are complying with the set requirements. This has been underscored by recent developments in the field of vehicle fuel economy and emission standards – from installation of cheat devices in vehicles (defaulting Volkswagen cars were programmed to perform better during emission test cycles) to manipulation of data (the Mitsubishi case involves manipulation of fuel efficiency numbers through the use of "self-determined" test formats). There is a need in the UAE to strengthen ESMA with more technical staff, higher budgetary allocations, and a stronger mandate, particularly for implementation of standards.

As the UAE pursues regulatory processes that contribute to sustainable lifestyles, new government entities may need to be set up to fulfil new roles and plug gaps in governance. At the same time, these processes need to be supported by actors beyond government structures, including business associations, private players, and even civil society organisations. Such cooperation is necessitated by the multi-dimensional nature of energy policy design and implementation, and the range of capacities and skills required. Governments often benefit from working in collaboration with non-governmental entities that bring technical skills and expertise in niche areas. Some illustrations can already be seen in the UAE.

The Dubai Integrated Energy Strategy set a target for Dubai on retrofitting of old buildings. The implementation of this target is being led by Etihad ESCO established for the purpose in 2013. Etihad ESCO is engaged in establishing a viable contracting market for energy service companies by executing building retrofits, increasing penetration of district cooling, building capacity of local energy service companies (ESCOs), and facilitating access to project finance. A non-governmental entity that has come to be recognised as a key supporting player on greening of both old and new buildings is the Emirates Green Building Council (EmiratesGBC). Established in 2006, EmiratesGBC helps facilitate the adoption of green building practices in Dubai. It tracks relevant policy developments, compiles technical resources, and helps build local skills through trainings on energy management and green building design. In 2015, the EmiratesGBC published new guidelines for retrofitting of existing buildings, endorsed by DSCE and Ministry of Public Works. The 'Technical Guidelines for Retrofitting Existing Buildings' cover energy and water consumption, indoor air quality, building materials and waste, and management techniques directed at lowering utility and labour costs (Debusmann Jr. 2016).

Another successful partnership between government actors and civil society is the Ecological Footprint Initiative (EFI), a partnership between the UAE Ministry of Climate Change and Environment, Environment Agency – Abu Dhabi (EAD),

ESMA, Global Footprint Network, and EWS-WWF. EFI serves as a model of policy development that champions a science-based and consultative paradigm of decision-making. One of the most important successes of the EFI has been the adoption of the UAE indoor lighting standard. Developed under the aegis of the EFI, the standard is informed by technical analysis and extensive stakeholder engagement. In 2016, the Initiative concluded a technical study on UAE vehicle fuel economy that provided the basis for a regulatory proposal on fuel economy policies. EWS-WWF, a local non-governmental organisation and an associate office of the World Wide Fund for Nature, functions as the Secretariat of the Initiative, leading policy research and supporting the government in stakeholder engagement. On standards development, it coordinates technical assessments covering product baseline; regulatory scenarios and associated energy, economic, and environmental savings; required policy frameworks; and risks and mitigation strategies. EWS-WWF, and its role on the EFI, provide an example of the critical role that a non-governmental organisation (NGO) can play – working in collaboration with government agencies to further the agenda of low-carbon development.

In addition to developing labels and standards, and thus facilitating product access, governments need to ensure access to after-sales maintenance and operation services that may not be particularly abundant especially in the case of new technologies entering the domestic market. Governments thus are required to work closely with energy service companies and help build local capacity for technology maintenance. Inadequate local capacities for after-sales servicing can become a strong deterrent to uptake of technologies, and is therefore an area where regulatory frameworks need to pay special attention. The service provider market needs to be regulated to eliminate unqualified actors.

Consumer awareness is another area where the benefits of cross-sectoral collaboration are immense. Governments can work with schools, universities, companies, and local societies and communities to reach consumers across different age groups. The 'Heroes of the UAE' campaign (2010–2014) is one example of a national-level campaign on energy and water conservation, jointly developed by EWS-WWF and EAD. The campaign provided conservation tips and toolkits to households, businesses, and schools on deployment of efficient technologies and day-to-day consumption behaviours, and led to the development of the Corporate Heroes programme that signed on private actors to reduce their energy and water consumption, supported and audited the process and results, and rewarded successes (EWS-WWF 2016).

It is critical for a multi-stakeholder effort to gather momentum to deliver the energy savings possible from sustainable lifestyles. In the absence of required institutional capacities and multi-stakeholder inputs, the transition to sustainable lifestyles would be a slow process short of optimal impact and reach.

Conclusion

Innovations in energy technologies, and new models of finance and governance, have opened up a host of sustainable lifestyle possibilities that are feasible and pragmatic. Combining energy-efficient product choices and efficient consumption behaviours can bring significant energy and carbon savings for the UAE, and regulatory interventions in the form of efficiency labels and standards are critical to achieve them.

Efficiency labels and standards – particularly for household electrical appliances, vehicles, and buildings – present a powerful government tool to alter lifestyles in the country. These programmes reduce information and transaction costs for consumers, promote supply of efficient products by manufacturers, and support market transformation. At the same time, consumer education and awareness programmes are required to build a case for sustainability and to make consumers realise their power as agents of change. Government support schemes that help alleviate the high upfront costs associated with efficient technologies, along with rational pricing of electricity and fuel, can create the right financial and monetary incentives for consumers to adopt efficient technology applications. Additionally, government entities need to establish demonstration projects and institute sustainable procurement policies, while ensuring that an integrated energy systems transformation is underway to help optimise energy and environmental benefits of regulations. A regulatory process that is informed by robust science, internalises consultation amongst government actors, and takes cognizance of private sector and community concerns, can help advance energy standards and labels in the UAE as well as bring attendant energy, economic, environmental, and public health benefits.

References

Abdullatif, Laila, and Tanzeed Alam. 2014. *UAE Regulation on Lighting Products and Recommendations to Implement Its Implementation*. EWS-WWF. Available at: http://d2ouvy59p0dg6k.cloudfront.net/downloads/policy_brief_wwf_template_en_final.pdf (Accessed 17 June 2016).

Abu Dhabi City Municipality. 2015, January 8. *Abu Dhabi City Municipality Retrofits Traditional Lighting System With LED Lights, Saves More Than AED 3m Per Annum*. Municipal System Portal – Emirate of Abu Dhabi. Available at: https://municipalgateway.abudhabi.ae/en/ADM/MediaCenter/News/Pages/news2015.08.01.aspx (Accessed 19 June 2016).

Abu Dhabi Urban Planning Council, and Municipality of Abu Dhabi City. 2016. *Estidama: A Comprehensive Guide of Procedures for Implementing Estidama in the Municipality of Abu Dhabi City*. Available at: www.adm.gov.ae/uploads/New%20Folder/Estidama_Brochure_en.pdf (Accessed 24 May 2016).

Afshari, Afshin, Christina Nikolopoulou, and Miguel Martin. 2014. Life-cycle analysis of building retrofits at the urban scale – A case study in United Arab Emirates. *Sustainability*, 6(1): 453–473.

Al Shamsi, Fatima Al Foora. 2016. *Making the Transition: How the UAE is Moving to New, Sustainable Forms of Energy Use*. UAE State of Energy Report 2016. Ministry of Energy, Abu Dhabi/Dubai.

Bin, Shui, and Hadi Dowlatabadi. 2005. Consumer lifestyle approach to US energy use and the related CO2 emissions. *Energy Policy*, 33: 197–208.

Bressand, Florian, Diana Farrell, Pedro Haas, Fabrice Morin, Scott Nyquist, Jaana Remes, Sebastian Roemer, Matt Rogers, Jaeson Rosenfeld and Jonathan Woetzel. 2007. *Curbing Global Energy-Demand Growth: The Energy Productivity Opportunity*. McKinsey Global Institute.

Available at: www.mckinsey.com/business-functions/sustainability-and-resource-productivity/our-insights/curbing-global-energy-demand-growth (Accessed 18 June 2016).

Building Efficiency Initiative. 2010, April 29. *Integrating Efficiency and Renewable Energy to Maximize Benefits*. Available at: www.buildingefficiencyinitiative.org/articles/integrating-efficiency-and-renewable-energy-maximize-benefits (Accessed 27 May 2016).

Debusmann Jr., Bernd. 2016. Emirates Green Building Council unveils new guidelines for retrofitting of buildings. *Khaleej Times*, June 18.

DEWA. 2016. *Smart Applications Via Smart Meters and Grids*. Website of DEWA. Available at: www.dewa.gov.ae/en/customer/innovation/smart-initiatives/smart-applications-via-smart-meters-and-grids (Accessed 29 May 2016).

DEWA, and Dubai Municipality. 2011. *Green Building Regulations and Specifications in the Emirate of Dubai*. Available at: www.dm.gov.ae/wps/wcm/connect/662c2fc7-03b4-41a5-aad0-c9d1959773a3/Green+Building+Regulations+and+Speci.pdf?MOD=AJPERES (Accessed 22 May 2016).

Energy Charter Secretariat. 2009. *Policies That Work: Introducing Energy Efficiency Standards and Labels for Appliances and Equipment*. Energy Charter Secretariat. Available at: www.energycharter.org/fileadmin/DocumentsMedia/Thematic/EE_Standards_and_Labels_2009_en.pdf (Accessed 31 May 2016).

ESMA. 2014. Conformity Assessment System for Lighting Products. UAE: ESMA.

Etihad ESCO. 2014. *About Etihad ESCO*. Website of Etihad ESCO. Available at: www.etihadesco.ae/about-etihad-esco/ (Accessed 31 May 2016).

EWS-WWF. 2014. *UAE Energy Efficiency Lighting Standard What Does It Mean for You?* EWS-WWF. Available at: http://d2ouvy59p0dg6k.cloudfront.net/downloads/lighting_standard_infographic_english.pdf (Accessed 22 May 2016).

EWS-WWF. 2016. *Heroes of the UAE*. Website of EWS-WWF. Available at: http://uae.panda.org/ews_wwf/achievements/heroesoftheuae_achievement/ (Accessed 30 May 2016).

Global Energy Efficiency Accelerator Platform. 2016. *Appliances and Equipment*. Sustainable Energy for All. Available at: https://se4all.net/eeh/content/appliances-and-equipment (Accessed 16 May 2016).

Hart, Craig A. 2013. Climate Change and the Private Sector: Scaling Up Private Sector Response to Climate Change. New York: Routledge.

IEA. 2014, October 8. *Global Energy Efficiency Market "An Invisible Powerhouse" Worth at Least USD 310 Billion Per Year*. Press Release. Available at: www.iea.org/newsroomandevents/pressreleases/2014/october/global-energy-efficiency-market-an-invisible-powerhouse-at-least-usd-310byr.html (Accessed 13 May 2016).

IEA. 2015a. Energy Balances of Non-OECD Countries. Paris: IEA, p. 5.

IEA. 2015b. *Energy Efficiency Market Report 2015*. International Energy Agency. Available at: www.iea.org/publications/freepublications/publication/MediumTermEnergyefficiencyMarketReport2015.pdf (Accessed 13 May 2016).

IEA. 2015c. Achievements of Appliance Energy Efficiency Standards and Labelling Programs: A Global Assessment. Paris: IEA, pp. 24, 32.

IEA. 2015d. *IEA Fossil Fuel Subsidies Database*. Available at: www.worldenergyoutlook.org/resources/energysubsidies/52 (Accessed 29 May 2016).

International Council on Clean Transportation, and Emirates Wildlife Society in association with WWF. 2016. *An Assessment to Help the UAE Develop Vehicle Fuel Economy Policies*. Technical Study Undertaken for the Ecological Footprint Initiative, EWS-WWF. Unpublished.

International Renewable Energy Agency. 2015. *Synergies Between Renewable Energy and Energy Efficiency: A Working Paper Based on REMap 2030*. IRENA. Available at: www.irena.org/DocumentDownloads/Publications/IRENA_C2E2_Synergies_RE_EE_paper_2015.pdf (Accessed 20 June 2016).

Karlsson, Per-Ola, Christopher Decker, and Jad Moussalli. 2015. *Energy Efficiency in the UAE: Aiming for Sustainability*. Report by Strategy& based on a workshop initiated and sponsored by the Energy Working Group of the UAE-UK Business Council. Available at: www.strategyand.pwc.com/media/file/Energy-efficiency-in-the-UAE.pdf (Accessed 15 May 2016).

Krane, Jim. 2010. *Energy Conservation Options for GCC Governments*. Dubai School of Government Policy Brief No. 18. Dubai School of Government, Dubai.

Meyers, S., J.E. McMahon, M. McNeil, and X. Liu. 2003. Impacts of US federal energy efficiency standards for residential appliances. *Energy*, 28(8): 755–767.

Molenbroek, Edith, Matthew Smith, Nesen Surmeli, Sven Schimschar, Paul Waide, Jeremy Tait, and Catriona McAllister. 2015. *Savings and Benefits of Global Regulations for Energy Efficient Products*. European Commission. Available at: https://ec.europa.eu/energy/sites/ener/files/documents/Cost%20of%20Non-World%20-%20Final%20Report.pdf (Accessed 18 May 2016).

The National. 2016. Abu Dhabi Executive Council approves Dh166m in projects. *The National*, May 08.

Prindle, Bill, Maggie Eldridge, Mike Eckhardt, and Alyssa Frederick. 2007. *The Twin Pillars of Sustainable Energy: Synergies Between Energy Efficiency and Renewable Energy Technology and Policy*. ACEEE Report No. E074. American Council for an Energy-Efficient Economy. Available at: http://citeseerx.ist.psu.edu/viewdoc/download?doi=10.1.1.545.4606&rep=rep1&type=pdf (Accessed 12 May 2016).

Rouchdy, Nadia, and Tanzeed Alam. 2015. *What Is Holding Back the Private Sector?* EWS-WWF. Available at: http://d2ouvy59p0dg6k.cloudfront.net/downloads/e_w_web_english_f.pdf (Accessed 29 May 2016).

Sharjah Electricity and Water Authority. 2015. *The Declaration of Sharjah City of Conservation*. SEWA. Available at: www.sewa.gov.ae/en/content.aspx?P=4JVpzOgumWxxDeo5mu1mhQ%3d%3d (Accessed 28 May 2016).

Todorova, Vesela 2011. A fifth of air-conditioning units face ban. *The National*, February 20.

UAE Ministry of Energy. 2016. *Case Study UAE*. UAE State of Energy Report 2016. Ministry of Energy, Abu Dhabi/Dubai.

UAE Ministry of Environment and Water. 2014. *UAE State of Green Economy*. UAE Ministry of Environment and Water, Abu Dhabi/Dubai.

United Nations. *Sustainable Development Goals*. Sustainable Development Knowledge Platform. Available at: https://sustainabledevelopment.un.org/?menu=1300. (Accessed 18 July 2016).

United Nations Environment Programme. 2016. *Why Buildings*. UNEP Sustainable Buildings and Climate Initiative. Available at: www.unep.org/sbci/AboutSBCI/Background.asp. (Accessed 24 May 2016).

van Leijen, Majorie. 2015. Will more UAE commuters use public transport? *Emirates 24/7*, July 23. Available at: www.emirates247.com/news/emirates/will-more-uae-commuters-use-public-transport-2015-07-23-1.597711 (Accessed 27 May 2016).

WAM. 2016, February 6. *RTA Plans to Convert 50% of Dubai Taxi Fleet to Hybrid Cabs by 2021: Al Tayer*. WAM. Available at: http://wam.ae/en/news/emirates/1395291233478.html (Accessed 31 May 2016).

Wiel, Stephens, and James E. McMahon. 2001. *Energy Efficiency Labels and Standards: A Guidebook for Appliances, Equipment and Lighting.* Washington, DC: Collaborative Labeling and Appliance Standards Programme.

The Abdullah Bin Hamad Al-Attiyah Foundation for Energy & Sustainable Development. 2015. Reversing the trend in domestic energy consumption in the GCC: Consequences of success & failure? *Industry Report November 2015*. Available at: http://thegulfintelligence.com/uploads/Publications/Industry%20Report.pdf (Accessed 06 May 2017)

The World Bank. 2014a. *Energy Use*. Website of The World Bank. Available at: http://data.worldbank.org/indicator/EG.USE.PCAP.KG.OE (Accessed 13 May 2016).

The World Bank. 2014b. *Electric Power Consumption*. Website of The World Bank. Available at: http://data.worldbank.org/indicator/EG.USE.ELEC.KH.PC (Accessed 1 June 2016).

The World Bank. 2015. *The Little Green Data Book 2015*. Available at: https://openknowledge.worldbank.org/bitstream/handle/10986/22025/9781464805608.pdf (Accessed 24 May 2016).

The World Bank and IEA. 2015. *Overview: Global Tracking Framework*. Available at: www.iea.org/media/freepublications/oneoff/GlobalTrackingFrameworkOverview.pdf (Accessed 16 May 2016).

Zawya. 2016, April 30. *DEWA Visits China to Visit Energy Projects in the UAE and Dubai*. Available at: www.zawya.com/story/DEWA_visits_China_to_boost_energy_projects_in_the_UAE_and_Dubai-ZAWYA20160430063748/ (Accessed 24 May 2016).

10 Sustainability assessment for real estate in the UAE

The case of Masdar City

Natalia Karayaneva and Mark Coleman

Introduction

The current state of the built environment is having a negative impact on the environment. UNEP (2011) estimates that 40% of global energy is used by buildings and that about 30% of greenhouse gas (GHG) is emitted by buildings globally. Beyond resource consumption and carbon emissions, the residential sector (70% of all buildings) has social and economic issues such as affordability, safety, walkability, access to public transit and the like (Lorenz 2011). Housing is one of humanity's basic needs alongside with nutrition and health. It influences the daily lives of people and affects future generations – therefore housing is a core part of sustainable development. On 1 January 2016, the 2030 Agenda for Sustainable Development with the 17 Sustainable Development Goals (SDGs) officially came into force after they were first adopted by the world leaders in September 2015 at a UN Summit. Sustainable city life is the 11th goal of SDGs that addresses the challenge to make cities inclusive, safe and sustainable. To achieve progress in sustainable urban development, many requirements should be met: affordable housing, sustainable urban infrastructure, sustainable public transportation, improved waste management, further investment in renewable energy and sustainable built environment (Wilson 2015).

Advancements in technology, energy, building products and materials, business models and development approaches have emerged and provoked a change in the status quo. Disruption is now viewed as a source of resilience. In the past decade, government, business and society have demonstrated greater awareness and a deeper understanding of anthropogenic-induced climate change. In the fall of 2015, nations met in Paris for COP21 to deliberate on how a global climate strategy and accord could be reached. Then, in December 2015, a historic global agreement was reached when 195 countries adopted the first-ever universal and legally binding global climate deal.

The backdrop to COP21 is a generational movement of people who are committing themselves to live with purpose and impact. A sustainability generation has emerged and is gaining force. Consumer markets for fair trade food, organic food, social investing, green building, renewable energy and cleaner transport have all demonstrated increases in market share and total value in the past 10 years.

A market study, "Consumer Trends in Sustainability", conducted by Solar City and Clean Edge noted that in 2011 93% of Americans had done something to conserve energy and 77% had done something to conserve water. Consumers are demanding more renewable energy and greener alternatives in the products and services they buy.

Promoting a sustainable housing for consumers and the industry has become an important policy consideration worldwide (Wong et al. 2010). Different countries have introduced green building assessment certificates, regulations and targets to drive energy-efficient and environmentally friendly housing. These green building certifications play both a role in determining guidelines for the design and construction and for consumer awareness (Kibert 2008).

Taking into account the attributes that affect the value of a residential building, the author suggests a simplified scheme shown at Figure 10.1, which illustrates those attributes that impact residents and produces environmental loads. For instance, the proximity of a building to public transportation adds value to the real estate assets, as well as delivers benefits to the residents and the environment. High levels of air pollution affect the value of nearby properties as well as negatively affect residents and the environment. Thus, these attributes should be considered

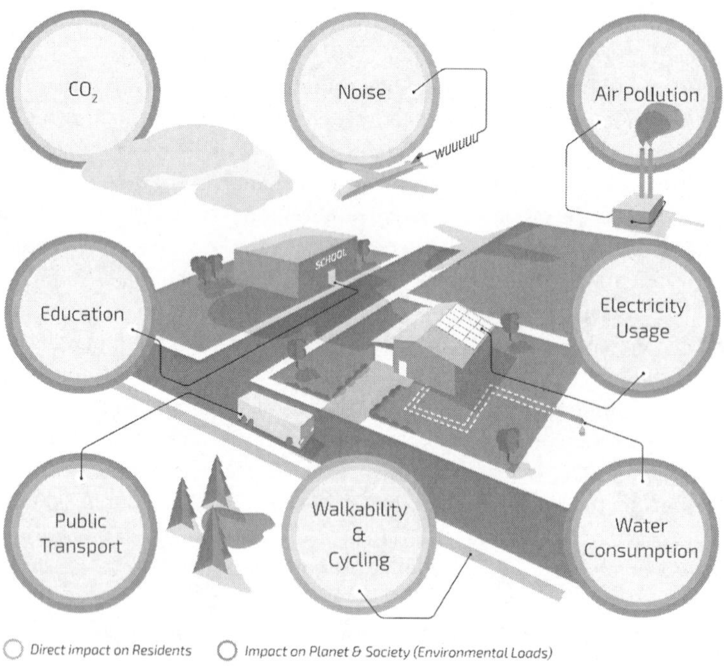

Figure 10.1 Key attributes for sustainability assessment and residential real estate value

Source: Natalia Karayaneva, 2015

in the sustainability assessment of buildings and delivered in understandable metrics to the consumers who make decisions when choosing a home.

How to measure sustainable housing

The necessity for pursuing sustainability in the real estate sector has been well established by researchers including Myers (2011), Lorenz (2011), Boyd and Kimmet (2005) and Sayce et al. (2004).

Green Building or *Sustainable Building* as a result of *Sustainable Construction* refer to both materials and processes which are resource efficient and environmentally and socially responsible throughout the entire building's lifecycle (Kibert 2008).

Today, more than 100 different energy and sustainability assessment systems, ratings and certifications (further all called SA tools) operate for the built environment in different countries (Fischlein and Smith 2010). Many researchers focus their attention on the analysis of assessment methodologies and of the reliability of sustainability metrics in real estate. Existing literature mostly covers studies on the several leading voluntary sustainability certifications for buildings, and government building energy performance assessment methods in different countries (Nelson 2012). The majority of studies on sustainability assessment are focused on the UK, US, and Australia's real estate markets. As far as the Gulf and other markets are concerned, analysts have mostly investigated the employment of the international BREEAM and LEED systems, as well as criticized their implementation into different markets (Ding 2008).

The benchmarking systems for the built environment have been illustrated by researchers as an important instrument in the drive for sustainable housing, as it allows targets to be set and encourages consumer demand for sustainable homes, and thus *encourages sustainable lifestyles* (Lorenz 2011).

Regardless of the advantages of the independent evaluation external assessment tools provide, the point-based method of scoring used by all current tools does not permit those sustainable projects which focus on particular criteria such as, for instance, embodied carbon emissions or water conservation (critical for the Gulf) to achieve high scores since those parameters are either missing or underestimated in some SA systems (Ding 2008). By contrast, the developers that follow conventional construction principles operate under the misconception widely held in the industry that achieving urban sustainability has basically to do with materials or equipment used in the construction phase (Bowen 2014). The world's acceptance that buildings should be sustainable or 'green' by simply using 'green' materials, incorporating high tech in buildings and obtaining green building certifications has misled the sector and its consumers from the real issues of the holistic concept of sustainability (Bowen 2014). Thus, researchers admit the need for a new holistic assessment approach to facilitate market participants with guidance in qualifying sustainable buildings (Ali and Nsairat 2009).

Though the current SA tools for buildings are designed to be comprehensive (Cole 1999), there are many constraints and limitations in the leading SA tools today. Ding (2008) claims that the main limitations of the existing SA tools include complexity, non-applicability to different locations and typology and inadequate consideration of a weighting system. In addition, Siew et al. (2013) criticize the developers of the tools for inadequate scores allocation for different types of projects. Furthermore, Baird (2009) concluded that there is a need to implement user performance attributes in the SA tools.

The lack of essential quantitative sustainability metrics are been considered and addressed by a number of researchers in the context of sustainability reporting and metrics. Nelson (2012, 18) discussed the metrics proposed by the Green Property Alliance, which in 2010 defined four categories that are the key output metrics for sustainability both for the industry and consumers:

- Energy use (e.g. kWh/m^2 area or occupancy/year)
- Carbon emissions (e.g. kg CO_2e/m^2 area or per occupant/year)
- Water consumption (e.g. m^3/m^2 area occupancy/year)
- Waste produced (e.g. tonnes/by reference to occupancy or area/year)

Thus, according to Nelson, the lack of proper outputs, consensus on standards and credibility of the tools' operators contribute to inefficient sustainability assessment for the real estate sector (2012).

Sustainability assessment worldwide: classification

This section examines the selection and the classification of SA tools related to residential real estate. There are over 100 SA tools in existence and currently in use in the world (Fischlein and Smith 2010). For the purpose of the study more than 90 tools related to residential real estate were reviewed and have been placed in a classification proposed in Figure 10.1.

More than 90 potentially significant tools were identified from recent studies. Screening criteria are developed to narrow down the list of SA tools. Fowler and Rauch (2006) in their research identified via a survey the main criteria for evaluating SA tools: measurability, applicability, availability, development, usability, system maturity, technical content, communicability, and cost. Nineteen SA tools for buildings are chosen to review according to the following screening criteria:

- from the point of applicability, tools are chosen for residential buildings and communities
- from the point of operating tools, only third-party assessment tools are selected

A quantitative method of collecting data was created to define the tools with the highest number of buildings assessed. After narrowing down the list of SA tools, a number of building SA tools and community SA tools is examined using the criteria to provide classification. The study will further consider almost all of the criteria suggested by Fowler and Rauch (2006) but will focus mainly on measurability (the outputs of the tools), availability (different locations) and applicability (typology of buildings, policy involvement and number of buildings).

Classification of the SA tools for residential real estate

After reviewing more than 90 SA tools and literature concerning frameworks of the tools (Burnett 2007), the classification of the tools that are most appropriate for the residential sector was devised and represented in Figure 10.2.

The classification will allow further to set the base for both quantitative and qualitative research.

Community assessment tools

Sustainability assessment for communities plays a significant role in the valuation of residential real estate, as certain indicators such as public transportation access, walkability and access to amenities are crucial indicators for consumer choice and property value.

The community SA tools are applicable for large real estate developments and as voluntary systems aim to facilitate developers to address the sustainability aspects. In a closer review of the credit criteria the SA tools for communities pay attention to resource efficiency, quality of buildings, safety, public transport access,

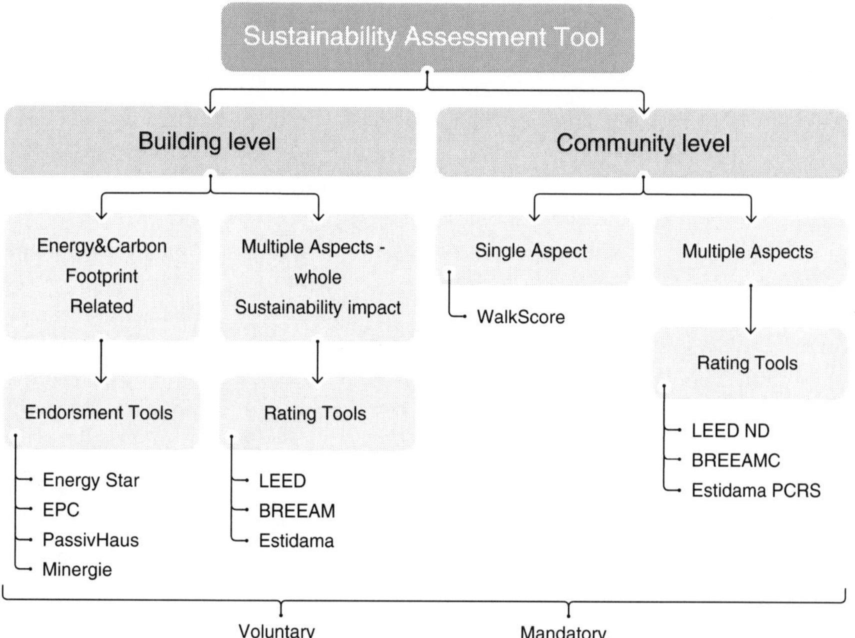

Figure 10.2 Classification of SA tools for real estate

air quality, noise pollution and access to amenities; however, underestimating walkability valuation is witnessed in many of the tools (Sharifi and Murayama 2013). In relation to walkability – a challenge in the Gulf – it is worth mentioning a related single aspect assessment tool – well adopted in the US and Canada and becoming global – WalkScore, which measures pedestrian access to amenities. Walkability level influences the property value (Pivo and Fisher 2011).

Sustainability assessment standards worldwide

The study collects data on methodological and contextual parameters for the researched SA tools and the quantity of certified buildings. Public online information about the quantity of the assessed buildings however is limited. The quantitative research sets out the following framework:

- Determination of the most widely used sustainability tools for buildings and communities, including the Gulf countries.
    - The collection of data on categorical variables for the selected sustainability assessment tools
    - The collection of data on quantitative variables – number of buildings assessed.

Among the range SA tools available for analyzing real estate, for the study 19 SA tools were chosen and reviewed in the table below. Among them LEED and BREEAM are the international tools used in the Gulf. Estidama and GSAS are the local tools used in the Gulf – UAE and Qatar accordingly. The selection of SA tools used the following baseline criteria: SA tools must have been used to assess a minimum of 300 buildings or SA tools must have been recognized as globally accepted, but without having any data available to the public.

In the Table 10.1 the information consists of both methodological (development basis, community assessment) and contextual (international adoption, policy involvement, number of assessed buildings) data.

Table 10.1 illustrates that the majority (12 of 19) of the researched SA systems (including Estidama) included community assessment tools, which demonstrates that their operators consider a holistic assessment approach. As far as the other methodological aspect, according to the table, six of the 15 multiple-aspect SA tools (the data on four of the SA tools is undisclosed) were created by modifying a single system or integrating multiple systems and thus are similar in methodological approach of the evaluating process.

Next, the data of Table 10.1 illustrates that governments have adopted SA tools in urban policies and as a prerequisite for obtaining any building permits at least for some sectors (government and commercial buildings), which will further increase sustainability awareness.

In order to statistically analyze the impact of the tools on the built environment it is essential to understand how many buildings the researched tools, including Estidama Rating System, were applied to. A request for the number

Table 10.1 Usage of the most widely used SA tools for residential buildings[1]

Sustainability Assessment tools for buildings	*Development basis and origin*	*Countries actively using*	*Involvement in policies*	*International applicability*	*Separate community assessment*	*Amount of buildings (period)*
Energy-focused endorsement tools						
EPC	Original, EU	EU, 27 countries	✓ M	✓	–	593,749 buildings by September 2015
Energy Star	Original, US	US, > 10 countries	✓	–	–	25,504 buildings by 2015
PassivHaus	Original, Germany	Mainly Germany and Austria, >15 countries	–	✓	–	> 30,000 buildings by 2013
Minergie	Undisclosed	France, Italy, Germany and US	✓	–	–	37,965 buildings by 2015
Multiple-aspect building assessment rating tools						
BREEAM	Original, UK	UK, Canada, > 50 countries	✓ PM	✓	✓	200,000 by 2012
CASBEE	Original, Japan	Japan	✓ PM	✓	✓	450 buildings by April 2015; >14,000 assessed projects by March 2014
DGNB	Original, Germany	Germany, >25 countries	–	✓	✓	1,281 by 2015
Estidama PRS	LEED, BREEAM, Energy Star + original, UAE	Abu Dhabi	✓ M	–	✓✓	12,920 2008–2015

(*Continued*)

Table 10.1 (Continued)

Sustainability Assessment tools for buildings	*Development basis and origin*	*Countries actively using*	*Involvement in policies*	*International applicability*	*Separate community assessment*	*Amount of buildings (period)*
GBTool	Original, Korea; 20 countries participated	Global	–	✓	–	N/A
GBL or 3 star	Undisclosed, China	China (Mainland)	✓	–	✓	1,409 buildings by 2015
Green Globes	BREEAM and Canadian version	Canada, US	✓	–	–	2,600 buildings by 2015
Green Mark Singapore	LEED	Singapore	✓	–	✓	836 by 2015
Green Star Australia	BREEAM, LEED	Australia, South Africa	✓	✓	✓	669 by 2015
GRIHA	Undisclosed, India	India	✓	–	✓	650 by 2015
HK BEAM	BREEAM	Hong Kong	✓	–	✓	319 by 2015
HQE	BREEAM; France	Mainly France, >5 countries in Europe, popular globally	–	✓	✓	266,000 by 2015
LEED	Original, US	US, China, Australia, Canada, India, Mexico; >30 countries	✓	✓	✓	Globally – 41,466 buildings and US – 63,588; China – 1,988 buildings 2015; Canada – 3,071 by 2015
NABERS	Undisclosed, Australia	Australia	✓	–	–	856 by 2015
GSAS (ex-QSAS)	Original, Qatar	The Gulf, Global		✓	✓	N/A

1 The information for the tools used in the table is taken from the official websites of the tool operators.

of Estidama certified building was initially sent to the Abu Dhabi UPC and no response was received. The necessary information was found at the stand of the UPC during the CityScape exhibition on 21st of April (Figure 10.3) and summarized in Table 10.2.

Analyzing the presented data in Table 10.1, it can be inferred that the majority of the SA tools, since they first were introduced 25 years ago (BREEAM 2015), have not produced a significant impact on the real estate market as of 2015 in terms of the number of certified buildings. Internationally, according to the

Figure 10.3 The display of the UPC with Estidama achievements

Source: (CityScape 2015)

Table 10.2 Number of Estidama certified buildings

Estidama certifications		
Type	*Number of buildings*	*Gross floor area*
Pearl rated villas	11,881	15.5 million m^2
Pearl rated buildings	921	
Pearl rated schools	118	
Total	12,920	

Source: Figure 10.3

collected data, 687,218 buildings were assessed by 4 energy-focused tools and 593,044 buildings were assessed/certified by multiple-aspect SA tools. These numbers are low and could be compared to a scale of one city with 1,053,713 buildings – namely, 8.4 million populated New York City. It could be assumed a range of roughly 250–500 million buildings in the cities, which are populated by 3.9 billion urban people. There are more than 428,270 buildings in six million populated Abu Dhabi (Alobaidi et al. 2015), among which, 12,920 are Estidama certified, which is an impressive achievement for the four years of the Estidama mandate. This takes into account that most of the 70 existing tools reviewed for the research have assessed fewer than 1,000 buildings – globally or in any particular country.

The graph on Figure 10.4 represents the number of assessed buildings by energy-focused endorsement tools and whole building rating tools; the number of the energy-focused certifications issued is higher than the number of the multiple-aspect building certifications issued. EPC is the most widely used among all the tools, which represents more than half a million assessed buildings. As for the multiple-aspect

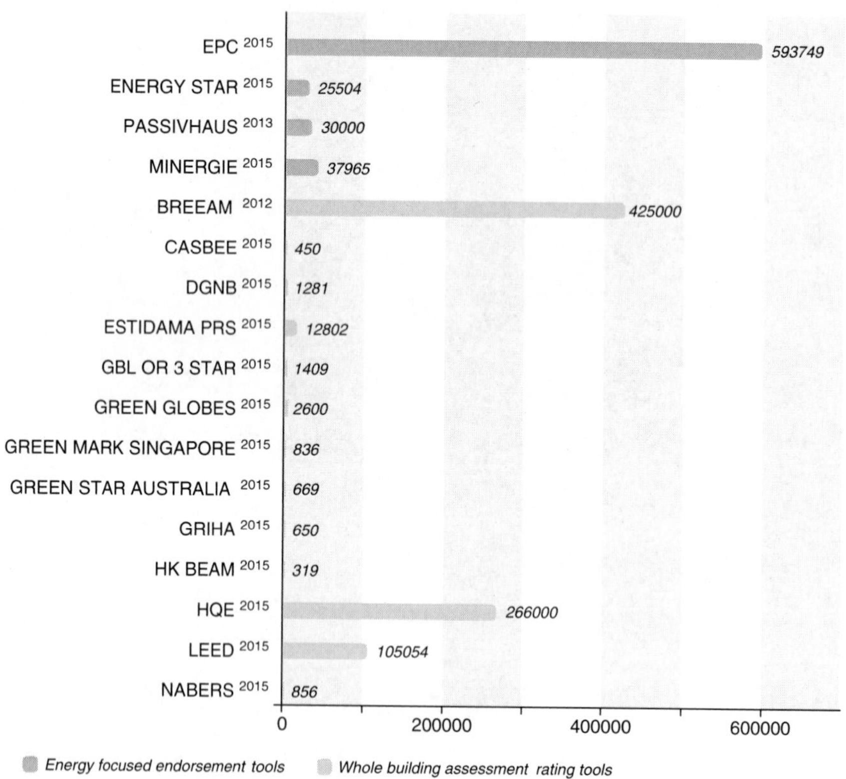

Figure 10.4 Number of buildings assessed; from the year of introduction to the year when the latest data was published

Source: Table 10.1

building assessment tools HQE, BREEAM, LEED and Estidama System, these assessment tools have the largest impact on buildings representing between 12,802 to 266,000 issued rating certifications. All other multiple-aspect tools have assessed less than 2,600 buildings. The analysis of the quantity of certified buildings and assessment tools in major markets demonstrates that SA tools have a higher quantitative impact on the real estate market when they are policy-driven (as for example the EPC in the EU countries and Estidama in Abu Dhabi).

The review of the tools and the compiled data demonstrated that *Estidama System stands out* in the list of internationally known tools, even though the tool was introduced only 7 years ago.

Among the selected multiple-aspect rating tools, only Estidama considers the operational cycle of all the four stages of the lifecycle of a building (UPC 2010). The other SA tools focus on only two stages: material acquisition and construction. This creates a distinctive aspect for Estidama because the audit and inspection are carried out at during the four key stages of the building lifecycle. During the construction and competition phases, the Pearl Operational Rating System is applied so that on site testing can be conducted in order to reduce defects and liability issues. Furthermore, this removes instances of non-compliance (UPC 2010).

Estidama stands out as the only mandatory tool among the multiple-aspect rating tools. The application of Estidama and LEED will be researched in the context of the selected real estate development Masdar City, which the highest sustainability targets as an eco-district in the region.

Sustainable housing in UAE

The UAE is one of the largest energy and water consumers due to cooling purposes in its harsh climatic conditions. Buildings account for 70% of this consumption (Saifur 2012). The government heavily subsidizes utility tariffs as follows: the electricity subsidy in residential buildings ranged from 55% to 90% and the water subsidy ranged from 79% to 100% as of 2015 (see Figure 10.3). Water and electricity generation are closely linked in the UAE as they tend to be produced in natural gas fired co-generation power plants (UPC 2015). With natural gas sources increasing in price and the oil price falling, it is becoming expensive for the government to maintain the provision of water and electricity. It is estimated that such subsidies cost the government US$ 17 billion in 2014 (Augustine 2015). Some subsidy reduction initiatives were taken at the beginning of this year for the first time in 13 years for non-UAE-nationals (Bouyamoun 2015). The increase in utility bills has affected non-UAE-nationals and accounts for 20% to 175% depending on the type of building and consumption (Augustine 2015). Linking this case to investment of the government into efforts for green building incentives will be suggested further.

Reducing overconsumption and increasing awareness about sustainability in the residential sector in the region is critical (Issa and Abbar 2015) and thus related and adequate sustainability assessment tools for buildings are needed. As shown in Figure 10.5, residential and commercial buildings cost almost 70% of the energy consumption in the UAE. A study made by Issa and Abbar (2015) has reviewed

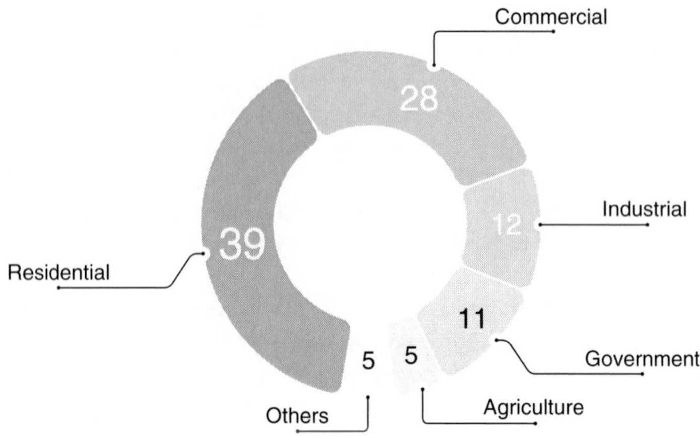

Figure 10.5 Energy consumption by sector in the UAE

Source: Adapted from Saifur (2012)

and analyzed the major building codes and green building ratings in Gulf countries and concluded that further development of tools and reformation of the building codes are required. A brand developed tool alone for the whole region will not solve the existing constraints in assessing buildings due to differing regulations for obtaining building permits (Issa and Abbar 2015). In the UAE, Dubai and Abu Dhabi have introduced different strategies and tools for sustainable housing.

Institutional setup of the green buildings councils in UAE and GCC

With record-breaking construction projects valued at $1.67 trillion in 2013 in the GCC, the development of green building policies has also strived in the region, which is developing towards sustainability in the post-oil era (Issa and Abbar 2015).

The GCC has three well-established green building policies:

Abu Dhabi: mandatory Estidama building certifications managed by the Abu Dhabi Urban Planning Council

Dubai: mandatory green building codes for all governmental projects from 2011 and for all private projects from 2014 – Green Building Regulations managed by Dubai Municipality;

Qatar: GSAS (Global Sustainability Assessment System) applicable in the entire region managed by GORD (Gulf Organization for Research and Development, a subsidiary of the QATARI DIAR Real Estate Investment Company) since 2009

The main aim of these councils is to improve the quality of new construction and performance of buildings by reducing the energy, water and materials consumption (Dubai Municipality 2014). Green building codes and SA tools in the region demonstrate the efforts and investments of governments in embedding sustainability in the construction industry. In UAE only one local SA tool has been adopted widely, namely Estidama Pearl Rating System in Abu Dhabi.

Estidama

'Estidama' is the Arabic word for sustainability. Estidama Systems are the tools for all new buildings and communities and is a part of 'Abu Dhabi Vision 2030', a new large-scale urban master plan for the city (UPC 2015). Abu Dhabi has one of the fastest growing urban expansions to account for the explosion in population growth, which stood at 2.12 million in 2011 (Alobaidi et al. 2015). Furthermore, it also has one of the highest GDPs per capita in the world with only 15% of the UAE-nationals (Cugurullo 2013). In 2010, the number of residential buildings comprised 165,072 among the overall 428,270 building stock (Alobaidi et al. 2015).

UPC introduced the mandatory assessment of all new buildings prior to issuing building permits. Estidama PRS received a government mandate in July 2010 and has been implemented essentially free of charge – provided by the government to ensure all new projects are included. The construction industry has been actively trained to accelerate the spread of awareness through the industry and wider population (UPC 2015).

Estimada PRS is a mandatory rating system developed by the Abu Dhabi's UPC, which stands out in the group of multiple-aspect assessment tools. Estimada consists of four different rating systems and this study will examine two of these: the Pearl Building Rating System and the Pearl Community Rating System (UPC 2015).

Due to the cost of implementation, assessment systems are being criticized in a 'greenwashing' context of new urbanism (Low 2008). In contrast to the international LEED and BREEAM certification systems, expenses for the Estidama certification are covered by the government. The consumer awareness about energy conservation issues, climate change and sustainable living are seen as the main drivers in increasing the demand for sustainable homes in the UAE (UPC 2015). Current research also aims to demonstrate a lack of consumer-focused attributes – insufficient output metrics – the SA systems, which might be one of the reasons for low awareness and low consumer demand for green buildings in the residential sector in contrast to the increasing demand for green buildings in the educated commercial real estate market (DeFrancesco and Levy 2008). The present paper will support this argument for Masdar City and explore additional issues, such as the lack of holistic approach in the SA methods.

Case study: Masdar City

The most ambitious project of Abu Dhabi to address sustainability is Masdar City – a settlement that aims to become one of the most sustainable communities in the region by 2030 (Alusi et al. 2011). Masdar consists of five entities including 'Masdar City', which is the developer of the site (Masdar 2015), and is the central focus of this study. A mandatory green building certification Estidama, introduced by

Abu Dhabi's UPC in 2010, and the international tool LEED have been used to assess buildings in Masdar City (AlNaqbi et al. 2012).

Although Masdar City is suggested in this study as a project of a sustainable settlement, it is often mentioned by academics in a negative context (i.e. Cugurullo 2013; Hodson and Marvin 2010; Lau 2012). Masdar City's stakeholders aim to create the first truly sustainable community, which benefits from the environmental advantages of traditional Arabian design (Lau 2012). However being a project owned by the Abu Dhabi governmental company, it may be seen as one of those Arabian urban projects defined by David Harvey, which

> have emerged in the Middle East in places like Dubai and Abu Dhabi as a way of mopping up the capital surpluses arising from oil wealth in the most conspicuous, socially unjust and environmentally wasteful ways possible.
>
> (Harvey 2012: 12)

Masdar City is being criticized because the increasing popularity of sustainability stimulates its commoditizing which in consequence leads to city 'greenwashing'. Moreover, its recent development could be defined as socially regressive as it breaks the communication with nearby communities and thus is considered unsustainable long term (Hodson and Marvin 2010).

Masdar City's stakeholders have a goal to set an international example for sustainable urban development for a city for 100,000 people. This sustainable neighborhood has a scope for further development and the prospective demand for sustainable homes can only be forecasted and examined as one of the many aims of the stakeholders. This is the reason this study examines the implementation of local and international sustainability tools applied to Masdar City and the perspective of the developers on driving consumer demand for sustainable lifestyle.

Currently less than 1,000 residents, who are mainly students of the Masdar Institute, inhabit Masdar City. The buildings completed are those of the campus, offices, Siemens HQ and IRENA Global HQ. The last building completed in 2015 is IRENA Global HQ with a building rating of 4 pearls by PRS and its own performance calculations: annual energy consumption/m^2 GFA – 121 kWh/m^2/year and embodied carbon in materials – 410 kgCO_2/m^2 (Masdar 2015).

The first building certified by the Estidama Pearl Building Rating System in Masdar is the IRENA HQ's building (Masdar 2015). The building was completed in January 2015 and was the first building in Abu Dhabi to achieve a PBRS 4 Pearls certification. Other buildings were not assessed by any rating system until LEED was used for the Siemens HQ, which was opened in January 2014 (Masdar 2015). The building achieved a LEED Platinum certification and is on target for receiving an Estidama PBRS 3 Pearls (of maximum 5) certification. The only residential buildings completed are the students' dorms, which have not been certified. Through the qualitative method the case study below will examine how the Masdar stakeholders are addressing the application of both mandatory PBRS and PCRS and voluntary LEED, as well as how targets are set for the buildings and the community to validate the high level of sustainability.

The research methodology

This study has aims to identify the role and constraints of sustainability assessment for real estate. To accomplish this, further investigation of the viability of SA will be required by asking a range of questions such as:

1 What is the role of SA tools for consumers, developers and the industry?
2 What is missing in the SA tools to assess adequately sustainable developments such as Masdar City?
3 What are the advantages of government-driven SA tools such as Estidama?

As far as Masdar City is not finished and not permanently inhabited, industry expert perceptions become central to the explanation of these research questions.

The research used a case study method with qualitative data collecting from a group of interviewees. The selected group of experts (both UAE and non-UAE nationals) have in-depth knowledge of sustainability and regional standards. The group was selected by their expertise and involvement in sustainability strategy for Masdar City, in-depth knowledge of the applied to Masdar City systems Estidama and LEED in both design and construction stages. Table 10.3 describes the six experts interviewed for this study.

Table 10.3 Interviewees and their roles

Intervewees	*Position*	*Role*	*Domain of knowledge*
1	An executive of Masdar City	Decision-making in designing process	Sustainable design; Estidama; LEED
2	An executive of Masdar City	Master planning; third-party developers	Real Estate development; Masdar; Estidama
3	A representative of the Department of Municipal Affairs	Development of international building code and standards	Estidama; LEED; green building standards; policy
4	A former employee of Masdar City, government representative	Sustainability strategy	Masdar; sustainability strategy; policy
5	A former member of Abu Dhabi Sustainability Group	Involvement in the Abu Dhabi Vision 2030 and the Urban Planning Council Framework Development Plan	Sustainability strategy; policy
6	An architect of a building achieved the highest *Platinum* LEED and 5 *Pearls* Estidama	Designing within the guidelines of both LEED and Estidama systems	Estidama; LEED; policy

The interviews were conducted in English in the period between 2 and 10 June 2015 in Abu Dhabi and lasted between 30 to 60 minutes each, with a set of pre-defined and non-predefined open-ended questions. The interviews were transcribed in more than 13,000 words.

To answer the above-mentioned research questions the research questionnaire was designed comprising semi-structured open-ended questions such as:

- What are the pros and cons of Estidama's Pearl Rating system for developers and for consumers?
- What are the main advantages and disadvantages of LEED for Masdar City?
- Can the consumer awareness about sustainability outcomes be the main driver in attracting residents to sustainable housing as Masdar City today or in the future?
- Through which indicators do you think people would be accustomed to when it comes to the sustainability of Masdar City today, by 2020?
- Should Estidama PRS use the essential metrics as energy performance and carbon footprint?

Results

Interviewee 1 derived the idea that '*what is happening between the buildings*' is essential for evaluating sustainability in real estate (Interviewee 1 2015). The multi-faceted placemaking attributes of an urban space are essential for livable communities (Jacobs 1965). Focusing on the way residents will socially interact, the means by which they will reach their work and schools, and the way the out-of-building conditions will affect their lifestyles will be part of Masdar's community. Smaller Masdar City developers are considering applying for Community PRS when the stage is appropriate (Interviewees 1 and 2 2015). Sixty percent of the building stock of Masdar City is planned to be residential and to be inhabited by 50,000 people (Interviewee 1 2015) and thus is eligible for the certification. The second interviewee said that the 4 pearls rating is the desired target to be achieved for the community assessment (Interviewee 2 2015). The perception of a sustainable community for Masdar City illustrated in Figure 10.6 is an urban place, where residents can 'Live, Play, Work and Learn'. This is why creating jobs, businesses and institutes are in the core of Masdar development and are indicative of these valuable community components and must be assessed and illustrated to end-users (Interviewee 1 2015).

Interviewees 1, 2, 5 and 6 (2015) were confident that one day people could be attracted by the sustainability characteristics of a place like Masdar City, while Interviewee 4 claimed this will never happen in the Gulf context because of the faux ideals of seeking 'luxury' attributes, which correlates to the consumption an excess amount of energy for cooling and water desalinization. In contrast, the

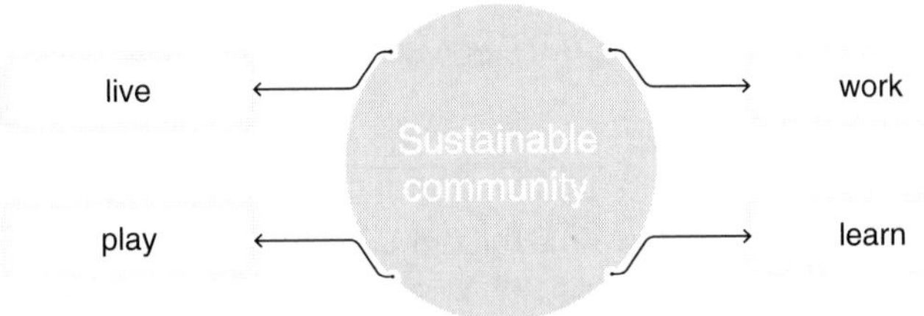

Figure 10.6 Masdar City's perception of a sustainable community

Interviewee 6 (2015) admitted that there is demand for places in Abu Dhabi where people can avoid the *'motorized' lifestyle* and luxurious trends and can simply walk and meet neighbors. The need to evaluate access to public transportation and walkability will be quite challenging for the climate conditions of the area and particularly for Masdar City given its remote location, which is considered 'very bad' (Interviewees 1 and 4 2015). All interviewees shared the idea that a tool that assesses the level of walkability such as WalkScore in the US and Canada would be worth applying to Abu Dhabi and would be well adopted by citizens, when the industry matures.

Besides governmental minimum requirements, Masdar City developers set their own sustainability benchmarks for third-party developers that wish to develop in Masdar. One of the main criteria is that they need to achieve the minimum 3 Pearls level of Estidama PRS (Interviewee 2 2015). Large international companies such as Etihad Airlines, Siemens and IRENA are tenants, customers or third-party developers at Masdar City (Masdar.ae). The contractors and designers of their buildings are more familiar with LEED and would prefer to use it for the building guidelines (Interviewee 3 2015), however Masdar sets the targets according to Estidama – as it is required – and compliance to the requirements are facilitated by the Masdar City developer team's know-how (Interviewees 1 and 2 2015). The developer is hoping that the overall average rating of all buildings will achieve 4 Pearls (Interviewee 2 2015).

The Masdar developer is using many metrics and KPIs for sustainability to achieve their sustainability targets. Using Estidama and LEED as indicators of some aspects of sustainability, the developer is not aiming to achieve the maximum results because they put too much emphasis on categories that are not assessed by these particular tools such as embodied energy or not properly weighted aspects (water in LEED, walkability in Estidama). The developers identified the lack of a holistic approach of the rating tools as a shortcoming, a fact raised by both the academics in the field (e.g. Bowen 2014) and the interviewees:

> From our experience, the disadvantage of an assessment system is that it predefines what are your sustainability criteria and it takes your path to go after the credits, because you are required to achieve a certain level of credits or a

> certain rating and this leads to a possibility that you are going after from a design point of view, certain technical features of a building rather than looking at the building holistically and how it reacts to the environment holistically.
>
> (Interviewee 1 2015)

Besides the sustainability criteria within the Estidama PRS, the Masdar City developer places emphasis on several additional green indicators (such as targets for the quantity of embodied carbon and the minimization of the construction costs), which illustrates that the perception of the sustainable built environment might be different for developers even in the same climate and market conditions (Interviewee 1 2015).

The role and impact of SA tools

For consumers

The usage of rating tools is not very widespread in terms of the number of certified buildings as the quantitative analysis of this research illustrates. Some researchers have demonstrated that the residential sector has experienced less demand for green certifications by comparison this demand in the commercial sector (DeFrancesco and Levy 2008). Nonetheless, interviewees believe that in the future, *Masdar City will attract customers for residential buildings via the sustainability narrative* because of the focus on the holistic approach of the placemaking concept and a set of sustainability KPIs including Estidama level. Thanks to policies such as 'Abu Dhabi Vision 2030' that promote a sustainable lifestyle, the residents of Abu Dhabi will acquire sustainability awareness and initiate demand for green homes. Most researchers (Nelson 2012; Lorenz 2011; Kimmet and Boyd 2004) and interviewees suggest that usage of green building rating tools should be encouraged by urban policies, and this will produce significant impacts on sustainability awareness of consumers.

Critics of the tools call for public participation (Sharifi and Murayama 2013) and consumer-focused adaptation of the current tools and possible devising of new instruments (Ismail et al. 2012). The interviewees (Interviewee 1, 2 and 3 2015) indicated the need for new outputs in the SA tools to be incorporated – for example essential metrics such as energy and water consumption and embodied carbon, which was considered to be missing in the current tools in previous research (Ding 2008).

Interviewee 1 called for a need of the essential quantitative metrics to be understandable for end-users, such as the fuel consumption for cars (Interviewee 1 2015). The time will come when people will ask:

'What is the kWt per m^2 annually for this home?' (Interviewee 1 2015)

All the interviewees have concluded this need. As far as the implementation of these essential metrics are concerned, Interviewee 1 assumes that the demand for measuring tools should be driven by end-users (2015). Interviewee 3 (2015) suggested that it would be difficult to implement new metrics in Estidama's systems, but most of the interviewees believe it should be done (Interviewees 1, 2, 3, 4 and 6 2015), even if this will cause further delay in the construction sector (Interviewee 3 2015).

For the government

Researchers claim that the improvement of tools and metrics will be rewarded through payback from more efficient building operations (e.g. Nelson 2012), which was also suggested by interviewees in the context of the new urban policy of Abu Dhabi, where the government aims to improve the building stock and reduce expenditures for utility subsidies (Interviewees 5 and 6 2015). Thus, a new positive role of a SA tool has appeared, namely, to deliver savings in governmental expenditures (Interviewees 5 and 6 2015). However, metrics need to be understandable to the populace in order for people to have a better understanding of their energy usage and impacts, which is missing from Estidama and other leading SA tools (Interviewees 1, 5 and 6 2015).

The quantitative analysis of the number of the assessed buildings suggests that *government-driven* tools such as Estidama in UAE are generally effective over others.

For the construction and the real estate sectors (and Masdar)

Interviewees 1, 3, 5 and 6 (2015) admitted that in the case of Abu Dhabi industry awareness had been advanced thanks to the application of Estidama. The contribution of the current tools to fostering demand for sustainable homes is unknown (Braganca et al. 2010; Kibert 2008). However, the supply side is affected positively in terms of the number of developers certifying their new buildings (Kibert 2008). Thus, the impact of the mandatory tools, as claimed by academics (e.g. Braganca et al. 2010) and Interviewees 3 and 6 (2015) leads to a quality improvement of the building stock.

SA tools are being criticized both for contextual and methodological inadequacies (Ding 2008; Bowen 2014). Some studies have attempted to prove the necessity of new tools for the residential sector both at the building level (Bowen 2014) and the community level (Ismail et al. 2012). The comparative analysis and the experts' perceptions have illustrated that Estidama is outstanding for its methodological approach of assessing the entire 4 lifecycles of buildings and that the system includes a performance audit of the assessed buildings, which is an advantage and could be implemented in other tools. The interviewees (Interviewee 1, 2 and 3 2015) firmly indicated the need for improvement. The interviewees concluded that globally recognized SA tools are still needed in the Gulf for international projects such as Masdar City because of their international recognition and reputation.

One negative impact on the real estate sector in Abu Dhabi due to the introduction of Estidama was the construction delays (Interviewee 3 2015) and the additional costs of the design and approval processes (Interviewee 3 and 6). In the case of Estidama the costs of the application of the SA tools cannot be put in the context of 'greenwashing' as other researchers have attempted to do for the voluntary tools such as LEED and BREEAM (e.g. Alves 2009). Most of the tool operators charge for the assessment process, while Estidama is an example of a free tool (UPC 2015). However, the industry payers suggest that this expense for green certification is anyway relatively low among design expenses, where other simulation and modelling tools represent higher expenses for sustainable projects such as Masdar City (Interviewee 6 2015).

Nelson (2012: 18), after revising the constraints of metrics for SA, concluded that sustainability is a new concept for the industry and that the SA tools need to be *modified and adapted in order to remain viable*. In addition interviewees claim that the industry is yet to achieve maturity.

Barriers for sustainable housing development in the GCC

Despite the extensive opportunities in the Gulf to invest in sustainable construction – from the financial perspective to time and efforts – the building sector in the region is faced with the most challenging circumstances. From natural constraints to man-made problems, the GCC countries have struggled to implement sustainability into green building policies. One of the significant challenges is the lack of awareness in the industry and the consumers, and another is lack of transparency within institutions. Fortunately, the Gulf countries achieved a high level of education. According to The UN Development Programme's report in 2014, which has categorized countries by their Human Development Index (HDI), an indication of education, quality of life and overall welfare, the GCC countries have high and very high HDI. Although human development is not necessarily correlated with high sustainability awareness levels, it allows the industry to involve highly educated specialists to construct quality buildings and the population to understand the government's sustainability strategies.

Another challenge that Saudi Arabia, the UAE and Qatar are facing is the overconsumption behavioral patterns that have to be addressed for the sustainable development of the real estate sector. The Kingdom of Saudi Arabia and the UAE's water consumption significantly exceeds the world's average. These countries consume more water than the countries that are rich in surface water – a contradictory and problematic fact. The water and energy overconsumption is indirectly caused by the government subsidies for the utility bills that prevent the behavior shift in the region.

Although the existing green building regulations in UAE are effective for the new construction, there is a challenge in dealing with the existing building stock that was constructed before the policies came into force. Retrofitting existing buildings to be more energy and water efficient has proven to be a financially lucrative investment but there are financing barriers to the widespread implementation of retrofit programmes. Dubai has established a comprehensive framework by the Dubai Supreme Council of Energy called 'Efficiency' to encourage energy-efficient building retrofitting and decrease the energy demand by 30% by 2030 in the city (Dubai Supreme Council of Energy 2016).

The Gulf countries have shown tremendous progress, from governmental efforts to private developments. This however does not change the fact that much more needs to be done in embedding sustainability in the process of urban development achieving transparency of the market, data accessibility and efficient data infrastructure for the effective governance.

Blockchain for real estate record – progress in Dubai

In November 2016 the UN started to discuss how blockchain – the new technological phenomenon as the "Internet" used to be in 1990s – can introduce solutions for sustainable development (coindesk.com). Thus, Sustainable Development Goal 9 points to safe and secure digital infrastructure as a crucial driver of economic growth and development, where blockchain could play the crucial role.

The blockchain technology, the underlying innovation of Bitcoin, will allow countries around the world to develop a comprehensive real-time database for real estate records (Tapscott and Tapscott 2016). Particularly, blockchain used for electronic title deeds will revolutionize the entire real estate purchase process, enabling secure and automated online asset transfer.

The current challenge in the real estate market is the lack of international standard for an electronic property rights registry. Each state keeps its own register and establishes national rules of property deeds. In the classical "pre-electronic" and "pre-blockchain" era, we would require to gather governments from different countries to sign an international convention that would establish standards and other procedures. They would implement standards for cross-border property rights transactions in the electronic registry and launch it on a central server. No state would agree to transfer its right to manage a server and a process to another state (Konashevich 2017).

In the case of blockchain, those procedures are not required because the network is decentralized. It means no country controls the network. The "law" of leger is a protocol; once developed and launched, it provides secured work for a system. Blockchain is secured by cryptography. The only thing required from a government is to recognize the electronic ledger legally and provide national procedures of property rights verification and user identification.

Benefits for governments

Here is how the blockchain for title deeds will benefit the governments in each country. First, the immutable public records stored on blockchain will prevent corruption amongst public service officials and politicians. Second, since all records are hashed, any mistakes can be traced and corrected, which ensures that final records are accurate and current. And third, a transparent process with a clean, accurate and secure record of land titles will help attract and increase foreign investment (Couse 2016). It is estimated that foreigners bought $43 billion of residential homes in Dubai (the UAE buyers bought $25 billion of homes in the US and Europe in 2016), thus the economical development of Dubai further benefitting from foreign investors and supporting technology.

Besides the transparency benefits, private investors, both domestic and foreign, will have the innovative facility to buy and resell properties remotely via a customer-centric interface, which will add a healthy liquidity to the particular market in the countries that adopt the blockchain ledger.

In a significant endorsement of blockchain technology, the Dubai government will see all of its administration documents on blockchain by 2020. Under the new initiative to go all-in on blockchain technology, Hamdan bin Mohammed became the first influential blockchain advocate in the region.

Blockchain protocol provides rules for servers ("nodes"), which interact with each other in a decentralized way. Open and verifiable "smart contract" is a set of national rules and algorithms, which provide property registry operating. Each country has its own smart contract and is free to write, change or cancel it. Governments announce which of the smart contracts is valid. National smart contracts provide possibility for electronic transactions by allowing identified parties no matter from what country ownership rights are transfered.

The blockchain ledger and the blockchain-enabled smart contracts allow countries to adopt a new standardized comprehensive real-time database for real estate, delivering the following benefits:

Secure asset transfer: absolutely secure transfer of assets by enforcing international data standards for property transfer and providing an additional standardized distributed ledger to the existing title registrars in the US, EU and other countries. With blockchain technology, property title records cannot be manipulated or adjusted without consensus of all participants.

Cost effective: by reducing the need for human interaction during the real estate transaction process, foreign investors can seamlessly buy and resell properties online while minimizing cost, error and fraud.

Transparency: application of blockchain in real estate registries to allow countries to develop a real-time database of property title portfolios accessible by anyone or within a permissioned environment.

The blockchain technology, however, is not the most appropriate solution for pure stamping (hashing) documents without asset transfer and/or identity-verified association involved. Heavy energy consumption is required for transactions on blockchain, which is computing intensive, demanding storage of data and energy to maintain and execute. The ledger supporting asset transfer with insignificant number of annual transactions on blockchain is the sustainable solution for real estate. A number of companies started to develop and implement the blockchain ledger for land registries in 2016 such as ChromaWay for Sweden; Ubitquity for Georgia, US; and Propy and ConsenSys for Middle Eastern countries.

Conclusions and recommendations

The present study focused on answering a question: how viable are the sustainability assessment methods for real estate and their role in consumer demand for sustainable housing in the GCC?

The main finding from the quantitative analysis was that an insignificant share of the building stock worldwide has been assessed in terms of sustainability for the last 25 years and only a few SA tools in the world are widely used: energy-focused mandatory tool EPC, applied in the EU; multiple-aspect tools, such as internationally recognized LEED, BREEAM, and HQS; and local government-driven Estidama. The findings were supplemented by the findings from expert interviews on the case study of Masdar City. The research discovered important evidence to improve the SA tools by implementing building performance assessment, essential metrics on embodied carbon footprint and water and energy consumption, and holistic community metrics. Also, the expert interviews identified new knowledge in how the Abu Dhabi mandatory urban policy improved sustainability awareness, empowering developers, designers and authorities to consider green building practices.

SA tools need to be government driven or at least implemented into policies and mandatory schemes to produce awareness for consumers and the industry. The findings of the case study on application SA tools to Masdar City are applicable for sustainable projects in other countries as well. The recommendation of the prior studies followed by the current research is that the residential sector should be strongly encouraged to assess and value sustainability. Consumers should be able to access understandable metrics in order to fully comprehend the benefits and receive a stable incentive to demand such sustainable projects as Masdar City. Even though a sustainable home is fundamentally not possible to measure holistically, – a point debated by academics (Muldavin 2008) and supported by interviewees – better sustainability metrics and tools would be vital to foster sustainable housing supply and demand.

As for extending the conducted research, it will be important to evaluate the potential return on the investment of the Abu Dhabi government in the development and application of the mandatory SA tool for the new buildings. The government has developed and applied the SA tool Estidama without charging developers – presumably by linking its implementation to potentially reducing expenditures for electricity and water subsidies. Further, a study on enhancement of people's awareness about sustainable housing thanks to Estidama and a study on demand for sustainable projects such as Masdar City could be conducted.

Based on the findings for the sustainability imperatives and assessment challenges for Masdar City, the following policy recommendations for the GCC countries are suggested:

- Mandatory rating systems such as Estidama and GSAS to be adopted to improve the baseline building performance and setting higher sustainability goals
- Embodied carbon emissions to be assessed for the new constructions
- Affordability requirements implemented into the new construction
- Community involvement when creating local building SA tools or codes
- Understandable sustainable housing metrics for consumers
- Increasing awareness about the artificially low energy and water tariffs for the populace to reduce overconsumption patterns
- Industry training: providing workshops, hands-on exercises, detailed user guides and tools
- Comprehensive programmes for retrofitting the existing building stock to energy efficiency
- Financial programmes to overcome the cost barriers. Costs for some of the high-efficiency technology such as chillers, LED-lighting and glass are expected to decrease as the demand increases after the green building requirements become mandatory
- Transparency on the assessment process and its results for the consumers and the industry players
- Transparency on real estate records delivered by blockchain-enabled infrastructure

The transition towards more sustainable development will require political undertakings for the implementation of new sustainability and well-being indicators for the necessary transformation to ensure a sustainable planet for future generations (Sen 2010). Particularly the sustainability indicators in the residential sector, as this paper illustrates, need to be improved: they are imperfect but viable and could incentivize the sustainable housing demand as a part of the behavioral change towards a sustainable lifestyle, which is especially needed in the Gulf.

References

Ali, H.H., and S.F. Al Nsairat. 2009. Developing a green building assessment tool for developing countries – Case of Jordan. Building and Environment, 44: 1053–1064.

AlNaqbi, A., W. AlAwadhi, A. Manneh, A. Kazim, and B. Abu-Hijleh. 2012. Survey of the existing residential buildings stock in the UAE. *International Journal of Environmental Science and Development*, 3(5): 491–496.

Alobaidi, K.A., A.B.A. Rahim, A. Mohammed, and S. Baqutayan. 2015. Sustainability achievement and Estidama Green Building regulations in Abu Dhabi vision 2030. *Mediterranean Journal of Social Sciences*, 6(4): S2.

Alves, I. M. 2009. Green Spin Everywhere: How Greenwashing Reveals the Limits of the CSR Paradigm. Journal of Global Change and Governance, 2(1): 1-26.

Alusi, A.A., G.R. Eccles, C.A. Edmondson, and T. Zuzul. 2011. *Sustainable Cities: Oxymoron or the Shape of the Future?* Working Paper 11–062, Harvard Business School.

Augustine, B.A. 2015, August 2. UAE energy subsidy reforms to boost public finances. *Gulf News*. Available at: http://m.gulfnews.com/business/sectors/banking/uae-energy-subsidy-reforms-to-boost-public-finances-1.1559972 (Accessed 5 September 2015).

Baird, G. 2009. Incorporating user performance criteria into Building Sustainability Rating Tools (BSRTs) for buildings in operation. *Sustainability*, 1(4): 1069–1086.

Bouyamoun, A. 2015. UAE takaful industry must stand out more, chiefs say. *The National*, April 13. Available at: www.thenational.ae/business/economy/uae-takaful-industry-must-stand-out-more-chiefs-say (Accessed 1 September 2015).

Bowen, F. 2014. After Greenwashing: Symbolic Corporate Environmentalism and Society. Cambridge: Cambridge University Press.

Boyd, T., and P. Kimmet. 2005. *The Triple Bottom Line Approach to Property Performance Evaluation*. Paper Presented at PRESS Conference, 23–27 January, Melbourne, Australia.

Braganca, L., R. Mateus, and H. Koukkari. 2010. Building sustainability assessment. *Sustainability*, 2(7): 2010–2023.

Breeam, 2015. Building Research Establishment Environmental Assessment Method. Available at homepage: www.breeam.com

Burnett, J. 2007. City buildings-eco-labels and shades of green. *Landscape and Urban Planning*, 83(1): 29–38.

CityScape. 2015. *Display Panel on UPC Exhibition Stand Shown at the CityScape Exhibition*. ADNEC Centre, Abu Dhabi, UAE, 21–25 April 2015 (Accessed 22 April 2015).

Coindesk. 2016. Available at: www.coindesk.com/united-nations-blockchain-sustainability-solutions/ (Accessed 20 Decemeber 2016).

Cole, R.J. 1999. Building environmental assessment methods: Clarifying intentions. *Building Research & Information*, 27(4–5): 230–46.

Couse, A. 2016. *World Economic Forum, JLL*. Available at homepage: www.jll.com.

Cugurullo, F. 2013. The business of Utopia: Estidama and the road to the sustainable city. *Utopian Studies*, 24(1): 66–88.

DeFrancesco, A.J. and D. Levy. 2014. The impact of sustainability on the investment environment. Journal of European Real Estate Research, 1(1): 72–87.

Deutsche Gesellschaft für Nachhaltiges Bauen (DGNB). 2015. Available at: www.dgnb.de, (Accessed 5 September 2015).

Ding, G.K.C. 2008. Sustainable construction – The role of environmental assessment tools. *Journal of Environmental Management*. School of the Built Environment Faculty of Design, Architecture & Building University of Technology, Sydney, Australia. 86(3):451–64.

Dubai Supreme Council of Energy; Software. Available at: www.dubaisce.gov.ae/default.aspx

Fischlein, M., and T. Smith. 2010. Rival private governance networks: Competing to define the rules of sustainability performance. *Global Environmental Change*, 20(3): 511–522.

Fowler, K.M. and E.M. Rauch. 2006. *Sustainable Building Rating Systems – Summary*. (The Pacific Northwest National Laboratory) operated for the U.S. Department of Energy by Battelle, PNNL-15858.

Green Rating for Integrated Habitat Assessment (GRIHA). 2015. Available at: www. Grihainida.org (Accessed 10 September 2015).

Harvey, D. 2012. Rebel Cities: From the Right to the City to the Urban Revolution. London: Verso.

Hodson, M., and S. Marvin. 2010. Urbanism in the anthropocene: Ecological urbanism or premium ecological enclaves? *CITY: Analysis of Urban Trends, Culture, Theory, Policy, Action*, 14(3): 298–313. Routledge, London.

High Environmental Quality (HQE). 2015. Available at homepage: www.behqe.com (Accessed 2 September 2015).

Ismail, M. H., J. Doak, D. Nicholson, R. Yao, and A. Yates. 2012. *Sustainable Community Tools: What do Tool Users Really Want?*. Henley Business School, University of Reading, United Kingdom.

Issa, N., and S.A. Abbar. 2015. *Sustainability in the Middle East: Achievements and Challenges*. Dubai, United Arab Emirates: AESG.

Jacobs, J. 1965. The death and life of great American cities., New York, NY: Vintage Books.

Kibert, C.J. 2008. Sustainable Construction: Green Building Design and Delivery. Hoboken: Wiley.

Kimmet, P., and T. Boyd. 2004. An Understanding of Triple Bottom Line Evaluations and the Use of Social and Environmental Metrics. CRC for Construction Innovation Project.

Konashevich, O. 2017. *Whitepaper for Decentralized Blockchain Ledger for Real Estate*. Ávailable at: www.propy.com/whitepaper.

Lau, A. 2012. Masdar City: A Model of Environmental Sustainability. Stanford University, Stanford, CA

Lorenz, D. 2011. Property Valuation and Sustainability. Stockholm: RICS.

Low, T.E. 2008. Light Imprint: Integrating Sustainability With New Urbanism. CNU Green Council Report, pp. 28–30.

Masdar. 2015. Available at homepage: www.masdar.ae (Accessed 1 September 2015).

Muldavin, S. 2008. Quantifying "Green" Value: Assessing the Applicability of the CoStar Studies. Green Buildings Finance Consortium, California.

Myers, D. 2011. *Economics and Property*. Oxford: Elsevier.

Nelson, A. 2012. Building Labels vs. Environmental Performance Metrics: Measuring What's Important About Building Sustainability. RREEF Research Strategic Outlook.

Pivo, G., and J.D. Fisher. 2011. The walkability premium in commercial real estate investments. *Real Estate Economics*, 39(2): 185–219.

Regulation and Supervision Bureau (RSB). 2013. Customer Tariffs & Charges. Available at: www.rsb.gov.ae/uploads/ReportWEConsumption.pdf (Accessed 1 September 2015).

Saifur, R. 2012. UAE power capacity outpaces demand. GulfNews. Available at: http://gulfnews.com/business/economy/uae-power-capacity-outpaces-demand-1.1068506 (Accessed 1 September 2015).

Sayce, S., L. Ellison, and J. Smith. 2004. *Incorporating Sustainability in Commercial Property Appraisal: Evidence From the UK*. Paper presented at the European Real Estate Society Conference, 2–5 June, Milan.

Sen, A. 2010. *Beyond GDP: Measures of Welfare and Sustainability*. Univesita Ca' Foscari Venezia [online]. Available at: www.youtube.com/watch?v=tKgLwqmB6Go (Accessed 7 September 2015).

Sharifi, A., and A. Murayama. 2013. A critical review of seven selected neighborhood sustainability assessment tools. *Environmental Impact Assessment Review*, 38: 73–87.

Siew, R.Y.J., M.C.A. Balatbat, and D.G. Carmichael. 2013. A review of building/infrastructure sustainability reporting tools (SRTs). *Smart and Sustainable Built Environment*, 2(2): 106–139.

Solar City and CleanEdge, Consumer Trends in Sustainability: Insights to Grow Your Market Share and Defend Your Brand. Available at: www.solarcity.com/sites/default/files/reports/reports-consumer-trends-in-sustainability.pdf (Accessed 1 June 2016).

Tapscott, A., and D. Tapscott. 2016. Blockchain Revolution: How the Technology Behind Bitcoin Is Changing Money, Business, and the World. Penguin, New York, NY.

UNEP. 2011. Towards a Green Economy: Pathways to Sustainable Development and Poverty Eradication. Nairobi: United Nations Environmental Program (UNEP).

United Nations (UN). 2015. Available at: www.un.org/en/development/desa/news/population/world-urbanization-prospects-2014.html (Accessed 5 September 2015).

United States Green Building Council (USGBC). 2015. Available at homepage: www.usgbc.com, (Accessed 5 September 2015).

Urban Planning Council (UPC). 2010. Pearl Rating System Design & Construction for Estidama Version 1.0. UPC, Abu Dhabi, UAE.

Urban Planning Council (UPC). 2015. Available at homepage: upc.gov.ae (Accessed 5 September 2015).

Wilson, A. 2015. *SDG Number 11: Make Cities and Human Settlements Inclusive and Sustainable.* Available at: https://unstats.un.org (Accessed 7 July 2016).

Wong, J.M.W., S.T. Ng, and A.P.C. Chan. 2010. Strategic planning for the sustainable development of the construction industry in Hong Kong. *Habitat International*, 34(2): 256–263.

Part IV

The socio-economic perspective

11 Energy consumption and transition dynamics to a sustainable future under a rentier economy

The case of the GCC states

Abdullah Kaya, Nazli Choucri, I-Tsung Tsai and Toufic Mezher

Introduction and outlook of GCC states

In this chapter, the political system and prevalent rentier economy of the Gulf Cooperation Council (GCC) states will be analyzed in order to assess those states' transition to a sustainable energy future. There are two important pillars, namely demand and supply, for a sustainable energy transition to take place in the GCC. First, cheap utility prices (water, oil, and electricity) have been a part of "rentier agreement" between the ruler and the citizens. This has partially led to excessive demand and waste of energy in those states. We analyze recent trends of change in utility prices and dynamics of energy consumption in these states. Second, sustainable energy transition needs the introduction of sustainable energy production forms. This will require a change in decade-old energy infrastructure of the GCC states which could be very challenging due to idiosyncratic economic, industrial, and political structures of these states.

The chapter follows with the prevailing political and economic system of the GCC states. Energy consumption dynamics and recent change in utility prices are analyzed in the second section. Development of sustainable energy forms in the GCC is discussed in the third section, which is followed by a conclusion.

Political system

Six Arab countries located in the Arabian Peninsula by the Persian Gulf are Bahrain, Kuwait, Oman, Saudi Arabia, Qatar and UAE together constitute the GCC (Hvidt 2011). The political systems of these six countries are monarchies, with Kuwait, Qatar, and UAE ruled by emirs; Oman ruled by a sultan; and Bahrain and Saudi Arabia ruled by kings. The Democracy Index is published by the Economist Intelligence Unit (EIU); the score of 1 is for absolute authority and the score of 10 is for the maximum democracy. The 2012 report classifies all GCC states as countries with absolute political systems (Table 11.1) based on the democracy scores of GCC.

Table 11.1 GCC Democracy Index

Country/Year	*2012*
Bahrain	2.53
Kuwait	3.78
Oman	3.26
Qatar	3.18
Saudi Arabia	1.71
UAE	2.58
Norway (Highest)	9.93
North Korea (Lowest)	1.08

Most national councils of GCC states have limited rights and executive power. While the national councils of Kuwait and Bahrain have more executive and legislative power, appointments of critical ministries and approval of large projects are directly managed by the rulers or the committees appointed directly by the rulers (Kaya and Tsai 2016; Hanieh 2015).

Rentier agreement

GCC states are classified as rentier states in which revenue from selling of hydrocarbon reserves plays a vital role in those societies (Ross 2001). The governments of GCC distribute accrued wealth to their people through subsidies, free education and health schemes and high-paying public jobs in exchange for the political rights known as "rentier social contract" or "rentier agreement" or "ruling agreement" (Herb 2005). Additionally, there is little or no tax in the GCC states since the state doesn't need taxation due to revenue from hydrocarbons (Herb 2005).

Productive and commodity circuits in the economic structure of GCC states

Productive circuit

As indicated earlier, GCC states sit on top of significant hydrocarbon reserves while possessing little agricultural land and other mineral resources (Rogner 1997). Due to easily accessible and cheaper-to-produce oil reservoirs of the GCC region compared to deep-offshore, shale, or tar sands oils, money generated from exporting hydrocarbon products constitute a significant revenue for the GCC governments (Fasano-Filho and Wang 2002). All the upstream exploration, drilling, transportation, and production rights of hydrocarbon resources are under the control of the government in all of the GCC states (Kaya and Tsai 2016).

It is, hence, not surprising that revenues from selling hydrocarbon constitute a significant part of government revenue, country exports, and the overall economy in the GCC states, as shown in Table 11.2 (Hvidt 2013).

Table 11.2 Percentages of hydrocarbon revenue in export, state budget and GPD in 2011

Country	*% of export earnings*	*% of state budget*	*% of GDP*
Bahrain	69	86	24
Kuwait	90	93	45
Oman	65	77	41
Qatar	91	80	46
Saudi Arabia	85	85	50
UAE	69	77	32

In the 1980s, GCC states started initiatives to diversify their hydrocarbon business by investing into downstream operations in oil and gas industries through, for example, building state-of-the-art petrochemical complexes. Saudi Basic Industries Corporation (SABIC), a subsidiary of Aramco as the national oil company of Saudi Arabia, is one of the leading petrochemical companies in the world (Hertog 2010). Similar to SABIC, other GCC states have established successful petrochemical companies which delivered good profits thanks to strict and autonomous management (granted by the ruler) and the advantage of cheap oil and gas as raw material for production. Following the successful diversification into downstream hydrocarbon industries, the Gulf states gradually expanded their business into capital intensive and high energy-intensive manufacturing such as aluminium and steel production. "Coke and refined petroleum products", "Chemical products", "Non-metallic mineral products", "Manufacture of basic metals" are categorized as high energy-intensive manufacturing sectors. Further investment and creation of state-owned enterprises (SOEs) are directed towards natural monopoly areas such as airlines and telecommunication industries where the Gulf states captured significant returns for their investments (Hertog 2010). To conclude, GCC states have either nationalized or developed monopoly entities to engage almost all of the productive industries, first starting with hydrocarbon industries. This strategy was critical in empowering the state to supply its citizens with various economic privileges as a part of the rentier agreement. This economic circle, which is entirely under state control, is named as "productive circuit" (Hanieh 2015).

Commodity circuit

There is no significant manufacturing of capital goods used for production (i.e. machinery and heavy equipment) in the GCC states. This has resulted in the imports of necessary capital goods from advanced economies. Rapidly improving economic conditions of GCC citizens and expatriate workers has also created huge demand for basic consumer goods such as food products, automobiles, home appliances, and apparels (Hanieh 2015). Due to lack of industrial base, most of the consumer goods are imported as well. The state has given exclusive licenses to the family businesses established by the locals to perform importing of some capital goods and most of the consumer goods as part of the rentier agreement. The Dubai ruler has granted "exclusive import licenses and business contracts" to the famous merchant families in Dubai such as Al Ghurairs, Al Futtaims and Al Rostamanis (Krane 2009: 70). Large family conglomerates in the GCC countries are a common feature and mostly operate in "commodity circuit" (Hanieh 2015, Chapter 3). Regular citizens are also awarded with economic privilege through sponsorship systems (known as "kafala" in Arabic) which require foreign entities to have a local partner with a majority stake of ownership in a business (Fargues 2011).

Energy consumption dynamics in the GCC states

Energy consumption per capita in the GCC states

GCC states have very high energy consumption figures (per capita) compared to the other Arab nations, wealth nations, and the world average in general. Figure 11.1 highlights the stark difference of the GCC countries compared to the rest of the world based on World Bank Database.

High energy use in the GCC states can be attributed to many different factors. Generous utility subsidies under rentier agreement may be one of the most important reasons for excessive use of electricity, oil, and gas in the GCC states (Mezher et al. 2014). Diversification into high energy-intensive industries such as steel and aluminium manufacturing under "productive circuit" strategy may contribute excessive energy use in the GCC states as described above. The region's very hot climate, desalination due to lack of potable water, low level of development in public transportation and high GPD per capital levels are partly the reason for excessive energy use in the GCC states. In fact GCC states have very energy dense economies compared to the world average or OECD average (comprised of 34

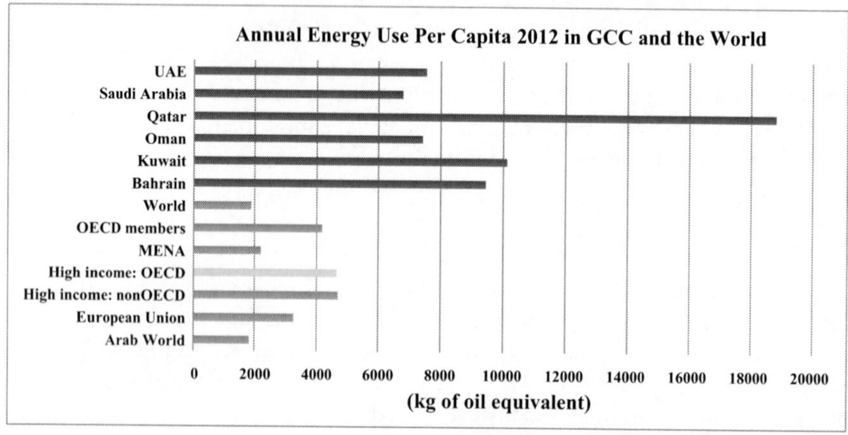

Figure 11.1 Annual energy use per capita in GCC states and selected regions and income groups

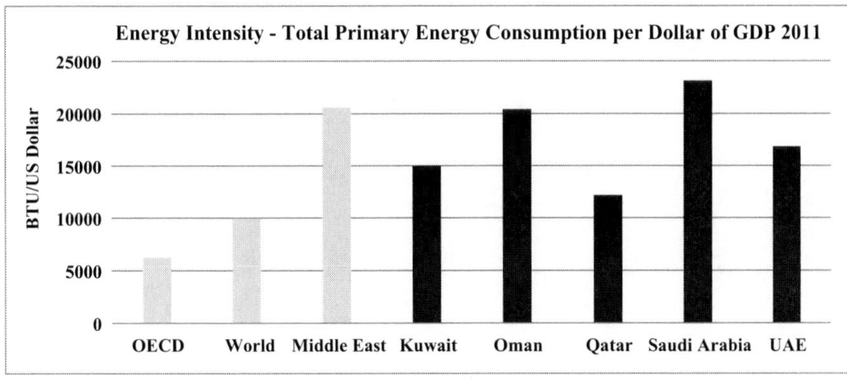

Figure 11.2 Total primary energy consumption per dollar of GDP created in the GCC

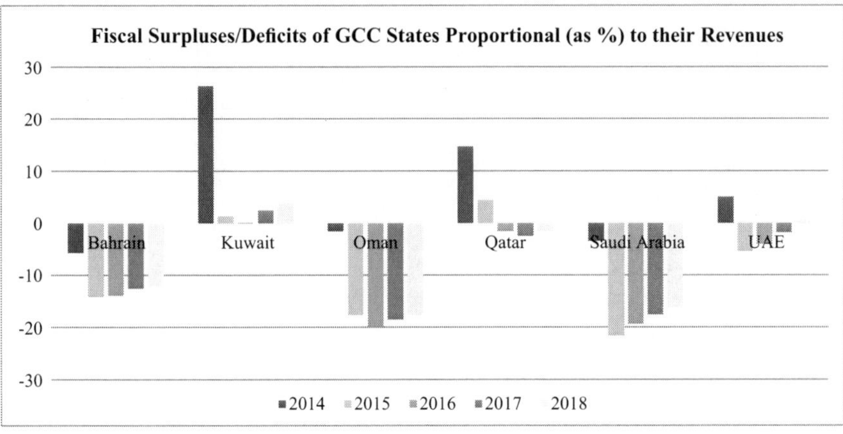

Figure 11.3 Fiscal surpluses/deficits of GCC states proportional to their revenues from year 2014 to 2018

countries having high GDP per capita income), as depicted in Figure 11.2 (AFEX 2015).

Nevertheless, there are some changes in the GCC states regarding generous subsidies and excessive use of energy and water subsequently. The recent collapse in oil prices have caused the most GCC states to run significant budget deficits and this is expected to be the case for the coming years, as shown in Figure 11.3, which is based on the IMF database.

With the exception of Kuwait, all the GCC states are expected to run significant budget deficits under low oil prices. Bahrain, Oman, and Saudi Arabia are suffering most due to their relatively bigger populations compared to oil revenues (Kaya and Tsai 2016).

In order to respond to the budget deficit, the GCC states decreased energy subsidies which appeared in the form of cheap electricity, water, and gasoline prices. GCC states have reduced the misalignment between the pump prices for gasoline and the international benchmark oil prices. Figure 11.4 shows prices increase for the gasoline in comparison with the subsidized rates in the GCC states.

Some GCC states (UAE, Saudi Arabia, and Qatar) have increased the electricity tariffs charged to the residential and commercial entities while other GCC states are planning to increase (Boersma and Griffiths 2016). Nevertheless current electricity tariffs are still far below than those of European Union (EU)

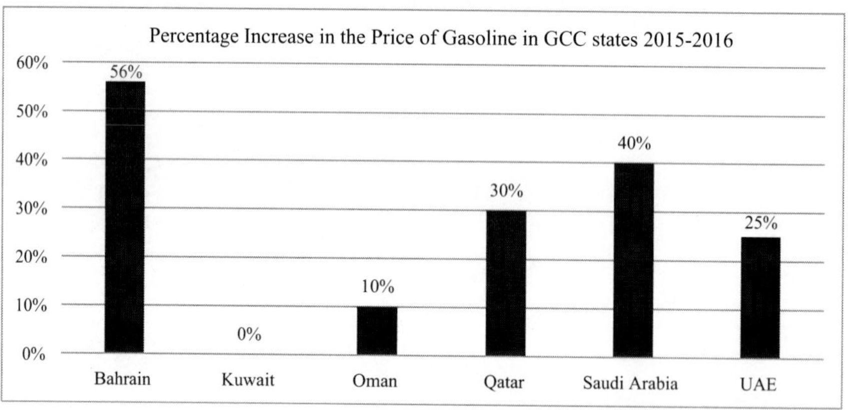

Figure 11.4 Percentage increase in the price of gasoline compared to its previous price either in year 2015 or 2016

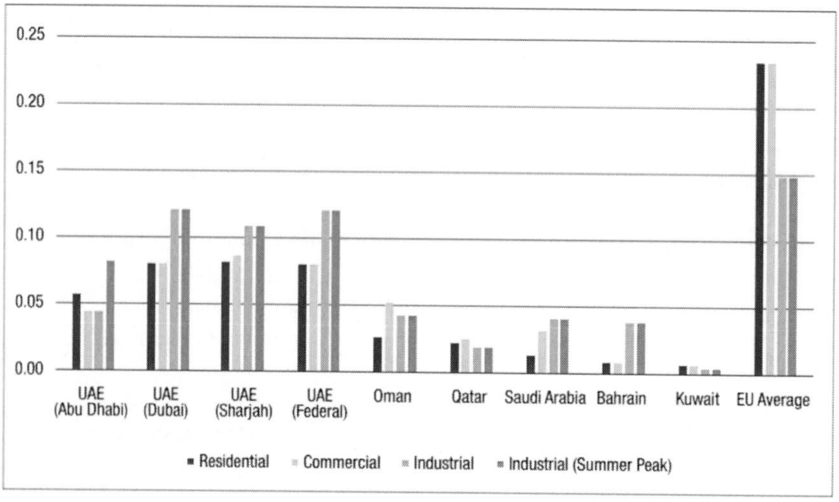

Figure 11.5 Electricity tariffs in the GCC states and the EU average

countries, to which GCC states have similar GDP per capita on average, as shown in Figure 11.5.

Future of energy consumption dynamics in the GCC states

Cheap utility prices due to the rentier economic system, industrialization in energy-intense production sectors, and the region's hot climate are the primary factors behind the high energy use in the GCC states compared to the Middle East Region, OECD countries, or the world average (Figure 11.1). The recent collapse in oil prices has caused the GCC states to take some austerity measures which have caused spikes in gasoline prices, electricity, and water tariffs. However, further increase in utility and gasoline prices in line with the value of energy in international markets may be tricky, especially in relatively less wealthy GCC states (Bahrain, Oman). It has been stated by Gengler and Lambert (2016):

> Most in the region remain broadly opposed in principle to the notion of benefit retrenchment, whatever the economic or environmental imperative. Many ordinary citizens perceive that they are being asked to make financial sacrifices disproportionate to their level of wealth compared to societal elites, and this in order to solve a problem derived from policies and decisions most played no significant role in shaping. In Qatar, for instance, a nationally representative survey conducted in September 2015 found strong resistance to the idea of Qataris paying for part or all of their electricity and water usage, even when the policy is explicitly framed against the backdrop of environmental and economic challenges.

Overall energy price in the GCC states is still much lower comparatively and recent increases may not change the energy consumption fundamentals of the region. Expected increase in population and economic activity along with low levels of energy efficiency are likely to dominate the energy consumption trends in the GCC, where there was a continuous upward trend since 2000.

More importantly, CO_2 emissions of GCC states will increase along with their energy consumption unless a significant change in energy production dynamics occurs. While, for example, a complete removal of water and electricity subsidy in Abu Dhabi is expected to reduce 7.2% of carbon emissions in the Emirate (Wang et al. 2016), investments in clean, efficient and renewable energy technologies (CERET) have been quite low until recently (Reiche 2010). The Gulf countries used to actively oppose any international binding agreement on reduction of carbon emissions (Jamil et al. 2016). Lately, there is a growing interest in the region for utilization of renewable energies in electricity production (Jamil et al. 2016). In the next section, the possibility of deploying CERET in the GCC states will be discussed regarding the rentier economic structure.

Development of CERET for a sustainable energy transition in the GCC

The entry barriers for CERET towards sustainable energy transition in the GCC

Deployments of renewable/clean energies along with energy-efficient technologies are important for the GCC states to curb their carbon emissions and will allow them to export more hydrocarbons with less domestic fossil-fuel consumption. These changes are likely to introduce new business opportunities, market structures, and industrial development which may challenge the status quo of productive and commodity circuits in the rentier states of GCC. Due to the rentier nature of the socio-political system, it is reasonable for GCC states to introduce market entry barriers for CERET (Kaya and Tsai 2016). We will first discuss theories for why there could be entry barriers for the new technologies in the GCC states before analyzing development dynamics of CERET in the GCC states.

There are various theories on the rationality of the introduction of entry barriers (Djankov 2009). "The helping hand" model postulates that governments regulate the entry conditions to prevent market failures (Djankov et al. 2002). A government may introduce entry barriers to block the entry of low-quality products or prevent the occurrence of undesirable externalities. This policy helps the incumbent firms strengthen their position vis-à-vis the new technology developer. "The capture theory" asserts that incumbent firms in an industry or sector tend to support regulations that block the entry of new firms or technologies to the market (Djankov 2009). As incumbent firms or economically strong power blocks tend to control the political power, they can effectively promote regulations that introduce entry barriers (Acemoglu 2008). Meanwhile, the "Tollbooth Theory" explains why there are more entry barriers in less democratic countries compared to the democratic countries (Djankov 2009). This theory claims that regulations and entry barriers are set in place by politicians and bureaucrats to extract money (bribe, rent) from the firms. Different than "the capture theory", which emphasizes the incumbent firms as the beneficiary of energy barrier, "the Tollbooth Theory" suggests that it is the politicians and bureaucrats who benefit from the introduction of entry barriers.

The Heritage Foundation's 2014 "Economic Freedom (EF)" report published data regarding business freedom in each country (Hall et al. 2014). Each index is scaled from 0 to 100 where 0 represents minimum level of freedom to do business and 100 represents maximum freedom to do business. From the 2014 EF report, "Business Freedom", "Trade Freedom", and "Investment Freedom" are chosen and their averages (labelled as "Average EF") to assess entry barrier levels in the GCC states. For the year 2014, the GCC states had similar (Kuwait, Qatar, Saudi Arabia, and UAE) or better (Bahrain and Oman) performance in those indexes compared to the world average. Figure 11.6 shows the level of business freedom in the GCC states in 2014.

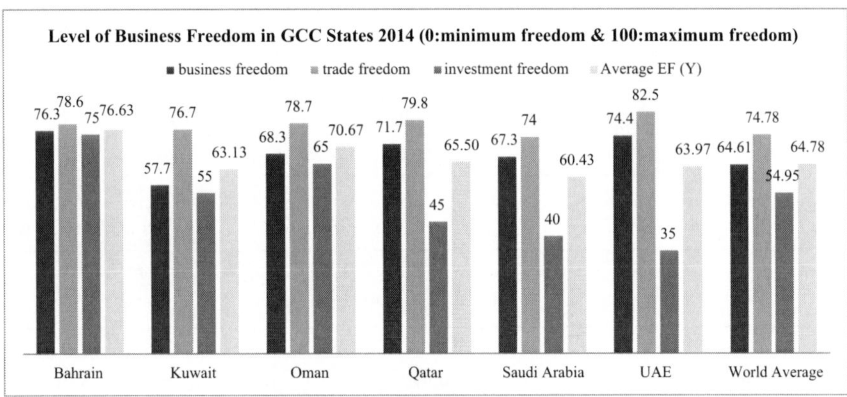

Figure 11.6 Level of business freedom in the GCC states 2014

While the GCC states generally have good performance regarding the "Trade Freedom" index, they have very low-level performance in "Business Freedom" and "Investment Freedom". This result is not very unlikely since we explained before that the "productive circuit" and "commodity circuit" areas are highly protected in the GCC by the state and the citizens respectively. This is a direct result of "rentier agreement" prevailing in the GCC states' economic and political structure, where critical business and investment opportunities are reserved either for the state or for the elites.

Panel data regression analysis for entry barriers in the GCC states

A panel data regression analysis is conducted to analyze the determinants of entry barriers in the GCC states. We use the EF index as a proxy to measure the level of entry barriers in those countries. The EF report provides performance for the GCC states from 2000 to 2014, which allows us to conduct a panel data regression analysis by using the index of entry barrier levels as the dependent (affected) variable. For the factors affecting the level of entry barriers, we use the Democracy Index (score) provided in Table 11.1, similar to previous studies (Djankov et al. 2002). Since a rentier state's fortunes are tightly linked to the price of its rent, oil price fluctuations may play a role in the level of entry barriers the GCC states. Finally, GDP per capita is added as a third factor to estimate the effect of economic prosperity on entry barriers in the GCC states.

Table 11.3 shows regression results. It is found that that the level of democracy has no statistical significant effect on the level of business freedom (or entry barriers) in the GCC states for the selected period for the pooled regression. However, oil price has a significant and negative effect on the level of entry barriers. A 1 dollar increase in oil prices results in 0.08 points increase in level of business

Table 11.3 Entry barriers in the GCC states, panel data analysis

Panel data regression of entry barriers in the GCC states						
	Regressors					
	Democracy score (EIU)		*Oil price (Brent US$/barrel)*		*GDP/capita (in 1000 USD)*	
Dependent variable:	*Random effects model*	*Fixed effect*	*Random effects model*	*Fixed effect*	*Random effects model*	*Fixed effect*
General business freedom	1.55 (1.08)	– –	0.08*** –(0.02)	0.045* –(0.03)	–0.1** (0.04)	0 –

Notes

General business freedom is the average of "business freedom", "trade freedom" and "investment freedom" indexes.

Oil price is for the Brent International Petrol and measured as US$ per barrel. The source of the data is eia.gov.

GPD per capita is measured in current US$ for each country. The source of data is databank.worldbank.org/data.

Standard errors are provided in the brackets.

"*": p < 0.05; "**": p < 0.01; "***": p< 0.001. (Level of significances for the regressors)

freedom. This result may indicate that GCC states are pursuing more market friendly economic policies and put less restriction when the oil revenues are high. Interestingly, higher GDP per capita results in more entry barriers in the GCC states, which may indicate that when GDP per capita is high, the state may feel less pressure to introduce market reforms to attract private investment or push for economic diversification. However, the effect of GDP per capita on entry barriers disappears in the fixed effect model.

A negative relationship between economic growth and high entry barriers has been proposed and analytically shown recently (Aghion et al. 2007). Autocratic governments tend to erect more entry barriers for the high value-added (advanced, closer to the technological front) sectors of the economy rather than the sectors with low value added (Aghion et al. 2007). While democratic countries have lower entry barriers for the advanced sectors, autocratic regimes have higher entry barriers for those sectors. For that reason, democratic regimes have generally more dynamic and competitive advanced sectors compared to the autocratic regimes which may contribute positively to the overall economy. In the European Union, renewable energy sectors had a productivity level similar to the manufacturing industry average, which usually comprises advanced manufacturing.

CERET are high value-added businesses and could face potential entry barriers in the GCC states. This could prevent creation of competitive industries and markets related to CER technologies in the GCC states. In fact investment into CERET is low compared to the world in the GCC states with the exception of a few initiatives with data taken from Eurostat and the study by Ragwitz et al. (2009).

The state itself may try to capitalize on high value-added CERET by localizing the manufacturing and utilizing for electricity and water production. This strategy could result in extension of the "productive circuit" similar to the previous extensions into petrochemicals and basic metal businesses. In fact, the Emirate of Abu Dhabi has taken separate but important initiatives towards localizing the manufacture and deployment of CERET while remaining GCC states are still in planning stages (Jamil et al. 2016). The success and continuation of these initiatives are yet to be seen. Different than petrochemical and basic metal industries, the GCC states don't have any comparative advantage in high value-added and competitive sectors of CERET. Manufacturing high value-added CERET by state can be costly and result in failure as opposed to the previous initiatives (petrochemical and basic metals) in the GCC states. By importing know-how of international companies and aggressively supporting Research and Development (R&D) efforts of local companies, the Norwegian government could be a very good example for the GCC states (Cherif and Hasanov 2014). Instead of being the main agent in manufacturing and production, Cherif and Hasanov (2014) suggests that GCC states can "*act as a venture capitalist and foster public-private collaboration to design and implement strategies that go beyond the comparative advantage sectors and target high value-added sectors with large potential spillovers and productivity gains.*" For example, Dubai's successful biddings to subcontract its solar energy power plant could be role model for the region to deploy and utilize CERET for electricity or water production (Sgouridis et al. 2016).

Conclusion

The rentier agreement prevailing in the GCC states has taken a hit by the recent collapse in the oil prices. To decrease the budget deficit due to very low oil prices, the GCC governments have phased out some subsidies for utilities and gasoline. Nevertheless, current price levels for utilities and gasoline are still below the world average in all the GCC states to varying degrees. In the UAE, for example, the price of gasoline is no longer subsidized but is still low compared to EU countries because there are no added taxes. Very low electricity and water rates, and cheap gasoline prices incentivized overconsumption and waste in those countries such that they are among the highest per-capita energy consumers in addition to high level of carbon emissions. Significant reduction in energy consumption per capita in the GCC states seems unlikely even after removal of the subsidies due to high GDP per capita, the region's hot climate, low efficiency in energy consumption, and the presence of energy-intense industries (productive circuit). Instead, growing population and economies will increase overall energy consumption in those states along with carbon emissions unless energy production and conservation dynamics change. Rentier economic systems in the GCC states where the political rights are traded off with economic privileges can play a decisive role in whether these countries transition to a more sustainable energy consumption and production dynamics by utilizing CERET instead of fossil fuels. Development and deployment of CERET may require a competitive and dynamic economic system as well as low entry barriers for newcomers. Despite having good performance for a free trade index, GCC states have high entry barriers for the business and investment opportunities compared to the world average. A regression analysis shows that entry barriers in the GCC states increase when rent revenues (oil price) decrease, and GDP per capita is high while there is no effect of democracy level. Implicit entry barriers and lack of comparative advantage may slow down CERET industries' development in the GCC states. However, sharp decreases in the cost of CERET may incentivize the Gulf States to deploy these technologies instead of fossil fuels, which can be exported.

References

Acemoglu, Daron. 2008. Oligarchic versus democratic societies. *Journal of the European Economic Association*, 6(1): 1–44.

Arab Future Energy Index (AFEX). 2015. *"Energy Efficiency" Report*. Available at: www.rcreee.org/sites/default/files/afex_ee_2015_engish_web_0.pdf

Aghion, Philippe, Alberto F. Alesina, and Francesco Trebbi. 2007. *Democracy, Technology, and Growth*. www.nber.org

Boersma, Tim, and Steve Griffiths. 2016. *Reforming Energy Subsidies: Initial Lessons From the United Arab Emirates*. Research paper, Energy, Security and Climate Initiative at Brookings.

Cherif, Reda, and Fuad Hasanov. Soaring of the Gulf Falcons: Diversification in the GCC Oil Exporters in Seven Propositions. No. 14–177. International Monetary Fund, 2014.

Djankov, Simeon. 2009. *The Regulation of Entry: A Survey*. The World Bank Research Observer: lkp005.

Djankov, Simeon, Rafael La Porta, Florencio Lopez-de-Silanes, and Andrei Shleifer. 2002. The regulation of entry. *Quarterly Journal of Economics*, 117(1), pp. 1–37.

Fargues, Philippe. 2011. Immigration without inclusion: Non-nationals in nation-building in the Gulf States. *Asian and Pacific Migration Journal*, 20(3–4): 273–292.

Fasano-Filho, Ugo, and Qing Wang. 2002. Testing the Relationship Between Government Spending And Revenue: Evidence From GCC Countries. Vol. 2. International Monetary Fund.

Gengler, Justin, and Laurent A. Lambert. 2016. Renegotiating the ruling agreement: Selling fiscal reform in the GCC. *The Middle East Journal*, 70(2): 321–329.

Hall, Joshua C., and Robert A. Lawson. 2014. Economic freedom of the world: An accounting of the literature. *Contemporary Economic Policy*, 32(1): 1–19.

Hanieh, Adam. 2015. *Capitalism and Class in the Gulf Arab States*. Palgrave Macmillan, Chapters 2 & 3. Basingstoke, UK: Palgrave Macmillan.

Herb, Michael. 2005. No representation without taxation? Rents, development, and democracy. *Comparative Politics*: 37(3), pp. 297–316.

Hertog, Steffen. 2010. Defying the resource curse: Explaining successful state-owned enterprises in rentier states. *World Politics*, 62(2): 261–301.

Hvidt, Martin. 2011. Economic and institutional reforms in the Arab Gulf countries. *The Middle East Journal*, 65(1): 85–102.

Hvidt, Martin. 2013. *Economic Diversification in the GCC Countries: Past Record and Future Trends*. London, UK: London School of Economics. http://eprints.lse.ac.uk/

Jamil, M., Farzana Ahmad, and Y.J. Jeon. 2016. Renewable energy technologies adopted by the UAE: Prospects and challenges – A comprehensive overview. *Renewable and Sustainable Energy Reviews*, 55: 1181–1194.

Kaya, A. and Tsai, I., 2016. Inclusive Economic Institutions in the Gulf Cooperation Council States: Current Status and Theoretical Implications. Review of Middle East Economics and Finance, 12(2), pp. 139–173.Krane, Jim. 2009. City of Gold: Dubai and the Dream of Capitalism. Macmillan. London, UK: St. Martin's,

Mezher, Toufic, Steve Griffiths, Mohammad Abu Zahra, and Zeina Abbas. 2014. Outlook for a power generation fuel transition in the MENA region. *Journal of Energy Engineering*, 141(3): 04014026.

Ragwitz, Mario, Wolfgang Schade, Barbara Breitschopf, Rainer Walz, Nicki Helfrich, Max Rathmann, Gustav Resch, Christian Panzer, Thomas Faber, Reinhard Haas, Carsten Nathani, Matthias Holzhey, Inga Konstantinaviciute, Paul Zagamé, Arnaud Fougeyrollas, and Boris Le Hir 2009. *The Impact of Renewable Energy Policy on Economic Growth and Employment in the European Union*. Brussels, Belgium: European Commission, DG Energy and Transport.

Reiche, Danyel. 2010. Energy Policies of Gulf Cooperation Council (GCC) countries – possibilities and limitations of ecological modernization in rentier states. *Energy Policy*, 38(5): 2395–2403.

Rogner, Hans-Holger. 1997. An assessment of world hydrocarbon resources. *Annual Review of Energy and the Environment*, 22(1): 217–262.

Ross, Michael L. 2001. Does oil hinder democracy? *World Politics*, 53(3): 325–361.

Sgouridis, Sgouris, Ayu Abdullah, Steve Griffiths, Deger Saygin, Nicholas Wagner, Dolf Gielen, Hannes Reinisch, and Dane McQueen. 2016. RE-mapping the UAE's energy transition: An economy-wide assessment of renewable energy options and their policy implications. *Renewable and Sustainable Energy Reviews*, 55: 1166–1180.

Wang, Yanxiang, Shaikha Ali Almazrooei, Zhanna Kapsalyamova, Ali Diabat, and I-Tsung Tsai. 2016. Utility subsidy reform in Abu Dhabi: A review and a Computable General Equilibrium analysis. *Renewable and Sustainable Energy Reviews*, 55: 1352–1362.

12 Economic value of the Abu Dhabi coastal and marine ecosystem services

Estimate and management applications

James Blignaut, Myles Mander, Roula Inglesi-Lotz, Jane Glavan and Stephen Parr

Introduction

The Abu Dhabi coastal and marine resources, like many other coastal and marine resources (Lopes and Videira 2013), offer a range of ecosystem goods and services to their users. These include a range of regulating, supporting, cultural and provisioning services such as waste dilution, water quality maintenance, source of water supply, food, and recreation. The Abu Dhabi coastline is also unique in the sense that it provides non-renewable resources such as oil. The way humans are using these services, however, often leads to conflicts. Opening waterways for oil tankers using dredging, for example, often increases sediment pollution that inhibits coral growth and reduces recreation options (Burt et al. 2011; Burt 2014). When either visiting the city or considering marketing material concerning the city, it should be self-evident though that the Abu Dhabi authorities actively market the city as a preferred destination for high-value individuals and corporations. Through this concerted effort, supported by various publications, the authorities commit to maintain and provide a good and functioning marine and coastal environment. While not intuitively obvious, and perhaps not even explicitly intended, it is the amenity value of the coastal and marine resource that are especially highlighted as service offerings to residents and visitors.

Here, we are interested in the economic value beach hotels derive from the Abu Dhabi city coastal and marine ecosystem and resources. The city is being marketed as a destination of choice for the global traveller and business person, with beach and sea views, recreation, and sport opportunities as attractions (Abu Dhabi Urban Planning Council 2013; Abu Dhabi Urban Planning Council 2014a; Abu Dhabi Urban Planning Council 2014b; Environment Agency – Abu Dhabi 2014). Urban development, however, including a concomitant increase in the number of red algae blooms, threatens this image (see also AGEDI 2008; Al Shehhi et al. 2014; Burt et al. 2011; Burt 2014; Cheung et al. 2012; Foster and Foster 2013; Ghaffour et al. 2013; Grandcourt et al. 2011; Sheppard et al. 2010; Zhao and Ghedira 2014). We therefore embarked on estimating the economic value of Abu Dhabi's coastal ecosystem services, specifically its amenity values, to its hotel industry using both a WTA compensation for a deterioration in quality of coastal amenity values, as well as a WTP to contribute to a hypothetical restoration fund to avoid a loss in these amenity values.

The chapter first considers the specific Abu Dhabi context, then discusses the research method, and then follows with the results and discussion thereof.

Background

The Abu Dhabi Emirate is currently home to approximately 1.4 million people of which close to 50% are located within the city (Statistics Centre – Abu Dhabi 2014). Due to the very arid and even hostile nature of the Abu Dhabi hinterland, urban growth has been concentrated along the coast – the only location in the Emirate with abundant water supply, albeit saline. Not only does the coastal and marine environment host people, it also hosts the oil industry. This industry is largely focused on the marine environment as an associated transport sector consisting of ports, extensive dredged channels, and shipping routes. Consequently, there is a comprehensive and intensive use of the marine environment for economic inputs such as oil, shipping routes, water for desalination, fish harvesting, recreation, and general coastal amenity services linked to culture and relaxation. The marine ecosystems are also recipients of the outputs of development, such as the residential settlements, mining, and manufacturing, in the form of, among others, wastewater discharge, thermal cooling water discharge, brine discharge, dredging spoil, ballast discharge, and accidental petro-chemicals pollution (Burt 2014). The coastal and marine resources are working hard to provide a range of services to the visitors, residents, and citizens of Abu Dhabi.

It is also not surprising that the Abu Dhabi Urban Structure Framework (also known as 'Capital 2030') (Abu Dhabi Urban Planning Council 2014a) suggests that the demand for marine ecosystem goods and services in Abu Dhabi Emirate is likely to increase dramatically given that the population is expected to increase by 233%, from 1.4 million to 3.1 million by 2030, with further growth in associated factors such as hotels rooms (645%), industry (275%), commercial office space (436%), retail space (365%), and residential units (281%).

The future development set aside, economic development activities of the past 30 years has already led to significant impacts on the environment. There has, for example, been an increase in surface water temperatures, salinity, nutrient levels, sediment, resource harvesting, and chemical pollution in recent years (AGEDI 2008; Al Shehhi et al. 2014; Burt et al. 2011; Burt 2014; Cheung et al. 2012; Foster and Foster 2013; Ghaffour et al. 2013; Grandcourt et al. 2011; Sheppard et al. 2010; Zhao and Ghedira 2014). The state of marine ecological assets has subsequently declined due to these pressures leading to a large reduction in fish stocks (Cheung et al. 2012; Grandcourt et al. 2011), coral reefs (Burt et al. 2011; Sheppard et al. 2010), and a decline in the Socotra cormorant (*Phalacrocorax nigrogularis*) colonies (BirdLife International 2014).

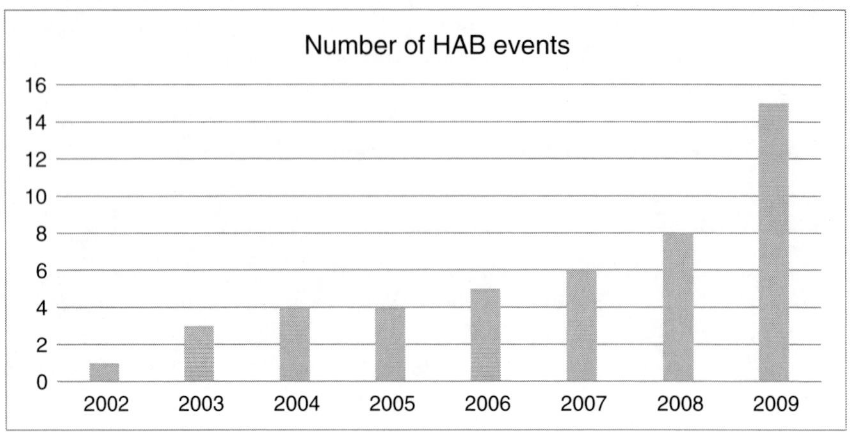

Figure 12.1 Number of harmful algal bloom (HAB) events per year

Source: Environment Agency – Abu Dhabi (2014)

One of the ecological responses to declining marine functionality has been an increase in intensity, frequency, and duration of harmful algal blooms (HAB, also called red tides) and inshore eutrophication (Environment Agency – Abu Dhabi 2014) (see Figure 12.1); see also Burt et al. (2011) and Feary et al. (2013). The red tides lead to toxic water conditions and large-scale fish die-offs, resulting in poor water quality, odours, and poor beach conditions (i.e. unsafe and unsuitable for recreation and general use).

This decline in marine functionality and associated increase in disservices of poor water quality is in stark conflict with the 'Capital 2030' (Abu Dhabi Urban Planning Council 2014a) vision of Abu Dhabi being a world-class city that, through careful planning, will conserve the city's environmental and cultural amenities. This statement is further substantiated by the overarching principles of urban development planning in a way that recognises and entrenches the city's natural capital as one of the main pillars of development (Abu Dhabi Urban Planning Council 2014a):

- Abu Dhabi will be a contemporary expression of an Arab city, which has people living, doing, and thriving in healthy supportive proximity to each other.
- Abu Dhabi will continue its practice of measured growth reflecting a sustainable economy, rather than an uncontrolled growth.
- Abu Dhabi will respect, be scaled to, and be shaped by the natural environment of sensitive coastal and desert ecologies.
- Abu Dhabi will manifest its role and stature as a capital city.
- Abu Dhabi's urban fabric and community infrastructure will enable the values, social arrangements, culture, and mores of this Arab community.

The current development trajectory and the historic evidence with respect to changes in the quality and quantity of coastal and marine resources imply that change is required for these official commitments to be upheld. In support of these commitments this study endeavours to investigate the amenity value of Abu Dhabi's coastal and marine resources to its beachfront hotels. We do so, using a double-bound continuous choice contingent valuation method using voting cards. We consider both the willingness to accept (WTA) compensation for any value loss in amenity as a result of a decline in the quality of the coastal and marine resources and the willingness to pay (WTP) to avoid future damages by contributing to a hypothetical restoration fund.

Contingent valuation

Coastal and marine resources are highly productive yet fragile. This has the unfortunate consequences that i) they are being used by many users for various reasons and ii) they do suffer degradation as a result of the use very easily. In an attempt to capture both the use and benefits humans derive from these resources, they have been the subject of many economic valuation assessments (Barbier et al. 2011; Carandang et al. 2013; De Groot et al. 2010; De Groot et al. 2012; Lange and Jiddawi 2009; Lopes and Videira 2013; Luisetti et al. 2011; Samonte-Tan et al. 2007; Tuya et al. 2014; Van der Ploeg and De Groot 2010; Vassallo et al. 2013; Vo et al. 2012; Voke et al. 2013; Wattage and Mardle 2008). Studies such as these are of great help within the context of assessing broad ranges of the value of ecosystem goods and services (see Annexure 1). Herein it is obvious that the value of coastal and marine resources, especially those linked to aesthetic and recreational values, is very high. In the Abu Dhabi context, however, specific policy questions require context-specific estimates of the value of ecosystem goods and services. This necessitates site-specific valuation.

Given the threats to the amenity values people derive from the coastal and marine resources within the Abu Dhabi Emirate, and specifically for Abu Dhabi city, we are interested in analysing the possible costs of such threats. This has become an important consideration given the rapid rate of economic development, as mentioned earlier, and the fact that the city is being marketed as a destination of choice for the global traveller and business person using amenity values, such as beach and sea views, recreation and sport opportunities, and facilities, as attractions (Abu Dhabi Urban Planning Council 2013; Abu Dhabi Urban Planning Council 2014a; Abu Dhabi Urban Planning Council 2014b; Environment Agency – Abu Dhabi 2014). The consequences of urban growth, however, include an increase in waste, energy, and water use. Furthermore, there is active reclamation of the ocean leading to an increase in the canalisation of the coastal area, reducing water flow; as a result, the city has seen an increase in eutrophication and the number of harmful algae bloom events as discussed above (see also AGEDI 2008; Al Shehhi et al. 2014; Burt et al. 2011; Burt 2014; Cheung et al. 2012; Foster and Foster 2013; Ghaffour et al. 2013; Grandcourt et al. 2011; Sheppard et al. 2010; Zhao and Ghedira 2014).

Marketing the city using its coastal and marine resources, among others, as incentives for the global traveller to opt for Abu Dhabi as a destination of choice, leads the investor and the traveller to an expectation of, or perceived entitlement to, the direct and indirect benefits of the 'free', non-marketed ecosystem services supplied by the ocean, as communicated in the planning documents.

While there is a range of well-documented valuation techniques (Dixon et al. 1994), the method favoured by many when seeking to estimate the direct and indirect value of non-marketed commodities is that of contingent valuation studies (Bowers 1997; Callan and Thomas 1996; Kahn 1997; Rao 2000). This is since contingent valuation studies provide a stated preference by the interviewee as to his/her perceived value of a resource and/or the change in value given a specific scenario. Two types of contingent valuation studies can be identified, namely the willingness to pay (WTP) for a service, an improvement in a condition, and/or the avoidance of a deterioration; and/or the willingness to accept (WTA) compensation for the loss of and/or deterioration in the service. The contingent valuation method has also been successfully applied to estimate the economic value of coastal and marine resources in the past within different countries and continents, such as Japan, Mexico, China, and the United States (Barr and Mourato 2009; Huang et al. 2013; Petrolia and Kim 2011; Zhai and Suzuki 2009). As elaborated on by Huang et al. (2013) and Zhai and Suzuki (2009), the WTA and WTP estimates of the same study and/or scenario should, according to neo-classical economics, render the same value. In practice, however, that is never the case (Ebert 2013; Flachaire et al. 2013; Tunçel and Hammitt 2014; Zhao and Kling 2004). Empirical evidence indicates that the WTP method renders values that are considerably lower than that of the WTA method.

Given the natural tendency of the WTA method to render upper-bound estimates of the economic value of a resource and/or amenity, WTP is generally favoured as a more conservative estimate (Arrow et al. 1993). This is true unless one is dealing with perceived entitlements and/or property rights. When a person has an actual and/or perceived property right to an amenity, it would be less appropriate to ask whether the person would be willing to pay for, for example, the avoidance in the loss of a condition he/she has an entitlement to. According to Zhai and Suzuki (2009), based on Pearce (2002), the general rule is as follows:

> Choose WTP for a quantity increase if the individuals in question do NOT have a property right to the post-change situation; Choose WTA for a quantity decrease if the individuals in question have a property right to the pre-change situation.

The important question that arises in this context is whether a "property right" can be assigned to public goods. Pearce (2002) answers as follows:

> While it is reasonably straightforward to determine the rules about which measure to use given the existence of well-defined property rights, it is far less

> easy to determine what property rights exists. The reason for this is that "property rights" relate not just to legal ownership of physical assets, but to rights to secure some flow of benefits. In other words, "property" = "benefits" and "rights" refer to the right to secure those benefits without being prevented from doing so. Rights therefore imply a duty on the part of everyone else not to prevent those benefits being secured.
>
> Pearce (2002)

As is in the cases of China (Huang et al. 2013) and Japan (Zhai and Suzuki 2009), it can be argued that the beach users, coastal residents, and property owners of Abu Dhabi have a high expectation that could be considered a right to the amenity values of the coastal and marine resources. This is since Abu Dhabi is being marketed to prospective investors, residents, and tourists as having access to high-quality coastal and marine resources. This is clearly demonstrated in, among others, the following statement on the historic role of Abu Dhabi's natural resources and continued commitment to its future protection and state (Environment Agency – Abu Dhabi 2014):

> Abu Dhabi has demonstrated commitment to improving the living standards of its citizens and other residents across several fronts. The leadership of the Abu Dhabi has the foresight to realise that well-being and utility depends not just on Gross Domestic Product (GDP) and disposable income, but also on broader accounting concerns including environmental sustainability and preservation of ecological and cultural heritage. This echoes the words of the late Sheikh Zayed who was a firm believer in the need to protect the environment, stating that it was a gift to the current generation to be passed on to future generations.
>
> 'We cherish our environment because it is an integral part of our country, our history and our heritage. On land and in the sea, our forefathers lived and survived in this environment. They were able to do so only because they recognised the need to conserve it, to take from it only what they needed to live and to preserve it for succeeding generations. We are responsible for taking care of our environment & wildlife, protect it and preserve it not only for the sake of our current generation, but also for the sake of our children and grandchildren. It is our duty to be loyal to our ancestors as well as our successors. With God's will, we shall continue to work to protect our environment and our wildlife, as did our forefathers before us. It is a duty, and, if we fail, our children, rightly, will reproach us for squandering an essential part of their inheritance, and of our heritage.'
>
> The Late Sheikh Zayed bin Sultan Al Nahyan, Founding father of the United Arab Emirates
>
> (February 1998, on the occasion of the Annual Environment Day)

Based on the above statement, and many other similar declarations with regard to the role of the natural environment in the past and the continued importance and support thereof in the future, which validates the users' expectation, we embark on estimating the economic value of Abu Dhabi's coastal amenity values to its beachfront hotels. This is done by considering both the WTA compensation for a deterioration in quality of the coastal amenity values, and the WTP and/or contribute to a hypothetical restoration fund to avoid a loss in these amenity values (see also Barr and Mourato 2009). The focus, however, is on the former.

Materials and method

Survey

A survey using a double-bound continuous choice contingent valuation method with voting cards considering both the willingness to accept (WTA) compensation for any value loss in amenity as a result of a decline in the quality of the coastal and marine resources and the willingness to pay (WTP) to avoid future damages by contributing to a hypothetical restoration fund was employed. The questionnaire commenced with a general introduction about the current state of the coastal and marine resources, marketing material, the government's vision, and examples of real and recent pollution in the form of harmful algal blooms (HABs) (used as a proxy to illustrate the potential impact of a decline in water quality) – all supported with photographs. The general introduction was followed by a section of questions enquiring about the current operational aspects of the hotel. This was then followed by a referendum-style double-bound continuous choice contingent valuation survey seeking to determine the willingness to accept (WTA) compensation for a loss in amenity services. Interviewees were shown voting cards in an increasing order. In the case of the real estate survey, the interviewees were asked to provide a percentage answer (or bid) based on the following question:

> What would be the minimum compensation required for the direct and indirect losses to avoid any net loss to your enterprise as measured against the impact, where impact is measured as:
>
> > *Impact = (current occupancy rate * current unit rate) – (new occupancy rate * new unit rate)* (the impact factor therefore measures the marginal change in the hotel's turnover before the event [at the current occupancy and unit rates] compared to the turnover after the event)

In this case 'current' is defined as up to before the change and the 'new' as after the change in amenity services. What was therefore sought is the level of compensation required (in percentage terms) in the 'before' and 'after' scenarios in relation to the impact on the business's operation.

Following the determination of the WTA compensation, a hypothetical restoration scenario was sketched and the interviewees were asked whether they would be willing to pay an annual fee to a restoration fund that would mitigate the pollution and ensure a constant supply of amenity services. Should the interviewee answer 'yes', a similar referendum-style double-bound continuous choice method using voting cards was used to determine the level of contribution the interviewee would make. In all cases, once the upper-bound of the voting cards was reached, it was followed by an open-ended question as to the interviewee's preference.

The survey was conducted between 16 October 2014 and 13 November 2014 whereby the financial managers of the hotels were interviewed. The sampling strategy was to engage all hotels on or close to the beach. Only one beachfront hotel in Abu Dhabi city refused to participate in the survey. Twenty-four hotels were interviewed. This is 27% of the total number of Abu Dhabi hotels and 96% of Abu Dhabi's beach hotels. It is assumed to represent 100% of Abu Dhabi's beach hotels.

Model

For the econometric part of this study, we planned to estimate a Tobit model as frequently used in similar applications in the literature. For example, Huang et al. (2013) examined the public demand for ecosystem improvement at Hongze Lake in China by assessing respondents' willing to pay for a future improvement in the water quality of the lake and their willingness to accept specific compensation in the absence of improvement efforts. Barr and Mourato (2009) and Petrolia and Kim (2011) both used a Tobit model to investigate WTP and WTA for marine protection in Mexico and welfare changes from future coastal wetland losses in Louisiana, respectively. The Tobit model would be ideal for this study to evaluate the integrated representation of the effects of WTP and WTA for two reasons: i) it can combine the best features of the linear regression and ii) it is appropriate when a large number of observations on the dependent variable hover around zero (Huang et al. 2013; Zhai and Ikeda 2006; Zhai and Suzuki 2009). The number of observations in this study (24 out of a possible 25) is relatively small for this type of estimation. We therefore decided to proceed with the estimation of various parametric and non-parametric hypothesis testing to evaluate the possible existence of association among WTA and WTP and various factors.

Table 12.1 presents the various tests that will be employed in the analysis depending on the nature of each of the series. Here we explain that each of the various tests will be chosen based on the variable's nature (categorical or numerical) and distribution (normally distributed or not). In essence, depending on these factors for the pair of variables tested, the appropriate test is chosen.

Table 12.2 describes the dependent variables (WTA and WTP), the independent variables (property, rooms, room_perc, unit_rate_average, lifespan) and their nature (categorical or numerical according to the questionnaire completed by the respondents).

Table 12.1 Bivariate hypothesis testing

	Variable 1	*Variable 2*	*Appropriate test*[1]
1	Categorical (2 or more categories)	Categorical (2 or more categories)	Chi-squared test or Fischer's exact for small samples
2	Numerical (normally distributed)	Categorical (2 categories)	Unpaired t-test
3	Numerical (normally distributed)	Categorical (2 or more categories)	ANOVA
4	Numerical (normally distributed)	Numerical (normally distributed)	Pearson's correlation
5	Numerical (skewed)	Categorical (2 categories)	Wilcoxon rank-sum
6	Numerical (skewed)	Categorical (2 or more categories)	Kruskal-Wallis[2]
7	Numerical (skewed)	Numerical (skewed)	Spearman's rho[3]

1 Gibbons, J. D., and Chakrabati, S. "Non-parametric statistical inference," *International Encyclopedia of statistical science* (Heidelberg: Springer Berlin, 2014), 977–979.

2 Kruskal, W. H., and Wallis, W. A. "Use of ranks in one-direction variance analysis," *Journal of the American Statistical Association* 47 (1952): 583–621.

3 Caruso, J. C., and Cliff, N. "Empirical size, coverage and power of confidence intervals for Spearman's Rho", *Educational and Psychological Measurement* 57 (1997): 637–654.

Table 12.2 Description of the variables

Variable	*Description*	*Type of variable*
WTP	The amount that the respondents are willing to pay for restoration	Numerical
WTA	The minimum compensation required for the direct and indirect losses to avoid any net loss to their enterprise as measured against the impact (impact = (current occupancy rate * current unit rate) – (new occupancy rate * new unit rate))	Numerical
rooms	Number of rooms	Numerical
room_perc	Average occupancy rate per year	Numerical (percentage)
unit_rate_average	Weighted average of the rate for 2014	Numerical
lifespan	Expected lifespan of the operation from 2014	Numerical

Results

Estimates of the willingness to accept and to pay

The survey results for the hotels are provided in Table 12.3.

Table 12.3 Summary of Abu Dhabi hotel surveys

	Hotels						
	Min	*Max*	*Ave*	*Std. Dev.*	*Total orsum*	*Yes*	*No*
Number of observations					24		
Number of rooms	189	565	348	109.9	8 242		
Current occupancy rate (%)	48%	88%	72.8%	10.8			
Unit rate (AED)*	350	2300	793	458.9			
Expected period before major refurbishment (years)	1	50	12.8	11.7			
Would the scenario of reduced amenity values affect your business						20	4
Would you seek compensation for the loss						20	0
Of those saying yes, the number proving new financial data:						15	5
Of those saying yes and providing new financial data:							
New occupancy rate (%)	18%	80%	54.1%	15			
New unit rate (AED)*	340	2300	771.4	637.5			

Note (*): Exchange rate considered for this report is AED3.67 = 1US$

Table 12.4 Hotels: estimate of the WTA compensation for changes in amenity services

	*Stated by 15 hotels**	*Elevated to 20 hotels**
Stated annual WTA	AED 414 131 051 US$ 112 842 248	AED 517 663 814 US$ 141 052 810
NPV of WTA over 13 years @ SDR of 2%	AED 6 219 259 810 US$ 1 694 621 201	AED 7 774 074 762 US$ 2 118 276 502
NPV of WTA over 13 years @ SDR of 2%	AED 4 699 713 950 US$ 1 280 576 008	AED 5 874 642 438 US$ 1 600 720 010
NPV of WTA over 13 years @ SDR of 5%	AED 3 890 170 257 US$ 1 059 991 896	AED 4 862 712 821 US$ 1 324 989 869

Note (*): AED3.67 = 1US$

Based on the information provided by the hotels, it was possible to estimate the WTA compensation (see Table 12.4). The WTA is estimated using the following formula for each of the hotels that provided data, both individually and aggregated:

> ((current occupancy rate * current unit rate) – (new occupancy rate * new unit rate)) * number of rooms * 365 days * impacted percentage

The aggregate (total) WTA for the 15 hotels that provided financial data is estimated to be US$113 million per year. Elevated by 25% to make provision for the hotels that indicated they will require compensation but did not provide financial information, this number is estimated at US$141 million per year, or 35% of average turnover. This is 9% of the total revenue for all of Abu Dhabi's hotels in 2013, which is estimated to be US$1.5 billion (www.arabianbusiness.com/abu-dhabi-targets-3-1m-tourists-during-2014-536809.html). This also equates to an average NPV of between US$1.3 and US$2.1 billion assuming discount rates of 5% and -2% respectively over the period of 13 years, which is the average period before major refurbishment will take place. However, a note on the discount rate is warranted. While capital development and financial projects tend to have higher discount rates (5% to 10%) to reflect the current scarcity of the resource and the declining time value of money, this does not reflect the characteristics of natural capital. Natural capital tends to be increasingly scarce due to transformation, with a declining quantity, and is used by increasingly more people. Consequently, the demand for the services derived from natural capital tends to increase over time. Hence, it has been argued that negative discount rates may be appropriate when dealing with ecosystem services that are of high and increasing value due to increasing demand (Blignaut and Aronson 2008; Brouwer et al. 2008; Dasgupta and Maskin 2005; Gowdy et al. 2013; Hoel and Sterner 2006; Price 2000; Rees et al. 2007). As a rule of thumb the negative discount rate is the rate equal to the population growth rate to keep the per capita value of the ecosystem goods and services constant over time.

Of the 17 hotels indicating that they would be willing to contribute to a restoration fund, only nine provided data on WTP. This ranged from AED 10 000 to AED 2 000 000 per year totalling AED 2 984 000 (US$813 000). This number could be doubled to make provision for the hotels stating that they would make a contribution to the restoration fund, but failed to indicate a value. This is, however, still only about 1.2% of what the hotels would require in the form of compensation through the WTA indicator; a clear indication of the high premium and expectations the hotels are placing on the coastal amenity. It should also be seen in the context of Abu Dhabi's tax policy where there is limited precedent or culture for companies to make financial contributions to the authorities.

Model results

Before proceeding with examining the existence of association between WTP or WTA and various other factors, we need to test the normality hypothesis of all the numerical variables in order to assess which test will be used (see Table 12.1). Table 12.5 presents the results of the normality test. The first column mentions the variable, the second column gives the adjusted chi-squared, while the third column indicates the associated p-value. In the last column, the conclusion for each variable is given (the null hypothesis can be rejected if the statistic > critical value or p-value<α %level of significance).

As seen in Table 12.5, both dependent variables (WTA and WTP) are numerical and non-normally distributed so options/test 5–7 (Table 12.1) are applicable. All the dependent variables are numerical, so from Table 12.1, only option 7/Spearman's rho statistic tests will be used here (see Table 12.6 for the results).

Table 12.5 Normality test (Ho: normally distributed series)

Variable	*Adjusted-chi squared*	*p-value*	*Conclusion*
Rooms	2.390	0.3034	Normally distributed
room_perc	0.330	0.8490	Normally distributed
unit_rate_average	11.400	0.0033	Skewed
lifespan	8.670	0.0131	Skewed
WTP	13.930	0.0009	Skewed
WTA	5.530	0.0628	Skewed

Table 12.6 Bivariate hypothesis testing (Ho: no association between the two variables) Spearman's rho statistic

Dependent variable	*Associated variable*	*Statistic*	*p-value*	*Conclusion*
WTP	rooms	0.1757	0.6511	Do not reject Ho: no association
	room_perc	−0.8277	0.0059	Reject Ho→ association
	unit_rate_average	0.4036	0.3214	Do not reject Ho: no association
	lifespan	0.2857	0.4561	Do not reject Ho: no association
WTA	rooms	0.3791	0.2014	Do not reject Ho: no association
	room_perc	−0.0304	0.9215	Do not reject Ho: no association
	unit_rate_average	0.9107	0.0000	Reject Ho→ association
	lifespan	0.3047	0.3114	Do not reject Ho: no association

Table 12.6 shows the results of the Spearman's rho test for each pair of variables and the conclusion that can be derived from each. The null hypothesis tested is that there is no association between the two variables and can be rejected when the Spearman's rho statistic is higher than its critical values or the p-values are smaller than α (level of significance) zero. From these findings, we conclude that only the average occupancy rate per year (unit_rate_average) showed some evidence of association with the minimum compensation required for the direct and indirect losses to avoid any net loss to their enterprise (WTA), as well as the annual contribution over the respondents' enterprises' expected lifetime that they would be willing to make towards the dedicated restoration fund.

Conclusion

Abu Dhabi is one of the world's youngest but fastest growing metropolies. To achieve this standard, the city is marketing itself actively as a destination of choice to the foreign investor and promises, among others, well-managed coastal and marine resources and its continued functioning. However, there is recent evidence that indicates serious deterioration in the resource quality and its continued ability to render a wide range of services to its user population, for example, the rapid increase in harmful algae bloom outbreaks.

In this study we used a contingent valuation assessment of 24 of Abu Dhabi's 25 beachfront hotels to determine the amenity value these hotels are deriving from the coastal and marine resources. To estimate such, we use the value of the perceived impact of frequent and prolonged outbreaks of harmful algae blooms (or red tides) on the business as well as the hotel operators' willingness to accept compensation in the event of such an outbreak, and their willingness to make a contribution to a restoration fund to avoid such outbreaks.

The willingness to accept (WTA) compensation is estimated at US$141 million per year, or 35% of the average turnover. This is 9% of the total revenue for all of Abu Dhabi's hotels in 2013 and equates to an average NPV of between US$1.3 and US$2.1 billion over the average period before major refurbishment will take place. The WTP, however, is only about 1.2% of what the hotels would require in the form of compensation through the WTA indicator; a clear indication of the high premium and expectation the hotels are placing on the coastal amenity. This should be seen in the context of i) the hotels having a perceived entitlement to a clean and functioning ecosystem given the marketing drive advertising such and the strong impetus towards attracting new investment based on, among others, an assured quality environment; and ii) Abu Dhabi's tax policy, where there is limited precedent or culture for companies to make financial contributions to the authorities.

The amenity value of Abu Dhabi's coastal and marine resources is therefore substantial. The risk of the resources not playing its vital role is highly detrimental to the environment, society, and the economy at large. The potential knock-on effect of this goes far beyond the beachfront hotels, affecting the entire economy. Extreme and diligent care to restore and maintain Abu Dhabi's marine and coastal resources is therefore of the utmost importance if the dream on which the city is built, is to be realised.

Acknowledgement

The programme of work was prepared for the Abu Dhabi Global Environmental Data Initiative (AGEDI), which is a partnership between the Environment Agency-Abu Dhabi and UNEP, under the Contingent Ecosystem Services Valuation project for Abu Dhabi. The authors are grateful for the implementation services provided by project consultant Hyder Consulting Middle East Ltd and acknowledge the fact that the survey team, comprising members of staff from Hyder Consulting (Stephen Parr, Natalie Jones, Senna Sabir) and AGEDI (Jane Claire-Gavan, Rawan Mamoun, Hedaya Ali Al Ameri) have conducted the survey. The outcomes of the findings have been achieved due to the willingness of those being surveyed to share their expertise and thoughts. Collaboration between all stakeholders has resulted in learning opportunities for all parties and contributions from every individual involved are graciously acknowledged. The authors remain responsible for the content of this chapter, yet they cannot accept any responsibility for any use of or reliance on the contents of this report by third parties.

Annexure 1 Estimates of the value of coastal and marine ecosystem services: Summary: 2013USD/ha

			Food	*Fresh water supply*	*Raw material*	*Genetic resources*	*Medicinal resources*	*Ornamental resources*	*Influence on air quality*	*Climate regulation*	*Moderation of extreme events*	*Regulation of water flows*	*Waste treatment/water purification*	*Erosion prevention*	*Nutrient cycling*	*Lifecycle maintenance (nursery services)*	*Gene pool protection (conservation)*	*Aesthetic information*	*Recreation and tourism*	*Inspiration for culture, art and design*	*Spiritual experience*	*Cognitive information (education and science)*
Coral reefs	De Groot et al. (2012)	min	–		10	37 130		18		93	4		95	1 497			7	2 476	–			4
		max	6 937		72 275	37 130		1 747		2 462	116 998		95	344 282			103 816	30 729	1 668 452			7 223
		median	174		275	37 130		328		1 450	1 701		95	172 890			1 234	5 184	1 755			128
	Samonte-Tan et al. (2007)	min	468														191		233			37
		max	1 877														368		1 699			128
	De Groot et al. (2010) TEEB (2010)	min	–					169			2						89	2 488	0			1
		max	1 973					391			15 945						36 624	30 879	1 195 397			7 258
		median	30					359			3 146						2 421	16 683	1 247			102
Sea grass, shallow seas, continental shelves, shores & beaches, intertidal zone	De Groot et al. (2012)	min	1		1					538				28 502		104	202		–		23	24
		max	16 845		39					538				28 502		292	202		789		23	24
		median	458		1					538				28 502		257	202		58		23	24
	Samonte-Tan et al. (2007)	min	9																			
		max	138																			
	Vassallo et al. (2013)	min												2 198 944								
		max												2 198 944								
	Barbier et al. (2011)	min			27									265								
		max			27									265								
	De Groot et al. (2010) TEEB (2010)	min	24								83 119								221			
		max	24								83 119								45 243			
		median	24								83 119								22 732			

(*Continued*)

Annexure 1 (Continued)

			Food	*Fresh water supply*	*Raw material*	*Genetic resources*	*Medicinal resources*	*Ornamental resources*	*Influence on air quality*	*Climate regulation*	*Moderation of extreme events*	*Regulation of water flows*	*Waste treatment/water purification*	*Erosion prevention*	*Nutrient cycling*	*Lifecycle maintenance (nursery services)*	*Gene pool protection (conservation)*	*Aesthetic information*	*Recreation and tourism*	*Inspiration for culture, art and design*	*Spiritual experience*	*Cognitive information (education and science)*
Tidal marshes & mangroves	De Groot et al. (2012)	min	–	1	–	11	7			7	2		6	211	50	5	10		22			
		max	21 058	4 805	4 739	11	669			206	36 280		719 176	14 691	50	139 190	24 778		31 849			
		median	262	332	104	11	338			34	2 514		4 715	1 377	50	1 266	2 039		616			
	Vo et al. (2012)	min	40	40						116			7 873	4			20					
		max	623	339						116			7 873	4 045			20					
	Samonte-Tan et al. (2007)	min	18											776		280	22					
		max	38											776		280	22					
	Barbier et al. (2011)	min			559									4 977								
		max			676									4 977								
Mangroves	De Groot et al. (2010) TEEB (2010)	min	0		3		2			2	41			108		55			553			
		max	229		919		39			879	3 022			158		67 013			553			
		median	28		29		20			441	1 801			133		940			553			
Saltwater wetland	De Groot et al. (2010) TEEB (2010)	min									307					34			44			
		max									4 269					2 655			78			
		median									2 288					295			61			
Tidal marsh	De Groot et al. (2010) TEEB (2010)	min									9 339					2 520						
		max									9 339					2 520						
		median									9 339					2 520						
Estuaries	De Groot et al. (2010) TEEB (2010)	min	1		0											37						
		max	257		0											37						
		median	129		0											37						

References

Abu Dhabi Urban Planning Council. 2013. *Al Gharbia 2030 Regional Long Range Plan – Draft Concept Report*. Abu Dhabi: Abu Dhabi Urban Planning Council.

Abu Dhabi Urban Planning Council. 2014a. *Plan Abu Dhabi 2030 – Urban Structure Framework Plan*. Abu Dhabi: Abu Dhabi Urban Planning Council.

Abu Dhabi Urban Planning Council. 2014b. Plan Maritime 2030 – Abu Dhabi Coastal and Marine Framework Plan – Charette 1 Proceedings Book – Existing Conditions, Constraints and Opportunities. Abu Dhabi: Abu Dhabi Urban Planning Council.

AGEDI. 2008. *Marine and Coastal Environments of Abu Dhabi Emirate*. Abu Dhabi: Environment Agency – Abu Dhabi.

Al Shehhi, M.R., I. Gherboudj, and H. Ghedira. 2014. An overview of historical harmful algae blooms outbreaks in the Arabian Seas. *Marine Pollution Bulletin*, 86: 314–324.

Arrow, K., R. Solow, P.R. Portney, E.E. Learner, R. Radner, and H. Schuman. 1993. Report of the NOAA panel on contingent valuation. *Federal Register*, 58: 4601–4614.

Barbier, E.B., S.D. Hacker, C. Kennedy, E.W. Koch, A.C. Stier, and B.R. Silliman. 2011. The value of estuarine and coastal ecosystem services. *Ecological Monographs*, 81(2): 169–193.

Barr, R., and S. Mourato. 2009. Investigating the potential for marine resource protection through environmental service markets: An exploratory study from La Paz, Mexico. *Ocean & Coastal Management*, 53: 568–577.

BirdLife International. 2014. *Species Factsheet: Phalacrocorax Nigrogularis*. Available at: www.birdlife.org.

Blignaut, J.N., and J. Aronson. 2008. Getting serious about maintaining biodiversity. *Conservation Letters*, 1(1): 12–17.

Bowers, J. 1997. Sustainability and Environmental Economics. Harlow: Longman.

Brouwer, R., P. Van Beukering, and E. Sultanian. 2008. The impact of the bird flu on public willingness to pay for the protection of migratory bird. *Ecological Economics*, 64(3): 575–585.

Burt, J.A. 2014. The environmental costs of coastal urbanization in the Arabian Gulf. *City*, 18(6): 760–770.

Burt, J.A., S. Al-Harthi, and A. Al-Cibahy. 2011. Long-term impacts of coral bleaching events on the world's warmest reefs. *Marine Environmental Research*, 72(4): 225–229.

Callan, S.J., and J.M. Thomas. 1996. *Environmental Economics and Management.* Boston: Irwin Press.

Carandang, A.P., L.D. Camacho, D.T. Gevaña, J.T. Dizon, S.C. Camacho, C.C. De Luna, F.B. Pulhin, E.A. Combalicer, F.D. Paras, R.J.J. Peras, and L.L. Rebugio. 2013. Economic valuation for sustainable mangrove ecosystems management in Bohol and Palawan, Philippines. *Forest Science and Technology*, 9(3): 118–125.

Caruso, J.C., and N. Cliff. 1997. Empirical size, coverage and power of confidence intervals for Spearman's Rho. *Educational and Psychological Measurement*, 57: 637–654.

Cheung, W., D. Zeller, M. Palomares, M. Al-Abdulrazzak, V. Lam, M. Paleczny, and D. Pauly. 2012. *A Preliminary Assessment of Climate Change Impacts on Marine Ecosystems and Fisheries of the Arabian Gulf.* A report to Climate Change Research Group/LLC.

Dasgupta, P., and E. Maskin. 2005. Uncertainty and hyperbolic discounting. *American Economics Review*, 95: 1290–1299.

De Groot, R.S., L. Brander, S. Van Der Ploeg, R. Costanza, F. Bernard, L. Braat, M. Christie, N. Crossman, A. Ghermandi, L. Hein, S. Hussain, P. Kumar, A. McVittie, R. Portela, L.C. Rodriguez, P. Ten Brink, and P. Van Beukering. 2012. Global estimates of the value of ecosystems and their services in monetary units. *Ecosystem Services*, 1: 50–61.

De Groot, R.S., P. Kumar, S. Van der Ploeg, and P. Sukhdev. 2010. Estimates of monetary values of ecosystem services. Appendix 3. In *The Economics of Ecosystems and Biodiversity (TEEB): Ecological and Economic Foundations*, edited by P. Kumar. London: Earthscan.

Dixon, J.A., L.F. Scura, R.A. Carpenter, and P.B. Sherman. 1994. *Economic Analysis of Environmental Impacts.* London: Earthscan.

Ebert, U. 2013. The relationship between individual and household measures of WTP and WTA. *Social Choice and Welfare*, 40: 367–390.

Environment Agency – Abu Dhabi. 2014. *The Abu Dhabi Environment Vision 2030 – A Sustainable Future for Abu Dhabi.* Abu Dhabi: Environment Agency – Abu Dhabi.

Feary, D., J. Burt, A. Bauman, S. Al Hazeem, M. Abdel-Moati, K. Al-Khalifa, D. Anderson, C. Amos, A. Baker, A. Bartholomew, R. Bento, G. Cavalcante, C. Chen, S. Coles, K. Dab, A. Fowler, D. George, E. Grandcourt, R. Hill, D.M. John, D.A. Jones, S. Keshamurthy, H. Mahmoud, M. Moradi Och Tapeh, P.G. Mostafvi, H. Naser, M. Pichon, S. Purkis, B. Riegl, K. Samimi-Namin, C. Sheppard, J.V. Samiei, C.R Voolstra and J. Wiedenmann. 2013. Critical research needs for identifying future changes in Gulf coral reef ecosystems. *Marine Pollution Bulletin*, 72: 406–416.

Flachaire, E., G. Hollard, and J.F. Shogren. 2013. On the origin of the WTA – WTP divergence in public good valuation. *Theory*, 74: 431–437.

Foster, K.A., and G. Foster. 2013. Demography and population dynamics of massive coral communities in adjacent high latitude regions (United Arab Emirates). *PLoS*, 8(8): e71049.

Ghaffour, N., T.M. Missimer, and G.L. Amy. 2013. Combined desalination, water reuse, and aquifer storage and recovery to meet water supply demands in the GCC/MENA region. *Desalination and Water Treatment*, 51(1–3): 38–43.

Gibbons, J.D., and S. Chakrabati. 2014. Non-parametric statistical inference. In *International Encyclopedia of Statistical Science*, 977–979. **Lovric**, M. (Ed.). Heidelberg: Springer Berlin.

Gowdy, J., J.B. Rosser, and L. Roy. 2013. The evolution of hyperbolic discounting: Implications for truly social valuation of the future. *Journal of Economic Behaviour and Organisation*, 90: 94–104.

Grandcourt, E., T. Abdessalaam, A. Al Shamsi, S. Hartmann, and F. Francis. 2011. An evaluation of the management effectiveness of a stock re-building strategy for a multi-species demersal trap fishery in Abu Dhabi, United Arab Emirates. *Open Journal of Marine Science*, 1(3): 82–97.

Hoel, M., and T. Sterner. 2006. *Discounting and Relative Prices: Assessing the Future Damage.* Resources for the Future, Discussion Paper 06–18. Washington: Resources for the Future.

Huang, L., J. Ban, B. Duan, J. Bi, and Z. Yuan. 2013. Public demand for remediating a local ecosystem: Comparing WTP and WTA at Hongze Lake, China. *Lake and Reservoir Management*, 29(1): 23–32.

Kahn, J.R. 1997. The Economic Approach and Environmental and Natural Resources. Orlando: Dryden Press.

Kruskal, W.H., and W.A. Wallis. 1952. Use of ranks in one-direction variance analysis. *Journal of the American Statistical Association*, 47: 583–621.

Lange, G.-M., and N. Jiddawi. 2009. Economic value of marine ecosystem services in Zanzibar: Implications for marine conservation and economic development. *Ocean & Coastal Management*, 52: 521–532.

Lopes, R., and N. Videira. 2013. Valuing marine and coastal ecosystem services: An integrated participatory framework. *Ocean & Coastal Management*, 84: 153–162.

Luisetti, T., R.K. Turner, I.J. Bateman, S. Morse-Jones, C. Adams, and L. Fonseca. 2011. Coastal and marine ecosystem service valuation for policy and management: Managed realignment case studies in England. *Ocean & Coastal Management*, 54: 212–224.

Pearce, D. 2002. *The Role of "Property Rights" in Determining Economic Values for Environmental Costs and Benefits.* Available at: http://webarchive.nationalarchives.gov.uk/20140328084622/www.environment-agency.gov.uk/commondata/acrobat/wtawtp_pearce_1485692.pdf.

Petrolia, D., and T. Kim. 2011. Preventing land loss in coastal Louisiana: Estimates of WTP and WTA. *Journal of Environmental Management*, 92: 859–865.

Price, P. 2000. Discounting compensation for injuries. *Risk Analysis*, 20: 839–849.

Rao, P.K. 2000. *Sustainable Development.* Oxford: Blackwell Press.

Rees, W.E., J. Farley, E. Vesely, and R. De Groot. 2007. Valuing natural capital and the cost and benefits of restoration. In *Restoring Natural Capital: The Science, Business and Practise*, edited by J. Aronson, S. Milton, and J.N. Blignaut. Washington, DC: Island Press.

Samonte-Tan, G.P.B., A.T. White, M.A. Tercero, J. Diviva, E. Tabara, and C. Caballes. 2007. Economic valuation of coastal and marine resources: Bohol Marine Triangle, Philippines. *Coastal Management*, 35(2–3): 319–338.

Sheppard, C., M. Al-Husaini, F. Al-Jamali, F. Al-Yamani, R. Baldwin, and J. Bishop. 2010. The Gulf: A young sea in decline. *Marine Pollution Bulletin*, 60(1): 13–38.

Statistics Centre – Abu Dhabi (SCAD). 2014. *Statistical Year Book of Abu Dhabi.* Abu Dhabi: Statistics Centre.

Tunçel, T., and J.K. Hammitt. 2014. A new meta-analysis on the WTP/WTA disparity. *Journal of Environmental Economics and Management*, 68: 175–187.

Tuya, F., R. Haroun, and F. Espino. 2014. Economic assessment of ecosystem services: Monetary value of seagrass meadows for coastal fisheries. *Ocean & Coastal Management*, 96: 191–187.

Van der Ploeg, S., and R.S. De Groot. 2010. *The TEEB Valuation Database – a Searchable Database of 1310 Estimates of Monetary Values of Ecosystem Services.* Wageningen: Foundation for Sustainable Development. Available at: www.es-partnership.org/esp/80763/5/0/50.

Vassallo, P., C. Paoli, A. Rovere, M. Montefalcone, C. Morri, and C.N. Bianchi. 2013. The value of the seagrass Posidonia oceanica: A natural capital assessment. *Marine Pollution Bulletin*, 75: 157–167.

Vo, Q.T., C. Kuenzer, Q.M. Vo, F. Moder, and N. Oppelt. 2012. Review of valuation methods for mangrove ecosystem services. *Ecological Indicators*, 23: 431–446.

Voke, N., I. Fairley, M. Willis, and I. Masters. 2013. Economic valuation of the recreational value of the coastal environment in a marine renewable deployment area. *Ocean & Coastal Management*, 78: 77–87.

Wattage, P., and S. Mardle. 2008. Total economic value of wetland conservation in Sri Lanka identifying use and non-use values. *Wetlands Ecology and Management*, 16: 359–369.

Zhai, G.F., and S. Ikeda. 2006. Flood risk acceptability and economic value of evaluation. *Risk Analysis*, 26: 683–694.

Zhai, G.F., and T. Suzuki. 2009. Evaluating economic value of coastal waterfront in Tokyo Bay, Japan with willingness-to-accept measure. *Water Resources Management*, 23: 633–645.

Zhao, E., and C.L. Kling. 2004. Willingness to pay, compensating variation, and the cost of commitment. *Economic Inquiry*, 42(3): 503–517.

Zhao, J., and H. Ghedira. 2014. Monitoring red tide with satellite imagery and numerical models: A case study in the Arabian Gulf. *Marine Pollution Bulletin*, 79: 305–313.

13 Economic and GHG emission policy co-benefits for integrated waste management planning across the GCC

Lead Authors
Paul Dumble and Nagwa El Karawy

Contributing Authors
Amr Osama Abdel-Aziz and Ahmed Wafiq Abolnasr

Background

The Gulf Cooperation Council (GCC) was established in 1981 as a trade bloc for member states: Saudi Arabia, Kuwait, Bahrain, Oman, Qatar and United Arab Emirates (UAE). The GCC consensually develops unified regulations in areas such as the environment, economy and political affairs. In 1997, the publication of *General Regulations of Environment in the GCC States* provided a framework for the implementation of rules and regulations on environmental issues.[1] Significant health with wider community and land environmental impacts, as described by Al-Maaded et al. (2012: 186–194) and Cointreau (2006), arise from large-scale dumping of waste (Ansari 2012a; Luomi 2014). Reviewing regional waste management, Nefisa Abou-Elseoud (2008: 125) noted that some Arab countries had "*embarked on the application of an integrated environment management approach towards waste*", adding that there were many challenges, including:

- Lack of surveys, statistics and consequently data and information
- Limited technical infrastructure, plans and strategies
- Insufficient financial resources

Deficiencies in reporting data, planning and waste management capacity is not unique to GCC countries (ISWA 2013). However, this situation has changed little with Ibrahim Abel Gelil (2014: 11) noting that "*In many Arab countries, the capacity and the infrastructure for environmentally sound management of . . . and wastes is lacking.*" Saleh Ansari (2012a) argues that there is a need to improve understanding of climate change impacts, the vulnerability of society, economy, waste management and the environment, and "*advocates the use of a new waste hierarchy*" as policy options supporting the developing Integrated Waste Management (IWM) systems in the GCC countries to reduce greenhouse gases (GHG's) identifying key strategy drivers for the GCC region including;

- Articulating the need for resources to address MSW issues,
- Understanding how development of IWM capacity can stabilise and reduce emissions from municipal solid waste (MSW), to
- Finding ways to progress the aspirational political and environmental visions.

This study utilises core data from a wide range of data sources referenced within academic studies, reports, strategies, website reports (e.g. Zafar 2015) and government entities.[2] Historical difficulties have been found in obtaining consistent and sufficient data on waste in the GCC region (Hasawi 1999: 22–34), as recorded in an Economic and Social Commission for Western Asia (ESCWA) regional report (Blickensdörfer-Wieland 2005), noted in a global commentary (ISWA 2013), noted more recently in a study (Nizami et al. 2015) and with significant periodic data gaps in accessible databases (UNSD 2016: UNFCCC 2016).

The model developed for this study builds on environmental and lifecycle principles related to methane emissions adopted within established emission assessment models (IPCC 2006c; Alexander, Burkin and Singleton 2005; Gentil 2006) in a region where MSW disposal emissions are affected by the dry tropic climatic conditions of the region with average annual rainfall below 100 mm (Almazrour et al. 2012) with high evapotranspiration rates.

Objectives

For the purposes of this chapter, the model will be used to

- Address GCC MSW data deficiencies
- Identify and assess the potential economic and emission co-benefits from the development of IWM capacity in the GCC, setting out the scale and time frames
- Provide the basis for ongoing discussions and actions to address barriers to the development of IWM

This chapter takes the debate on the development of IWM in the GCC from "this is what we should do to reduce MSW emissions" based on data inconsistencies, to an argument that says "this is what is needed to mitigate MSW emissions and here are our best IWM intervention capacity estimates and timescales. What is stopping us from getting on with this?" The model described in this study changes everything not just for MSW management in the GCC countries but almost every developing and undeveloped country across the world.

Methodology

Development of the WTEEM tool

The waste, technology, economics and emission model (WTEEM) is a decision-making tool designed and developed by the lead authors to assess the impacts from the future adoption of a range of waste collection, treatment and disposal technologies necessary for the development of IWM systems.

The model evolved from spreadsheets developed by the authors for the UNEP Geo6 West Asia Assessment (UNEP 2016: 92–99) to provide a realistic planning assessment for regional and country MSW. Papers published in the region while developing the policy and strategic context contain very little detail to support practical IWM capacity interventions that would mitigate the climate change impacts of MSW (Ansari 2012a; Luomi 2014).

WTEEM tool and other emission tools

The WTEEM tool differs from the IPCC (2006c) *Waste Model* and *LandGEM* (RTI 2010: 2–4) in estimating degradable organic carbon (DOC) from characterisation and compositional features. The *LandGEM* model uses assumed default factors including fixed values to estimate the degradable organic carbon fraction and does not take account of soil oxidation of the methane emissions (RTI 2010: 2–2). The *IPCC Waste Model* also uses default assumptions (IPCC 2006a: 2–4 to 2–17; IPPC 2006b: 3.6–3.22) where there is no data on MSW organic composition to determine the DOC (IPPC 2006a, Table 2.5). The *WRATE* (Waste Resource Assessment Tool for the Environment) model provides a broader lifecycle and environmental emission assessment (Gentil 2006), though it lacks, as with the *IPCC Waste Model* and *LandGEM*, an economic and time context to assess the necessary financial, planning capacity and range of treatment capacity needed for effective IWM development.

Characterising GCC MSW

To address data deficiencies, the WTEEM characterisation and compositional databases have been populated from a variety of resources with data pertinent to GCC countries taken from global reviews (Hoornweg and Bhada-Tata 2012), regional reviews (Abou-Elseoud 2008: 111–126; Al Ansari 2012b; Al-Maaded et al 2012: 186–194), media sources such as *EcoMENA* (Zafar 2015) and GCC country studies or reports including Palanivel and Sulaiman (2014: 96–102; QDB 2015; Rawa Al-Jarallah and Esra Aleisa 2014: 953–954).

The model uses a six-component characterisation – Organic; Plastic; Paper and Cardboard; Glass; Metal; and Other that is used in Hoornweg and Bhada-Tata (2012: 90–94) as the basis to build up a detailed 11 waste type characterisation for the *IPCC Waste Model* and estimate a 30 waste type characterisation (see: Burnside International Ltd 2014), shown in Figure 13.1. Gaps in characterisation of specified waste types are filled using regional averages or details or estimates found in studies and reports (Al-Jarallah and Aleisa 2014: 954; Al-Maaded et al. 2012: 186–194; Dumble, Williams and Lowe 2011; Environment Agency 2008).

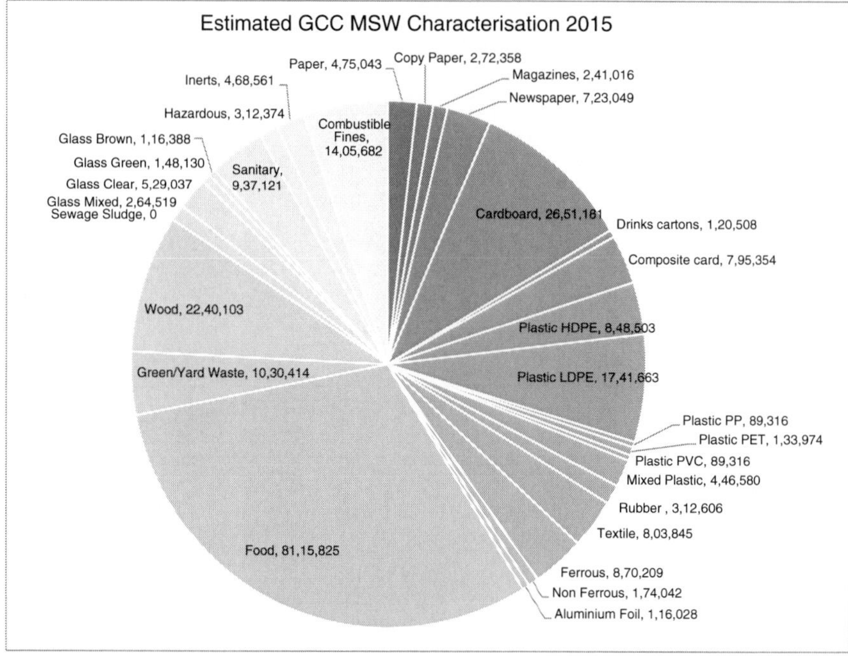

Figure 13.1 Estimated GCC MSW quantities and characterisation in 2015

Source: Paul Dumble

MSW organic, physical and chemical composition

Supporting databases were established, with weighted averages used to estimate compositional data for each waste type. The organic solids content is calculated by segmenting country MSW characterisations into the chemical components of organic solids (carbon, hydrogen, oxygen, nitrogen and sulphur or CHONS), inert solids and moisture Tchobanoglous et al. 1993; Vounatsos et al. 2012: 14–37; World Bank 1999. The organic fraction is also segmented into biodegradable and non-biodegradable components, lignin, hemicellulose, cellulose with other organics such as protein and synthetic carbon wastes taken from wide range of studies detailing both MSW and a wide range of waste types (Colt et al. 1995; Barlaz 2006: 321–333; Staley and Barlaz 2009; Zheng et al. 2013: 2632–2640; Wang et al. 2015: 70–90) as shown in Table 13.1.

Modern consumable plastics have little inert content, as shown in the chemical solids, ash and moisture contents for a wide range of plastics in the European Life study (Vounatsos et al. 2012: 14–37), which included a wide range of paper wastes. The World Bank (1999) advice on thermodynamic assessment for municipal waste incineration provides a useful reference point for the physical content of waste

Table 13.1 Estimated organic, chemical and physical composition of GCC MSW in 2015

MSW organic chemical composition/Mg					
	Carbon	*Hydrogen*	*Oxygen*	*Nitrogen*	*Sulphur*
GCC	6,436,963	830,081	3,484,788	136,735	20,072
Bahrain	209,475	26,967	136,892	6,028	945
Kuwait	532,736	68,750	283,643	11,177	1,442
Oman	370,172	47,589	205,928	6,072	806
Qatar	347,182	44,904	199,797	9,180	1,239
Saudi Arabia	3,662,528	470,655	1,966,562	75,407	10,803
UAE	1,309,920	170,628	687,445	29,196	4,832

MSW organic composition/Mg						
	Lignin	*Hemicel-lulose*	*Cellulose*	*Protein*	*Other natural*	*Synthetic*
GCC	1,684,041	869,089	3,307,992	167,213	1,791,643	3,088,662
Bahrain	73,034	36,297	130,605	9,274	75,885	55,212
Kuwait	135,637	70,332	264,168	13,352	144,535	269,725
Oman	96,484	52,457	207,731	5,672	89,016	179,206
Qatar	100,825	50,237	178,370	12,816	110,579	149,475
Saudi Arabia	963,182	498,481	1,867,611	89,553	1,006,544	1,760,585
UAE	311,625	159,283	653,742	37,298	366,874	673,199

MSW physical composition/Mg				*MSW/Mg*
	Organic	*Ash*	*Moisture*	*Arising's*
GCC	10,908,640	4,197,467	11,366,388	26,472,495
Bahrain	380,308	156,847	483,871	1,021,025
Kuwait	897,748	238,323	879,694	2,015,764
Oman	630,567	295,473	564,682	1,490,722
Qatar	602,303	257,873	676,358	1,536,533
Saudi Arabia	6,185,955	2,447,476	6,182,575	14,816,007
UAE	2,202,021	806,662	2,583,760	5,592,444

Source of compositional estimates data: Paul Dumble, WTEEM Tool

types that better reflect levels in known regional MSW characterisations and compositions (CDR 2015: 26).

MSW methane emission estimates

First order degradation emissions are calculated using time-based emission iterations of annual MSW characterisation and arising data set out by the 2006 IPPC guidelines (IPCC 2006a; IPCC 2006b; RTI International 2010: 2–2).

$$M=\sum_{x=S}^{T-1} W_x\left(M_{cf}\times DOC\times DOC_f\times M_f\times {}^{16}\!/_{12}\right)_x\left(e^{-k(T-x-1)}-e^{-k(T-x)}\right)$$

Equation 1 (adapted from RTI International 2010: 2–2)

Where:

M: CH_4 generation (Mg/yr)
X: Year of waste disposal
S: Start year of the inventory calculation
T: Inventory year for which emissions are calculated
W*x*: Quantity of waste disposed at the solid waste disposal site (Mg)
M*cf*: Methane correction factor, typically 1 for managed landfills
DOC: Degradable organic carbon (Mg of Carbon in waste/Mg waste)
DOC*f*: Fraction of DOC decomposed (fraction), generally assumed to be 0.5
M*f*: Fraction by volume of CH_4 in landfill gas, generally assumed to be 0.5
K: Decay rate constant (yr^{-1}).

Annual methane emissions are built up from the summation of annual emissions from previous years with at least 5 half-lives (calculated from $Log_n 2/k$). Annual methane emission reports are provided periodically by GCC countries in annual reports (UNFCCC 2016). Equation 1 is adapted for the model as;

$$M=\sum_{x=S}^{T-1} W_x\left(M_f\times DOC_m\times {}^{16}\!/_{12}\right)_x\left(e^{-k(T-x-1)}-e^{-k(T-x)}\right)$$

Equation 2

Where:

DOC_m = degradable organic carbon calculated from

$$DOC_m=\sum_{wt}\left(\left(Q_{L+H+Cl+P+Ot+Sy}\right)-\left(Q_{L+Sy}\right)\right)_{wt}\times\sum_{ncwt}\left({}^{Q_C}\!\big/\!_{\left(Q_c+Q_H+Q_O+Q_N+Q_S\right)}\right)_{ncwt}$$

Equation 3

Where:

Q: Mass (Mg)
Wt: waste type
ncwt: natural carbon waste type
L: Lignin, HC: Hemicellulose, Cl: Cellulose, P: Protein, Ot: other natural organic, Sy: Synthetic
C: Carbon, H: Hydrogen, O: Oxygen, N: Nitrogen, S: Sulphur

IPCC guidance provides assumptions for the calculation of the DOC, and k, the decay constant. The tropical dry climate decay *k* constant is 0.065 for bulk MSW. However, a weight adjusted waste specific k constant (IPCC 2006b Chapter 3, Table 3.3: 3–17) was calculated to provide a better assessment of significant GCC MSW characterisation differences.

An oxidation factor (Ox) of 0.1 is used for managed landfills sites and 0.0 for unmanaged sites (IPCC 2006b, Table 3.2: 3–15). This factor applied in the model by multiplying the annual methane output from the first order equation by (1-Ox). A methane correction factor (M_{cf}) can be used (IPCC 2006b, Table 3.2: 3–14), varying from 1 for managed landfills to 0.4 to 0.8 for unmanaged sites dependant on waste depth and aerobic disposal options.

The differences in organic content of both natural and synthetic carbon and the physical composition data are developed as weighted averages providing MSW characterisation-sensitive estimates of organic solids, inert solids and moisture content (see: Table 13.1).

Methane emissions are converted into CO_{2eq} multiplying the quantity of emissions of CH_4 by the 100 year Global Warming Potential (GWP_{100}) (Forster et al. 2007). Methane global warming potential of 21 is used in this work, though this can be varied to revised GWP_{100} values 23, 25 and 34 (IPCC 2001; IPCC 2006a; IPCC 2013).

IWM systems and processes

Source segregated collections have been segmented into three basic types:

- Dry waste,
- Green wastes (mainly for composting) and
- Food wastes (which can be treated by composting or anaerobic digestion methods),

The dry wastes are taken to clean materials recycling facilities (MRF) where they are separated into fractions such as plastic bottles (PET), plastic film (LDPE), paper and cardboard, ferrous and non-ferrous metals. A study of MRF's in England, Europe and North America (WRAP 2006) found rejects levels between 12% and 15%.

Composting and anaerobic digestion from source segregated collections

Composting and anaerobic digestion treatment from source segregated green and food wastes is growing (De Baere and Mattheeuws 2011: 416 to 453) with regulatory frameworks and financial incentives for adoption of such processes (California EPA 2011). A facility in Canada integrates the two technologies to maximise economic and environmental benefits (Kraemer and Gamble 2014: 32). Composting and anaerobic digestion significantly reduces emissions that would occur if the waste was landfilled. Small quantities of residual methane and nitrogen oxide emissions may arise from composting operations (Beck-Friis et al. 2000: 317–331).

Mechanical treatments

Mechanical heat treatment (MHT) can take several forms, such as that of an autoclave (120–140°C) where steam under pressure is used to thermal dry the waste and sterilise the waste. A variant of this is a thermal drying process operating between 140–160°C.[3] Another is a low temperature process <90°C that pulps the paper wastes,[4] and washes the residual waste. Other treatments used to stabilise organic wastes include mechanical treatment with bio-treatment (MT+Bio) and mechanical biological treatment (MBT) as shown in Defra (2013).

For modelling purposes it is assumed that each waste type, collected as a residual waste from the segregated waste stream or as an unsegregated mixed waste, is fed into the available treatment capacity. This is to ensure that each residual waste stream passes through a bio drying or thermal process that will bio-stabilise or thermally stabilise (sterilise or burn) the waste types containing organic solids. Where the MSW is not bio-treated or sterilised it is assumed that this is rejected and sent to landfill.

The bio (drying) treatment process in composting, MBT or MT+Bio is principally aerobic with the emission of water and carbon dioxide (CO_2) taking into account process and transport emissions from MRF's, bio-treatment (composting and AD), MBT and incineration technologies (Teichmann and Schempp 2013). While nitrogen oxide has a much larger GWP_{100} than methane (RTI 2010), it is assumed that these emissions from aerobic and anaerobic processes are not significant when compared to landfill MSW methane emissions.

From *WRATE* style assessments (Papageorgiou et al. 2009; Zaman 2010) the waste planner's impression is that net emissions below zero are likely from adoption of an IWM technology option. In the future, planners will be required to demonstrate how MSW emissions are mitigated and controlled. MSW mitigation projects focus on methane recovery from solid waste disposal (UNFCCC 2016).

Waste to Energy

Waste to Energy (Defra 2013) is the penultimate treatment option before land disposal in the waste hierarchy.[5] This option is used to treat residual MSW that is not treated by MT+Bio, MBT and MHT methods and to provide an energy recovery option for refuse derived fuel (RDF) produced from MBT processes and as process energy for MHT processes. A review of the health impacts for proposed incineration facilities is normally required for planning applications (Defra 2004), setting out necessary standards for emission control. A *WRATE* assessment for an incineration planning proposal in the UK was shows net emission reductions greater than an alternative MBT process, due to the inclusion of savings from combined heat and power (SLR Global Environmental Solutions 2010). The net reduction claimed seems high considering other assessments reviewed above, with the *WRATE* modelling appearing to be prone to the subjectivities or assumptions of the modeller.

Lined landfill with gas collection

The IPCC (2006a) guidance identifies variable range of 35% to 70% for landfill methane recovery. Across China, landfill methane recovery rates of 43% are reported for Class I landfills (Bo-Feng Cia et al. 2014). For UK landfill emissions Defra 2013 provide a figure of 75% of methane emissions (used for modelling) that are captured by landfill gas engines.

Landfill sites without gas recovery

In the GCC countries managed sites, usually unlined, are controlled by the competent authority. The nuisance and health aspects of controlled and uncontrolled dumping (Luomi 2014) including GHG emission and leachate contamination (Cointreau 2006) provide this as the lowest cost option (Arif 2012: 22–23). However, the environmental consequences short and medium term or from the legacy of the GWP_{100} warming potential are unacceptable to the communities these sites are intended to serve.

Economic MSW cost estimates for GCC MSW management

Collection, process, transport and waste facility data and costs are based gate fees from a range of sources (Dumble, Williams and Lowe 2011), including data from global review and regional reviews (Hoornweg and Bhada-Tata 2012: 46; Cointreau-Levine and Coad 2000) by and media commentary[6] from a financial perspective on recent Lebanese MSW IWM tender submissions in the summer of 2015 (CDR 2015).

Results

Modelling MSW treatment and disposal technology capacity methane emission scenarios

It is necessary to understand the reduction of disposal MSW methane emissions taking into account the available IWM capacity and the residual waste that is sent for disposal over a period of time. The reduction of the GHG MSW methane emissions is primarily about climate change mitigation. The *WRATE*, *IPCC Waste Model* or EPA *LandGEM* models have not been used to provide clear mitigation analysis (Bogner et al. 2007), limiting the waste planners view, context and perspective.

Key growth factors and arising's that influence future changes to quantities and value of MSW are shown in Table 13.2. Price inflation relative to the current US$

Table 13.2 GCC MSW arising's and key growth factors adapted to 2015

Country	*WGR (2015) kg/capita/day*	*% MSW growth rate*	*% population growth rate*	*% urban population*	*% GDP growth rate*
GCC countries	1.37*	4.21*	2.60	83.9%	5.10
Bahrain	2.02*	3.00	1.93	88.7%	3.90
KSA	1.28*	4.20	2.40	82.3%	5.68
Kuwait	1.45*	3.00	1.73	98.3%	3.93
Oman	0.88*	5.00	9.10	73.4%	3.20
Qatar	1.84*	4.20*	5.18	98.8%	6.73
UAE	1.68*	4.70*	0.50	84.3%	5.25
Data sources	*P. Dumble (Lead Author), WTEEM tool adapted estimates or literature sources provide from Zafar 2014; Ansari 2012a: Ansari 2012b; Dornier Consulting 2008, Al-Jarallah and Esra 2014; QDB 2015; Al-Maaded et al. 2012; Dumble Williams and Lowe 2011; SCAD 2014		Index Mundi. 2014, World Bank 2015b	World Bank 2015a	World Bank 2015b

rate[7] of 1.10% is set at a higher rate 2.0% for modelling purposes. The modelling of the development of infrastructure is made from the *Baseline Capacity* of a mix of existing IWM facilities expressed in Table 13.3 based on the *Estimated % Maximum Levels* of technology capacity that can be implemented annually in the model and as a proportion of the *100% Annual Planned Capacity Increase.* This is the increase over the established % waste growth levels which is adapted as a proportion for modelling purposes. The maximum level of source segregated recycling is determined from the characterisation and composition of the MSW (see: Table 13.1) and the maximum recycling level of each waste type (Fisher et al. 2006, Table 5.1: 13). The year 2 intervention level is where there is no existing capacity in year 1 for a type of IWM facility. CDM landfill (with gas recovery) quantities as a percentage of the total MSW by weight are estimated from registered UNFCCC CDM (2016) data.

The baseline capacity was estimated from the MSW by destination data. However, this is very limited as it is only found in specialist regional and international sources (Zafar 2015; QDB 2015; UNSD 2016). The primary treatment capacity is based on processing about 80% of the non-source segregated MSW through mechanical treatment options (MT+Bio, MHT, MBT) resulting in the residual capacity being taken up by a Waste to Energy option. This is further increased by the feed of organic residuals for energy recovery from MHT an MBT processes.

Food waste is important as it represents about 30.7% of the GCC MSW. This is modelled at a 30% *Annual Planned Capacity Increase* rate for the segregated

Table 13.3 WTEEM tool IWM capacity parameters

Treatment		*Baseline capacity**	*100% annual planned capacity increase**	*Year 2 intervention level**	*Estimated % maximum levels by weight**
Source segregated collection	Dry	0.8%	20.0%	1.0%	27.3%
	Compost		20.0%	1.0%	6.2%
	Food		30.0%	2.0%	19.9%
Primary treatment	MT + Bio	8.2%	8.2%	1.0%	11.6%
	MBT	0.0%	0.0%	2.0%	19.6%
	MHT	0.8%	0.8%	1.0%	6.1%
	Waste to energy	1.3%	1.3%	1.0%	9.3%
Disposal	Landfill (CDM)	13.8%	13.8%	1.0%	15.2%
	Dumpsite	75.1%	75.1%	Reduce	0.0%
Data sources		Paul Dumble: WTEEM tool settings. based on baseline data from aggregated data sources including Zafar (2015), QDB (2015), UNSD (2016) and Landfill (CDM) data from UNFCCC Reports			

collection supporting the UN17 Global Goals and the 2030 Agenda for Sustainable Development requiring urgent action to combat climate change ensuring sustainable consumption and production patterns. This sets an objective to *halve per capita global food waste at the retail and consumer level, and reduce food losses along production and supply chains by 2030.*[8]

Figure 13.2 shows the modelling of methane emissions based on existing (the do-nothing scenario) and projected increases in the IWM capacity (43%) increase from 2015, showing historical (from 1970) and future emissions from 1970 to 2050. The example shown shows the necessary capacity intervention to reduce annual disposal methane emissions by 51,617GgCO$_{2eq}$ and achieve stabilisation of the disposal emissions at 46,947GgCO$_{2eq}$ in 2050. The cost of these options is shown on the *Annual MSW Budget* chart to the right, with an increase in 2050 from the current GCC MSW Budget estimate of US$1.30 billion in 2015 to US$6.08 billion for the do-nothing scenario and US$21.65 billion in 2050 for the IWM capacity increase scenario.

The decoupling of annual disposal emissions is shown in the *Annual MSW Methane Emissions and GDP* chart with the relative MSW costs as % of GDP on the *Annual MSW Budget as % of GDP* chart to the right showing an increase from 0.08 to 0.22% in the GCC MSW budget by 2050 for the IWM capacity increase option, with a drop to 0.06% for the do-nothing option in the same period. The annual emission reduction costs fall to US$301,572/GgCO$_{2eq}$ by 2050 (rising due to inflation) with some variation due to the impact of modelled changes of specific waste treatment technology capacity.

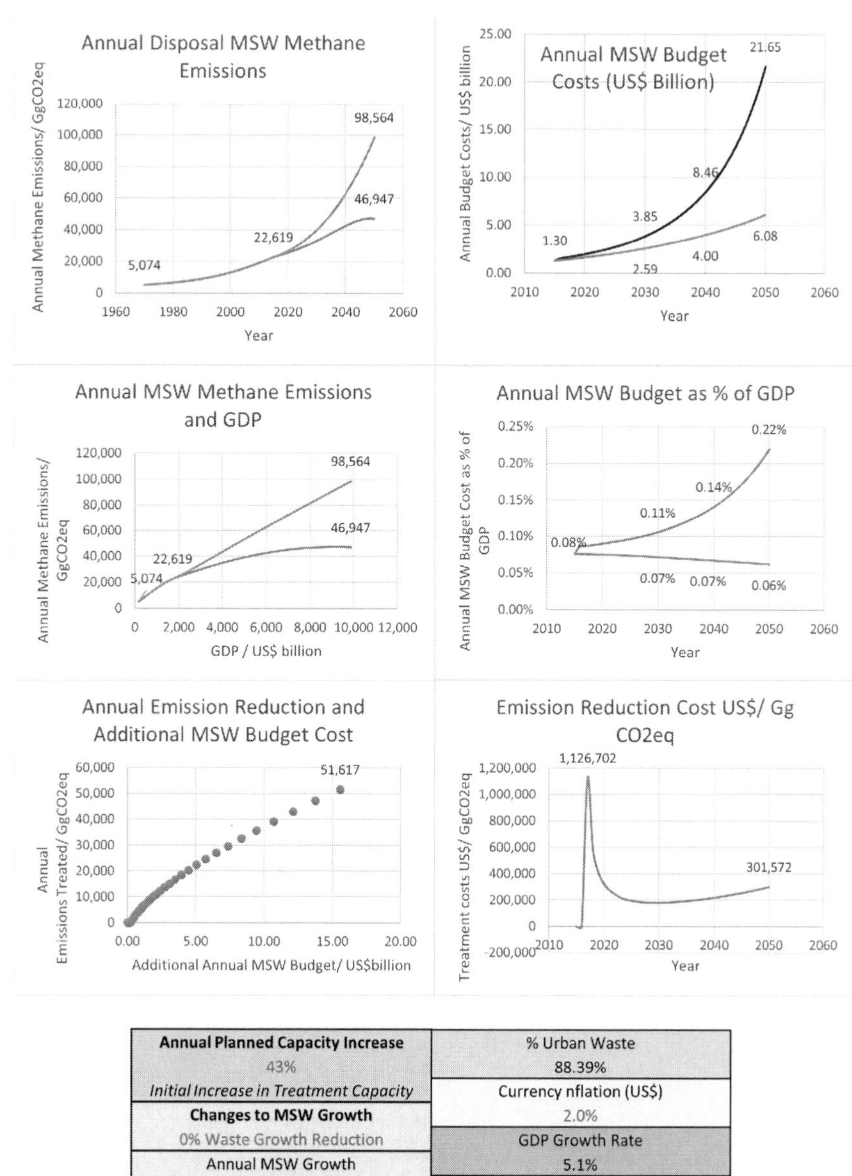

Annual Planned Capacity Increase 43% *Initial Increase in Treatment Capacity*	% Urban Waste 88.39%
Changes to MSW Growth 0% Waste Growth Reduction	Currency nflation (US$) 2.0%
Annual MSW Growth 4.2%	GDP Growth Rate 5.1%
Population Growth Rate 2.60%	Climate Dry Tropical

Figure 13.2 IWM capacity changes to stabilise disposal methane emissions with GCC MSW budget costs

Source: Paul Dumble

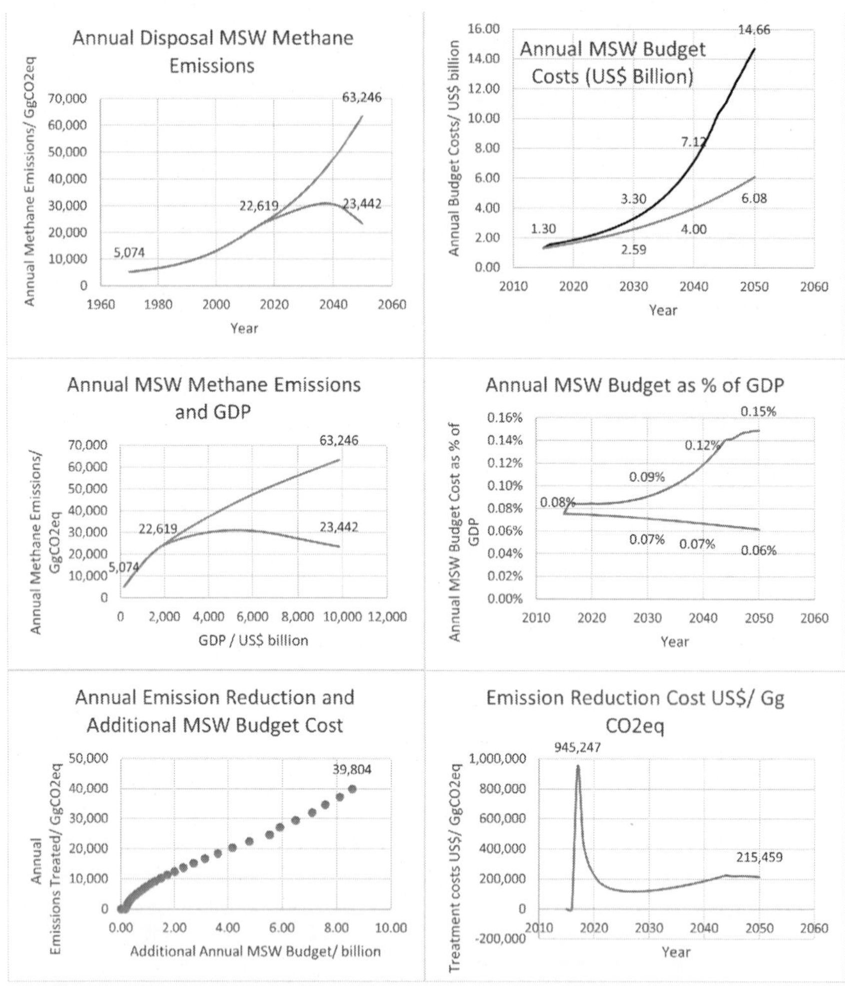

Annual Planned Capacity Increase	% Urban Waste
43%	88.39%
Initial Increase in Treatment Capacity	Currency Inflation (US$)
Changes to MSW Growth	2.0%
40% Waste Growth Reduction	GDP Growth Rate
Annual MSW Growth	5.1%
2.5%	Climate
Population Growth Rate	Dry Tropical
2.60%	

Figure 13.3 Impact of waste growth reduction policies on stabilisation and no action options

Source: Paul Dumble

The impact of prioritising waste reduction at the top of the waste hierarchy is shown in Figure 13.3 as a percentage of Waste Growth Reduction applied to the data in Figure 13.2. The annual waste growth is reduced by an achievable 40% to 2.5%, which is close to the *% Population Growth Rate* change (2.6%). This reduction affects both scenarios with disposal emissions for the do-nothing option falling by 35,318GgCO_{2eq} and the stabilised emissions from the IWM capacity increase falling by an additional 23,505GgCO_{2eq} to a level that is just above the 2015 disposal methane emission level.

Reduction of MSW methane emissions can be achieved through policies encouraging waste reduction such as extended producer responsibility (Pauli 2010) and through supply chain interventions such as reducing and reusing quantities of raw materials used in manufacture, remanufacture of consumables and other supply chain initiatives (Government of Western Australia 2005).

In terms of annual budget the 40% waste growth reduction has lowered the GCC annual MSW budget from US$21.65 (0.22% of GDP) to 14.66 billion (0.13%) with a saving in the emission reduction cost of US$86,113 as it drops to US$215,459/GgCO_{2eq}.

Previous regional disposal emission assessments of this type from literature provided estimates of disposal emissions up to 2030 and 2050 that were based on likely implementation of specific treatment infrastructure (Bogner et al. 2007: 597–598). This study sets out a progressive increase in a range of IWM capacity needed for stabilisation and reduction of disposal methane emissions by 2050, providing a clear view of the impact of two policy interventions; the development of IWM capacity and reducing waste growth at the regional level.

Reliability and sensitivity of data for modelling

To ensure that sufficient data has been collected for the modelling and to address the issues raised by the lack of regular reporting, consistency and the availability of regional waste management data, the data obtained for this study has been widely researched and the most reliable sources. Data was crosschecked with other available sources to ensure that this was reasonably consistent and accurate, taking into account the normal variances that occur in waste management where quantities of waste types may vary by 10% to 30% or more (IPCC 2006a: 2.14). Factors reflecting process efficiency and rejects have been adopted in the modelling impacting through increased levels of methane emissions. The annual MSW methane emission values estimated by the model are about 30% lower than the unmitigated growth adapted values extrapolated to 2015 for MSW methane emission data submitted by GCC countries in the period 1994 to 2007 (UNFCCC 2016).

The inflation adapted annual gates fees used in this study assume a public-private partnership arrangement (e.g. design, build and operate) with 10% equity funding and commercial debt funding rate of 8%. A 1% change in the debt interest rate would add about ±6.0% to the debt cost and ±1.5% to the total cost of a

7-year collection contract and ±18.2% to the debt cost and ±2.5% to the total contract value of a 25-year treatment facility. Inflation has been modelled at 2%, above the current US$ inflation rate of 1.1%.[9] An accumulative change in inflation from 2015 to 2050 of -1% would decrease 2050 costs by 28.5% with an increase from +1% rise of 39.7% for the stabilisation option. The results in this chapter are therefore presented as the best currently available estimates.

Discussion

This study, in considering the whole MSW management system encompassing future IWM development in the form of collection, treatment and disposal, has provided a new and novel way for waste planners to visualise not only what is needed but also the timescales involved in achieving meaningful MSW climate change mitigation. The charts from the modelling clearly show the stabilisation and reduction of regional MSW disposal emissions from policy interventions that will be required to drive the necessary IWM waste capacity development and producer responsibility initiatives that will reduce waste growth.

To do nothing could allow annual disposal methane emissions to rise to 98,564GgCO_{2eq} by 2050, about 4 times the 2015 level. There are significant co-benefits from implementation of these two policy interventions from the reduction of 75,122GgCO_{2eq} of annual disposal emissions in 2050, returning emissions to around 2015 levels. The combination of these two policy strands effectively reduces the annual projected MSW budget cost for stabilisation of disposal methane emissions by 32.2% or US$6.99 billion by 2050. The cost of reducing MSW emissions drops to a minimum after about 12 years, reaching US$117.458/Gg$CO_{2eq}$ in 2050 for the stabilisation option, rising to US$215,459/Gg$CO_{2eq}$ in 2050 for the combined policy approach.

These two policy approaches illustrate a synergy that could stabilise and reduce MSW methane emissions to 2015 levels and deliver considerable annual MSW budget savings. It is clear from modelling of the emission and economic co-benefits identified in this study that action is required now, with GCC annual MSW management budgets requiring an initial boost of 17.5% to 19.0% to initiate regional IWM capacity development with ongoing increase of annual budgets varying from to 5.0% to 9.8% until 2050 to maintain, install and operate the necessary facilities.

To address policy deficiencies identified by Abou-Elseoud (2008), Ansari (2012a) and Gelil (2014), there is a role for the GCC in coordinating and encouraging member countries to improve data management systems and communications supporting ongoing IWM development in the region. This study provides an understanding of what is required and the timescales essential for effective strategic planning and articulation of the necessary range and capacity of IWM services, combined with producer responsibility initiatives to deliver effective mitigation of MSW climate change emissions and also to address health, land and other concerns inherent in reviewed literature.

There are financial barriers to the development of IWM; for the first time future annual MSW mitigation budgets have been presented that now move the discussion into how the resources necessary for stabilisation and reduction of emissions and conservation of resources are secured and applied.

The modelling presents an opportunity for the GCC to lead in establishing a new global target or benchmark definition for waste-related climate change mitigation based on the timescales for stabilisation and reduction of MSW disposal emissions as a sustainable development goal (or SDG).

Acknowledgement

The authors would like thank Dr Morton Barlaz, North Carolina State University for his guidance on organic composition issues.

Notes

1 Translation of regulations (University of Notre Dame, Indiana, US) provided at http://www3.nd.edu/~ggoertz/rei/rei880/rei880.147tt1.pdf
2 Government Entities such as; SCAD, *Statistics Centre – Abu Dhabi*, available from www.scad.ae/SCADDocuments/SYB%202015%20En%20V4.pdf
3 See Orchid in: Defra. Mechanical Heat Treatment of Solid Wastes, 2013, available at www.gov.uk/government/uploads/system/uploads/attachment_data/file/221040/pb13891-heat-treatment-waste.pdf.
4 An example of pulping technique demonstrated by: Vickers Seerdrum Ltd, Biomass Recovery from Waste Organics Extraction from Municipal Solid Waste, Updated January 2016, available at www.seerdrum.com/
5 Originally proposed by: Ad Lansink. Waste hierarchy**,** in motion to Dutch Parliament in 1979, entered Dutch law in 1993. See: http://scp.eionet.europa.eu/facts/factsheets_waste/2006_edition/Netherlands in the Environment Management Act in 1993 accessed 13 December 2013
6 L. Saadeh. "Solid Waste Management in Lebanon", Blominvest Bank, August 29 2015, article available at http://blog.blominvestbank.com/wp-content/uploads/2015/08/Solid-Waste-Management-in-Lebanon.pdf
7 See: Trading Economics, accessed 30/5/16 at www.tradingeconomics.com/united-states/inflation-cpi
8 See: http://uneplive.unep.org/portal
9 Trading Economics, accessed 30/5/16 at www.tradingeconomics.com/united-states/inflation-cpi

References

Abou-Elseoud Nefisa. 2008. Waste management in Arab environment future challenges. In *Arab Environment Future Challenges*, edited by Mostafa K. Tolba and Najib W. Saab, Chapter 8, pp. 111–126. Arab Forum for Environment and Development. Available at: www.afedonline.org/afedreport/full%20english%20report.pdf

Al Ansari, Saleh M. 2012a, February. Improving solid waste management in Gulf co-operation council states: Developing integrated plans to achieve reduction in greenhouse gases. *Modern Applied Science*, 6(2): 60–68. doi:10.5539/mas.v6n2p60

Al Ansari, Saleh M. 2012b. Municipal solid waste management systems in the Kingdom of Bahrain. *International Journal of Water Resources and Environmental Engineering*, 4(5): 150–161. ISSN 1991–637Xal, doi:10.5897/IJWREE12.022

Alexander, Amy, Clint Burkin, and Amanda Singleton. 2005. *Landfill Gas Emissions Model (LandGEM) Version 3.02 User's Guide, Section 3.4.* US Environmental Protection Agency 2005, p. 48. Available at: http://www3.epa.gov/ttncatc1/dir1/landgem-v302-guide.pdf

Al-Jarallah, Rawa, and Esra Aleisa. 2014. A baseline study characterizing the municipal solid waste in the State of Kuwait. *Waste Management*, 34(2014) 952–960. doi:10.1016/j.wasman.2014.02.015

Al-Maaded, Mohammed, N.K. Madi, Ramazan Kahraman, A. Hodzic, and Gozde Ozerkan. 2012. An overview of solid waste management and plastic recycling in Qatar. *Journal of Polymers and the Environment*, 20: 186–194. doi:10.1007/s10924-011-0332

Almazrour, Mansour, M. Nazrul Islam, P.D. Jones, H. Athar, and M. Ashfaque Rahman. 2012 July. Recent climate change in the Arabian Peninsula: Seasonal rainfall and temperature climatology of Saudi Arabia for 1979–2009. *Atmospheric Research*, 111: 29–45, doi:10.1016/j.atmosres.2012.02.013

Arif, Sherif. 2012. *The Solid Wastes Management Situation in Mashreq and Maghreb Countries: Update on Challenges and Opportunities.* Sweepnet, 57pp. Available at: www.giz.de/en/downloads/giz2012-enSWEEP-Netregional-report.pdf

Barlaz, Morton. 2006. Forest products decomposition in municipal solid waste landfills. *Waste Management*, 26: 321–333. doi:10.1016/j.wasman.2005.11.002

Barlaz, Morton A. 2008. *Critical Review of Forest Products Decomposition in Municipal Solid Waste Landfills.* National Council for Air and Stream Improvements, 2004, NCASI, 48pp. Available at: www.ncasi.org/Downloads/Download.ashx?id=3158

Beck-Friis, B., M. Pell, U. Sonesson, H. Jonsson, and H. Kirchmann. 2000. Formation and emission of N2O and CH4 from compost heaps of organic household waste. *Environmental Monitoring and Assessment*, 62: 317–331. ISSN: 1573–2959, doi:10.1023/A:1006245227491

Blickensdörfer-Wieland, Inka. 2005. *An Assessment of the Situation of Environment Statistics in the ESCWA Countries – Data Gaps.* UNSD- ESCWA, 2005, 61pp. Available at: http://unstats.un.org/UNSD/environment/envpdf/escwaassessfinal2005.pdf

Bogner, Jane M., C. Abdelrafie Ahmed, A. Diaz, Q. Faaij, S. Gao, K. Hashimoto, and T. Zhang. 2007. Chapter 10, Waste management. In *Climate Change 2007: Mitigation. Contribution of Working Group III to the Fourth Assessment Report of the Intergovernmental Panel on Climate Change*, 585–618. Cambridge: Cambridge University Press. Available at: www.ipcc.ch/pdf/assessment-report/ar4/wg3/ar4-wg3-chapter10.pdf

Burnside International Ltd. 2014. Preliminary Draft Waste Charaterization Report, Mangrove Pond Green Energy Complex, pp26, Jan 2014, accessed 4/6/2015 at https://barbadosunderground.files.wordpress.com/2015/11/2-10-32-burnside-waste-characterization-draft-report-january-2014.pdf

California EPA. 2011. *Method for Estimating Greenhouse Gas Emissions Reductions From Compost From Commercial Organic Waste.* California Environmental Protection Agency, November 14, 2011, 24pp. Available at: www.waterboards.ca.gov/centralvalley/board_decisions/tentative_orders/1504/9_recology/17_recology_disch_evidence/recology_ex06.pdf

CDR. 2015, March. *Collection and Disposal of Municipal Waste in Lebanon. Part IV Project Information Memorandum.* Republic of Lebanon, El-Khoury, R. & Partners (Council for Development and Reconstruction 2015), 185pp.

Cia, Bo-Feng, Jian-Guo Liu, Qing-Xian Gao, Xiao-Qin Nie, Dong Cao, Lan-Cui Liu, Ying Zhou, and Zhan-Sheng Zang. 2014. Estimation of methane emissions from municipal solid waste landfills in China based on point emission source. *Advances in Climate Research*, 5(2): 81–91. doi:10.3724/SP.J.1248.2014.081

Cointreau, Sandra. 2006. Occupational and Environmental Health Issues of Solid Waste Management. Special Emphasis on Middle- and Lower-Income Countries. Urban Sector Board, World Bank, 48pp., Washington DC.

Cointreau-Levine, Sandra, and A. Coad. 2000. *Private Sector Participation in Municipal Solid Waste Management.* Swiss Centre for Development Cooperation in Technology and Management, 124pp. Available at: http://sandracointreau.com/wp-content/uploads/2011/02/Cointreau-2001-PSP-Guide-for-SKAT-WB-without-photos.pdf (Accessed 13/7/2016).

Colt, J., W. Driscoll, and R. Freed. 1995. *Work Assignment 239, Task 2: Carbon Sequestration in Landfills.* ICF Memo, ICF. Available at: www.epa.gov/epawaste/conserve/tools/warm/pdfs/ICF_Memo_Carbon_Sequestrati on_in_Landfills.pdf (Accessed 4 September 2015).

De Baere, L., and B. Mattheeuws. 2011. *State of the Art of Anaerobic Digestion of Municipal Waste in Europe.* In Proceedings of the International Conference on Solid Waste 2011- Moving Towards Sustainable Resource Management, Hong Kong SAR, P.R. China, 2–6 May 2011, pp. 416–453. Available at: www.iswa.org/uploads/tx_iswaknowledgebase/12_Anaerobic_Digestion.pdf

Defra. 2004. *Review of Environmental and Health Effects of Waste Management: Municipal Solid Waste and Similar Wastes.* Enviros Consulting Ltd and University of Birmingham with Risk and Policy Analysts Ltd, Open University and Maggie Thurgood. Available at: www.gov.uk/government/uploads/system/uploads/attachment_data/file/69391/pb9052a-health-report-040325.pdf

Defra. 2013. *Mechanical Biological Treatment of Municipal Wastes, 2013.* Available at: www.gov.uk/government/uploads/system/uploads/attachment_data/file/221039/pb13890-treatment-solid-waste.pdf

Dornier Consulting. 2008, January. *Treatment and Recycling of Municipal Solid Waste in Riyadh, Jeddah, Damman – Kingdom of Saudi Arabia.* Phase A-A2 Alternatives for Recycling and Treatment, Ministry of Municipal and Rural Affairs.

Dumble, Paul, Karl S. Williams, and Chris N. Lowe. 2011. *Key Sustainability Criteria Supporting the Development of Abu Dhabi's Integrated Waste Management Systems.* CRWM – Communications in Waste and Resource Management. Available at: www.ciwm.co.uk/CIWM/InformationCentre/CWRMJournal/CWRMpapers/CWRM_ Current_Papers.aspx

Environment Agency. 2008, October. *An Updated Lifecycle Assessment Study for Disposable and Reusable Nappies.* Science Report, SC010018/SR2, ISBN: 978-1-84432-927-4, 32pp. Available at: www.gov.uk/government/uploads/system/uploads/attachment_data/file/291130/scho0808boir-e-e.pdf

Fisher, Karen, Michael Collins, Simon Aumônier, and Bob Gregory. 2006, December. Carbon Balances and Energy Impacts of the Management of UK Wastes. Defra R&D Project WRT 237, 71pp. Available at: http://waste.ccac-knowledge.net/document/carbon-balances-and-energy-impacts-management-uk-waste-streams

Forster, P., V. Ramaswamy, P. Artaxo, T. Berntsen, R. Betts, D.W. Fahey, J. Haywood, J. Lean, D.C. Lowe, G. Myhre, J. Nganga, R. Prinn, G. Raga, M. Schulz, and R. Van Dorland. 2007. Changes in Atmospheric Constituents and in Radiative Forcing. In *Climate Change 2007: The Physical Science Basis. Contribution of Working Group I to the Fourth Assessment Report of the Intergovernmental Panel on Climate Change*, edited by Solomon, S., D. Qin, M. Manning, Z. Chen, M. Marquis, K.B. Averyt, M.Tignor, and H.L. Miller. Cambridge, UK and New York, NY: Cambridge University Press.

Gelil, Ibrahim Abdel. 2014. *Proposal for an Arab Strategic Framework for Sustainable Development 2015–2025.* Arab High Level Forum on Sustainable Development Amman, 2–4 April 2014, Economic and Social Commission for Western Asia (ESCWA), 16pp. Available at: http://css.escwa.org.lb/SDPD/3315/2.pdf

Gentil, Emmanuel. 2006. *WRATE: Waste LCA for Municipal Waste Strategies*. Golders Associates. Available at: www.iswa.org/uploads/tx_iswaknowledgebase/2c_-_1130_-_P_-_Gentil_-E_ISWA_2006_Paper_UK.pdf

Government of Western Australia. 2005. *Extended Producer Responsibility, Policy Statement: A New Approach to Waste Reduction*. Available at: www.wastenet.net.au/Assets/Documents/Content/Information/050628_epr_policy.pdf

Hasawi, Hamad. 1999. *Investigation of Municipal Waste Management in the GCC States*. Thesis submitted for the degree of Doctor of Philosophy, Volume1, Thesis 3505, pp. 22–34, British Library (can be accessed through web site).

Hoornweg, Daniel, and Perinez Bhada-Tata. 2012. *What a Waste: A Global Review of Solid Waste Management*. Washington, DC: © World Bank, 98pp. Available at: https://openknowledge.worldbank.org/handle/10986/17388 License: CC BY 3.0 IGO.

Index Mundi. 2014. Available at: www.indexmundi.com (Accessed 2015)

IPCC. 2001. Climate Change 2001: The Scientific Basis. Contribution of Working Group I to the Third Assessment Report of the Intergovernmental Panel on Climate Change, edited by J.T. Houghton,Y. Ding, D.J. Griggs, M. Noguer, P.J. van der Linden, X. Dai, K. Maskell, and C.A. Johnson. Cambridge, UK and New York, NY: Cambridge University Press, 881pp. Available at: www.grida.no/publications/other/ipcc_tar/?src=/climate/ipcc_tar/wg1/247.htm

IPCC. 2006a. Chapter 2, Waste generation, composition and management. In *IPPC Guidelines for National Greenhouse Gas Inventories*, authored by Riitta Pipatti, Chemendra Sharma, Masato Yamada, Joao Wagner Silva Alves, Qingxian Gao, G.H. Sabin Guendehou, Matthias Koch, Carlos López Cabrera, Katarina Mareckova, Hans Oonk, Elizabeth Scheehle, Alison Smith, Per Svardal, and Sonia Maria Manso Vieira, pp. 2–4 to 2–23. Available at: www.ipcc-nggip.iges.or.jp/public/2006gl/pdf/5_Volume5/V5_2_Ch2_Waste_Data.pdf

IPCC. 2006b. Chapter 3: Solid waste disposal. In *IPPC Guidelines for National Greenhouse Gas Inventories*, authored by Riitta Pipatti, Per Svardal, Joao Wagner Silva Alves, Qingxian Gao, Carlos López Cabrera, Katarina Mareckova, Hans Oonk, Elizabeth Scheehle, Chhemendra Sharma, Alison Smith, and Masato Yamada. Contributing Authors Jeffrey B. Coburn, Kim Pingoud, Gunnar Thorsen, and Fabian Wagner, pp. 3.6–3.40. Available at: www.ipccnggip.iges.or.jp/public/2006gl/vol5.html

IPCC. 2006c. *IPCC Publications: Guidelines for National Greenhouse Gas Inventories*. Volume 5, Waste Assessment Tool. Available at: www.ipcc-nggip.iges.or.jp/public/2006gl/vol5.html (Accessed 14 April 2016).

IPCC. 2013. Climate Change 2013: The Physical Science Basis. In *Contribution of Working Group I to the Fifth Assessment Report of the Intergovernmental Panel on Climate Change*, edited by Stocker, T.F., D. Qin, G.-K. Plattner, M. Tignor, S.K. Allen, J. Boschung, A. Nauels, Y. Xia, V. Bex, and P.M. Midgley. Cambridge, UK and New York, NY: Cambridge University Press, 1535pp. Available at: www.climatechange2013.org/images/report/WG1AR5_ALL_FINAL.pdf (Accessed 13 July 2016).

ISWA. 2013. *ISWA Report 2013*. International Solid Waste Association, ISWA General Secretariat Auerspergstrasse 15/41, A-1080, 2013, 60pp., Vienna, Austria. Available at: www.ccacoalition.org/ar/file/644/download?token=1bmiInsr

Kraemer Tom and Scott Gamble 2014. BioCycle November 2014, Vol. 55, No. 10, p. 32. Presentation, SWANA Northwest Symposium April 29, 2015 http://swanaoregon.org/images/Lopez_Integr_AD_and_Composting.pdf

Luomi, Marie. 2014. *Mainstreaming Climate Policy in the Gulf Cooperation Council States*. Oxford Institute for Energy Studies, February 2014, ISBN 978-1-907555-91-6, 73pp. Available at: www.oxfordenergy.org/wpcms/wp-content/uploads/2014/02/MEP-7.pdf

Nizami, A., M. Reha, O.K.M. Ouda, K. Shahzad, Y. Sadef, T. Iqbal, and I.M.I. Ismail. 2015. An argument for developing waste-to-energy technologies in Saudi Arabia. *Chemical Engineering Transactions*, 45, 337–342. doi:10.3303/CET1545057

Palanivel Thenmoxhi, Murugalan, and Hameed Sulaiman. 2014. *Generation and Composition of Municipal Solid Waste (MSW) in Muscat, Sultanate of Oman*. Singapore: ICESD, pp. 96–102. doi:10.1016/j.apcbee.2014.10.024

Papageorgiou, A., J.R. Barton, and A. Karagiannidis. 2009. Assessment of the greenhouse effect impact of technologies used for energy recovery from municipal waste: A case for England. *Journal of Environmental Management*, 90(10): 2999–3012. doi:10.1016/j.jenvman.2009.04.012

Pauli, Gunter. 2010. *The Blue Economy 10 Years, 100 Innovations, 100 Million Jobs Report to the Club of Rome*. Paradigm Publications, ISBN 9780912111902, review. Available at: www.paradigm-pubs.com/sites/www.paradigm-pubs.com/files/active/1/TBEBooklet.pdf

QDB. 2015. *Qatar: Solid Waste Management, Phase 1 Assessment* (Presentation). Qatar Development Bank. Available at: www.qsa.gov.qa/eng/News/2013/related/24-62013/Day_1/4_Qatar-Solid%20Waste%20Mgmt%20V5.pdf (Accessed 15 December 2015).

RTI International. 2010. Greenhouse Gas Emissions Estimation Methodologies for Biogenic Emissions From Selected Source Categories: Solid Waste Disposal, Wastewater Treatment, Ethanol Fermentation, U.S. (Environmental Protection Agency 2010). Sector Policies and Programs Division Measurement Policy Group, 43pp. Available at: www.epa.gov/ttnchie1/efpac/ghg/GHG_Biogenic_Report_draft_Dec1410.pdf

SCAD. 2014. *Statistical Yearbook of Abu Dhabi 2015, Period of Reference 2014.* Statistics Centre – Abu Dhabi (SCAD). Available at: www.scad.ae/SCADDocuments/SYB%202015%20En%20V4.pdf

SLR Global Environmental Solutions. 2010, August. *Greatmoor Energy From Waste Facility, Environmental Permit.* Waste Recycling Group, 18pp. Available at: www.fccenvironment.co.uk/assets/files/pdf/Greatmoor/permit-application/sec6-enviro-permit-app/greaup3734ht-ep-app-s6-batot-apx6.pdf

Staley, B.F., and Morton A. Barlaz. 2009. Composition of municipal solid waste in the United States and implications for carbon sequestration and methane yield. *Journal of Environmental Engineering*, 10, 901–909. doi:10.106/ASCE(EE)1943-7870.0000032

Tchobanoglous, G., H. Theisen, and S. A. Vigil. 1993. *Integrated Solid Waste Management: Engineering Principles and Management Issues*, 2nd ed., McGraw-Hill. ISBN 0070632375, 9780070632370, 978pp. (CHONS taken from: US Dept of Ed, Health and Welfare 1969).

Teichmann, Dorothee, and Christian Schempp. 2013. *Calculation of GHG Emissions of Waste Management Projects*. Staff Working Paper, JASPERS Knowledge Economy and Energy Division, 30pp. Available at: www.jaspersnetwork.org/download/attachments/4948011/13-03-11%20JASPERS%20WP_Methodology%20for%20GHG%20Emission%20Calculation_Waste%20Calculation_FINAL.pdf?version=1&modificationDate=1366389231000&api=v2

UNEP. 2016. *GEO-6 Regional Assessment for West Asia*. United Nations Environment Programme, Nairobi, Kenya. ISBN: 978-92-807-3548-2, 92–99pp. Available at: http://uneplive.unep.org/media/docs/assessments/GEO_Regional_Assessments_West_Asia_High_resv3.pdf

UNFCCC. 2016. *Greenhouse Gas Inventory Data – Detailed Data by Party, Non Annexed Parties, Category:6.A*. Available at: www.ipcc-nggip.iges.or.jp/public/2006gl/pdf/5_Volume5/V5_3_Ch3_SWDS.pdf.

UNSD. 2016. *UNSD Environmental Indicators, Waste*. U. N. Division, Producer. Available at: http://unstats.un.org/unsd/ENVIRONMENT/qindicators.htm

Vounatsos, P., K. Atsonios, M. Agraniotis, K. Panopoulos, and Panagiotis Grammelis. 2012. *Energy Waste*. LIFE Project Number LIFE09 ENV/GR/000307, 40pp. Available at: http://energywaste.gr/pdf/D4.1%20-%20Report%20on%20RDF-SRF%20gasification%20properties%20.pdf

Wang, X., F.B. De la Cruz, F. Ximenes, and M.A. Barlaz. 2015. Decomposition and carbon storage of selected paper products in laboratory scale landfills. *Science of the Total Environment*, 532: 70–90. doi:10.1016/j.scitotenv.2015.05.132

World Bank. 1999. *World Bank Technical Guidance Report, Municipal Solid Waste Incineration*. 103pp. Available at: www.worldbank.org/urban/solid_wm/erm/CWG%20folder/Waste%20Incineration.pdf

World Bank. 2015a. *The Little Green Data Book 2015*. Washington, DC: World Bank. doi:10.1596/978-1-4648-0560-8. License: Creative Commons Attribution CC BY 3.0 IGO.

World Bank. 2015b. *GDP and Population Data*. Available at: http://data.worldbank.org/country

WRAP. 2006, September. An Introduction to MRFs and Comparison of Sorting Operations Based on Site Visits to Selected Facilities in England, Europe and North America, MRFs Comparison of Efficiency and Quality. WRAP, 74pp. Available at: www.wrap.org.uk/sites/files/wrap/MRF_v6_19Dec06_LC.pdf (accessed 13 July 2016).

Zafar, S., 2015, Solid Waste Management in Oman. Article available at http://www.ecomena.org/solid-waste-oman/

Zaman, A.U. 2010. Comparative study of municipal solid waste treatment technologies using life cycle assessment method. *International Journal of Environmental Science and Technology*, 7(2): 225–234. ISSN: 1735–1472, doi:10.1007/BF03326132, available at: www.bioline.org.br/pdf?st10022

Zheng, W., K. Phoughthong, and F. Lu. 2013. Evaluation of classification method for biodegradation of solid wastes. *Waste Management*, 33(2013): 2632–2640. doi:10.1016/j.wasman.2013.08.015

14 Motivating sustainable consumption behaviour through education, incentive programs, and green policies in Saudi Arabia

Hadeel Banjar

Introduction

Consumer behaviour plays an important role in protecting the environment. Our choices, our consumption, and disposal patterns can make a direct or indirect impact on the environment. Encouraging a sustainable consumption behaviour in the society could help in reducing the level of consumption, which leads to a reduction in energy consumption and use of natural resources. At the same time, it will raise the level of awareness in the community. The United Nations Development Program (2010) has indicated that:

> Consumption clearly contributes to human development when it enlarges the capacities and enriches the lives of people without adversely affecting the well-being of others. It clearly contributes when it is as fair to the future generations as to the present ones. And it clearly contributes when it encourages lively, creative individuals and communities. But the links are often broken and when they are consumption patterns and trends are inimical to human development . . . Consumption patterns today must be changed to advance human development tomorrow.
>
> (UNEP 2010: 15)

One of the important concepts that play a role in shaping a sustainable lifestyle is sustainable consumption. Sustainable consumption is not a new concept, as it was developed in 1992 at the Rio Earth Summit and has become one of the important concepts and goals for sustainable development in the United Nations (Mathews 2012).

Sustainable Consumption and Production (SCP)

Sustainable Consumption and Production (SCP) was first defined by the Oslo Symposium in (1994):

> The use of services and related products, which respond to basic needs and bring a better quality of life while minimizing the use of natural resources and

> toxic materials as well as the emissions of waste and pollutants over the life cycle of the service or product so as not to jeopardize the needs of further generations.
>
> (Norwegian Ministry of Environment 1994)

The author of the current study focuses on sustainable consumption only through targeting the social dimension.

Sustainable consumption 10-year-framework

The 10-year framework of programs on sustainable consumption and production patterns (10YFP) is a global framework of action that aims to enhance international cooperation to shift towards sustainable consumption and production (SCP). It supports the access to technical and financial supports for developing countries, as well as national policies and resource efficiency (Executive Committee of the Regional Council of Government Experts on SCP, UNEP, and 10YFP Secretariat. 2015).

Marrakech process on sustainable consumption and production

The Marrakech Process is a global system that aims to develop implementing policies on sustainable consumption and production and support the improvement of a 10YFP on SCP. It helps countries shift their economies to green economies, promotes environmentally friendly business models and motivates consumers to live more sustainable lifestyles (ESA n.d.).

Education for Sustainable Development (ESD)

According to the UN conference Environment and Development in Rio de Janeiro 1992, education was one of the main ways of providing sustainable development. The concept of 'Education for Sustainable Development' is a learning approach that aims to provide people with knowledge and the appropriate education to create and foster sustainability, as well as to build a sustainable future (UNESCO n.d.).

Green policy

According to Dr Abdel Raouf (2014):

> The concept of Green Policy is known as the policy that protects the environment and its resources, achieves social justice, and promotes the living standards. Moreover, the green policy aims to transform the (conventional economics), which is called the (brown economy) to the (economy of the future), or the (green economy) to achieve sustainable development.
>
> (Abdel Raouf 2014)

The green economy has several characteristics, such as reducing the amount of pollution and greenhouse gases emissions, as well as preventing the degradation of ecosystems. Furthermore, it can be applied based on the capabilities of a state and it does not reduce the ability of developing countries to exploit their natural resources (Abdel Raouf 2014).

The ultimate goal of the green policy is to protect the environment and it should not have any negative effects on other sectors. Decision-makers and the authorities in a country have to create green policies that ensure the use of natural resources in a sustainable manner without harming people or the environment (Abdel Raouf 2014). One of the main themes for the 2012 conference (Rio + 20), in the context of sustainable development and poverty eradication, was the access to energy efficiency and renewable energy. It highlights the role of renewable energy in the transition to a green economy (Abdel Raouf 2014).

The current chapter aims to discuss promoting sustainable consumption behaviours of water and energy through education, incentive programs, and green policies in Saudi Arabia. Changing consumer behaviour to a sustainable behaviour requires four main stages. First, one must identify the challenge to achieve sustainable consumption. Second, one must promote sustainable consumption through education. Third, one must set appropriate incentive programs that help in realizing sustainable consumption. Fourth, one must implement green policies to promote a sustainable lifestyle in the country.

The current consumption levels in Saudi Arabia

Energy consumption

Saudi Arabia is an arid and dry land in most of its parts, while the southern part of Saudi receives monsoon rains usually in the summer season (MFA 2016). Saudi Arabia is the second-largest country among the Arab countries, with a total population around 31,015,999 in 2015, including 20,774,906 who are nationals (GAS 2016). The economy of Saudi Arabia depends on oil and it is considered to be the largest oil producer and exporter globally. Saudi Arabia consumed about 2.9 million barrels of oil per day in 2013. And in the first quarter of 2014, Saudi Arabia exported around 1.5 million bbl/d of total petroleum to the United States (U.S. EIA 2014).

Saudi Arabia is the biggest energy consumer in the Middle East. In the last five years, there has been a significant increase in energy demand in Saudi Arabia by an average of 7.5%. About 58% of the total electricity supply in the country depended on oil in 2013 (Hino 2015). Energy and electricity sectors are considered the biggest emitter of CO2 in the country. Also, energy and electricity accounted for about 50% of the CO2 emissions in Saudi Arabia, followed by the transportation sector with 30% and the industrial/construction sector with 20% (Taher and Al-Hajjar 2014).

Furthermore, Saudi Arabia consumes oil products more than industrialised countries such as Germany. Also, Saudi Arabian oil consumption per capita equals the United States' consumption per capita. It is a huge challenge that Saudi Arabia faces with the increase in oil consumption as well as the increase in demand (R.A. 2012). There was a significant increase in oil consumption between 1970 and 2015 that has led to an increase in carbon emissions in the same period, which has a negative impact on the environment (Alkhathlan and Javid 2015).

Electricity production and consumption

Electricity consumption has increased in Saudi Arabia in the last decade by about 7–8% per year due to the high use of air conditioning in the summer and low electricity tariffs. The residential sector consumes about 50% of the total production, the industrial sector consumes about 21%, commercial sector 15%, and governmental agencies consume about 12% (Nachet, Aoun 2015; Electricity & Cogeneration Regulatory Authority 2015). Furthermore, the Saudi electricity market has increased in the last 20 years and it is expected to grow by 5% per year in the next coming years (U.S. Department of Commerce 2016). Saudi Arabia depends mostly on fossil fuel to generate electricity, accounting for 99.9% in 2012, and it ranked as the 10th country globally in high carbon dioxide emission in 2012. Also, the Saudi's consumption of refined petroleum is greater than the production amount in 2012 (CIA n.d.) (see Table 14.1).

Water consumption

The domestic water consumption in Saudi Arabia was around 2.1 billion cubic meters/year in 2004. Eighty-eight percent was used by the agriculture sector, 3% for the industrial sector, and household consumption accounts for 260 litres/capita each day. There was an increase in water demand in various sectors in Saudi Arabia for the past 30 years and predictions up to 2025 (Iitgn 2013). Water demand will continue to increase and it will be 40% greater than today by 2030. Furthermore, the population of Saudi Arabia is expected to grow and reach about

Table 14.1 Saudi Arabia reliance on oil and a comparison in oil consumption and production in 2012

Production			*Consumption*		
Electricity production	*Refined petroleum products – production*	*Electricity from fossil fuel*	*Electricity consumption*	*Refined Petroleum products – consumption*	*Carbon dioxide emissions from energy consumption*
255.4 billion kWh (2012 est.)	1.971 million bbl/day (2012 est.)	99.9% of total installed capacity (2012 est.)	231.6 billion kWh (2012 est.)	2.961 million bbl/day (2013 est.)	582.7 million Mt (2012 est.)

Source: CIA (Central Intelligence Agency) "The World Fact Book." www.cia.gov/library/publications/the-world-factbook/geos/sa.html

40,444,000 by 2035, with 59.3 per capita of water supply (m3/person/year) (Al-Ferra 2015).

The government of Saudi Arabia announced on 29 December 2015, that by 2020 there will be an increase in the prices of fuels gradually, which includes: natural gas, gasoline, diesel, and electricity and water (*OGJ Online*, January 11, 2016). The Council of Ministers has decided to amend the water pricing for the residential, commercial, and industrial sector due to the excessive water consumption rates per capita. Also, the water pricing has not been modified throughout the past 15 years, despite the increase in the costs of water desalination and water consumption (*Saudi Press Agency*, December 12, 2015).

(Sustainable Development Goals) Goal 12: ensure sustainable consumption and production patterns

According to the Agenda 21 of the 'Earth Summit 1992', the main causes of environmental degradation are the unsustainable consumption and production patterns. Thus, there is a demand to change lifestyle and unsustainable consumption patterns, which is the most effective strategy in solving many environmental issues (Abdel Raouf and Banjar 2016). Changing unsustainable consumption patterns in the GCC countries and in Saudi Arabia specifically is considered one of the highly important targets since the GCC countries overuse oil products, water, and energy. Achieving sustainable consumption in the GCC countries requires a collaboration among private, public sectors, and civil society. One of the most effective ways of changing unsustainable behaviour is raising awareness regarding the importance of sustainable consumption through conducting lectures, research, and development (Abdel Raouf and Banjar 2016).

Goal number 12 aims not only at achieving environmentally sound management but also reducing waste and limiting emissions on air, water, and soil (Abdel Raouf and Banjar 2016). Also, good governance plays a crucial role in fighting against corruption and developing appropriate policies that promote sustainable consumption; for instance, laws that support sustainable consumption such as licensing for sustainable products and the adoption of environmental and energy efficiency labels (Abdel Gelil and Saab 2015).

In addition, Goal number 12 of the SDGs aims to ensure sustainable consumption and production patterns; it is about promoting resource and energy efficiency. More importantly, it is one of the essential goals of 2030 and it is linked to the other 16 goals as well. According to United Nations Sustainable Development, Goal 12 includes several targets: "12.2 By 2030, achieve the sustainable management and efficient use of natural resources. 12.8 by 2030, people all over the world will have the appropriate knowledge and awareness for sustainable development and lifestyles in harmony with nature." Also, target 12.c of Goal 12 has the following focus: "Rationalise inefficient fossil-fuel subsidies that encourage wasteful consumption by removing market distortions, in accordance with national circumstances, including by restructuring taxation and phasing out those harmful subsidies, where they exist, to reflect their environmental impacts." (UNSD SDGs n.d.).

Sustainable consumption requires a societal change through a systematic method that focuses on the development of humans based on ecological, social, and economic dimensions (ICSU and ISSC 2015). This means in order to achieve sustainable consumption and production, there is a need to focus on changing the current consumption behaviour on both the household level and the government level. Moreover, it aims to promote sustainable infrastructure and provides suitable jobs, which makes people's lives better. This means that implementing this goal helps in achieving the other 16 goals and in reducing poverty levels. At the same time, this goal helps in reducing environmental and social costs and supports economic competitiveness (UNSD SDGs n.d.). This goal is targeting a vast action in public and private sectors, citizens, and civil society. Irresponsible consumption and production will increase the waste production and deplete a great amount of energy and natural resources. In addition, to achieve SDGs, one must achieve this goal by first setting the appropriate policies (UNSD SDGs n.d.).

Furthermore, achieving this goal requires a significant change of behaviour on the government level, business level, and individual level. Governments should present new legislation that restricts excessive consumption of natural resources and minimises waste generation. This goal includes the general principles of sustainable development and the 2030 framework would have been ineffective without it (Adeel 2015). World leaders admitted the sustainable development path in September 2015 by agreeing on seventeen Sustainable Development Goals (SDGs) with 169 targets. The SDGs are officially known as "Transforming Our World: The 2030 Agenda for Sustainable Development". The following year, in April 2016, Saudi Arabia presented its "KSA Vision 2030" that comes to continue the sustainable development path and to achieve the SDGs by the year 2030 (Abdel Raouf and Banjar 2016).

The Saudi Vision 2030

Saudi Arabia was presented the KSA Vision 2030 on 25 April 2016 by Prince Mohammad bin Salman bin Abdulaziz Al-Saud. It is an ambitious vision that has multiple targets which include various aspects: social, economic, and environmental. Saudi Arabia has established a transparent vision that aims to build the best future for the Kingdom. The Vision 2030 is based on three themes. The first theme is a vibrant society, which has a high priority to achieve this vision. This theme aims to make the better life of Saudi society by living with Islamic principle of moderation and supporting the society by empowering social and healthcare system. The second theme is a thriving economy. This theme helps in creating an education system that is aligned with market demands and provides economic opportunities for the entrepreneur as well as small and large businesses. The third theme is an ambitious nation, which aims to build a transparent, responsible, and high-performing government (Vision 2030 Kingdom of Saudi Arabia 2016).

More importantly, Saudi Arabia's vision 2030 aims to achieve environmental sustainability by reducing the levels of pollution, increasing the efficiency of waste management, becoming a sustainable country without depending on oil by 2020, reducing water consumption by supporting the optimal use of water resources, encouraging the use of treated and renewable water, and optimising the investment of aquatic wealth by rationalising water consumption and the use of treated and used water. The Saudi 2030 vision aims to provide high-quality services of electricity and seeks to add 9.5 gigawatts of renewable energy for local production due to the high level of domestic consumption of energy by 2030 (Vision 2030 Kingdom of Saudi Arabia 2016).

In addition, the new water tariff is within the framework of the Kingdom's Vision 2030, which seeks to improve the environment of Saudi Arabia by preserving the environment and protecting natural resources, which are moral, religious, and human responsibilities toward the environment. One of the most important goals within the vision axes 2030 are the rationalisation of water consumption and the use of treated and renewable water (Vision 2030 Kingdom of Saudi Arabia 2016). The Ministry of Water and Electricity in Saudi Arabia has applied the new water tariffs on 10 January 2016 to achieve energy efficiency and water conservation. The increasing rate has reached up to 1754% and 4238% per capita. The highest three countries in water consumption are the US (666 litres/day), Canada (431 litres/day), and Saudi Area (265 litres/day) (*Arabian Business*, January 10, 2016). Furthermore, Dr Abdullah Al Shehri has pointed out that the new electricity tariff in residential, industrial, and commercial sectors is designed to rationalise electricity consumption and to reduce the reliance on the state. Only the electricity bills with SR 300 or more will be affected gradually (*Alweeam*, January 2, 2016).

The Consumer Protection Association (CPA)

According to a survey conducted by the Consumer Protection Association (CPA) regarding the new water tariff via Twitter, about 50% of the participants stated that there is a significant increase, roughly 11-fold, in the current water bills compared to the previous bills, while 20% of the participants have noticed an increase by 6–10 times, 16% of the participants have noticed an increase by 2–5-fold, and only 14% have noticed an increase by 1–2 times (CPA 2016).

Sustainable consumption

There are several interlinked targets among SDG 12 and KSA Vision 2030. "Sustainable consumption" is the main factor among Sustainable Development Goals and the KSA Vision 2030. The Saudi Vision 2030 focuses on reducing oil dependency and becoming a sustainable country without oil by 2020. Also, the vision aims to reduce water consumption by supporting the optimal use of water resources and encouraging the use of treated and renewable water (Saudi Gazette 2016). Furthermore, the Saudi vision aims to provide high-quality services such as water, and electricity. Through rationalising water consumption and the use of treated and used water, and adding 9.5 gigawatts of renewable energy for local production due to the high level of domestic consumption of energy by 2030, these goals aim to achieve target 12.2 of Goal 12 of the SDGs, which states: "By 2030, achieve the sustainable management and efficient use of natural resources" (*Arab News*, April 26, 2016).

Also, the new water and electricity tariffs are within the framework of the Kingdom's Vision 2030, which aim to achieve energy efficiency and conservation of natural resources and to promote rational use. This new water and electricity policy is linked to target 12.c of Goal 12, which states:

> Rationalize inefficient fossil-fuel subsidies that encourage wasteful consumption by removing market distortions, in accordance with national circumstances, including by restructuring taxation and phasing out those harmful subsidies, where they exist, to reflect their environmental impacts, taking fully into account the specific needs and conditions of developing countries and minimizing the possible adverse impacts on their development in a manner that protects the poor and the affected communities.
>
> (UNSD SDGs n.d.)

The researcher of this chapter aims to provide a suitable solution that reflects the common goals of Goal 12 of SDGs and the KSA Vision 2030 by motivating sustainable consumption in Saudi Arabia through education, incentive programs, and green policies (see Table 14.2).

Table 14.2 The common goals of SDG 12 and the Saudi Vision 2030 that support motivating sustainable consumption in Saudi Arabia

KSA Vision 2030	*SDG 12*
1- Rationalizing water consumption and the use of treated and used water. 2- Add 9.5 gigawatts of renewable energy for local production by 2030. 3- Focus on reducing oil dependency. A country without oil by 2020.	12.2 By 2030, achieve the sustainable management and efficient use of natural resources
4- The new water and electricity tariff are within the framework of the Kingdom's Vision 2030. To achieve energy efficiency and conservation of natural resources and promote a rational use.	12.c Rationalize inefficient fossil-fuel subsidies that encourage wasteful consumption by restructuring taxation and phasing out those harmful subsidies, and develop it in a way that protects the poor and the affected communities.

Source: United Nations Sustainable Development. Sustainable Development Goals, Goal 12: Ensure sustainable consumption and production patterns. doi:www.un.org/sustainabledevelopment/sustainable-consumption-production/#

Global (2016). *Saudi Vision 2030*. Global Research Strategy Report. Kuwait: Global Investment House. doi:www.gulfinthemedia.com/files/article_en/779463.pdf

Islamic ethics toward environmental protection

Protecting the environment

The Holy Quran and the Prophetic teachings have clarified the relation between humans and the universe as a relation based on thinking of the world – a relation between humans and the universe based on sustainable utilisation to benefit humans, as well as a relation based on protecting nature to benefit other creatures (Bagader et al. 2011). Islamic beliefs mostly focus on environmental protection and protection of natural resources, as well as prohibit any source of pollution and misuse or destruction. Muslims are encouraged to support sustainable development and are prohibited from over-exploitation of natural resources. Humans and other creatures equally have the right to benefit from these resources (Al-Banna 2016). Islamic teachings support planting trees and protecting the environment. Prophet Muhammad (Peace be upon him) said: "If a Muslim plants a tree or sows seeds, and then a bird, or a person or an animal eats from it, it is regarded as a charitable gift (Sadaqah) for him" (Saheeh Al-Bukhari, Saheeh Muslim) (Muslim News 24 n.d.).

Regulations and penalties

Dr Qaradawi emphasizes the importance of setting regulations and penalties against any kinds of environmental damage. There is a lack of environmental protection in the Arab and Islamic societies, and religious advice is not enough. Thus, people need encouragement to preserve the environment and confront those corruptors in their societies (*Al Khaleej*, February 17, 2012). Dr Mohi Eddin Abdel Halim, Professor of Islamic Media at the University, discusses the importance of moral values and teaching the young generation how to protect the environment. The media and educational institutions play a major role in providing useful knowledge to people on how to protect the environment (*Al Khaleej*, January 10, 2010).

Moreover, God has placed a specific quantity of the natural resources that matches the total demand of these resources in the universe. This means there is an existence of environmental balance in the natural ecosystem. The Holy Quran says: "Verily, all things have We created by measure" (Quran 55:7) (Akhtar 1996). In addition, Islam is against any kind of corruption, such as littering, deforestation, or toxic waste. These environmental crimes have a negative impact on humans in the long run. The Quran has warned Muslims against corruption: "And do not desire corruption in the land. Indeed, God does not like corrupters." (Quran 28:77) (Ashtankar 2015). Therefore, agriculture, industry, and waste management should be developed in a sustainable manner to avoid any environmental damage.

Literature review

This section addresses various case studies regarding the important role of education, policies, and incentive programs in motivating sustainable consumption all over the world. The aim of this chapter is to design a framework of an action plan to promote and motivate sustainable consumption in Saudi Arabia. Moreover, the current study focuses on the role of education, incentives, and policies that help in changing the current unsustainable consumption patterns. The United Nations Secretary General's High-Level Panel on Global Sustainability (2012) recently wrote that "sustainable development is not a destination, but a dynamic process of adaptation, learning and action. It is about recognising, understanding and acting on inter-connections – above all, those between the economy, society, and the natural environment" (United Nations Secretary-General's High-Level Panel on Global Sustainability 2012). Changing unsustainable behaviour demands time, intentions, and motivations. Previous studies suggested that education is one of the main factors in changing unsustainable behaviours and attitudes toward the environment.

The (sustainable consumption) survey by Arab Forum for Environment and Development (AFED)

The sustainable consumption survey was conducted by AFED and covered 22 Arab countries. Participants were asked 27 questions regarding food, water, energy consumption, and environmental issues. About 72% of the participants agreed that Arab countries are facing water scarcity. Seventy-seven per cent of the participants stated that water consumption in the Arab countries is one of the highest. And 46% of the participants stated that there is a lack of awareness which causes the increase in water and energy use (Abdel Gelil and Saab 2015).

A case study in ownership and regulation in the Portuguese region of Madeira

According to a study conducted in the Portuguese region of Madeira, the study aims to find out to what extent water bills service is educating and encouraging consumers about the importance of consuming water sustainably and to inform them about water shortage issues. A questionnaire was distributed to 386 households in the Madeira region. The results show that water bills lack educational information. Also, the results suggest that redesigning the water bills may have a positive change on consumption behaviour. The majority of domestic users have an incomplete perception about the items included in the bills. In contrast, a small group of participants was aware of the amount of water they were consuming and how much money they were paying for the service. This small group is more conscious in adopting environmentally friendly behaviour and more sustainable consumption (Martins and Moura e Sa 2011).

A teaching intervention at University of Corunna, A Coruña, Spain

A study conducted at the University of Corunna, A Coruña, Spain aimed to increase the awareness level of trainee teachers regarding sustainable consumption by establishing a teaching strategy design. The study covered a sample size of

94 trainee teachers at the Faculty of Educational Sciences, University of A Coruña. The participants were enrolled in a "teaching environmental education" class; 72% of them were female, 23% were male, and the average age was 21 years of age. The study aims to evaluate the participants' backgrounds with environmental impacts of consumerism, their behavioural intentions before (pre-test) and after (post-test), and their perspectives on sustainable consumption. The results were analyzed using statistical analysis. The results of the study show a positive change after (post-test) in the participants' behaviour through consuming responsibly to reduce their ecological footprint. The participants also show a significant increase in their knowledge of environmental issues and consumerism impacts (Álvarez-Suárez et al. 2013).

An empirical study to motivate a behavioural change in Germany

An empirical study was conducted in Germany to study the influence of financial rewards for (eco-driving) on fuel consumption. The researchers designed a comparative experience with both a monetary and a non-monetary incentive for eco-driving among 86 employees of light commercial vehicles in different branches of a German logistics company. The study divided the participants into three groups: a control group with no incentives, whereas the second and third group were treatment groups (a monetary incentive and a non-monetary incentive). The three groups were from different branches of the same company in three different states (Schalla and Mohnen 2015).

There were 24 participants in the first group, while the second group had 22 and the third group had 40. The second and third groups were rewarded for eco-driving. These incentives were given to the drivers as (financial rewards) in cash or as a non-financial reward which was equal to the financial reward, such as cinema tickets, passes for social events, or restaurant coupons. The experiment was conducted for six months, during which the first three months passed without introducing incentives and during the remaining three months the drivers received incentives. Fuel consumption was calculated individually for each driver. The results of the study show that non-financial incentives have a strong influence on drivers for fuel-efficient driving compared to the financial incentives. Fuel consumption declined by 5% after introducing the non-monetary incentives and declined by 3.5% after providing the monetary incentives (Schalla and Mohnen 2015).

Methodology

This section describes the methodology approach for this research. The researcher chose a quantitative method of analysis. The methodology section includes the purpose, research questions, instruments, and data analysis.

Purpose of the study

The main purpose of this study is to encourage sustainable consumption behaviour of water and energy in Saudi Arabia through education, incentives, and green policies. The researcher aimed to investigate the current consumption behaviour of consumers in Saudi Arabia, their perceptions regarding their consumption behaviour and its impact on the environment, whether they have enough knowledge regarding environmental issues or not, and whether the consumers are willing to change their consumption behaviour to more sustainable behaviour if there is a suitable environmental course at a University level as a motivation and suitable incentives. Finally, the researcher aimed to find the suitable green policy or policies that will help with consuming water and energy in a more sustainable manner.

Research questions

1 What are the current consumption patterns of water and electricity in Saudi Arabia?
2 Are consumers in Saudi Arabia willing to change their consumption behaviour to more sustainable behaviour if there is a suitable environmental course at a University level?
3 Are incentive programs useful tools in changing current consumption behaviour in Saudi Arabia?
4 What is the suitable green policy that helps to change the current consumption behaviour of water and electricity to more sustainable behaviour in Saudi Arabia?

Quantitative

The researcher of this project aimed to distribute an online survey questionnaire to investigate the current consumption patterns of water and energy among consumers in Saudi Arabia. The researcher selected the Makkah region to distribute the survey. The methodology of this study consists of collecting quantitative data by distributing 3,000 online survey questionnaires among consumers in Saudi Arabia from different backgrounds and age groups ranging between 24 and 64. The survey consisted of 19 questions with open-ended and multiple-choice, close-ended questions. The first five questions were general questions about gender, age, nationality, the highest degree of school the participants have earned, and income. The second part of the survey focused on the awareness level of the participants and their perceptions regarding the importance of education in changing consumption behaviour. The third part of the survey focused on gathering information on the participants' consumption patterns of water and energy. The fourth part of the survey focused on investigating the public's opinion about current water and energy policies. The fifth part of the survey focused on finding a relation between suitable incentives and changing consumption behaviour.

Analysis of the data

The researcher used Excel to analyze and graph the collected data. The Excel software is a very efficient tool to analyze and manage the findings of the questionnaire.

Results and discussion

A total of 784 questionnaires were completed by participants in the Makkah region (Makkah and Jeddah City). The researcher distributed an online survey by email to a number of universities, companies, and governmental organizations. Female participants accounted for 66% of respondents, while male participants accounted for 34%. The majority of respondents were Saudi citizens, and only 15% of the respondents were non-Saudi residents (see Table 14.3).

The participants' age group ranged between 18 and 64. About half of the participants were in age group 25–34, followed by age group 35–44 with 25%. And about 12% of the participants were in age group 18–24, and 10% in age group 45–54. A small number of respondents was in the age group 55–64 (see Table 14.4).

The results show that more than half of the respondents have earned a Bachelor's degree, followed by 17% of the participants having completed high school while 16% of the participants have earned a Master's degree. Only a small number of participants have earned a Doctorate degree. Moreover, the results show that about 26% of the respondents earn between SR 3,000–6,000 a month, and 23% of the respondents earn less than SR 3,000 a month, while 21% of the respondents declared that they earn between SR 7,000–10,000 a month. Then the participants were asked about the top three environmental issues in Saudi Arabia. About 28% of the respondents choose a lack of water resources, followed by traffic congestion with 20% and air pollution with 18% (see Figure 14.1).

Questions 7, 8, 9, and 10 of the survey focused on the participants' perceptions regarding the importance of education in changing their consumption behaviour. Around 46% of the respondents declared that they have studied a course related

Table 14.3 Gender and nationality of the participants

Participants		*Number of participants*	*Percentage*
Gender	Male	270	34%
	Female	514	66%
Nationality	Saudi	664	85%
	Non-Saudi	120	15%

Table 14.4 Age group of the participants

Age group	*Number of participants*	*Percentage*
18–24	94	12%
25–34	382	49%
35–44	198	25%
45–54	78	10%
55–64	32	4%

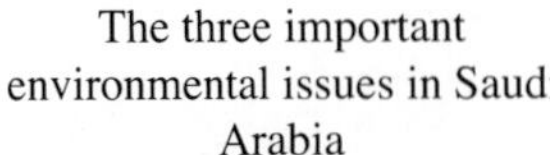

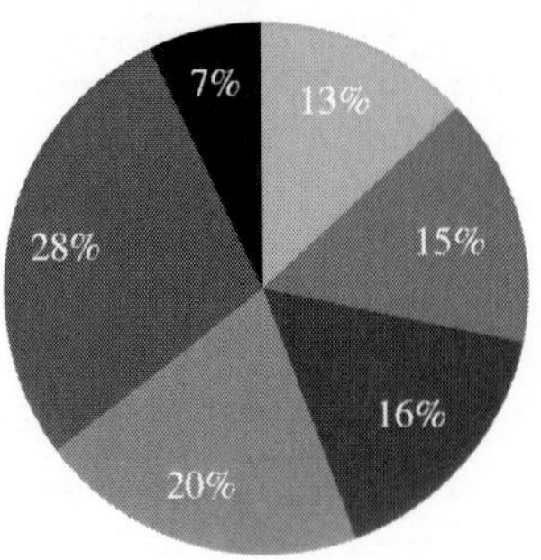

Figure 14.1 The three important environmental issues in Saudi Arabia

to the environment, while more than half of the participants stated that they have not taken any course related to the environment. The results show that about 47% of the participants prefer media to gain knowledge regarding environmental issues and to raise awareness, while 31% of the participants believe that high school courses or University courses are a more suitable method to gain knowledge regarding environmental issues. Only a low percentage of the participants (16%) choose workshops and lectures as a suitable approach to gain knowledge regarding environmental issues.

The participants suggested having strict environmental laws and regulations for environmental protection. Education plays an important role, especially at a very young age. Social media and documentaries also are important tools that provide sufficient knowledge regarding environmental issues. Furthermore, a number of respondents believe that different environmental protection associations have to be more involved in creating events, workshops, and volunteering opportunities to raise awareness within society (see Figure 14.2).

Furthermore, about 78% of the participants believe that education has a great influence on changing current consumption behaviours, while only 10% of the participants believe that education does not have an influence on changing current consumption behaviours. The participants suggested that schools should provide a suitable and improved curriculum that focuses on the environmental issues and promotes a rational consumption behaviour for water and energy.

About 68% of the participants believe that the electricity and water campaigns are useful tools that provide enough knowledge regarding water and electricity issues for the public. However, about 19% of the respondents believe that these campaigns are not useful tools. And 13% of the participants stated that these campaigns should be more improved and available to the whole society. Moreover,

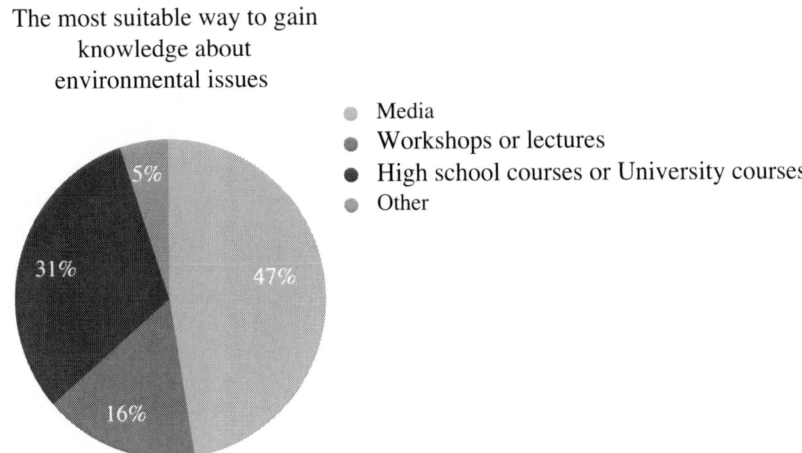

Figure 14.2 The most suitable way to gain knowledge about environmental issues

a number of respondents stated that there is a need for effective water and electricity campaigns that encourages consumers to consume wisely.

Questions 11, 12, and 13 focus on the monthly payment of water and energy (electricity and gas) bills. The results show that about 43% of the participants pay between 50–200 SR for electricity per month, another 40% of the participants pay between 200–400 SR per month, and only 17% of the respondents pay more than 500 SR. While 37% of the participants pay between 300–500 SR for gas and transportation per month, and 32% of the participants pay between 100–250 SR, 31% pay more than 500 SR. More than half of the respondents pay between 50–200 SR for water per month, and 31% pay between 200–400 SR. Only 12% of the respondents pay more than 500 SR per month.

Questions 14, 15, and 16 focus on the participants' perceptions regarding the new water and electricity prices and whether it affects them in a positive or negative way. More than half of the participants believe that the increase in oil prices in Saudi has affected and increased other services as well as increased their costs of living. However, 28% of the participants stated that the increase in oil prices did not affect them at all.

About 46% of the respondents believe that the sudden increase in water and electricity prices may not help them to consume less water and electricity due to lack of awareness and the increasing demand for electricity, especially in this hot climate. However, 43% of the participants believe that the increase in water and electricity prices will help them to consume water and electricity more wisely. About 94% of the participants agreed that the increase in water and electricity prices will affect low-income families negatively. Only a small percentage of the participants believe that the increase in water and electricity prices will not affect low-income families.

The last two questions of the survey aimed to identify the participants' perceptions regarding the suitable incentive and their willingness in changing their consumption behaviour if suitable incentives were provided. More than 81% of the participants stated that they are willing to reduce their current consumption behaviour of water and energy if there were appropriate incentives provided.

The author suggested in the last question a number of incentives to provide to consumers as an encouragement to consume water and energy in a sustainable manner. About 35% of the participants chose health insurance due to the high costs of hospitals and medical services, while 32% of the participants preferred pre-paid electricity cards and 26% of the participants chose cash as a suitable incentive (see Figure 14.3).

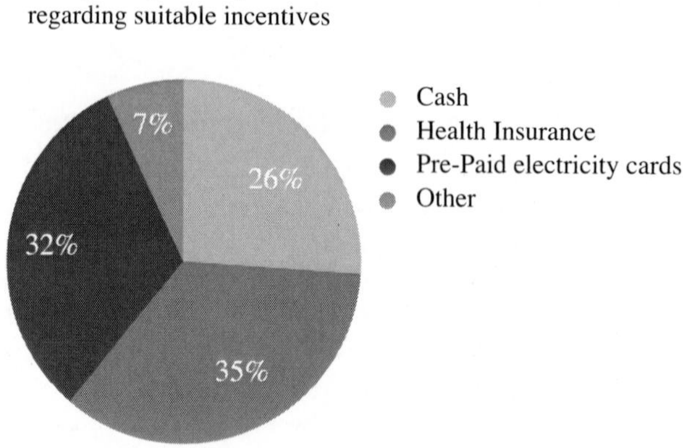

Figure 14.3 The participants' opinions regarding suitable incentives

Discussion

This section discusses the results of the research. The first research question of this study asked: what are the current consumption patterns of water and electricity in Saudi Arabia? The findings of this study indicated that a great number of consumers think that the current consumption behaviour of water and energy in Saudi Arabia is not sustainable due to a lack of awareness in this regard.

The second research question asked: are consumers in Saudi Arabia willing to change their consumption behaviour to more sustainable behaviour if there is a suitable environmental course at a University level? The results show that there is a lack of awareness of environmental issues in the society. At the same time, there is a strong demand for raising awareness and providing information among the society regarding environmental issues through social media, University courses, appropriate school curriculum, and workshops and lectures. Furthermore, there is a demand to develop the current electricity and water campaigns and to explain to the public the negative impact of over-consuming water and electricity.

The third research question asked: are incentive programs useful tools in changing the current consumption behaviour in Saudi Arabia? The findings of the survey show that a high percentage of the participants welcome the idea of receiving incentives as a motivating tool for consumers to help them consume water and energy in a sustainable manner. Also, the previous studies show the powerful influence of incentives in changing people's behaviour. Moreover, the results of the current study support the concept of providing incentives in exchange for changing current consumption behaviours to more sustainable consumption behaviours.

The fourth research question asked: what is the suitable green policy that helps to change the current consumption behaviour of water and electricity to a more sustainable behaviour in Saudi Arabia? The author focused on the new tariff of water and electricity that aims to rationalise the consumption of water and electricity in Saudi. The results of this study show that the new tariff could have a positive impact on changing the current consumption behaviour. However, removing the subsidies and increasing the prices of water and electricity will affect low-income families negatively. In addition, the climate of Saudi Arabia is extremely hot. Thus, under these circumstances, it is a very challenging goal to reduce electricity consumption, even with the removal of the subsidies and an increase in the prices. Therefore, there is a necessity for a green policy that is suitable for the life standards of consumers in Saudi Arabia and for the climate.

Policy recommendations

General recommendations

- Raise the level of awareness in the media and the use of the appropriate technology that helps improve the conservation of water and energy.
- Distribute and provide the rationalisation tools that help reduce water and electricity consumption.

Education

- Education is the ultimate solution for any issue. The Ministry of Education has to create a mandatory school curriculum that values the environment and is formulated in a way that helps students appreciate nature and understand environmental issues. More importantly, this curriculum has to teach the students to consume in a more sustainable manner (theoretical and practical).
- Provide mandatory courses for students at University level.
- Provide mandatory courses and lectures for teachers and professors at school and University levels.

Incentives and green policies

Incentives and green policies are overlapping and both can be designed in a way that accomplishes this goal. Thus, there is a need to promote suitable policies by the government or specific entities such as Water and Electricity Corporation, and then to provide the eligible audience with suitable incentives. Several studies show that people tend to change their consumption behaviour whenever there are suitable incentives provided to them. Also, a number of studies have declared that incentives have a great influence on changing people's behaviour.

In behavioural psychology, incentives and rewards have powerful effects on changing people's behaviour, more than punishments. Therefore, there should be compatible green policies that encourage people to change their consumption behaviour. Furthermore, a good policy requires a collaboration among the private sector, public sector, and civil society to ensure the use of natural resources in a sustainable manner and to protect the environment. There is a need to identify the relevant stakeholders and engage institutions, share their knowledge, and develop the appropriate policy that encourages sustainable consumption. Based on the results of the current study, the author proposed a number of recommendations:

1 (Green Home) Public Fund Authority

According to the results of the current study, the author recommends that the government creates a green policy that mandates homeowners to use environmentally friendly materials in their new buildings and to implement low energy house standards. The first low energy house in the Aqaba Residence Energy Efficiency (AREE) in Jordan is considered a great example of a residential project that is designed to support energy efficiency (Elgendy 2010). Also, the policy should mandate homeowners to use rationalisation tools in the new buildings, which will help reduce water consumption. The government could provide the appropriate incentives to the homeowners who use environmentally friendly materials and take into account the standards of low energy houses in their new houses. In contrast, the homeowners who do not use the environmentally friendly materials and do not take into account the standards of low energy houses will have to pay taxes to the government.

The researcher recommends collecting these taxes in the "Green Home", which is a public fund authority. Then, the collected taxes will be used to subsidise low-income families in building houses by using environmentally friendly materials and implementing the standards of low energy houses with the newest technologies that support energy and water efficiency. In addition, these taxes can be used to improve the existing houses and make them more energy and water efficient (see Figure 14.4).

2 Based on the results of the current study, the following recommendations are proposed by the researcher and participants. Governmental incentives can be provided to people either as monetary or non-monetary incentives. Consumers can receive incentives when their water bills or electricity bills reach a certain level. For instance, the water and electricity company can

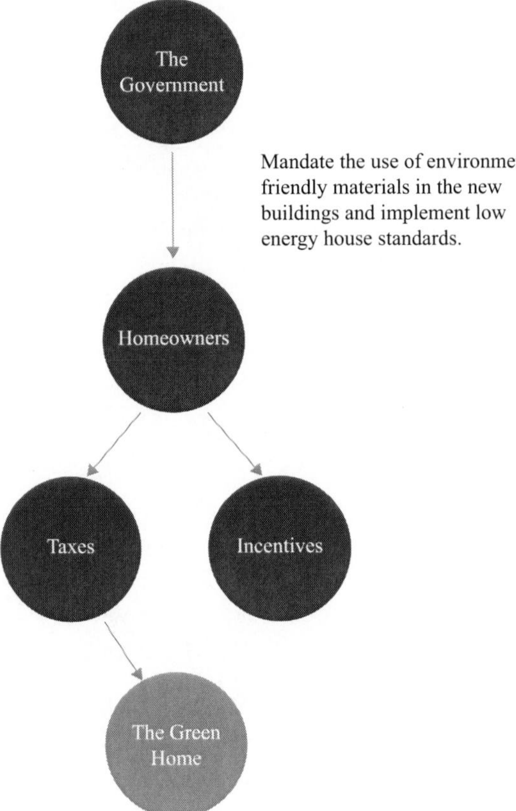
The Government
Mandate the use of environmentally friendly materials in the new buildings and implement low energy house standards.
Homeowners
Taxes
Incentives
The Green Home

Figure 14.4 The "Green Home" outline

calculate the reference value per house and take into consideration important factors (e.g. number of family members, the size of the house). If the average of water consumption or electricity consumption is below the reference value per house, consumers can receive incentives.

3 The researcher recommends a number of incentives such as cash, health insurance, and pre-paid electricity cards. Furthermore, the participants suggest deducting a portion of the water or electricity bill that equals the rate of reduction in consumption.

4 It is necessary to mandate the labelling of energy performance on electronic devices that help decrease electricity consumption.

Conclusion

Saudi Arabia needs to switch to a new direction to achieve sustainable development by realising sustainable solutions and policies that are appropriate to the Saudi climatic conditions, as well as suitable for the people's life standards. This chapter discusses promoting sustainable consumption behaviour through education, incentive programs, and green policies in Saudi Arabia. Changing the consumer behaviour to a sustainable behaviour requires implementing suitable school curriculum for the public, establishing incentive programs that promote sustainable consumption, and realising a green policy that supports sustainable consumption. In this chapter, the main issue is unsustainable consumption behaviour of water and electricity in Saudi Arabia. The social dimension is the primary dimension that has the ability to develop a sustainable development in Saudi Arabia.

The current issue faces three main challenges

- Lack of sufficient knowledge and awareness regarding environmental issues.
- Lack of motivation that helps in changing the current consumption behaviour.
- Lack of environmental policies that aim to protect natural resources and the environment.

Therefore, there is a demand to shift to a new direction in order to achieve sustainable consumption behaviour, within the framework of the KSA Vision 2030 and supporting Goal 12 of SDGs.

Furthermore, according to the survey conducted by the Consumer Protection Association and the results of the current study, the new water policy has increased consumers' monthly water bills. Also, the new policy of water and electricity that aims to achieve water and energy efficiency could have a negative impact on low-income families. As the climate in Saudi Arabia is extremely hot, this new policy might not accomplish the desired goal. Therefore, there is a clear demand to establish appropriate green policies that have several benefits:

1 Promote water and energy efficiency.
2 Protect the environment and natural resources.
3 Suitable for consumers' life standards in Saudi Arabia (does not affect low-income families) and suitable for the climate.
4 Promoting green policies can help reduce the temperature in buildings, reduce energy consumption, and cut energy bills.

Appendix A

Survey questionnaire

1 What is your gender?
Male ______ Female ______

2 How old are you?
18–24 25–34 35–44 45–54 55–64

3 What is your nationality?
A. Saudi B. Non-Saudi

4 What is the highest degree of school you have completed?
A. High school B. Bachelor's degree
C. Master's degree D. Doctorate degree

5 What is your income?

1. less than SR 3000
2. SR 3000–6000
3. SR 7000–10,000
4. SR 11,000–15,000
5. SR 16,000–20,000
6. More than SR 20,000

6 Which of the following do you consider the top 3 environmental issues in Saudi Arabia?
1. Desertification 2. Solid waste 3. Air pollution
4. Traffic congestion 5. Lack of water resources 6. Lack of food resources

7 Have you taken any class during your studying related to the environment?
A. Yes B. No

8 What is the most effective way to gain knowledge about environmental issues and raise awareness? (please explain your answer when you choose D)
A. Media B. Workshops or lectures
C. High school courses or University courses D. Other

9 Do you believe that education has a positive influence on changing the current consumption behaviour of water and energy, as well as raising awareness regarding environmental issues? Please explain your answer.
A. Yes B. No C. Other

10 Do you think that the electricity and water campaigns are useful tools that provide useful knowledge regarding water and electricity issues to the public? Please explain your answer.
A. Yes B. No C. Other

11 How much do you pay for electricity in a month?
A. 50–200 SR B. 200–400 SR C. More than 500 SR

12 How much do you pay for gas? transportation? in a month?
A. 100–250 SR B. 300–500 SR C. More than 500 SR

13 How much do you pay for water per month?
A. 50–200 SR B. 200–400 SR C. More than 500 SR

14 Does the increase in oil prices affect your spending habits? Explain your answer.
A. Yes B. No C. Other

15 Do you think the sudden increase in water and electricity prices will help you to consume less (water and electricity)? Explain why?
A. Yes B. No C. Other

16 Do you think the sudden increase in water and electricity prices may affect low-income families negatively?
A. Yes B. No

17 Do you think there is a relation between the environmental issues and your consumption of water and energy?
A. Yes B. No C. I don't Know

18 If the government provide consumers in Saudi with suitable incentives in order to reduce their consumption patterns of water and energy, would you reduce your water and electricity consumption?
A. Yes B. No C. I don't Know

19 If there are suitable incentives in exchange for consuming less water and energy, which of these incentives would you rather choose? Please explain your answer when you choose D.
A. Cash B. Health Insurance C. Pre-Paid electricity cards
D. Others

References

Abdel Gelil, Ibrahim, and Najib Saab. 2015. *Arab Environment: Sustainable Consumption. Annual Report of Arab Forum for Environment and Development (AFED).* Beirut: Technical Publications. Available at: www.afedonline.org/Report2015/English/ENglish2015L.pdf

Abdel Raouf, Mohamed. 2014. السياسة الخضراء لموازنة أهداف الطاقة والبيئة حالة دولة الإمارات العربية المتحدة [*Green Politics to Balance the Goals of Energy and Environmental Status of the United Arab Emirates*]. Abu Dhabi: Emirates Center for Strategic Studies and Research.

Abdel Raouf, Mohamed, and Hadeel Banjar. 2016. Sustainable Development Goals (SDGs) Challenges and Opportunities for The GCC Countries. Gulf Research Center.

Adeel, Zafar. 2015, September 20. *Consumers Can be the Vanguard of Sustainability*. United Nations University. Available at: http://unu.edu/publications/articles/consumers-vanguards-sustainability.html

Akhtar, Muhammad. 1996. Towards an Islamic approach for environmental balance. *Islamic Economic Studies*, 3(2). Available at: www.irti.org/English/Research/Documents/IES/137.pdf

Al-Banna, Fatima. 2016, May 31. *Islam and Environment Protection*. EcoMENA, Echoing Sustainability. Available at: www.ecomena.org/islam-environment/

Al-Ferra, Taha. 2015. Water security in the Gulf region. *Al Jazeera Center for Studies*, March 31. Available at: http://studies.aljazeera.net/en/dossiers/2015/03/20153318534835257.html

Al Khaleej. 2010. حماية البيئة من التلوث فريضة إسلامية [Environmental protection is an Islamic obligation]. *Al Khaleej*, January 10. Available at: www.alkhaleej.ae/supplements/page/91cb1561-267d-4c0c-bd72-777c6c716d4b

Al Khaleej. 2012. حماية البيئة من التلوث واجب ديني [Protecting the environment from pollution is a religious responsibility]. *Al Khaleej*, February 17. Available at: www.alkhaleej.ae/supplements/page/edd2d2ab-94e7-4e53-ad7e-180ce435a810

Alkhathlan, K., and Muhammad Javid. 2015. Carbon emissions and oil consumption in Saudi Arabia. *Renewable and Sustainable Energy Reviews*, 48: 105–111. doi:10.1016/j.rser.2015.03.072

Álvarez-Suárez, Pedro, Pedro Vega-Marcote, and Ricardo Garcia Mira. 2013. Sustainable consumption: A teaching intervention in higher education. *International Journal of Sustainability in Higher Education*, 1: 3–15. doi:10.1108/IJSHE-06-2011-0044

Alweeam. 2016. تنظيم الكهرباء: الفواتير التي تزيد على "300" ريال ستتأثر بقرار التعرفة الجديدة [Electricity regulation: Bills that over "300" sr will be affected by the new tariff decision]. *Alweeam*, January 2. Available at: www.alweeam.com.sa/377566/تنظيم-الكهرباء-الفواتير-التي-تزيد-على/

Arabian Business. 2016. تطبيق التعرفة جديدة للمياه في السعودية وتوجه لإصدار فواتير شهرية [The application of the new tariff for water in Saudi Arabia and issue a monthly bills]. *Arabian Business*, January 10. Available at: http://arabic.arabianbusiness.com/business/energy/2016/jan/10/404475/

Arab News. 2016. The vision document that charts new course for Saudi Arabia. *Arab News*, April 26. Available at: www.arabnews.com/saudi-arabia/news/915676#

Ashtankar, O.M. 2015. Islamic perspectives on environmental protection. *International Journal of Applied Research*, 2(1): 438–441. Available at: www.allresearchjournal.com/archives/2016/vol2issue1/PartG/2-1-57.pdf

Bagader, Abubakr, Abdullatif El-Sabbagh, Mohamad Al-Glayand, and Mawill Samarrai. 2011. Environmental protection In Islam. *IslamReligion*, 19. Available at: www.islamreligion.com/articles/307/viewall/environmental-protection-in-islam/

Central Intelligence Agency (CIA). *The World Fact Book*. Available at: www.cia.gov/library/publications/the-world-factbook/geos/sa.html

Consumer Protection Association. 2016. التعريفة الجديدة لاستهلاك المياه [*The New Tariff of Water Consumption*]. Available at: https://cpa.org.sa/?program_content=4846-2

Electricity & Cogeneration Regulatory Authority. 2015. *Activities and Achievements of the Authority in 2014.* Riyadh: King Fahd Library Indexing During Publication.

Elgendy, Karim. 2010. The first low energy house in Jordan. *Carboun Middle East Sustainable Cities*, March 1. Available at: www.carboun.com/sustainable-design/the-first-low-energy-house-in-jordan/

ESA. *The Marrakech Process*. Available at: http://esa.un.org/marrakechprocess/

Executive Committee of the Regional Council of Government Experts on SCP, UNEP, and 10YFP Secretariat. 2015. Regional Strategy on Sustainable Consumption and Production

(SCP) for the 10YFP Implementation in Latin-America and the Caribbean (2014–2022). Available at: www.pnuma.org/english/scp_strategy/Regional_SCP_Strategy_160415.pdf

General Authority for Statistics, Kingdom of Saudi Arabia (The Total Population, 2016) Available at: www.stats.gov.sa/en/node

Global. 2016. *Saudi Vision 2030.* Global Research Strategy Report. Global Investment House, Kuwait. Available at: www.gulfinthemedia.com/files/article_en/779463.pdf

Hino, Yukari. 2015. Saudi Arabia field report: Another potential oil crisis in the Middle East. *Brookings*, July 2. Available at: www.brookings.edu/blog/markaz/2015/07/02/saudi-arabia-field-report-another-potential-oil-crisis-in-the-middle-east/

ICSU, ISSC. 2015. *Review of the Sustainable Development Goals: The Science Perspective.* Paris: International Council for Science (ICSU). Available at: www.icsu.org/publications/reports-and-reviews/review-of-targets-for-the-sustainable-development-goals-the-science-perspective-2015/SDG-Report.pdf

Iitgn. 2013. *Fresh-Water Modeling for Saudi Arabia.* Iitgn. Available at: www.iitgn.ac.in/mcm/solutions/Team%2019075.pdf

Martins, R., and Patricia Moura e Sa. 2011. Promoting sustainable residential water use: A Portuguese case study in ownership and regulation. *Policy Studies*, 3: 291–301. doi:10.1080/01442872.2011.561697

Mathews, Charles. 2012. *Towards a Framework for Sustainable Consumption in China.* London: Centre for Environmental Policy, Imperial College London.

Ministry of Foreign Affairs. 2016. *About Saudi Arabia.* Ministry of Foreign Affairs. Available at: www.mofa.gov.sa/sites/mofaen/ServicesAndInformation/aboutKingDom/Pages/KingdomGeography46466.aspx

Muslim News 24. Protection of environment: An important aspect in Islam. *Muslim News 24.* Available at: http://muslimnews24.com/protection-of-environment-an-important-aspect-in-islam/

Nachet, Said, and Marie-Claire Aoun. 2015. *The Saudi Electricity Sector: Pressing Issues and Challenges.* Paris: Ifri. Available at: www.ifri.org/sites/default/files/atoms/files/note_arabie_saoudite_vf.pdf

Norwegian Ministry of Environment, Oslo Symposium, 1994. Available at: https://sustainabledevelopment.un.org/topics/sustainableconsumptionandproduction.

OGJ editors. 2016. Saudi Arabia, UAE lead GCC subsidy reform. *Oil and Gas Journal*, January 11. Available at: www.ogj.com/articles/2016/01/saudi-arabia-uae-lead-gcc-subsidy-reform.html

R.A. 2012. Oil burning their wealth. *The Economist*, April 5. Available at: www.economist.com/blogs/freeexchange/2012/04/oil

Saudi Gazette. 2016. Full text of Saudi Arabia's vision 2030. *Al Arabiya*, April 27. Available at: https://english.alarabiya.net/en/perspective/features/2016/04/26/Full-text-of-Saudi-Arabia-s-Vision-2030.html

Saudi Press Agency. 2015. زيادة تعرفة المياه والكهرباء طفيفة . وأسعار الوقود الأقل عالميًا [Slight increase in water and electricity tariff and less fuel prices globally.] *Saudi Press Agency*, December 12. Available at: www.spa.gov.sa/viewstory.php?newsid=1433312

Schalla, D., and Alwine Mohnen. 2015. Incentives for energy-efficient behavior at the workplace: A natural field experiment on eco-driving in a company fleet. *Energy Procedia*, 75: 2626–2634. doi:10.1016/j.egypro.2015.07.348

Taher, Nahed, and Bandar Al-Hajjar. 2014. *Energy and Environment in Saudi Arabia: Concerns and Opportunities.* Basel, Switzerland: Springer.

UNESCO. Education for Sustainable Development Unit (USD). Available at: www.unescobkk.org/education/esd-unit/definition-of-esd

United Nations Environment Programme. 2010. *Here and Now! Education for Sustainable Consumption*, 32pp. Available at: www.unep.org/pdf/Here_and_Now_English.pdf

United Nations Secretary-General's High-Level Panel on Global Sustainability. 2012. *Resilient People, Resilient Planet: A Future Worth Choosing, Overview.* New York: United Nations. Available at: www.un.org/gsp/report/. http://uscib.org/docs/GSPReportOverview_A4%20size.pdf

United Nations Sustainable Development. Sustainable Development Goals. *Goal 12: Ensure Sustainable Consumption and Production Patterns*. Available at: www.un.org/sustainabledevelopment/sustainable-consumption-production/#

U.S. Department of Commerce, International Trade Administration. 2016. *Top Markets Report Smart Grid Country Case Study, Saudi Arabia.* Available at: www.trade.gov/topmarkets/pdf/Smart_Grid_Saudi_Arabia.pdf

U.S. Energy Information Administration. 2014. *Country Analysis Brief: Saudi Arabia.* U.S. Energy Information Administration, 19pp. Available at: www.eia.gov/beta/international/analysis_includes/countries_long/Saudi_Arabia/saudi_arabia.pdf

Vision 2030 Kingdom of Saudi Arabia. 2016a. Available at: http://vision2030.gov.sa/ar/node/259

Part V

Conclusion

15 Outlook towards the future of sustainability in the Gulf

Elie Azar and Mohamed Abdel Raouf

Introduction

In September 2015, leaders from around the world, including the GCC, have committed to a sustainable development path by agreeing on 17 Sustainable Development Goals (SDGs) with 169 targets for the next 15 years. The SDGs were clubbed under the title "Transforming Our World: the 2030 Agenda for Sustainable Development". They have sparked numerous debates and are currently inspiring an increasing number of countries in their quest for alternative development pathways. The SDGs are something the GCC states simply cannot afford to ignore.

From a Gulf perspective, the key question that begs answering is: why should the GCC countries embark on a transition to sustainability through the SDGs and why should they do so at this point in time? Moreover, how could the GCC states benefit from the SDGs? The simple answer is that the GCC countries have seen their economies expand and diversify tremendously in the last decade. However, as these economies have grown, economic, social, and environmental challenges have grown as well. As a result, the SDGs represent important modules for the GCC countries to tackle their challenges and chart the way forward in a more sustainable manner.

SDGs and the need for 'good governance'

From a GCC perspective, what are the essential conditions for realizing SDGs? To answer this question, many drivers and enablers are needed such as technology and innovation, funding mechanisms, behavioural and cultural changes, and effective governance.

In fact, 'good governance' is a fundamental requirement for a sustainable development transition. Good governance can help induce changes in current behaviours and encourage investments in green growth strategies. At the core of good governance are 'green policies', which governments should employ to encourage and support the shift towards sustainability. A green policy can be defined at the macro level as "a policy that balances between natural resource utilization and environmental protection, while seeking to achieve social equity and raise the well-being of the society" (Abdel Raouf 2013). In simple terms, it is a policy that has a green economy as its central objective, with the ultimate goal of achieving sustainable development.

It is worth mentioning that green policies are context-specific and should always account for the local cultural, economic, and social considerations of a country. Also, green policies may and should evolve over time as the above-mentioned circumstances change and develop. Furthermore, a truly effective green policy will not only generate economy-wide impacts but will also have positive or favourable impacts across different sectors such as infrastructure or healthcare. Therefore, when designing such policies, a cross-sectoral approach is needed to maximize benefits across sectors while minimizing and mitigating unintended consequences. For instance, an aggressive investment in biofuels might negatively impact water and food resources, and should, therefore, be accounted for.

A 'mix' of green policy instruments is needed in the GCC and may include some or all of the following: market instruments (e.g., subsidy reform, green taxes, and permit markets), legal instruments (e.g., environmental legislation and sustainable trade agreements), sustainable public procurement strategies, integrated water management strategies, sustainable land use and urban planning, monitoring and accountability measures, as well as awareness and educational campaigns.

More importantly, as the principle of good governance dictates, the design and execution of policies should involve the participation of all relevant stakeholders, starting with key government agencies and integrating inputs from non-governmental organizations, scholars, businesses, and professional organizations, among others (Abdel Raouf 2011).

From challenges to opportunities

In recent years, the GCC countries have enacted a number of sustainability-driven visions and strategies to provide a better future for their citizens. As shown in Table 15.1, all six GCC countries have developed visions and strategies, which have led to numerous green initiatives and projects across the region.

The initiatives presented in Table 15.1 indicate a clear desire of the GCC states to incorporate sustainability in their visions and plans for the future. However, the reality is that the actual path towards meeting the SDGs is still very long and additional efforts and action are needed. The challenges are many and include economies that continue to be heavily dependent on oil, high energy and water usage characterized by wasteful consumption patterns, car-oriented mobility, rapid population growth, rapid urbanisation, education and employment challenges, extreme climatic conditions, lack of local industries, and limited entrepreneurship and innovation activities.

In the GCC, the economy and natural resources are inextricably linked. All business sectors depend upon natural resources for their success – be it the petroleum, tourism, or even the services sectors. One specific focus of the GCC has been, and will remain to be, on economic development as the countries are aware that through such development, they will be in a better position to eradicate poverty, create jobs, and increase prosperity. However, economic development in itself is insufficient. Instead, the emphasis must be on sustainable economic development

Table 15.1 Sustainability-driven visions and strategies in GCC countries

Country	*Visions and strategies*	*Main aim*
Saudi Arabia	Saudi Vision 2030	It is a package of social and economic policies that are designed to free the Kingdom from dependence on oil exports and to build a prosperous and sustainable economic future by focusing on country's strength and policies.
UAE	UAE Vision 2021; Green economy strategy; Abu Dhabi vision 2030	A number of sustainable strategies that aim to make the UAE among the best countries in the world by the Golden Jubilee of the UAE Union.
Kuwait	Kuwait's Vision: The Year 2030	The objective is to enlighten and spread the vision of a long-term development plan as well as transform Kuwait's currently unsustainable economy into a sustainable one.
Bahrain	The Economic Vision 2030	A comprehensive economic vision for Bahrain, providing a clear direction for the continued development of the Kingdom's economy and, at its heart, a shared goal of building a better life for every Bahraini.
Qatar	The Qatar National Vision 2030 (QNV 2030)	Transform Qatar into an advanced society capable of achieving sustainable development by 2030. The plan's development goals are divided into four central pillars: economic, social, human, and environmental development.
Oman	Oman Vision 2040	To diversify its economic activities from oil and gas sector to tourism sector and other services sectors. In short, it aims at developing a sustainable economic development for Oman.

Source: Compiled by authors

that is inclusive, addressing the needs of the poor, the vulnerable, women, men, youth, and indigenous people (e.g., Bedouins). Furthermore, growth should not come at the expense of environmental sustainability, which in addition to pollution and carbon emissions includes the protection of biodiversity.

Given the historic key role of the energy sector in the socio-economic development of the region, it can be argued that a drastic transformation in this sector is a precondition for any progress towards sustainable development. Greening the energy portfolio of GCC, coupled with investments in smart grids, infrastructure, and cities is very likely to a have positive 'spill-over effect' on other sectors, boosting the economy and creating green jobs. The drastic decline in oil prices since the end of 2014 has made this transition even more urgent, reaffirming the need for an alternative path to the current oil-driven growth that GCC states have followed over the past decades.

Taking into consideration the achievements at the UN Climate Conference in Paris on 12 December 2015 (COP 21), where a historical and ambitious agreement was reached by 195 nations to cut emissions, combat climate change, and unleash actions and investment towards a low-carbon economy and sustainable future, progress on the SDGs can be realised too. The agreement provides a real chance for the Arabian Gulf states to cooperate with all partners locally, regionally, and globally to address the challenges ahead. Overall, there are tremendous benefits to be gained from moving forward on the path towards sustainability. The global supporting context, through initiatives such as COP21 and the SDGs, provides a unique opportunity for the GCC states to take immediate action and initiate the overdue sustainable transition.

Concluding remarks

In this book, we have presented important research activities conducted by GCC scholars and institutions. Such efforts, which need to be highlighted and promoted further, cover themes and sectors that are very critical to support and help achieve the SDGs.

The first theme was "infrastructure management and solutions" where research efforts on water management, infrastructure, and urban design were presented and discussed. The following theme of the book tackled "standards and policies" to benchmark and promote energy efficiency and sustainability throughout key sectors such as the built environment. The third and last theme covered was the "socio-economic perspective" or dimension of sustainability. Economic instruments and models were presented, followed by discussions on how to alter the current unsustainable behaviours that are dominant in the GCC, mainly through tools such as educational programs and incentive schemes.

Finally, a comprehensive analysis of the state of sustainability research in the Gulf helped identify two important gaps that can guide future research efforts. First, there is a lack of diversification in the research on sustainability in the Gulf, which is mostly focused on technical energy and water challenges. Future efforts should include research in disciplines such as the social sciences, where the sociological and psychological barriers to altering current behaviours can be investigated and better understood. The sustainability challenges we are facing are in fact multi-disciplinary in nature and, therefore, require a holistic approach to be properly addressed. Finally, another gap in current research efforts is the lack of cooperation between GCC researchers and institutions. Creating collaboration channels between the GCC government and academic institutions is crucial to promote the exchange of ideas and lessons learned. While the GCC states currently share the challenges and dangers of climate change, they also can, through joint efforts and resources, become leaders in sustainable development and share successes in the transition towards a sustainable future for the region and their citizens.

References

Abdel Raouf, Mohamed. 2011. Rio Plus 20 a window for the Arab World. *Gulf News*, 28 October. Available at: http://gulfnews.com/

Abdel Raouf, Mohamed. 2013, June. *Green Policy to Balance Energy and Environment Needs: The Case of the United Arab Emirates.* Abu Dhabi: The Emirates Center for Strategic Studies and Research (ECSSR) (in Arabic).

Index